An Introduction to the Com
and Analysis of Greek Prose

Why learn to write in a dead language? Because a really good understanding of a language can only be attained by using it actively. Unlike earlier textbooks aimed at schoolboys, this work addresses modern adults who want to understand concepts fully as they learn. Drawing on recent scholarship where appropriate, and assuming no prior background except some reading knowledge of Greek, the course combines a structured review of paradigms and vocabulary with clear and comprehensive explanations of the rules of Greek syntax. Large numbers of exercises are provided, both with and without key: a complete set of cumulative exercises and another set of non-cumulative exercises for those who prefer to dip into specific sections. The exercises include, as well as English sentences and paragraphs for translation, Greek sentences and passages for translation, analysis, and manipulation. A full English–Greek vocabulary and list of principal parts are included.

ELEANOR DICKEY has taught Greek in Canada (University of Ottawa), the United States (Columbia University), and England (Oxford and Exeter), where she is currently Professor of Classics at the University of Reading and a Fellow of the British Academy. She is an expert on Greek and Latin linguistics and has published more than eighty scholarly works, including books on Greek forms of address, Latin forms of address, ancient Greek scholarship, and the Colloquia of the Hermeneumata Pseudodositheana (an ancient Latin and Greek textbook). Having fought hard to get the chance to learn to write Greek in order to become a first-class scholar, and having suffered considerably in the process, she cares passionately about giving others the gift of learning this valuable skill without the suffering she endured. Over decades of teaching the subject and working out how each element can most easily be absorbed by learners, she has distilled the result into this book, which can be used with or without a teacher and will make a good understanding of how to write Greek significantly easier to acquire.

An Introduction to the
Composition and Analysis
of Greek Prose

ELEANOR DICKEY

CAMBRIDGE
UNIVERSITY PRESS

CAMBRIDGE
UNIVERSITY PRESS

University Printing House, Cambridge CB2 8BS, United Kingdom

Cambridge University Press is part of the University of Cambridge.

It furthers the University's mission by disseminating knowledge in the pursuit of education, learning and research at the highest international levels of excellence.

www.cambridge.org
Information on this title: www.cambridge.org/9780521184250

© Eleanor Dickey 2016

First published 2016
4th printing 2017

Printed in the United Kingdom by TJ International Ltd. Padstow Cornwall

A catalogue record for this publication is available from the British Library

Library of Congress Cataloguing in Publication data
Dickey, Eleanor, author.
An introduction to the composition and analysis of Greek prose / Eleanor Dickey.
    pages   cm
Includes bibliographical references and index.
ISBN 978-0-521-76142-0 (hardback)
1. Greek language – Composition and exercises.   I. Title.
PA258.D54   2015
488.2'421 – dc23   2015012662

ISBN 978-0-521-76142-0 Hardback
ISBN 978-0-521-18425-0 Paperback

Dedicated to all my former students,
with profound gratitude
for what I have learned from them.

Contents

Preface

Greek prose composition, which was once cultivated primarily as an art form, is now increasingly valued for the practical benefits it brings to those who would like to read and understand ancient Greek texts. An active command of Greek, like that of any language, brings with it an increased fluency in comprehension and a greater appreciation of an author's choices and the reasons behind those choices. In addition, an ability to compose a correct Greek sentence is essential for those who intend to teach Greek. Yet it is still very difficult to learn this skill, particularly without access to a teacher who has been well trained in this particular area – and in some places few such teachers are available.

This book aims to make it easier for everyone to learn the basics of Greek prose composition well, with or without a teacher. It is aimed at students of any age who have a good passive knowledge of Greek (i.e. the equivalent of several years of continuous study) but assumes no active command of the language. A thorough review of declensions, conjugations, vocabulary, principal parts of verbs, etc. is built into the book: each chapter focuses not only on a particular syntactic construction or constructions, but also on a particular set of grammatical forms and vocabulary, and (with a very few unavoidable exceptions) no forms or constructions are used in chapters before the one of which they are the focus.

To derive maximum benefit from the exercises, the relevant vocabulary and grammatical forms should be memorized before each chapter is undertaken, so that the sentences can be done without consultation of reference works. Students starting to learn prose composition are often misled into believing that no memorization is necessary, but such deception is ultimately in no-one's interests: the rules of Greek grammar and syntax are so complex that it is impossible even to know what to look up unless one has done a fair amount of memorization, and looking up all the vocabulary, grammar, and syntax required for even a single sentence takes so long that discouragement is inevitable and very few sentences can be done. The author, as a student, wasted years over the non-memorization method and later wished bitterly that someone had told her how much more efficient it would be just to sit down and learn things by heart; it would have been the single most useful tip anyone could have given her, so she hereby passes it on.

The temptation to do prose composition without memorization, of course, derives from the impression – wholly reasonable when one is presented with a grammar and a large dictionary as one's basic reference works – that it is impossible to memorize all the necessary information and therefore pointless to begin. This book attempts to correct that problem by presenting a finite body of information, large enough to cover all the really important facts but small enough to be memorized in one semester. It is based ultimately on North and Hillard's *Greek Prose Composition*, but with a significant reduction in vocabulary (on the grounds that vocabulary, being the easiest thing to look up, is the least worthy direction in which to allocate precious memorization time) and a significant increase in the amount of explanation devoted to each construction (on the grounds that modern students prefer to understand rules rather than simply memorizing examples). I have the greatest respect for North and Hillard's work, from which I myself learned, but it is not easy to use, especially for non-native speakers of English and those working without a teacher, and it is aimed at students rather younger than and different in outlook from most of today's prose composition students. I hope that the present work will offer a more accessible introduction for modern readers. Like North and Hillard, I have presented a somewhat simplified version of the rules of Greek syntax and omitted many of the exceptions and complications mentioned in the larger grammars. Streamlining of this sort is essential in order to make it possible to master the main points in a reasonable amount of time, but readers should not assume that the exceptions I have omitted are wholly unimportant; for this reason it would be a good idea to do the recommended syntax reading from Smyth, which will give a more complete picture.

As necessary as memorization is consolidation. It is an inescapable fact that for most people, Greek grammatical forms and syntactic rules have a tendency to depart rapidly from the mind soon after being learned. One must simply accept this fact and learn the material repeatedly; to this end there are review exercises scattered throughout the book, and it is a good idea to re-memorize the vocabulary and forms of the relevant chapters before doing these exercises. One way to improve one's retention rate is to be scrupulous about correct accentuation, because once one has learned each form with its proper accent, one knows the form itself considerably more solidly than one does when one has learned only the form. For this reason a brief explanation of the accent rules and exercises in their use are provided, and all users of this book who do not already have a firm grasp of the accent system are encouraged to do these exercises before progressing to the chapters proper.

Essential as memorization, consolidation, and orderly progress are for students whose goal is to learn Greek properly, a book relying on the assumption that all its readers want to learn Greek properly can be inadequate for the needs of those who want to brush up on particular points without going through the whole course. For this reason this book also includes "practice exercises" on particular points of syntax; these exercises can be done without knowledge of the paradigms and vocabulary assumed for the main group of sentences, and (as much as possible) without knowledge of the previous chapters in this book. Users should be aware that if they do only these exercises and do not tackle the memorization and the main exercises, they will not actually learn very much.

This book departs from traditional prose composition books in its inclusion of exercises in the analysis of "real" Greek sentences as well as sentences for translation into Greek. While analysis is no substitute for translation into Greek, examining real, complex examples of the constructions one is studying helps one understand them better. By necessity, these exercises often employ vocabulary and constructions not yet covered in the book, but the examples provided in the text are restricted to familiar forms whenever practicable, to make them as easy as possible to understand.

This work is designed to fit a one-semester course meeting twice a week; in such a setting it is assumed that one chapter will be covered at each class meeting. The first chapter has no associated memorization to facilitate its being presented on the first day of class; it is recommended that memorization of paradigms and vocabulary (as indicated at the start of each chapter) be assigned for each subsequent class meeting and tested by means of a quiz at the start of each class. If the students do this memorization properly, one can translate the sentences at a brisk pace in class (skipping the practice exercises); if the students do not memorize the vocabulary adequately beforehand, the practice exercises can be used in class and the sentences (or such of them as do not have a key provided) reserved for homework. It is recommended that several tests be given during the semester to encourage re-memorization and consolidation. The material has been squeezed into eighteen chapters because no construction can afford to be the one that comes at the end of the semester and therefore is never consolidated; the exercises presented at the end of the book are intended to be done over several weeks at the end of the semester as a way of reviewing and consolidating the material learned earlier. They are vital if this material is to be successfully retained.

At the start of each chapter are listed not only the paradigms and vocabulary that should be memorized before the chapter is studied, but also recommended grammar and syntax reading. These selections are presented on the theory that it is helpful to have read all the way through a large grammar like that of Smyth, which gives a more nuanced explanation of the rules than can be presented here: the grammar readings consist of the material relevant to the paradigms covered in that chapter, and the syntax readings point to Smyth's treatments of the constructions covered in that chapter. Neither set of readings is essential, but students who do them will have a deeper understanding of the material and will know the limitations of the rules they learn from this book.

As this book is intended to be helpful to those who have no access to a teacher as well as to those who do, a partial answer key is provided; it is hoped that this compromise will make the book useful to the independent learner without spoiling its effectiveness in class settings. Generally speaking the answer key covers the first half of each practice exercise, the first ten sentences in each chapter, and the first analysis exercise. In certain chapters, however, the nature of the exercises has necessitated a different distribution of answers in order to assure that a student relying exclusively on the exercises to which answers are provided will be able to learn successfully.

Many people helped in the creation of this book. My first thanks go to Mabel Lang, who taught me Greek, David Raeburn, who taught me how to teach Greek, and Jasper Griffin, who taught me Greek prose composition. All my Greek syntax and composition students, at Oxford and at Columbia, have contributed something for which I am grateful, but Pedro de Blas and Ryan Fowler were particularly generous in helping with the actual construction of this book. Steven Kennedy and his students at the Maynard School in Exeter helpfully allowed me to test portions of the work in a school setting. Many thanks are also due to David Raeburn, Helma Dik, Martin West, Philomen Probert, Elizabeth Scharffenberger, Ralph Rosen, Carlos Carter, Gregory Mellen, and the Cambridge University Press readers for reading drafts of the work and making many useful criticisms. I am also very grateful to Martin West for providing me with the passage used in Appendix H, and to the Leverhulme Trust for generous funding that allowed me to finish this work. Particular thanks are due to everyone involved in the book's production at Cambridge University Press, especially the incredibly hard-working Christina Sarigiannidou and Iveta Adams as well as Henry Maas, the best proofreader I have ever encountered.

I must also acknowledge here my debts to published sources, for these are now so woven into the fabric of this book that specific footnotes are impossible. Most chapters are derived from a combination of Smyth, Goodwin, and North and Hillard, and the ultimate basis of the vocabulary list is M. Campbell, *Classical Greek Prose: A Basic Vocabulary*, though LSJ is an important secondary source. Goodwin's *Moods and Tenses*, Rijksbaron, and Cooper/Krüger have also provided material.

Useful reference texts

Grammars

The standard grammar in the USA is H. W. Smyth, *Greek Grammar* (Cambridge, Mass. 1920); equally good, and often preferred to Smyth in Britain, is W. W. Goodwin, *Greek Grammar* (London 1879; also a revised edition by C. B. Gulick, Boston 1930). There will soon be a new grammar, *The Cambridge Grammar of Classical Greek*, by Evert van Emde Boas, Albert Rijksbaron, Luuk Huitink, and Mathieu de Bakker; this is currently in preparation and I have not been able to see it. More complete than any English-language work are the two massive German authorities on Greek grammar: R. Kühner, B. Gerth, and F. Blass, *Ausführliche Grammatik der griechischen Sprache* (Hanover 1898–1904), and E. Schwyzer and A. Debrunner, *Griechische Grammatik* (Munich 1939–71). Grammars smaller than those of Smyth and Goodwin are generally not suitable for use with this book, as they oversimplify as much as I do (and in some cases more); in order to gain a good understanding of the Greek language from this book one should use it with a proper reference grammar to which one can appeal for more information to fill in the gaps I have left.

English–Greek dictionaries

The best are S. C. Woodhouse, *English–Greek Dictionary* (London 1910) and G. M. Edwards, *An English–Greek Lexicon* (Cambridge 1914), but most other printed lexica are also usable. Online English–Greek lexica are much less reliable and should generally be avoided, except for the online version of Woodhouse (www.lib.uchicago.edu/efts/Woodhouse/). When doing prose composition seriously one should avoid words that only occur in poetry; in a good dictionary words are marked as belonging to prose or to poetry. It is also usual to avoid post-Classical words; a good dictionary marks these or leaves them out entirely. A general rule for using English–Greek dictionaries is that any unfamiliar word found in them should be double-checked in a good Greek–English dictionary before being used.

Prose composition textbooks

Almost all the books that exist were designed for British schoolboys of a bygone era. Probably the best, and by far the most popular today, is M. A. North and A. E. Hillard, *Greek Prose Composition* (London 1898), followed by A. Sidgwick, *Sidgwick's Greek Prose Composition* (London 1876); both these books are still in print, and there are published answer keys to both. Most others are out of print. A perhaps more interesting option than North and Hillard is L. W. P. Lewis and L. M. Styler, *Foundations for Greek Prose Composition* (London 1934). A set of very easy sentences for translation by beginners (but with no rules or explanations) is provided as an introduction to North and Hillard by A. E. Hillard and C. G. Botting, *Elementary Greek Exercises* (London 1949); a similar work based on Xenophon's *Anabasis* is W. C. Collar and M. G. Daniell, *The Beginner's Greek Composition* (Boston 1893). A few tricky topics are covered in more detail in the highly respected work of A. H. Nash-Williams, *Advanced Level Greek Prose Composition* (London 1957). Radically different in approach and more recent, but unfortunately full of errors, is S. A. Stephens, *Greek Prose Composition* (Bryn Mawr 1996). A. T. Murray, *Greek Composition for Colleges* (Chicago 1902), contains no rules but offers a useful sequence of Greek passages for reading paired with closely related English passages for translation into Greek. W. H. Auden, *Greek Prose Phrase-Book* (London 1949), provides a list of idiomatic Greek expressions from Thucydides, Xenophon, Demosthenes, and Plato, classified by topic and listed under their English equivalents.

Specialized works

W. W. Goodwin, *Syntax of the Moods and Tenses of the Greek Verb* (Boston 1890): wonderfully clear presentation with well-chosen, comprehensible examples; still the standard reference.

A. Rijksbaron, *The Syntax and Semantics of the Verb in Classical Greek* (3rd edn., Amsterdam 2002): one of the few accessible works that take into account recent research on Greek syntax; very comprehensible, but much less detailed than Goodwin. Sometimes the rules presented here are significantly different from the ones found in older works, and it is not clear that the older works are necessarily wrong in such cases.

G. L. Cooper after K. W. Krüger, *Attic Greek Prose Syntax* (vols. i and ii, Ann Arbor 1998): enormous and comprehensive, but difficult to use and less authoritative than Goodwin; contains many misprints.

B. L. Gildersleeve and C. W. E. Miller, *Syntax of Classical Greek from Homer to Demosthenes* (New York 1900–11).

Y. Duhoux, *Le verbe grec ancien: éléments de morphologie et de syntaxe historiques* (2nd edn., Louvain 2000): fascinating study, not restricted to Attic prose.

J. D. Denniston, *Greek Prose Style* (Oxford 1952): illuminating on many specific topics.

J. D. Denniston, *The Greek Particles* (2nd edn., Oxford 1950): the Bible on the subject of particles; indispensable.

K. J. Dover, *The Evolution of Greek Prose Style* (Oxford 1997).

K. J. Dover, *Greek Word Order* (Cambridge 1960): a respected work on this subject, but by no means the last word.

H. Dik, *Word Order in Ancient Greek* (Amsterdam 1995): a new and exciting approach, but not universally accepted.

E. Dickey, *Greek Forms of Address* (Oxford 1996): more than you ever wanted to know about the use of the vocative.

H. W. Chandler, *A Practical Introduction to Greek Accentuation* (2nd edn., Oxford 1881): the standard English-language reference work on accentuation.

P. Probert, *New Short Guide to the Accentuation of Ancient Greek* (London 2003): an excellent introductory textbook on accentuation, with many more rules than are given here and exercises to match.

W. S. Allen, *Vox Graeca: A Guide to the Pronunciation of Classical Greek* (3rd edn., Cambridge 1987): a clear explanation of how Greek sounded at various periods and how we know about pronunciation.

B. Jacquinod (ed.), *Études sur l'aspect verbal chez Platon* (Saint-Etienne 2000): an alternative view of verbal aspect.

J. Bertrand, *La grammaire grecque par l'exemple* (Paris 1996): really a beginners' Greek book, but useful for more advanced students as well because of its collection of authentic ancient sentences illustrating each construction.

IMPORTANT NOTE

ALMOST EVERY RULE PRESENTED IN THIS BOOK HAS EXCEPTIONS, MOST OF WHICH ARE NOT MENTIONED.

Accentuation

There are three types of accent in Greek: acute (´), grave (`), and circumflex (˜).[1] Normally, each word has one accent. Which one it is, and where it appears, are the result of interaction between the word's basic accent and the rules that govern accentuation. A word will try to keep its basic accentuation unless prevented by some rule; if so prevented, it will prefer to change its type and remain on the same syllable than to change syllables.

Accent is determined partly by vowel quantity; it is therefore necessary to know which vowels are long and which short. Epsilon and omicron are always short; eta and omega are always long; alpha, iota, and upsilon are long in some words and short in others. The following combinations of vowels are diphthongs and count as one long vowel: ει, υι, αυ, ευ, ηυ, ου, ᾳ, ῃ, ῳ. The remaining diphthongs, αι and οι, count as one long vowel except when they are the *very last* letters of a word, in which case they count as one short vowel;[2] but in optative endings they are long even when at the very end of a word.[3] (Thus οι counts as long in ἀνθρώποις and παιδεύοι (optative), but short in ἄνθρωποι; αι counts as long in ἀγαθαῖς and παιδεῦσαι (optative), but short in ἀγαθαί and παίδευσαι (imperative).) All other combinations of vowels count as two separate vowels and therefore as two separate syllables.

To accent all words correctly one needs to know the quantities of doubtful vowels in final syllables. The most important of these are:

– almost all -ι, -ις, and -ιν endings are short;
– finite verb endings in -α, -ας, or -αν are short, except in contract verbs;
– all neuter plural noun and adjective endings in -α are short;
– the -ας ending in the first declension genitive singular is always long;

---

[1] Originally these represented a rising pitch, the failure of the pitch to rise on a syllable where that would otherwise be expected, and a pitch that rose and fell on the same syllable (hence the restriction of the circumflex to long vowels). Now, however, it is customary to pronounce all three types of accent like the English stress accent. If when memorizing vocabulary one says the word out loud with a stress on the accented syllable, one engages in the memorization process portions of one's brain that would otherwise remain unused, and this makes it possible to learn the position of accents more efficiently.

[2] For purposes of accentuation, that is; in scanning poetry any diphthong in any position counts as one long vowel.

[3] Also in locative adverbs (e.g. οἴκοι) and some interjections (e.g. αἰαῖ).

- the accusative plural ending -ας is long in the first declension but short in the third declension;
- first declension feminine nouns can have a nominative/vocative singular in short -α, in which case they also have a short -αν in the accusative, or in long -α, in which case the accusative -αν is also long. First-second declension *adjectives*, in the feminine, always have long -α and -αν.

NB: ultima = last syllable; penultimate = next to last syllable; antepenultimate = third syllable from the end.

I. Basic accents

The basic accent, i.e. the one found on the dictionary-entry form of a word, must be memorized except in the case of verbs. Most finite verb forms have recessive accents (i.e. the accent goes as close to the beginning of the word as possible).

II. Accent rules

A. Basic rules

1. An acute or grave may occur on a long or short vowel, but a circumflex can appear only on a long vowel. Thus ἀνήρ, ἀνὴρ, ἀνδρός, ἀνδρὸς, γῆ.
2. If an acute accent stands on the ultima, and that word is followed by another non-enclitic word (see C below for enclitics) without intervening punctuation, the acute changes to a grave. This is the only situation in which the grave accent is used. Thus ἀνὴρ καὶ γυνή but ἀνήρ, καὶ γυνή.[4]
3. An acute accent may stand only on one of the last three syllables of a word; if the last vowel is long, the acute may stand only on one of the last two syllables. (A word with a basic accent on the antepenultimate will move the accent to the penultimate if the last vowel is long.) Thus ἄνθρωπος but ἀνθρώπου.
4. A circumflex may stand only on one of the last two syllables of a word; if the last vowel is long, a circumflex may stand only on the ultima. (A word with a basic accent on the penultimate will change the accent to acute if the last vowel is long.) Thus δῶρον but δώρου; Κλεοφῶν.
5. If the accent is on the penultimate, and that syllable has a long vowel, and the ultima is short, the accent must be a circumflex. Thus δῶρον. (This rule is called the σωτῆρα rule.)

---

[4] Interrogative τίς and τί are exceptions to this rule: their accents never become grave.

To summarize the rules in tabular form, the possible accents are as follows ($\smile$ = a syllable with a short vowel, $-$ = a syllable with a long vowel, and x = a syllable with either vowel):

x x́ x $\smile$	x x x̆́ x	x x x x́
	x x ´ –	x x x x̀
	x x ≃ $\smile$	x x x ≃

Many words have a recessive accent, i.e. an accent that tries to be as close to the start of the word as possible. On words with three or more syllables, the possibilities for recessive accents are only x́ x $\smile$ and x x́ –, but for words of two syllables the possibilities for recessive accents are x̆́ x, ≃ $\smile$, and ´ –.

B. Paradigm-specific rules

1. Finite verb forms are nearly always recessive. Infinitives, participles, nouns, and adjectives usually have a persistent accent: i.e. the syllable on which the accent appears is not predictable by the recessive rules but must be learned separately, and if the word is inflected the accent tries to stay on the syllable where it appears in the dictionary-entry form. There are however some complications:

2. Nouns and adjectives of the first and second declensions, if they have the basic accent on the ultima, have an acute in the nominative, vocative, and accusative but a circumflex in the genitive and dative (both singular and plural, all genders). Thus ἀγαθός, ἀγαθοῦ, ἀγαθῷ, ἀγαθόν, ἀγαθέ, ἀγαθοί, ἀγαθῶν, etc.

3. Nouns (but not adjectives) of the first declension always have a circumflex on the ultima in the genitive plural, regardless of the natural accent. This also applies to the feminines of adjectives and participles that have third-declension masculine and neuter forms, but not to those that have second-declension forms (the underlying principle is that if the feminine genitive plural is identical to the masculine and neuter genitives plural, it is accented like them, and otherwise it has a circumflex on the ultima). Thus θαλαττῶν from θάλαττα, and πολιτῶν from πολίτης, but ἀξίων from ἀξία (fem. of ἄξιος, masc. gen. pl. ἀξίων; there is also a noun ἀξία, but this has the genitive plural ἀξιῶν); παιδευουσῶν from παιδεύουσα (masc. παιδεύων, gen. pl. παιδευόντων) but παιδευομένων from παιδευομένη (masc. παιδευόμενος, gen. pl. παιδευομένων).

4. Monosyllabic nouns of the third declension usually accent the stem in the nominative, vocative, and accusative, but the ending in the genitive and dative (all numbers). The stem accent is normally the same type as the basic accent, except where the basic rules forbid; the ending accent is normally acute except in the

genitive plural. Thus κλώψ, κλωπός, κλωπί, κλῶπα, κλῶπες, κλωπῶν, κλωψί, κλῶπας.

5.   First-declension feminines in short -α (all first-declension nouns in -α that do not have ε, ι, or ρ before the final -α, and a few that do have ε, ι, or ρ) and third-declension neuters in -ς (those declined like γένος) always have recessive accents (except in the genitive plural). Note that this rule makes it possible to tell whether the final -α of a first declension noun is long or short: ἄγκυρα and μοῖρα have short -α, but ἡμέρα must have a long -α, since if it were short, the recessive accent would be *ἥμερα. (NB: first-declension adjectives in -α and first-declension masculine nouns in -ας always have long α.)

6.   Πόλις and other words declined like it have an accent that violates the basic rules by staying on the same syllable throughout the paradigm, even in forms like πόλεως and πόλεων where it ought to move.

7.   Contract verbs (and other contracted words) have accents that reflect the uncontracted forms. When a contraction occurs, if the accented syllable is not one of those that contract, there is no effect on the accent: ἐτίμαε > ἐτίμα. If the accented vowel is the first of the two contracting vowels, the resulting contracted vowel will have a circumflex (τιμάω > τιμῶ); if the accent is on the second contracting vowel, the contracted vowel will have an acute (τιμαόμενος > τιμώμενος).[5] The same rules apply to contracted forms of non-contract verbs, as μενῶ (future of μένω) and λυθῶ (aorist passive subjunctive).

8.   Βασιλεύς and certain other words have their own paradigm-specific rules, which are also followed by other words that decline the way they do; these rules are best learned as part of the irregular declensions of the words concerned.

C. Rules for enclitics (τις, τε, ποτέ, ἐστί, etc.)

These words have no accent of their own and normally follow accented words, whose accents they affect.

1.   If the preceding word ends in an acute accent, the accent does not change to grave. Thus ἀγαθός τις, ἀγαθοί τινες.

2.   If the preceding word has an acute on the penultimate, a monosyllabic enclitic can be added without change, but a dissyllabic enclitic takes an accent on its ultima. Thus λόγος τις, but λόγοι τινές, λόγων τινῶν.

3.   If the preceding word has an acute on the antepenultimate, it adds a further acute on the ultima. Thus ἄνθρωπός τις, ἄνθρωποί τινες.

---

[5] This is because an acute on a long vowel represents an accent on the second half of the vowel, while a circumflex represents an accent on the first half of the vowel.

4. If the preceding word has a circumflex on the ultima, there is no change. Thus ἀγαθῶν τε, ἀγαθῶν τινων.
5. If the preceding word has a circumflex on the penultimate, it adds an acute on the ultima. Thus δῶρά τε, δῶρά τινα.
6. If several enclitics stand in a row, each one except the last takes an accent (on its second syllable, if dissyllabic). Thus ἐάν ποτέ τίς τί τινι διδῷ.
7. To summarize in tabular form, where "α" represents a syllable of the preceding word and "ε" a syllable of the enclitic:

-α-α-ά + ε or ε-ε	-α-α-ᾶ + ε or ε-ε
-α-ά-α + ε or ε-έ or ε-ῆ	-α-ᾶ-ά + ε or ε-ε
-ά-α-ά + ε or ε-ε	

D. Rules for proclitics (ἐκ, οὐ, εἰ, ὡς, ὁ, ἡ, οἱ, αἱ, etc.)

These words have no accents of their own and are accentually joined to the words that follow them. If followed by an accented word, they cause no changes; if followed by an enclitic, they take an acute accent from the enclitic. Thus ὁ ἄνθρωπος but εἴ τις, οἵ γε.

Exercise A (basic rules)

Add correct accents to the following words:

1. Finite verbs:

παιδευε, παιδευωσι, παιδευοιμι, παιδευετω, ἐπαιδευον, ἐπαιδευομεν, παιδευο-μαι, παιδευομεθα, παιδευῃ, παιδευωμεθα, παιδευησθε, παιδευοιμην, παιδευοιο, παιδευου, παιδευεσθω, παιδευσουσι, παιδευσοι, παιδευσοιεν, παιδευσεται, παιδευ-σομεθα, παιδευσοιτο, παιδευσοιμην, παιδευσοιμεθα, παιδευσοιντο, ἐπαιδευσα, ἐπαιδευσε, ἐπαιδευσαμεν, ἐπαιδευσαν, παιδευσαιμι, παιδευσαι (optative), παιδευ-σαι (imperative), παιδευσαιεν, παιδευσον, παιδευσατω, παιδευσατε, παιδευ-σαντων, πεπαιδευκα, πεπαιδευκατε, ἐπεπαιδευκη, ἐπεπαιδευκεσαν, πεπαιδευκοι, πεπαιδευκοιμεν, πεπαιδευμαι, πεπαιδευσαι, πεπαιδευται, πεπαιδευμεθα, πεπαιδευσθε, ἐπεπαιδευμην, ἐπεπαιδευσο, πεπαιδευσομαι, πεπαιδευσει, διδ-ωμι, διδωσι, δωμεν, διδοασι, διδομαι, δωται, διδοται, δωμεθα, διδομεθα, διδοιην, δωτε, διδοιημεν, ἐδωκα, δωνται, ἐδομεν, ἐδομην, ἐδοτο, δοιεν, δωσι, δοιησαν, δοισθε, δοσθω, δοσθε, δοιτο, δοντων, δοτω, δοιο, ἐθηκε, θειεν, ἐθηκας, ἐθου, θειτε, ἐθεμεθα, θειμεν, ἐθεμην, ἐθεσαν, θωσι, ἐθετε, ἐθηκα, θωμεν, θητε, θειησαν, θειητε, θειημεν.

2. Other words (note the following basic accents: στράτευμα, πόλεμος, κῆρυξ, γενναῖος, ἄξιος, ῥήτωρ, πολίτης (long ι), θάλαττα, καλός, παιδεύων, ἀνδρεῖος, δαίμων):

στρατευματος, στρατευματι, στρατευματα, στρατευματων, στρατευμασι, πολεμου, πολεμῳ, πολεμον, πολεμοι, πολεμων, πολεμοις, πολεμους, κηρυκος, κηρυκα, κηρυκες,

κηρυκων, κηρυξι, γενναιου, γενναιῳ, γενναιον, γενναιε, γενναιοι, γενναιων, γεν-
ναιοις, γενναιους, γενναια (fem.), γενναιας (gen.), γενναιᾳ, γενναιαν, γενναιαι, γενναιων, γενναιαις, γενναιας (acc.), γενναια (neut.), ἀξιου, ἀξιῳ, ἀξιον, ἀξιοι, ἀξιων,
ἀξιοις, ἀξιους, ἀξια (fem.), ἀξιας (gen.), ἀξιᾳ, ἀξιαι, ἀξιων, ἀξιαις, ἀξιας (acc.), ἀξια
(neut.), ῥητορος, ῥητορων, ῥητορ, ῥητορας, ῥητορες, πολιτου, πολιτην, πολιτα, πολι-
ται, πολιταις, πολιτας, θαλαττης, θαλαττῃ, θαλατταν, θαλατται, θαλατταις, θαλατ-
τας, καλον, καλοι, καλη, καλαι, καλα, καλους, παιδευοντος, παιδευοντες, παιδευον-
των, παιδευοντας, παιδευον (neut.), ἀνδρειου, ἀνδρειῳ, ἀνδρειον, ἀνδρειοι, ἀνδρειων,
ἀνδρειοις, ἀνδρειους, ἀνδρεια (fem.), ἀνδρειας (gen.), ἀνδρειᾳ, ἀνδρειαν, ἀνδρειαι,
ἀνδρειων, ἀνδρειαις, ἀνδρειας (acc.), ἀνδρεια (neut.), δαιμονος, δαιμονι, δαιμονα, δαι-
μον, δαιμονες, δαιμονων, δαιμοσι, δαιμονας.

3. Groups of words (note the basic accents κακός, σοφός, δῆλος, δέ, καί):
κακον δε, σοφον και, δηλου κακοι και σοφοι, σοφους δε κακους και δηλους, σοφην δε
και κακην.

Exercise B (paradigm-specific rules)

1. Given the natural accents ὁδός, φωνή, κακός, αἴξ, μάχη (short α), θήρ, φιλέω, νίκη
(long ι), χείρ, χώρα, παιδευθείς, παιδευσάμενος, μάντις, put the correct accents on the
following words:
ὁδου, ὁδῳ, ὁδον, ὁδοι, ὁδων, ὁδοις, ὁδους, φωνης, φωνῃ, φωνην, φωναι, φωνων,
φωναις, φωνας, κακου, κακῳ, κακον, κακοι, κακων, κακοις, κακους, κακη, κακης, κακῃ,
κακαι, κακαις, κακας, κακα, αἰγος, αἰγι, αἰγα, αἰγες, αἰγων, αἰξι, αἰγας, μαχης, μαχην,
μαχαι, μαχων, μαχας, θηρος, θηρι, θηρα, θηρες, θηρων, θηρσι, θηρας, φιλεις, φιλουμεν,
φιλουσι, φιλητε, φιλοιην, φιλοιη, φιλοιμεν, φιλοιεν, φιλει (indicative), φιλει (imperative),
φιλειτω, φιλειτε, φιλουντων, ἐφιλουν, ἐφιλεις, ἐφιλει, ἐφιλουμεν, φιλουμαι, φιλειται,
φιλωμεθα, φιλησθε, φιλοιμην, φιλοιο, φιλοιτο, φιλοιμεθα, φιλοισθε, φιλου, φιλεισθω,
φιλεισθε, φιλεισθων, ἐφιλουμην, ἐφιλου, ἐφιλειτο, ἐφιλουμεθα, νικης, νικῃ, νικην, νικαι,
νικων, νικαις, νικας, χειρος, χειρι, χειρα, χειρες, χειρων, χερσι, χειρας, χωρας (gen.),
χωρᾳ, χωραν, χωραι, χωρων, χωραις, χωρας (acc.), παιδευθεντος, παιδευθεντα,
παιδευθεντες, παιδευθεντων, παιδευθεισι, παιδευθεντας, παιδευθεισα, παιδευθεισης,
παιδευθεισῃ, παιδευθεισαν, παιδευθεισαι, παιδευθεισων, παιδευθεισαις, παιδευ-
θεισας, παιδευθεν, παιδευσαμενου, παιδευσαμενον, παιδευσαμενοι, παιδευσαμενων
(masc.), παιδευσαμενοις, παιδευσαμενη, παιδευσαμεναι, παιδευσαμενων (fem.),
παιδευσαμενας, παιδευσαμενα, μαντεως, μαντει, μαντιν, μαντεις, μαντεων, μαντεσι.

2. Work out from the rules the natural accents of the following:
γλωττα, μουσα, ἁμαξα, δοξα, ἁμιλλα, λεαινα, τραπεζα, ξιφος (neut., short ι), τειχος
(neut.), ἐτος (neut.), εὐρος (neut.), γηρας (neut.), κρεας (neut.).

3. Indicate whether the α in the final syllable of these first-declension words is long or short:

ὥρα, σκιά, μοῖρα, πρῷρα, τόλμα, μυῖα, βασιλεία, ψάλτρια, νεανίας, ταμίας, ἐλευθέρα, αἰσχρά, δικαία.

Exercise C (enclitics)

Given the basic accents καλός, δένδρον, μικρός, ζῷον, λέων, μάχη (short α), νῆσος, put the correct accents on the following phrases:
καλος τις, καλοι τινες, καλου τινος, καλων τινων, καλαις τισι, δενδρον τι, δενδρα τινα, δενδρων τινων, δενδρῳ τινι, δενδροις τε, μικροι τινες, μικρος τε και, μικρα γε ἐστι, μικρων τινων ποτε, ζῳου τινος, ζῳον τι, ζῳα τινα, ζῳων τινων, ζῳοις τε τισι, λεοντος τινος, λεοντων τινων, λεοντα γε, μαχη τις, μαχαι τινες, μαχων τινων, μαχαις τισι, μαχης γε, μαχης τινος, νησοι τινες, νησων τινων, νησον τε ποτε ἐστι, παιδευομαι τε, παιδευομεν γε ποτε, ἐπαιδευε τις ποτε, ἐπαιδευον τινα, παιδευετε τινας γε ποτε, παιδευει τινας, παιδευω γε, παιδευοι τινας, παιδευσετε τινα, παιδευσομεν γε τινα.

Exercise D (proclitics)

Put the correct accents on the following phrases:
εἰ τις ποτε παιδευοι, αἱ γε καλαι, εἰ τι οὐκ ἐχεις, ὁ γε αἰξ καλος ἐστι, ἡ γε κακη ἐστι, ἐκ τε δενδρων.

I | Articles

Recommended syntax reading: Smyth §1021–9, 1099–1153

The Greek definite article is one of the key structural elements of the language; although it is very often used to express the same thing as English "the," it also has several important grammatical functions, some of which will not become apparent until the next chapter.

A) The article is attached to nouns to indicate definiteness. Greek authors normally use the article for this purpose wherever one would use "the" in English;[1] where English would have the indefinite article "a/an," Greek has no article (or sometimes enclitic τις).

ὁ ἵππος τὰ βιβλία ἐσθίει.	The horse is eating the books.
ἵππος βιβλία ἐσθίει.	A horse is eating books.
ἵππος τις τὰ βιβλία ἐσθίει.	Some horse is eating the books. / A horse is eating the books.

Sometimes, however, an article is used with a noun that would not take one in English.

1) The article is used with plurals that refer to **whole classes**, though not with ones that refer to only some members of the class. It is also used when a singular noun stands for a whole class.[2]

οἱ Ἕλληνες θνητοί.	Greeks (i.e. Greeks in general) are mortal.
οἱ Ἕλληνες ἔφυγον.	The Greeks (i.e. those particular Greeks) fled.
Ἕλληνες τὸν χρυσὸν ἔκλεψαν.	Greeks (i.e. some Greeks) stole the gold.
ὁ ἄνθρωπος θνητός.	Man (i.e. humans in general) is mortal.

---

[1] The two exceptions are the special words mentioned in A5, which take an article in English but not in Greek, and the English adverbial "the" with comparatives ("all the better"; "the more the merrier"; "so much the worse"); this "the" is etymologically a different word from the definite article and should never be translated with a Greek article.

[2] There is a similar usage in English, e.g. "The dodo is extinct" or "He plays the violin."

2) **Names** of people[3] or places that the reader is expected to recognize, either from previous mention in the same text or because they are well known, often take the article, though often they do not.[4]

ὑπὸ τοῦ Σωκράτους ἐπαιδεύθη.	He was educated by Socrates.
ἡ Ἑλλὰς καλή.	Greece is beautiful.
Πολύιππος μὲν ἔφυγε, Μόνιππος δὲ οὔ·[5]	Polyippus fled but Monippus did not,
ὁ γὰρ Πολύιππος αἰσχρός ἐστιν.	for Polyippus is shameful.

3) The article is generally used with **abstract nouns** in making generalizations.

ἡ ἀρετή	excellence
ἡ ἐλευθερία	freedom
ἡ εἰρήνη ἀγαθή	peace is good
but	
ἐν εἰρήνῃ ἐζῶντο	they lived in peace

4) The article is regularly used to indicate unemphatic **possession**, where English would have "my," "your," "his," etc. This only works when the possession is inferable from context; usually this means that the possessor is mentioned in the sentence (or the preceding sentence) and the noun modified by the article has a meaning that indicates some type of relationship (kinship, friendship, superiority, subservience, familiarity, etc.).

ἐπαίδευσε τὸν ἀδελφόν.	He educated his brother.
ὁ δοῦλος ἔφερε τὸν δεσπότην.	The slave was carrying his master.

5) But Greek does not use the article with a few idiosyncratic words that, because they refer to something unique and well known, are considered to be already definite in themselves.

ἐν ἀγορᾷ	in the marketplace
βασιλεύς	the Persian king (as opposed to ὁ βασιλεύς, the king of a Greek state)

Preliminary exercise 1 (on A). Indicate whether or not articles would be used in Greek with the underlined words, and why.

a. Freedom is precious to everyone.
b. The traders in the marketplace often have their sons with them.

---

[3] The article can also be used with any person's name, whether or not it would be recognized, as part of an identification formula. Such formulae normally put the article after the noun, followed by an identifier such as a demotic or the genitive of the father's name: Πολέμαρχος ὁ Κεφάλου "Polemarchus, son of Cephalus."

[4] There is much debate about the criteria that determine its use and absence.

[5] Note that οὐ is accented when it is the last word in a sentence: οὔ.

    c.   Thieves took the gold from the temple.
    d.   Thieves are antisocial and should be severely punished.
    e.   Thieves are heading for the marketplace right now.
    f.   Humility was not an important virtue for the Greeks.
    g.   I need to find my sister.
    h.   Themistocles talked directly to the Persian king.
    i.   Yesterday we saw two brothers feeding the pigeons.
    j.   Yesterday we saw our brothers feeding pigeons.
    k.   Brothers share a special kind of love.
    l.   Three brothers were involved in the robbery.
    m.   Love is a transfiguring emotion.
    n.   The Athenians did not appreciate Socrates.

B) Substantivization. The primary function of an article attached to something other than a noun is to create a noun.

1) Any **adjective** (or participle: see chapter v) can be turned into a noun by adding an article, and these substantivized adjectives are usually considered to have an understood noun "man," "men," "woman," "women," "thing," or "things," according to their gender and number.[6] If the context makes it clear, however, another noun can be understood.

οἱ ἀγαθοὶ εὖ βουλεύονται.	The good deliberate well. / Good men deliberate well. / The good men are deliberating well.
τὴν κακὴν οὐ φιλῶ.	I do not like the bad woman.
οὐκ ἐθέλω τὰ αἰσχρὰ μανθάνειν.	I do not wish to learn (the) shameful things.
ὁ μὲν ἀγαθὸς ποιητὴς ἥκει, ὁ δὲ κακὸς οὔ.	The good poet has come, but not the bad one.

The neuter singular of a substantivized adjective can be used as an abstract noun.

τὸ δίκαιον	justice

2) The **articular infinitive** is the closest Greek equivalent of the English gerund (verbal noun in -ing). The infinitive is preceded by a neuter singular article.

τὸ νικᾶν καλόν.	Winning is good. / It is good to win.
τῷ φεύγειν οὐ μαθήσεσθε.	You will not learn by fleeing.

---

[6] There is an English parallel for this usage in phrases like "from the sublime to the ridiculous" or "Only the brave deserve the fair."

3) A wide variety of **other words** and word groups, including adverbs, prepositional phrases, and possessive genitives, can also be substantivized by the addition of the article; in such situations the gender is indicated only by the article.[7]

αἱ πάλαι οὐκ ἐπαιδεύοντο.	Women of long ago were not educated.
οἱ μετὰ τοῦ ἀγγέλου ἔφυγον.	The men with the messenger fled. / Those with the messenger fled.
τὰ τῶν θεῶν ἔφερεν.	He was carrying the things of the gods (i.e. the holy things).

4) The article can be used with μέν and δέ in two ways.

a) **Ὁ μέν ... ὁ δέ** (in any gender, number, and case) means "the one ... and/but the other" (in the plural, "some ... and/but others").

ὁ μὲν ἀπέδραμεν, ὁ δὲ ἔμεινεν.	One ran away, and the other remained.
τὰς μὲν ἐλύσαμεν, τὰς δὲ οὔ.	We freed some women but not others.

This meaning only applies when *nothing* except the μέν or δέ goes with the article; if there is anything else for the article to attach itself to, μέν and δέ no longer mean "the one" and "the other."

ὁ μὲν κακὸς ἀπέδραμεν, ὁ δ' ἀγαθὸς ἔμεινεν.	The bad man ran away, but the good one remained.

b) **Ὁ δέ** (in any gender and number, but always nominative), in the absence of ὁ μέν, is used to pick up a word that has recently been given in an oblique case and make it into the subject of the next sentence or clause; it is usually translated with "but he," "but she," or "but they."

τοὺς αἰχμαλώτους ἐλύσαμεν· οἱ δὲ οὐκ ἀπέδραμον.	We freed the prisoners, but they did not run away.
πολλῶν γυναικῶν ἐρῶ· αἱ δὲ ἐμοῦ οὐκ ἐρῶσιν.	I love many women, but they do not love me.

It is tempting to analyze these constructions as if the Greek article were simply a pronoun, and historically such an analysis would be accurate. However, in classical Attic the article cannot be used by itself as a pronoun; it is always attached to some other

---

[7] Though the three groups mentioned are by far the most frequent in this usage, almost anything can be substantivized. For example, at Plato, *Republic* 327c there is a substantivized protasis: οὐκοῦν, ἦν δ' ἐγώ, ἔτι ἐλλείπεται τὸ ἢν πείσωμεν ὑμᾶς, ὡς χρὴ ἡμᾶς ἀφεῖναι "So, said I, the possibility of our persuading you to let us go still remains" (literally "the if we persuade you that it is necessary to let us go is still left").

word. Therefore one cannot create a freestanding *οἱ "the men" or *τούς "them" on the analogy of οἱ ἀγαθοί "the good men" or οἱ δέ "but they."

> **Preliminary exercise 2 (on B).** Indicate whether or not articles would be used in Greek with (or for) the underlined words, and why.
>
> a. The good <u>man</u> tried to help the <u>prisoners</u>, but <u>they</u> threw <u>stones</u> at him.
> b. <u>Men</u> of long ago were shorter than we are, but <u>they</u> were also stronger.
> c. <u>Fighting</u> in bronze <u>armor</u> was hard work even for strong <u>men</u>.
> d. Two <u>boys</u> were in the burning <u>house</u>; the brave <u>man</u> saved <u>one</u> but not the <u>other</u>.
> e. The bad <u>men</u> will not be able to convince anyone by <u>lying</u> about where they were.
> f. <u>Lying</u> comes naturally to bad <u>men</u>.
> g. Bad <u>men</u> live by <u>stealing</u>, but <u>they</u> don't get a good living from it.
> h. Good <u>things</u> are hard to get.
> i. Some <u>women</u> love beautiful <u>things</u>, but <u>others</u> do not.
> j. Good <u>women</u> are faithful, but <u>they</u> are not always humble.
> k. The <u>things</u> in the <u>temple</u> were saved from the <u>fire</u>.

Sentences

Translate into Greek using the vocabulary below and the constructions discussed in this chapter; omit words in parentheses.

1. The horse is carrying his master.
2. One carries a book, the other (does) not.
3. The poets do not always deliberate well.
4. Poets do not find courage by sacrificing in the marketplace.
5. The young learn well.
6. The men in the marketplace wish to sacrifice a horse.
7. The women of today (= now) learn by deliberating.
8. The poet wishes to deliberate with his brother, but he (i.e. the brother) is sacrificing in the marketplace.
9. The poets educated their brothers.
10. Courage (is) not bad.
11. One is sacrificing, and the other is deliberating.
12. Men of modern times (= now) do not eat horses.
13. The women in the marketplace are carrying books.
14. The young man wishes to find his horse, but he (i.e. the horse) is carrying a poet in the marketplace.

15. Learning (is) good.
16. Young people learn badness by being educated in the marketplace.
17. Good women always wish to be educated.
18. Some find courage by eating, but others do not.
19. Poets educated the good men.
20. Masters do not carry their slaves.
21. Current affairs (= the now things) (are) not bad.
22. Some (women) (are) shameful, but others (are) not.
23. The men with the poet deliberated well.
24. Messengers found the young man.
25. I wish to educate the shameful man, but he does not wish to learn.
26. A horse is carrying the young woman.
27. Slaves always learn badness.
28. The slave educates his master well.
29. Horses do not eat books.
30. The young woman learned the good things.
31. Some learn courage by being educated, but others (learn) shameful things.
32. The good man wishes to find the messenger, but he (i.e. the messenger) is eating with the young men.
33. Messengers found some (women), but not others.
34. Horses do not learn courage by deliberating.
35. The good woman wishes to educate the horses, but they do not wish to learn.

Vocabulary for chapter 1 sentences

always	ἀεί	marketplace	ἀγορά, -ᾶς, ἡ
bad	κακός, -ή, -όν	master	δεσπότης, -ου, ὁ
book	βιβλίον, -ου, τό	messenger	ἄγγελος, -ου, ὁ
brother	ἀδελφός, -οῦ, ὁ	not	οὐ
(to) carry	φέρω	now	νῦν
courage	ἀνδρεία, -ας, ἡ	poet	ποιητής, -οῦ, ὁ
(to) deliberate	βουλεύομαι	(to) sacrifice	θύω
(to) eat	ἐσθίω	shameful	αἰσχρός, -ά, -όν
(to) educate	παιδεύω	slave	δοῦλος, -ου, ὁ
(to) find	εὑρίσκω	the	ὁ, ἡ, τό
good	ἀγαθός, -ή, -όν	well	εὖ
horse	ἵππος, -ου, ὁ/ἡ	(to) wish	ἐθέλω (+ inf.)
in	ἐν (+ dat.)	with	μετά (+ gen.)
(to) learn	μανθάνω	young	νέος, -α, ον

Analysis

Translate into English as literally as is possible without being incomprehensible and explain each underlined article (both what it goes with and what it means) and the lack of article with those underlined words that are not articles. The order of the sentences is meaningful, as together they make up the opening of Xenophon's *Anabasis*.

1. Δαρείου καὶ Παρυσάτιδος γίγνονται παῖδες δύο, πρεσβύτερος μὲν Ἀρταξέρξης, νεώτερος δὲ <u>Κῦρος</u>· ἐπεὶ δὲ ἠσθένει Δαρεῖος καὶ ὑπώπτευε τελευτὴν <u>τοῦ</u> βίου, ἐβούλετο <u>τὼ</u> παῖδε ἀμφοτέρω παρεῖναι.

    (πρέσβυς "old," ἀσθενέω "grow weak," ὑποπτεύω "anticipate," τελευτή "end," τὼ παῖδε ἀμφοτέρω is a dual, πάρειμι "be present")

2. <u>ὁ</u> μὲν οὖν πρεσβύτερος παρὼν ἐτύγχανε· Κῦρον δὲ μεταπέμπεται ἀπὸ <u>τῆς</u> ἀρχῆς ἧς αὐτὸν σατράπην ἐποίησε, καὶ στρατηγὸν δὲ αὐτὸν ἀπέδειξε πάντων ὅσοι ἐς Καστωλοῦ πεδίον ἀθροίζονται.

    (μεταπέμπομαι "summon," σατράπης "satrap" i.e. a kind of governor, ἀθροίζω "assemble, collect")

3. ἀναβαίνει οὖν <u>ὁ</u> Κῦρος λαβὼν Τισσαφέρνην ὡς φίλον, καὶ <u>τῶν</u> Ἑλλήνων ἔχων <u>ὁπλίτας</u> ἀνέβη τριακοσίους, ἄρχοντα δὲ αὐτῶν Ξενίαν Παρράσιον.

    (τριακόσιοι "three hundred")

4. ἐπεὶ δὲ ἐτελεύτησε Δαρεῖος καὶ κατέστη εἰς <u>τὴν</u> βασιλείαν Ἀρταξέρξης, Τισ- σαφέρνης διαβάλλει <u>τὸν</u> Κῦρον πρὸς <u>τὸν</u> ἀδελφὸν ὡς ἐπιβουλεύοι αὐτῷ.

    (καθίσταμαι i.e. "settle into," διαβάλλω "slander," ἐπιβουλεύω "plot against")

5. <u>ὁ</u> δὲ πείθεται καὶ συλλαμβάνει Κῦρον ὡς ἀποκτενῶν· <u>ἡ</u> δὲ μήτηρ ἐξαιτησαμένη αὐτὸν ἀποπέμπει πάλιν ἐπὶ <u>τὴν</u> ἀρχήν.

    (συλλαμβάνω "arrest," ἐξαιτέομαι "beg off")

6. <u>ὁ</u> δ' ὡς ἀπῆλθε κινδυνεύσας καὶ ἀτιμασθείς, βουλεύεται ὅπως μήποτε ἔτι ἔσται ἐπὶ <u>τῷ</u> ἀδελφῷ, ἀλλά, ἢν δύνηται, βασιλεύσει ἀντ' ἐκείνου.

    (ἀτιμάζω "dishonor," ἐπί + dat. "in the power of," ἤν = ἐάν)

7. Παρύσατις μὲν δὴ <u>ἡ</u> μήτηρ ὑπῆρχε <u>τῷ</u> Κύρῳ, φιλοῦσα αὐτὸν μᾶλλον ἢ <u>τὸν</u> βασιλεύοντα Ἀρταξέρξην.

    (ὑπάρχω "support")

8. ὅστις δ' ἀφικνεῖτο <u>τῶν</u> παρὰ βασιλέως πρὸς αὐτὸν πάντας οὕτω διατιθεὶς ἀπεπέμπετο ὥστε αὐτῷ μᾶλλον φίλους εἶναι ἢ <u>βασιλεῖ</u>.

    (διατίθημι "cause to be disposed toward oneself")

9. καὶ <u>τῶν</u> παρ᾽ ἑαυτῷ δὲ βαρβάρων ἐπεμελεῖτο ὡς πολεμεῖν τε ἱκανοὶ εἴησαν καὶ εὐνοϊκῶς ἔχοιεν αὐτῷ.

(ἐπιμελέομαι "take care," εὐνοϊκῶς ἔχω "be well disposed")

10. <u>τὴν</u> δὲ Ἑλληνικὴν δύναμιν ἤθροιζεν ὡς μάλιστα ἐδύνατο ἐπικρυπτόμενος, ὅπως ὅτι ἀπαρασκευότατον λάβοι <u>βασιλέα</u>.

(ἀθροίζω "gather," ἐπικρυπτόμενος i.e. "secretly," ὅτι ἀπαρασκευότατος "as unprepared as possible")

11. ὧδε οὖν ἐποιεῖτο <u>τὴν</u> συλλογήν· ὁπόσας εἶχε φυλακὰς ἐν <u>ταῖς</u> πόλεσι παρήγγειλε <u>τοῖς</u> φρουράρχοις ἑκάστοις λαμβάνειν <u>ἄνδρας</u> Πελοποννησίους ὅτι πλείστους καὶ βελτίστους, ὡς ἐπιβουλεύοντος Τισσαφέρνους <u>ταῖς</u> πόλεσι.

(συλλογή "raising of troops," φρούραρχος "commander of garrision")

II | Modifiers

Material to learn before using this chapter: first and second declensions, article, and οὗτος (Smyth §216, 222, 227, 231, 235, 238, 287, 289, 332, 333 οὗτος only); Vocabulary 2 and associated principal parts
Recommended grammar reading: Smyth §1–239
Recommended syntax reading: Smyth §1018–20, 1040–3, 1154–89, 2025–37.

Greek uses adjectives, genitives, and other modifiers in a variety of different ways. In most cases it is the modifier's relationship to the article, not its relationship to the noun modified, that provides the crucial information on its construction.

A) Without the article. If a noun does not have the article, adjectives and possessive genitives are simply placed next to it (either before or after, though after is more usual for genitives).

ἀγαθὸν βιβλίον / βιβλίον ἀγαθόν	a good book
βιβλίον τοῦ δεσπότου	a book of the master's

Sometimes, particularly with a long modifier, this construction is equivalent to an English relative clause:

νεανίας τῇ τοῦ ἀγγέλου ἀδελφῇ φίλος	a young man who is dear to the messenger's sister

B) Attributive position. When a noun has the article, adjectives that modify it directly take the attributive position; that is, they come within the article–noun unit. Prepositional phrases and possessive genitives are also often found in attributive position. There are several types of attributive position:[1]

---

[1] In addition to the two given here, there is a type in which the modifier is placed after the noun and the article appears only with the modifier (βιβλίον τὸ ἀγαθόν "the good book"; βιβλίον τὸ ἐν τῷ νεῷ "the book in the temple"; βιβλίον τὸ τοῦ δεσπότου "the master's book"). This usage is much rarer than the others.

1) **Between article and noun** (common):

τὸ ἀγαθὸν βιβλίον	the good book
τὸ ἐν τῷ νεῴ βιβλίον	the book in the temple
τὸ τοῦ δεσπότου βιβλίον	the master's book

2) **After the noun**, with the article repeated (very useful for dealing with long, complex modifiers):

τὸ βιβλίον τὸ ἀγαθόν	the good book
τὸ βιβλίον τὸ ἐν τῷ νεῴ	the book in the temple
τὸ βιβλίον τὸ τοῦ δεσπότου	the master's book

Sometimes, particularly with a long modifier, this construction is equivalent to an English relative clause:

ὁ νεανίας ὁ τῇ τοῦ ἀγγέλου ἀδελφῇ φίλος	the young man who is dear to the messenger's sister

3) Note also these complications:

a) A **possessive genitive** thus attached to a noun with an article usually has the article too.

τὸ τοῦ Ἀλεξίππου βιβλίον	Alexippos' book (even if Alexippos is unknown)

b) One genitive can **nest** within another, but not if they have articles of identical form.

τὸ τῆς τοῦ ξαίνοντος τέχνης ἔργον	the work of the art of the wool-carder
but not	
*τὸ τῆς τῆς γυναικὸς τέχνης ἔργον	the work of the art of the woman

c) When **several modifiers** are attached in parallel to a single noun, multiple attributive constructions may be used, or (more commonly, if both modifiers are of the same type) the modifiers may be joined by a conjunction.

τὸ ἀγαθὸν βιβλίον τὸ τοῦ δεσπότου	the master's good book
τὸ βιβλίον τὸ ἀγαθὸν καὶ μέγα	the good, big book
τὸ ἀγαθὸν βιβλίον τὸ μέγα	the good, big book

Preliminary exercise 1 (on A and B). Translate into Greek using only the following vocabulary: ἀγαθός, -ή, -όν "good"; νέος, -α, -ον "young"; δοῦλος, -ου, ὁ "slave"; ἀγορά, -ᾶς, ἡ "marketplace." Which of these phrases cannot be translated in this way, and why?

a.   a good slave (acc., 2 ways)
b.   the good slave (nom., 2 ways)
c.   the slave in the marketplace (acc., 2 ways)
d.   the good man's slave (dat., 2 ways)
e.   the young man's slave (nom., 2 ways)
f.   the young men's slaves (gen.)
g.   a young slave (dat., 2 ways)
h.   the good woman's young slave (dat., 2 ways)
i.   the good woman's slave (gen., 2 ways)
j.   the young women in the marketplace (dat., 2 ways)
k.   slaves of the young men (nom.)
l.   the slave of the woman in the marketplace (acc., 2 ways)
m.   slaves of the young woman (gen.)
n.   the young woman's good slave (nom., 2 ways)
o.   the young man's slave (gen.)
p.   the young men in the marketplace (gen., 2 ways)
q.   the good young slave (gen., 3 ways)

C) Predicate position

1) Adjectives, *but not other modifiers*, become predicates when they stand outside the article–noun unit; in most cases this means that the verb "be" must be understood. In such sentences, as in most situations where there is a predicate nominative in Greek, the nominative with the article is usually the subject and the one without the article is usually the predicate.[2]

τὸ βιβλίον ἀγαθόν.	The book is good.
ἀγαθὸν τὸ βιβλίον.	The book is good.

2) Predicate position can also be used with a pair of nouns to indicate that the verb "be" is understood; again the one with the article is usually the subject.

ὁ πολίτης ποιητής.	The citizen is a poet.
πολίτης ὁ ποιητής.	The poet is a citizen.

---

[2] When the predicate of such sentences comes before the subject, it is often emphatic.

3) In such circumstances the rule that the predicate does not take an article may conflict with the rule that certain types of noun prefer to take an article. This conflict usually (but not always) results in the dropping of the article.

τὸ σοφὸν οὐ σοφία.   Cleverness is not wisdom.

4) **Demonstrative pronouns** do not follow these rules. Demonstratives functioning as adjectives always require the article and stand in what would for another adjective be predicate position, but they do not have predicate meaning.

τοῦτο τὸ βιβλίον   this book (not "the book is this one" nor
                                      "this is the book")

But demonstratives functioning as pronouns stand alone and never take the article.

ἔδεσθε τοῦτο;   Are you going to eat that?

5) Certain adjectives do not have the normal attributive/predicate distinction but rather a different one. They have one meaning in attributive position and a different one in predicate position; in neither position do they require the reader to supply the verb "be."

ἐν τῇ μέσῃ ὁδῷ	in the middle road (e.g. of three roads)
ἐν μέσῃ τῇ ὁδῷ / ἐν τῇ ὁδῷ μέσῃ	in the middle of the road
τὸ ἄκρον ὄρος	the high mountain
ἄκρον τὸ ὄρος / τὸ ὄρος ἄκρον	the top of the mountain
ὁ μόνος παῖς	the only child
μόνος ὁ παῖς ἦλθεν	only the child came / the child alone came / the child came alone
μόνος ἦλθεν	he alone came / he came alone

> **Preliminary exercise 2 (on C).** Translate into Greek using only the following vocabulary: ἀδελφός, -οῦ, ὁ "brother"; λίθος, -ου, ὁ "stone"; δοῦλος, -ου, ὁ "slave"; ἀγαθός, -ή, -όν "good"; μόνος, -η, -ον "alone, only"; μέσος, -η, -ον "middle"; οὗτος, αὕτη, τοῦτο "this, that"; ἐν (+ dat.) "in, on."
>
> a.   The slave is good. (2 ways)
> b.   The brother is good. (2 ways)
> c.   The brother is a slave. (2 ways)
> d.   The slave is a brother. (2 ways)
> e.   this slave (nom.)

f.   those things (nom.)

g.   these stones (acc.)

h.   those women (dat.)

i.   this man (gen.)

j.   these brothers (acc.)

k.   the middle brother (nom.)

l.   on the middle stone

m.   in the middle of the stone (2 ways)

n.   the brother alone (nom.)

o.   the only brother (acc.)

p.   only the brother (gen.)

q.   the only slaves (dat.)

r.   only the slaves (gen.)

s.   the stones alone remained (2 ways, do not translate "remained")

t.   the only stone (nom.)

D) Genitives and prepositional phrases do not have the same attributive/predicate distinction as adjectives.

1) Genitives and prepositional phrases may appear in predicate position without a major difference in meaning from attributive position.

τὸ βιβλίον τοῦ δεσπότου   the master's book

2) Predicate position without predicate meaning is standard for genitives that are not possessive.

τῶν πολιτῶν οἱ κακοί   the bad ones of the citizens / the bad men among
                             the citizens

E) Modifiers of **articular infinitives** observe the attributive/predicate distinction, but with some complications.

1) Articular infinitives may be directly modified by adverbs or prepositional phrases (but not by adjectives or possessive genitives), and they may take objects (in the accusative or whatever case the verb in question normally takes; verbs meaning "be" or "become" take predicate accusatives). Such dependent words may come between the article and the infinitive, or after the infinitive, but not before the article.

ἀντὶ τοῦ τοὺς δούλους εὖ παιδεύειν	instead of educating the slaves well
τῷ ἄρχειν τῆς πόλεως	by ruling the city
διὰ τὸ ἀγαθοὺς εἶναι	on account of being good (said of a group of men)

2) Articular infinitives may take neuter singular adjectives in predicate position; because of the cumbersome nature of many articular infinitives, such predicate adjectives often precede the article rather than following the infinitive.

αἰσχρὸν τὸ ἐν τῷ νεῴ ἐσθίειν.	Eating in the temple is shameful.
οὐ πονηρὸν τὸ παιδεύειν δούλους.	Educating slaves is not bad.

3) They may take subjects; such subjects are always accusative and come between the article and the infinitive.

αἰσχρὸν τὸ νέους μὴ μανθάνειν.	For young men not to learn is shameful. / It is shameful for young men not to learn. / Young men's not learning is shameful.[3]
οὐκ ἀγαθὸν τὸ ἵππους ἐσθίειν λίθους.	It is not good for horses to eat stones.

4) If negative, they take μή between the article and the infinitive.

τὸ μὴ θύειν οὐκ ἀγαθόν.	Not sacrificing is not good.

(The second negative in this example is οὐ because it goes not with the infinitive but with the understood ἐστί.)

> **Preliminary exercise 3 (on E).** Translate into Greek using only the following vocabulary: λίθος, -ου, ὁ "stone"; δοῦλος, -ου, ὁ "slave"; ἀγαθός, -ή, -όν "good"; οὗτος, αὕτη, τοῦτο "this, that"; θύειν "to sacrifice"; ἐσθίειν "to eat"; μανθάνειν "to learn"; διά (+ acc.) "on account of"; μή "not"; οὐ "not."
>
> a.   by learning
> b.   on account of learning
> c.   by eating stones (2 ways)
> d.   on account of eating stones (2 ways)
> e.   Eating stones is not good.
> f.   Not eating stones is good. (2 ways)

---

[3] Watch out for this type of English possessive with a gerund; it cannot be translated with a Greek genitive.

g.   It is good for slaves to learn.
h.   For slaves not to learn is not good.
i.   by sacrificing these things (2 ways)
j.   on account of these men's sacrificing
k.   It is not good not to sacrifice those things.
l.   It is good for those men to sacrifice.

F) Substantivized adjectives, adverbs, etc. have a slightly different use of modifiers.

1) They may take as negatives, in attributive position, either οὐ or μή, with a difference in meaning: οὐ indicates specificity and μή indicates generality. (Substantivized forms that are not negative can be either general or specific.)

οἱ ἀγαθοὶ θύουσιν.	Good men sacrifice. (general) / The good men are sacrificing. (specific)
οἱ οὐκ ἀγαθοὶ οὐ θύουσιν.	The men who are not good are not sacrificing. (specific)
οἱ μὴ ἀγαθοὶ οὐ θύουσιν.	Men who are not good do not sacrifice. (general)

2) They may take adverbs or prepositional phrases in attributive position, when those words fundamentally modify the substantivized word itself rather than something else in the sentence; such constructions are usually equivalent to an English relative clause.

οἱ ἔτι καλοὶ φεύγουσιν.	The men who are still beautiful are fleeing.
versus	
οἱ καλοὶ ἔτι φεύγουσιν.	The beautiful men are still fleeing.

3) They may take adjectives in predicate position; these often come before the article (see G for why).

ἀγαθοὶ οἱ νῦν.	Men of the present day are good.

G) Principles of article usage. An article is assumed to go with the first noun after it that it could agree with; if there is no such noun, it goes with the first adjective that it could agree with; if there is none, it goes with the first other word to which it could be attached. Therefore "The good women are sisters" cannot be expressed with αἱ ἀγαθαὶ ἀδελφαί, because that would mean "the good sisters."

Everything between the article and the word it ultimately goes with is viewed as a unit and can be broken up only by postpositive particles. If a word that cannot occur in attributive position, such as a finite verb, is encountered, it usually signals that the attributive position is at an end and forces the article to be taken with something before it. Therefore "The good women are sisters" could also be expressed with αἱ ἀγαθαί εἰσιν ἀδελφαί. Even a negative can function in this manner under certain circumstances; αἱ ἀγαθαὶ οὐκ ἀδελφαί means "The good women are not sisters," because the negative cannot be taken with the noun (nouns do not take negatives), nor with the adjective (οὐ cannot normally go with a preceding word), and therefore signals the presence of the understood verb that it has to go with.

> **Preliminary exercise 4 (on F and G).** Translate into Greek using only the following vocabulary: καλός, -ή, -όν "beautiful"; κακός, -ή, -όν "bad"; ἀδελφή, -ῆς, ἡ "sister"; ἄγγελος, -ου, ὁ "messenger"; οἰκία, -ας, ἡ "house"; ἐν (+ dat.) "in"; μανθάνω "learn." Which of these sentences can have words in several different orders, and which can have only one order?
>
> a. The beautiful women are not learning.
> b. The man in the house is a messenger.
> c. Women who are not beautiful do not learn.
> d. The beautiful men are messengers.
> e. The women who are not beautiful are learning.
> f. The bad women are sisters.
> g. Men who are not bad learn.
> h. The women in the house are sisters.
> i. The men who are not bad are not learning.
> j. The beautiful women are sisters.
> k. Men who are not bad do not learn.
> l. The men in the house are bad.
> m. The bad men do not learn.
> n. The bad man is a messenger.
> o. The woman in the house is beautiful.

Sentences

Translate into Greek using only words and constructions so far covered.

1. The dawn is always beautiful, even in the middle of the road.
2. Of the men in this house, some have a mind and others do not.
3. It is never good, O friend, for masters to hit their horses.
4. Men who are not in the temple will not sacrifice now.
5. The slave with the poet was always carrying books out of the house on the edge of the sea (and) into this beautiful temple.
6. By sacrificing a young horse to the gods of the sea, the man in the middle house long ago learned the allotted portion of his sister.

7.   The men from the land of beautiful horses are again eating alone in an old house on the edge of the sea.

8.   Both peace, O good man, and freedom and excellence are dear to free men.

9.   The man in the middle of the messengers wishes to learn the language of the gods well.

10.   The beautiful and good men often wished to have this young woman educated, but she does not have a good mind.

11.   Both the sea and voyages are dear to those young men.

12.   Only things that are not new, O young man,[4] are old.

13.   The courage of the poet's brothers educated even the slaves in the marketplace.

14.   The messenger's only voyage (was) bad.

15.   By not fleeing from a poet, this young horse learned courage long ago.

16.   These women too learned excellence by deliberating in the gods' temple, and now they have freedom.

17.   Even dawn is not beautiful to men who are not free.

18.   Bad things are dear only to shameful people.

19.   The middle road after the temple also leads (i.e. carries) to the house of the master's friends.

20.   O friend, the free man's sister was about to eat that.

21.   Goodness and beauty are dear not only to free men.

22.   Slaves, O young man, are never citizens.

23.   Only the shameful citizen never had his sister educated.

24.   Young men who are dear to beautiful women often do not wish to learn excellence by being well educated.

25.   The shameful young slave threw that poet's book into the sea again.

26.   The citizen with the messenger never learned the free woman's language.

27.   O friend, peace is always good.

28.   A citizen's throwing stones is always shameful.

29.   The friends again delayed carrying that into the middle of the land.

30.   The citizen's horse again fled from the new temple.

31.   This messenger is not a citizen.

32.   Women who are not shameful wish to sacrifice often.

33.   Never learning excellence, O good man, is shameful.

34.   The government's new freedom is dear to these men too.

35.   The young poet's only sister has come to this temple again.

36.   These poets are now about to educate the good men among the citizens.

37.   Peace is not the allotted portion of the bad citizens.

---

[4] Use νεανίας, as there is no singular vocative of νέος.

38. The young man in the marketplace now is a god.
39. It is not shameful for slaves to throw stones.
40. The good citizen learned by finding books in the marketplace long ago.
41. The government of the messenger's land is good now too.
42. Educating young men in a temple, O friend, is always good.

Analysis

Translate into English as literally as is possible without being incomprehensible and explain the underlined words with reference to the rules in this chapter.

1. Σωκράτης δ' ἐπεὶ διομολογήσαιτο <u>τὸ μὲν ἐργάτην εἶναι</u> <u>ὠφέλιμόν</u> τε ἀνθρώπῳ καὶ <u>ἀγαθὸν</u> εἶναι, <u>τὸ δὲ ἀργὸν</u> βλαβερόν τε καὶ κακόν, καὶ <u>τὸ μὲν ἐργάζεσθαι ἀγαθόν</u>, <u>τὸ δὲ ἀργεῖν</u> κακόν, τοὺς μὲν ἀγαθόν τι ποιοῦντας ἐργάζεσθαί τε ἔφη καὶ <u>ἐργάτας ἀγαθοὺς</u> εἶναι, τοὺς δὲ κυβεύοντας ἤ τι ἄλλο πονηρὸν καὶ ἐπιζήμιον ποιοῦντας ἀργοὺς ἀπεκάλει.

    (Xenophon, *Memorabilia* 1.2.57; διομολογέομαι "agree," ἐργάτης "worker," ὠφέλιμος "useful," ἀργός "lazy" (supply εἶναι after this word), βλαβερός "harmful" (supply εἶναι after this word), ἐργάζομαι "work," ἀργέω "be lazy," κυβεύω "play dice," ἐπιζήμιος "causing loss," ἀποκαλέω "call")

2. διὰ γὰρ <u>τὸ πολλοὺς εἰρηκέναι</u> καὶ <u>πάντας ἀκηκοέναι</u> προσήκει μὴ καινὰ μέν, πιστὰ δὲ δοκεῖν εἶναι <u>τὰ λεγόμενα</u> περὶ αὐτῶν.

    (Isocrates, *Panegyricus* 30; προσήκει "it is fitting," μή goes only with καινά, treat λεγόμενος "said" as an adjective)

3. ὁ μέν γε δι' ὀργάνων ἐκήλει τοὺς ἀνθρώπους <u>τῇ ἀπὸ τοῦ στόματος δυνάμει</u>, καὶ ἔτι νυνὶ ὃς ἂν <u>τὰ ἐκείνου</u> αὐλῇ – ἃ γὰρ Ὄλυμπος ηὔλει, Μαρσύου λέγω, τούτου διδάξαντος – τὰ οὖν ἐκείνου ἐάντε <u>ἀγαθὸς αὐλητὴς</u> αὐλῇ ἐάντε φαύλη αὐλητρίς, μόνα κατέχεσθαι ποιεῖ καὶ δηλοῖ τοὺς τῶν θεῶν τε καὶ τελετῶν δεομένους διὰ <u>τὸ θεῖα εἶναι</u>.

    (Plato, *Symposium* 215c; ὁ μέν i.e. Marsyas, ὄργανον "instrument," κηλέω "charm," στόμα "mouth," αὐλέω "play," Ὄλυμπος is the name of a poet here, ἐάντε "whether," αὐλητής "professional *aulos* player," φαῦλος "cheap," αὐλητρίς "*aulos*-girl," κατέχεσθαι ποιέω "cause to be enchanted," τελετή "religious ceremony," θεῖος "divine")

4. καὶ <u>τοῖς δὴ μὴ πλουσίοις</u>, χαλεπῶς δὲ τὸ γῆρας φέρουσιν, εὖ ἔχει ὁ αὐτὸς λόγος, ὅτι οὔτ' ἂν <u>ὁ ἐπιεικὴς</u> πάνυ τι ῥαδίως γῆρας μετὰ πενίας ἐνέγκοι, οὔθ' <u>ὁ μὴ ἐπιεικὴς</u> πλουτήσας εὔκολός ποτ' ἂν ἑαυτῷ γένοιτο.

(Plato, *Republic* 330a; γῆρας "old age," φέρουσιν is a participle, ἐπιεικής "reasonable," πενία "poverty," πλουτέω "become rich," εὔκολος "contented")

5.   τὸ γὰρ νέον ὄντα τοσοῦτον πρᾶγμα ἐγνωκέναι οὐ φαῦλόν ἐστιν· ἐκεῖνος γάρ, ὥς
      φησιν, οἶδε τίνα τρόπον οἱ νέοι διαφθείρονται καὶ τίνες οἱ διαφθείροντες αὐτούς·
      καὶ κινδυνεύει σοφός τις εἶναι· καὶ τὴν ἐμὴν ἀμαθίαν κατιδὼν ὡς διαφθείροντος
      τοὺς ἡλικιώτας αὐτοῦ, ἔρχεται κατηγορήσων μου ὡς πρὸς μητέρα πρὸς τὴν
      πόλιν.

      (Plato, *Euthyphro* 2c; γιγνώσκω i.e. "discover," φαῦλος "insignificant," treat διαφ-
      θείρων "corrupting" as an adjective, κινδυνεύω "be likely," διαφθείροντος is geni-
      tive because it agrees with an ἐμοῦ understood from the preceding ἐμήν, ἡλικιώτης
      "age-mate," κατηγορέω "accuse")

6.   ὃς ἀντὶ μὲν τοῦ μὴ νομίζειν θεούς, ὡς ἐν τῇ γραφῇ ἐγέγραπτο, φανερὸς ἦν θερ-
      απεύων τοὺς θεοὺς μάλιστα τῶν ἄλλων ἀνθρώπων· ἀντὶ δὲ τοῦ διαφθείρειν
      τοὺς νέους, ὃ δὴ ὁ γραψάμενος αὐτὸν ᾐτιᾶτο, φανερὸς ἦν τῶν συνόντων
      τοὺς πονηρὰς ἐπιθυμίας ἔχοντας τούτων μὲν παύων, τῆς δὲ καλλίστης καὶ
      μεγαλοπρεπεστάτης ἀρετῆς, ᾗ πόλεις τε καὶ οἶκοι εὖ οἰκοῦσι, προτρέπων ἐπι-
      θυμεῖν· ταῦτα δὲ πράττων πῶς οὐ μεγάλης ἄξιος ἦν τιμῆς τῇ πόλει;

      (Xenophon, *Memorabilia* 1.2.64; the sentence, which describes Socrates, is
      one long relative clause without any main clause; ἀντί "instead of," νομίζω
      "believe in," γραφή "indictment," φανερός "manifest" (i.e. "obviously"), θερ-
      απεύω "serve," μάλιστα "most of" (i.e. "more than"), διαφθείρω "corrupt,"
      γραψάμενος "accuser," αἰτιάομαι "accuse," ἐπιθυμία "desire," μεγαλοπρεπέστα-
      τος "magnificent," οἰκέω "be governed," προτρέπω "turn toward")

7.   ΣΩΚΡΑΤΗΣ: Ἀλλὰ μὴν ὅ γε εὖ ζῶν μακάριός τε καὶ εὐδαίμων, ὁ δὲ μὴ τἀναντία.
      ΘΡΑΣΥΜΑΧΟΣ: Πῶς γὰρ οὔ;
      ΣΩΚΡΑΤΗΣ: Ὁ μὲν δίκαιος ἄρα εὐδαίμων, ὁ δ᾽ ἄδικος ἄθλιος.

      (Plato, *Republic* 354a; treat ζῶν "living" as an adjective, τὰ ἐναντία "the opposite";
      what rule is violated here, and why do you think it was violated?)

III | Tenses, voices, and agreement

....

Material to learn before using this chapter: ω-verbs, indicative and
 infinitive (Smyth §383–4: indicative and infinitive forms only);
 Vocabulary 3 and associated principal parts
Recommended grammar reading: Smyth §355–84
Recommended syntax reading: Smyth §925–6, 949–75, 996–1017, 1030–39,
 1044–62, 1703–58, 1850–1965

....

A) Tenses in the indicative generally indicate time, but Greek tenses do not always match their English equivalents.[1]

1) The Greek aorist is normally used not only where English has the simple past, but also in most cases where English uses the pluperfect and in many where English uses the perfect.[2]

ἔπεσεν	he fell
ἔπαθεν ὅτι ἔπεσεν	he suffered because he had fallen

2) The imperfect is more usual than the aorist for an action that is by nature continuous, even where English uses a simple past.

εἶχεν	he had

3) The Greek imperfect is also the equivalent of the English progressive and repetitive pasts.

ἐδίδασκεν	he was teaching / he used to teach

4) The Greek present is the equivalent of the English simple present and present progressive.

πίπτει	he falls / he is falling

---

[1] For further detail see Appendix B.

[2] A simple rule for beginners in prose composition is to avoid the Greek perfect and pluperfect altogether except for the verbs in A5. A more advanced rule is to ask oneself, when one sees an English perfect, whether it denotes a lasting result; only if so is the Greek perfect an option.

5) The Greek perfect refers to a present state that results from a completed action in the past. Although conventionally translated by the English perfect, it is much less common; most situations in which English would use the perfect call for an aorist in Greek. A few verbs, however, are common in the Greek perfect because their perfects have distinct meanings; these perfects are normally equivalent to English presents, not to English perfects.

τέθνηκεν	he is dead (cf. ἀποθνῄσκει "he is dying," ἀπέθανεν "he died")
ἕστηκεν	he stands (cf. ἵσταται "he sets up for himself," ἔστη "he stood")
μέμνηται	he remembers (cf. μιμνῄσκεται "he is reminded," ἐμνήσθη "he remembered")

6) In those verbs, the Greek pluperfect is usually equivalent to an English imperfect.

εἱστήκει	he was standing

B) Tenses in the subjunctive, optative, imperative, and infinitive normally indicate aspect – whether an action is viewed as a process or as an event – rather than time, except in indirect speech.[3]

1) Aorist aspect indicates an event, i.e. a single action; this means that for most verbs, the aorist is normal for non-indicative forms.[4]

θῦσαι	to sacrifice
ἁρπάσαι	to snatch

2) Present aspect indicates a process, i.e. something continuous or repeated; this means that for certain verbs, the present is normal for non-indicative forms.

ἔχειν	to have
ἄγειν	to be leading / to lead repeatedly

3) The perfect is rarely used in non-indicative forms, except for the special present-like perfects in A5; when it does appear with another verb, it represents a state.

τεθνηκέναι	to be dead
μεμνῆσθαι	to remember

---

[3] For tenses of participles see chapter v; for tenses in indirect speech see chapter x.

[4] Overall, the aorist is more common than the present in the subjunctive and optative moods (and also in the indicative), but the present is more common in the imperative, infinitive, and participle. Source: corpus-based study by Yves Duhoux, *Le verbe grec ancien* (Louvain 2000) p. 505.

4) The future does not represent an aspectual distinction and is used non-indicatively only in a few special constructions (see chapters x and xi).

C) **The active voice** is used like the English active; verbs in the active may be intransitive (i.e. not taking an object) or may take one or more objects. Some intransitive actives can also take an agent construction (traditionally represented in English by "at the hands of," since English cannot use "by" with an active verb).

ὁ ξένος τὸν υἱὸν ἔλυσεν.	The stranger freed his son.
ὁ ξένος ἀπέθανεν.	The stranger died.
ὁ ξένος ἀπέθανεν ὑπὸ τῶν πολεμίων.	The stranger died at the hands of the enemy. / The stranger was killed by the enemy.

D) **The passive voice** is used like the English passive and cannot take an object, though it can take a construction of agent or of means.

ὁ ξένος ὑπὸ τοῦ υἱοῦ ἐλύθη.	The stranger was freed by his son.

> **Preliminary exercise 1 (on A–D).** Translate into Greek using only the following vocabulary: ξένος, -ου, ὁ "stranger"; σοφός, -ή, -όν "wise"; διώκω, διώξομαι, ἐδίωξα, δεδίωχα, –, ἐδιώχθην "pursue"; ἀποθνῄσκω, ἀποθανοῦμαι, ἀπέθανον, τέθνηκα "die, be killed"; ὑπό (+ gen.) "by, at the hands of"; ὅτι "because."
>
> a.   The wise man pursued the stranger.
> b.   The wise man died at the hands of the stranger.
> c.   to pursue (viewed as a process)
> d.   The stranger was being pursued by the wise man.
> e.   The wise man was not pursuing the stranger, because he was dying.
> f.   The wise man was pursued by the stranger.
> g.   to die
> h.   The stranger will pursue the wise man.
> i.   to pursue (viewed as an event)
> j.   The wise man will be pursued by the stranger.
> k.   to be dying
> l.   The stranger did not pursue the wise man because he had died.
> m.   The wise man used to be pursued by the stranger.
> n.   The stranger is being pursued by the wise man.
> o.   to be killed
> p.   The wise man is dying at the hands of the stranger.

q. The wise man used to pursue the stranger.
r. The stranger was not pursued because he had died.
s. to be being killed

E) The middle voice is normally translated by an English active and often takes an object. A number of verbs have a separate middle meaning, and others use the middle simply to indicate action in one's own interest or otherwise with reference to oneself. The middle is not a reflexive and is equivalent to the English reflexive only with a few verbs (usually verbs of habitual physical activity applied to one's body or clothing). Often middle meanings are not predictable from the active meanings and need to be learned individually.

ὁ ξένος τὸν υἱὸν ἐλύσατο.	The stranger ransomed his son.
ὁ ναύτης τὸν οἰκέτην ἐφυλάττετο.	The sailor was on guard against the house-slave.
τὸ ζῷον λούεται.	The animal is washing itself.

The most common separate middle meanings[5] are:

αἱρέομαι "choose"	versus	αἱρέω "take"
ἀμύνομαι "resist," "punish"	versus	ἀμύνω "defend"
ἀπέχομαι "refrain from"	versus	ἀπέχω "be distant from"
ἀποδίδομαι "sell"	versus	ἀποδίδωμι "give back"
ἀπόλλυμαι "perish"	versus	ἀπόλλυμι "destroy"
ἅπτομαι "touch," "grasp"	versus	ἅπτω "fasten," "kindle"
ἄρχομαι "begin"	versus	ἄρχω "rule"
γαμέομαι "marry" (female subject)	versus	γαμέω "marry" (male subject)
γράφομαι "indict"	versus	γράφω "write"
διδάσκομαι "cause to be taught"	versus	διδάσκω "teach"
ἐπιτίθεμαι "attack"	versus	ἐπιτίθημι "put on"
καίομαι "burn" (intransitive)	versus	καίω "burn" (transitive)
λούομαι "wash" (intransive), "take a bath"	versus	λούω "wash" (transitive)
λύομαι "ransom"	versus	λύω "release"
μισθόομαι "hire"	versus	μισθόω "hire out"
ὀνίναμαι "derive benefit from"	versus	ὀνίνημι "benefit"
ὀργίζομαι "be angry"	versus	ὀργίζω "enrage"
παιδεύομαι "cause to be educated"	versus	παιδεύω "educate"

---

[5] This list is given here only for reference; all these words are listed in the Vocabulary with their different meanings, often with more information on usage than is given here. See also Smyth §1734.

παύομαι "stop" (intransitive)	versus	παύω "stop" (transitive)
πείθομαι "obey"	versus	πείθω "persuade"
στρέφομαι "turn" (intransitive)	versus	στρέφω "turn" (transitive)
συμβουλεύομαι "consult"	versus	συμβουλεύω "advise"
τιμωρέομαι "take vengeance on"	versus	τιμωρέω "avenge"
τρέπομαι "turn" (intransitive)	versus	τρέπω "turn" (transitive)
φαίνομαι "seem," "be obviously"	versus	φαίνω "show"
φέρομαι "win"	versus	φέρω "carry"
φυλάττομαι "be on guard against"	versus	φυλάττω "guard"
ψεύδομαι "lie"	versus	ψεύδω "deceive," "cheat"

F) Agreement is generally straightforward, but neuter plural subjects regularly take a singular verb.

τὰ ζῷα τέθνηκεν.   The animals are dead.

> **Preliminary exercise 2 (on E and F).** Translate into Greek using the vocabulary in E and F.
>
> a.   she marries
> b.   we choose
> c.   he lies
> d.   we guard
> e.   they win
> f.   the animals seem
> g.   she takes vengeance
> h.   we consult
> i.   he marries
> j.   the animals obey
> k.   you educate
> l.   they are angry
> m. we ransom
> n.   she takes a bath
> o.   he indicts
> p.   they take
> q.   we begin
> r.   he persuades
> s.   the animals defend

Sentences

Translate into Greek using only words and constructions so far covered.

1. After that lawsuit, the courageous juror had immediately been killed by his enemies.
2. Wild animals often suffer bad things at the hands of humans.
3. The noble man's enemy wished in vain to be dead.
4. Perhaps the animals were released by the (military) enemy.
5. After the victory some of the enemy were dead, but others were being guarded by hoplites.
6. The prudent hoplite is guarding his only son on the middle island, but he (i.e. the son) wishes to drive the enemy out of this land.
7. Perhaps the lazy sailor was killed by falling into the middle of the river.
8. The good man's sons are already leading animals.
9. The wild animals were seized by human beings.
10. The unworthy sailor is not yet dead.
11. The stranger wished in vain to take the gold out of his enemy's house.
12. After the battle some of the hoplites were dead at the hands of the enemy, and others were fleeing.
13. The unjust stranger is being killed by his son.
14. Those men had already eaten the fruit.
15. For unworthy women to kill courageous men is almost impossible.
16. O guest-friend, the man having authority over prizes is dead.
17. Wild animals had pursued the house-slave into the middle of the road.
18. The lazy animals are already dead.
19. The guest-friends had not yet died.
20. After the war the inhabitants of the island no longer wished to be dead.
21. O human being, the men (who are) able to judge this lawsuit are dead at the hands of their enemies.
22. The juror's sister is still unjust both (in) word and (in) deed.
23. Some women took baths, and others suffered a bad disease.
24. It is impossible to teach an animal virtue.
25. The house-slave alone was on guard against wild animals.
26. The noble gift is almost worthy of a prize.
27. The wild animal is not yet being released by the wise sailor.
28. Perhaps both the island and the river were seized immediately.
29. The stranger will judge the (military) enemies alone. (Two versions with two different meanings.)
30. Being on guard against sailors is still prudent.

31. We shall judge between the speeches of the just and the unjust men.
32. It is impossible to have good judgement always.
33. This wise man is having his only house-slave taught, but he (the slave) (is) not able to learn.
34. The unjust men wished to dissolve the works of the wise men and to arrive at the island.
35. One woman was dragging the gold out of the sea, and the other was washing (it) in the river.

Analysis

Translate into English as literally as is possible without being incomprehensible, and comment on the underlined words with reference to the material in this chapter.

1. αἱ μέντοι κάμηλοι ἐφόβουν μόνον τοὺς ἵππους, οὐ μέντοι κατεκαίνοντό γε οἱ ἐπ᾽ αὐτῶν ἱππεῖς, οὐδ᾽ αὐτοί γε ἀπέθνησκον ὑπὸ ἱππέων· οὐδεὶς γὰρ ἵππος ἐπέλαζε.

    (Xenophon, *Cyropaedia* 7.1.48, describing a battle; κάμηλος "camel," κατακαίνω "kill," ἱππεύς "horseman," πελάζω "approach")

2. τὸ γὰρ γνῶναι ἐπιστήμην που λαβεῖν ἐστιν.

    (Plato, *Theaetetus* 209e)

3. ὦ Σώκρατες, πότερον ἡμᾶς βούλει δοκεῖν πεπεικέναι ἢ ὡς ἀληθῶς πεῖσαι, ὅτι παντὶ τρόπῳ ἄμεινόν ἐστι δίκαιον εἶναι ἢ ἄδικον;

    (Plato, *Republic* 357a)

4. Κλέαρχος μέν, ὦ ἄνδρες Ἕλληνες, ἐπεὶ ἐπιορκῶν τε ἐφάνη καὶ τὰς σπονδὰς λύων, ἔχει τὴν δίκην καὶ τέθνηκε, Πρόξενος δὲ καὶ Μένων, ὅτι κατήγγειλαν αὐτοῦ τὴν ἐπιβουλήν, ἐν μεγάλῃ τιμῇ εἰσιν.

    (Xenophon, *Anabasis* 2.5.38; ἐπιορκέω "swear falsely," σπονδαί "treaty," καταγγέλλω "denounce," ἐπιβουλή "plot")

5. μετὰ δὲ ταῦτα ἀνελόντα τὰς ἄρκυς καὶ τὰ δίκτυα, ἀνατρίψαντα τὰς κύνας ἀπιέναι ἐκ τοῦ κυνηγεσίου, ἐπιμείναντα, ἐὰν ᾖ θερινὴ μεσημβρία, ὅπως ἂν τῶν κυνῶν οἱ πόδες μὴ καίωνται ἐν τῇ πορείᾳ.

    (Xenophon, *Cynegeticus* 6.26; ἀναιρέω "take up," ἄρκυς "net," δίκτυον "casting-net," ἀνατρίβω "rub clean," κυνηγέσιον "hunt," ἐπιμένω "wait," θερινός "of summer," μεσημβρία "midday," πορεία "journey"; the sentence is a command with the infinitive for imperative)

6. ἡγοῦμαι μέν, ὦ ἄνδρες δικασταί, οὐδεμίαν ὑμᾶς ποθεῖν ἀκοῦσαι πρόφασιν παρὰ
    τῶν βουλομένων Ἀλκιβιάδου κατηγορεῖν· τοιοῦτον γὰρ πολίτην ἑαυτὸν ἐξ
    ἀρχῆς παρέσχεν, ὥστε καὶ εἰ μή τις ἰδίᾳ ἀδικούμενος ὑπ’ αὐτοῦ τυγχάνει, οὐδὲν
    ἧττον προσήκει ἐκ τῶν ἄλλων ἐπιτηδευμάτων ἐχθρὸν αὐτὸν ἡγεῖσθαι.

    (Lysias, *Oration* 14.1; ποθέω “desire,” πρόφασις “excuse, explanation,” κατη-
    γορέω “accuse,” παρέχω “present . . . as,” προσήκει “it concerns him,”
    ἐπιτήδευμα “custom”)

7. ἡγοῦντο γὰρ ταῖς μὲν ταπειναῖς τῶν πόλεων προσήκειν ἐκ παντὸς τρόπου
    ζητεῖν τὴν σωτηρίαν, ταῖς δὲ προεστάναι τῆς Ἑλλάδος ἀξιούσαις οὐχ οἷόν τ’
    εἶναι διαφεύγειν τοὺς κινδύνους, ἀλλ’ ὥσπερ τῶν ἀνδρῶν τοῖς καλοῖς κἀγαθοῖς
    αἱρετώτερόν ἐστιν καλῶς ἀποθανεῖν ἢ ζῆν αἰσχρῶς, οὕτω καὶ τῶν πόλεων ταῖς
    ὑπερεχούσαις λυσιτελεῖν ἐξ ἀνθρώπων ἀφανισθῆναι μᾶλλον ἢ δούλαις ὀφθῆναι
    γενομέναις.

    (Isocrates, *Panegyricus* 95; ταπεινός “lowly, unimportant,” προσήκει “it belongs
    to,” προΐσταμαι “be the chief power,” αἱρετώτερος i.e. “better,” ὑπερέχω “rise
    above the others,” λυσιτελεῖ “it profits,” ἀφανίζομαι “disappear”)

8. τίνας οὖν, ἔφη, ὑπὸ τίνων εὕροιμεν ἂν μείζω εὐηργετημένους ἢ παῖδας ὑπὸ
    γονέων; οὓς οἱ γονεῖς ἐκ μὲν οὐκ ὄντων ἐποίησαν εἶναι, τοσαῦτα δὲ καλὰ ἰδεῖν καὶ
    τοσούτων ἀγαθῶν μετασχεῖν, ὅσα οἱ θεοὶ παρέχουσι τοῖς ἀνθρώποις· ἃ δὴ καὶ
    οὕτως ἡμῖν δοκεῖ παντὸς ἄξια εἶναι ὥστε πάντες τὸ καταλιπεῖν αὐτὰ πάντων
    μάλιστα φεύγομεν, καὶ αἱ πόλεις ἐπὶ τοῖς μεγίστοις ἀδικήμασι ζημίαν θάνατον
    πεποιήκασιν ὡς οὐκ ἂν μείζονος κακοῦ φόβῳ τὴν ἀδικίαν παύσαντες.

    (Xenophon, *Memorabilia* 2.2.3; εὐεργετέω “benefit,” γονεύς “parent,” μετέχω
    “share in,” παρέχω “provide,” φεύγω i.e. “try to avoid,” ἀδίκημα i.e. “crime”)

IV | Cases

Material to learn before using this chapter: declension of numbers (Smyth §349); Vocabulary 4 and associated principal parts
Recommended grammar reading: Smyth §347–54
Recommended syntax reading: Smyth §1279–1702

In most situations case is determined by the individual requirements of verbs and prepositions, but there are some independent uses of cases, and a few tricks having to do with English usage.

A) Time is divided into three categories.

1) The **time *at* which** something occurs is normally represented by the dative without a preposition ("dative of time when"); this is often equivalent to English "at" or "on."

τῇ δευτέρᾳ ἡμέρᾳ ἀφίκοντο.   They arrived on the second day.

But some words take a preposition in this construction:

ἅμα τῇ ἕῳ / ἅμ᾽ ἡμέρᾳ   at dawn (i.e. "together with the dawn/day")

2) The **time *within* which** something occurs is represented by the genitive without a preposition ("genitive of time within which"); this is often equivalent to English "within," "during," or "at."

δυοῖν ἡμερῶν ἀφίξονται.   They will arrive within two days.
τῆς νυκτὸς ἀφίκετο.   He arrived during the night. / He arrived at night.

3) The **time *for* which** something continues to happen is represented by the accusative without a preposition ("accusative of extent"); this is often equivalent to English "for" and sometimes to "during," but it is also used in situations where English would not use any preposition.

δύο ἡμέρας ἔγραφεν.   He was writing for two days.
ἔτι δύο ἔτη ἔζη.   He lived another two years.

B) Place is normally indicated by prepositions; these tend to take the dative for the place where something is located, the genitive for the place from which it moves, and the accusative for the place toward which it moves.

1) But certain words have special one-word forms to express these ideas (generally using -ι to indicate stationary position, -θεν to indicate motion from, and -δε or -ζε to indicate motion toward), and when a word has such a form, it is normally used instead of the prepositional phrase.

Ἀθήνησι μένει.	He is staying in Athens.
Ἀθήνηθεν ἔφυγεν.	He fled from Athens.
Ἀθήναζε ἀφίκετο.	He arrived at[1] Athens.
οἴκοι μένει.	He is staying home.
οἴκοθεν ἔφυγεν.	He fled his home.
οἴκαδε ἀφίκετο.	He arrived home.

2) **Extent** of space is expressed by the accusative without a preposition ("accusative of extent").

δύο σταδίους τὰ ζῷα ἤγαγεν.	He led the animals (for) two stades.
τρεῖς σταδίους ἀπέχει (ἀπὸ) τῶν Ἀθηνῶν.[2]	It is three stades distant from Athens.

3) **Dimensions** are expressed by the genitive of a number and a unit of measurement, with an accusative (actually an accusative of respect, see D below) of a noun indicating the appropriate dimension; although Greek has adjectives for "long," "wide," and "high," they are not normally used with numbers.

νεὼς ἑκατὸν ποδῶν τὸ μῆκος	a temple a hundred feet long (= a temple of a hundred feet with respect to its length)
ποταμὸς τεττάρων ποδῶν τὸ εὖρος	a river four feet wide (= a river of four feet with respect to its width)
ὄρος τριῶν σταδίων τὸ ὕψος	a mountain three stades high (= a mountain of three stades with respect to its height)

---

[1] Notice how the English here gives no hint of the motion implied by the Greek construction; such situations are common, so when translating into Greek it is important to check whether the Greek verb expresses motion.

[2] Notice that Ἀθήνηθεν is not used here, because there is no motion.

Preliminary exercise 1 (on A and B). Translate into Greek using the examples above and the following vocabulary: πέντε "five"; ἑπτά "seven"; τρίτος, -η, -ον "third"; τέταρτος, -η, -ον "fourth"; ἡμέρα, -ας, ἡ "day"; λίθος, -ου, ὁ "stone"; οἰκία, -ας, ἡ "house"; ἀφικνέομαι, ἀφίξομαι, ἀφικόμην, –, ἀφῖγμαι "arrive"; μένω, μενῶ, ἔμεινα, μεμένηκα "stay."

a. He will arrive at Athens on the third day.
b. The house is three stades distant from Athens.
c. a stone five feet high
d. He will arrive home within seven days.
e. They are staying in Athens for five days.
f. a house seven feet wide
g. He will arrive from home on the fourth day.
h. He will stay at home for five days.
i. a stone seven feet long
j. He will arrive from Athens within five days.
k. a house seven feet high
l. The stone is seven stades distant from Athens.
m. a stone five feet wide
n. They are staying in Athens for seven days.
o. a house five feet long

C) Agent, means, and accompaniment are sometimes confused because of the various uses of English "with" and "by."

1) When "by" refers to an animate **agent**, it is equivalent to ὑπό + genitive, unless the verb is in the perfect or pluperfect passive or is a verbal adjective (see chapter xvii), in both of which cases Greek uses the dative without a preposition ("dative of agent").

ὑπὸ ναύτου ἐβλήθη.	He was hit by a sailor.
ναύτῃ βέβληται.	He has been hit by a sailor.

2) When "by" or "with" refers to an **instrument**, i.e. an inanimate object, it is equivalent to the Greek dative without a preposition ("dative of means").

λίθοις αὐτὸν ἔβαλον.	They hit him with stones.
λίθῳ ἐβλήθη.	He was hit by a stone.

3) When "with" indicates **accompaniment**, it is equivalent to μετά with the genitive or σύν with the dative.

μετὰ ναύτου ἔφυγεν.   He fled with a sailor.

σὺν ναύτῃ ἔφυγεν.   He fled with a sailor.

4) When "with" is used of a **leader** in a military context, it is equivalent to ἄγων or ἔχων (with the accusative).

ἀφίκετο ἄγων ἑκατὸν ὁπλίτας.   He arrived with a hundred hoplites.

5) When "with" or another word such as "in" indicates the **way or fashion** in which something is done, and the object of "with" or "in" consists of two words (a noun and a modifier), it is equivalent to the dative without a preposition.[3] When the object is only one word, the prepositionless dative may be used for certain words (including σιγῇ "in silence," σιωπῇ "in silence," τῇ ἀληθείᾳ "in truth," τῷ ὄντι "in reality," ὀργῇ "in anger," (τῷ) ἔργῳ "in fact," (τῷ) λόγῳ "in word," προφάσει "ostensibly," βίᾳ "by force"),[4] but most take σύν with the dative (or, less often, μετά + gen. or πρός + acc.). This construction is sometimes almost interchangeable with the adverb.

σιγῇ ἔφυγον.   They fled in silence.

σὺν δίκῃ ἀπέθανεν.   He was justly killed. (almost = δικαίως)

τύχῃ ἀγαθῇ ἀφίκοισθε.   May you arrive with good fortune.

> **Preliminary exercise 2 (on C).** Indicate whether the underlined words would be translated into Greek with ὑπό + genitive, the dative, μετά/σύν, or ἄγων/ἔχων.
>
> The general arrived with only fifty soldiers, who were swiftly defeated by the enemy. He fought with great courage – I know, because I fought along with him – but not with good fortune, for he was hit by several arrows and his horse was killed by a spear-thrust. In the end he was captured by a gigantic cavalry officer who came with ten men when the general was already wounded. The men caught him with a rope, which they threw around him from a distance, but once they had secured him he was, with justice, treated with great respect. The other captives with him were, in truth, amazed at the way he endured his sufferings in silence, while they acknowledged their own with lamentations. But in reality the men with him indeed had more to complain about, for they were sometimes beaten with sticks by their guards, or flogged with whips by the torturers, while the general was always well treated by everyone, even if he was oppressed, like all the prisoners, by cold

---

[3] This is called "dative of manner" in many grammars, but "dative of accompanying circumstance" in Smyth.

[4] See Smyth §1527 for others.

and hunger. He was also grieved <u>by</u> the pain of his wounds, though these were eventually healed <u>by</u> the prison doctor (or perhaps, as the cure cannot be attributed <u>with</u> certainty to a particular source, simply <u>by</u> his own immune system), and <u>by</u> a feeling of responsibility for the plight of the others. Eventually the men who had been captives <u>with</u> him, having been sold as slaves <u>by</u> their captors, departed <u>with</u> much weeping and wailing, and the general was ransomed <u>by</u> his family. He was delighted to be back <u>with</u> his children, whom he amused <u>with</u> stories of his adventures.

D) Respect, or the extent to which something is true, can be expressed by either the dative or the accusative without a preposition ("dative of respect," "accusative of respect"), but the accusative is more frequent. It is important when using this construction not to create ambiguity with other uses of these cases. The accusative of respect is closely related to, and sometimes indistinguishable from, the **adverbial accusative**, which acts like an adverb.

ὁ ὁπλίτης ταχὺς τοὺς πόδας.	The hoplite is quick with respect to his feet.
τίνα τρόπον ἐσώθη;	In what way was he saved?
τίνι τρόπῳ ἐσώθη;	In what way was he saved?

E) Possession is normally indicated by the genitive, but it can also be expressed by the dative with a verb meaning "be" ("dative of possession"). The two are not completely interchangeable: the dative of possession is the equivalent of English "have" and the genitive is (usually) the equivalent of English "of" or "'s."

ἡ τοῦ πολίτου οἰκία ἐστὶ καλή.	The citizen's house is beautiful.
τῷ πολίτῃ οἰκία ἐστὶ καλή.	The citizen has a beautiful house.

F) Value. The genitive is used without a preposition to indicate the worth, value, or price of something ("genitive of price and value").

ἀργυρίου ἀποδόσθαι ἵππον	to sell a horse for money
ἱερὰ τριῶν ταλάντων	offerings worth three talents

> **Preliminary exercise 3 (on D, E, and F).** For each of the underlined words or phrases, indicate whether it would be translated in Greek as a dative/accusative of respect, a genitive of possession, a dative of possession, or a genitive of price and value.
>
> <u>I have</u> a statue worth <u>two talents</u>. It was a bargain: I bought it for <u>fifty minae</u>. It is very beautiful, especially in <u>its face</u>, and is supposed to have been made

by one of Pheidias' sons. It was formerly owned by a Spartan nobleman, who was not really very Spartan with respect to his tastes or his budget: he bought it for a talent and a half. He also had five other statues that were even more beautiful; I don't know how much they were worth, but they were all excellent in design, in workmanship, and in the quality of their materials. Eventually, of course, the Spartan authorities noticed that my friend was being un-Spartan with respect to his art collection; in what way they found out, I do not know for sure. They inspected my friend's house and forced him to sell his artworks at a loss: my statue was sold for fifty minae, as I said, and the others went for one talent each to statue dealers. It is said that he also had some black-figure vases, old-fashioned in their glazing technique but of very high quality with respect to their painting, and that these were sold not for money but for the good will of the authorities – in other words, given as a bribe so that the authorities would allow my friend to keep the non-Spartan servants he had, who were excellent with respect to their cooking skills and their sewing.

G) With verbs, adjectives, and adverbs. The cases taken by different words should be individually learned, but there are some general principles:

1) The genitive tends to be used with words of touching, beginning, desiring or aiming at, obtaining, missing, sense perception, eating, being full of, leading, ruling, ceasing, needing, separation, remembering, and forgetting. Verbs having to do with legal action often take a genitive of the crime or the penalty; verbs of emotion can take a genitive of the cause of the emotion.

2) The dative tends to be used with words of helping, pleasing, having negative emotions toward, meeting, obeying, pardoning, advising, association, accompaniment, and being like or unlike. The ethical dative and datives of advantage and disadvantage can be used to indicate someone's interest in the verbal action.

Sentences

Translate into Greek using only words and constructions so far covered; use the dative of possession (with ἐστί "is") instead of ἔχω. Be prepared to use the datives of manner "in reality" (τῷ ὄντι), "in anger" (ὀργῇ), "in truth" (τῇ ἀληθείᾳ), "justly" (σὺν δίκῃ), "in silence" (σιγῇ), and "by force" (βίᾳ). English perfects in these sentences should be translated by Greek perfects except where otherwise noted.

1.   At Athens, some people sometimes have animals worth a talent, and others have animals worth two drachmae.

2.   According to this man, it is in reality not impossible for jurors to be hit with fruits here.

3.   On the second day, with a hundred hoplites, he (i.e. the general) pursued the inhabitants for three stades to a river twenty feet wide.

4.   The sailor's sister, (who is) not prudent with respect to her judgement, has just now been[5] dragged home from here by her brother without her house-slaves.

5.   The men at the juror's house have a guest-friend at Marathon.

6.   The unjust ones among the strangers sometimes used to hit their slaves with stones in anger, but they (i.e. the slaves) have now fled here from Athens.

7.   The sailors' sons, the ones before the temple, never wish to take baths at home during the day.

8.   In truth ransoming with gold hoplites who are lazy with respect to the war is not prudent.

9.   Before the battle, some of these citizens sacrificed for six days, and others (sacrificed) for seven days.

10. The young men in Athens have been well educated by the wise men there.

11. After the victory, the enemy's hoplites fled for three days and arrived home late on the fourth.

12. The battle against the hoplites was five stades distant from the river.

13. The bad house-slaves were justly killed by disease within eight days.

14. At dawn on the third day we carried fruits, worth nine drachmae, from home four stades to the temple.

15. At dawn yesterday[6] the young men who were courageous with respect to their words alone suddenly fled their homes and fell into a river ten feet wide.

16. The stranger at the sailor's house has a son who is courageous with respect to his deeds.

17. Instead of guarding the islands, within six days he (the commander) will arrive at Athens with a thousand hoplites because of the war.

18. On the fourth day the men who are unjust both with respect to their deeds and with respect to their words seized by force the gifts in the temple fifty feet long.

19. No-one at Athens now has a slave worth five hundred drachmae.

20. Contrary to the words of the wise man, the messenger from the strangers did not arrive here within seven days.

21. After those speeches against voyages and the sea, no-one wished to flee elsewhere.

22. The land beyond the sea is countless stades distant from Athens.

---

[5] Requires the present tense in Greek.   [6] I.e. yesterday, together with the dawn.

23. The wild animals there used to be killed then by humans in silence.
24. The fruits here have been washed twice by the slaves at home.
25. Instead of being killed by disease at home, this man died at Marathon at the hands of the enemy.
26. You will teach the young man badness by not guarding the gold today.
27. The messenger from there has come to Athens twice because of the war on behalf of the citizens.
28. None of the noble women wished to arrive there early.
29. Those men were carrying stones over the river for ten days before the battle.
30. Instead of throwing books, a wise man teaches with beautiful words and noble deeds.

Analysis

Translate into English as literally as is possible without being incomprehensible, give the case of the underlined words, and explain the reason for each case.

1. παρὰ ταύτην τὴν πόλιν ἦν πυραμὶς λιθίνη, τὸ μὲν εὖρος ἑνὸς πλέθρου, τὸ δὲ ὕψος δύο πλέθρων.

   (Xenophon, *Anabasis* 3.4.9; πυραμίς "pyramid," λίθινος "made of stone," πλέθρον is a unit of measurement of *c.* 100 feet)

2. . . . ἀπῆλθεν εἰς Ἔφεσον, ἣ ἀπέχει ἀπὸ Σάρδεων τριῶν ἡμερῶν ὁδόν.

   (Xenophon, *Hellenica* 3.2.11)

3. τίς, ἦν δ᾽ ἐγώ, καὶ ποδαπός, καὶ πόσου διδάσκει; Εὔηνος, ἔφη, ὦ Σώκρατες, Πάριος, πέντε μνῶν.

   (Plato, *Apology* 20b, an inquiry about a teacher; ποδαπός "of what land," Πάριος "from Paros")

4. τῇ δ᾽ ὑστεραίᾳ ὁ μὲν Ἀγησίλαος ἀπέχων Μαντινείας ὅσον εἴκοσι σταδίους ἐστρατοπεδεύσατο . . .

   (Xenophon, *Hellenica* 6.5.16; ὅσον "nearly," στρατοπεδεύω "encamp")

5. καταβὰς δὲ διὰ τούτου τοῦ πεδίου ἤλασε σταθμοὺς τέτταρας παρασάγγας πέντε καὶ εἴκοσιν εἰς Ταρσούς, τῆς Κιλικίας πόλιν μεγάλην καὶ εὐδαίμονα, οὖ ἦν τὰ Συεννέσιος βασίλεια τοῦ Κιλίκων βασιλέως· διὰ μέσου δὲ τῆς πόλεως ῥεῖ ποταμὸς Κύδνος ὄνομα, εὖρος δύο πλέθρων.

   (Xenophon, *Anabasis* 1.2.23; ἐλαύνω "march," σταθμός is one day's journey for an army on foot, παρασάγγης is a unit of measurement (about 3 ½ miles), Συέννεσις is the king's name and -ιος a genitive ending, βασίλεια (neut. pl.) "palace," ῥέω "flow," πλέθρον is a unit of measurement of *c.* 100 feet)

6. εἶχον δ᾽ οἱ Χαλδαῖοι γέρρα τε καὶ <u>παλτὰ</u> δύο· καὶ πολεμικώτατοι δὲ λέγονται <u>οὗτοι</u> τῶν περὶ ἐκείνην τὴν <u>χώραν</u> εἶναι· καὶ <u>μισθοῦ</u> στρατεύονται, ὁπόταν τις <u>αὐτῶν</u> δέηται, διὰ τὸ πολεμικοί τε καὶ πένητες εἶναι· καὶ γὰρ ἡ χώρα <u>αὐτοῖς</u> ὀρεινή τέ ἐστι καὶ ὀλίγη ἡ τὰ <u>χρήματα</u> ἔχουσα.

(Xenophon, *Cyropaedia* 3.2.7; γέρρον "wicker shield," παλτόν "light spear," μισθός "wages," στρατεύομαι "serve in army," ὀρεινός "mountainous," χρῆμα "useful produce"; pay attention to the ἡ near the end)

7. ἃ μὲν τοίνυν, ἦν δ᾽ ἐγώ, ζῶντι τῷ <u>δικαίῳ</u> παρὰ θεῶν τε καὶ ἀνθρώπων <u>ἆθλά</u> τε καὶ μισθοὶ καὶ δῶρα γίγνεται πρὸς ἐκείνοις τοῖς <u>ἀγαθοῖς</u> οἷς αὐτὴ παρείχετο ἡ <u>δικαιοσύνη</u>, τοιαῦτ᾽ ἂν εἴη.

(Plato, *Republic* 613e–614a; ἆθλον "prize," μισθός "wage," πρός "in addition to," παρέχομαι "provide")

8. ἦν δὲ ἡ μὲν κρηπὶς λίθου ξεστοῦ κογχυλιάτου, τὸ <u>εὖρος</u> πεντήκοντα <u>ποδῶν</u> καὶ τὸ <u>ὕψος</u> πεντήκοντα. ἐπὶ δὲ <u>ταύτῃ</u> ἐπῳκοδόμητο πλίνθινον <u>τεῖχος</u>, τὸ μὲν <u>εὖρος</u> πεντήκοντα <u>ποδῶν</u>, τὸ δὲ <u>ὕψος</u> ἑκατόν· τοῦ δὲ <u>τείχους</u> ἡ περίοδος ἓξ παρασάγγαι.

(Xenophon, *Anabasis* 3.4.10–11; κρηπίς "foundation," λίθος κογχυλιάτης "shelly marble," ξεστός "polished," ἐποικοδομέω "build up," πλίνθινος "made of brick," περίοδος "circumference," παρασάγγης is a unit of measurement, about 3½ miles)

V │ Participles

Material to learn before using this chapter: participles (Smyth §383–4
(participles only), 305–10); Vocabulary 5 and associated principal
parts
Recommended grammar reading: Smyth §300–10
Recommended syntax reading: Smyth §2039–2148

Participles are much more common and more important in Greek than in English.
Many types of subordinate clause have participial equivalents, and in some cases the
participial versions are more common than the ones with finite verbs. The ability to
choose between participial and finite-verb expressions as needed allows Greek authors
to attach many subordinates to a single main clause without ambiguity or stylistic infe-
licity and is thus one of the cornerstones of Greek prose writing.

A) Attributive participles are usually equivalent to a restrictive (defining) relative
clause;[1] they usually take an article and are the only type of participle construction to
do so.[2]

1) **Adjectival** participles are used with a noun and are frequently found in attributive
position; their negative is οὐ.

ηὖρον τὸν γράφοντα δοῦλον.	They found the slave who was writing.
ὁ δοῦλος ὁ γράφων κλέπτης.	The slave who is writing is a thief.

2) **Substantival** participles have only an article, masculine or feminine for people and
neuter for things or abstractions; they function like substantivized adjectives (chapter II
section F), and therefore their negative is οὐ if specific or μή if general.

ὁ φεύγων αἰσχρός.	The man who is fleeing is shameful. / The man who flees (i.e. anyone who flees) is shameful.
ηὖρον τοὺς οὐ γράφοντας.	They found the (specific) people who were not writing.

---

[1] For clues to identifying restrictive relative clauses see chapter VIII note 2; until that point all relative clauses in
this book will be restrictive.

[2] They are used without an article when they modify an expressed noun that does not have the article, like the
adjectives in chapter II A.

ηὗρον τοὺς μὴ γράφοντας.	They found (all) those who were not writing. / They found whoever was not writing. / They found such men as were not writing.
τὰ γεγραμμένα ἀγαθά.	What has been written is good. (either specific or general)

Preliminary exercise 1 (on A 1–2). Translate into Greek using participles and the following vocabulary: δοῦλος, -ου, ὁ "slave"; φεύγω, φεύξομαι, ἔφυγον, πέφευγα "flee"; φυλάττω, φυλάξω, ἐφύλαξα, πεφύλαχα, πεφύλαγμαι, ἐφυλάχθην "guard."

a. The slaves who are not guarded will flee.
b. The slaves who were guarded (use present participle) did not flee.
c. Those who are guarded will not flee.
d. The (specific) people who are not guarded will flee.
e. Whoever is not guarded will flee.
f. Such people as were not guarded fled.
g. The slaves who fled are (now) being guarded.
h. Whoever has fled will be guarded.
i. The (specific) people who did not flee are not being guarded.
j. The slaves who did not flee will be guarded.
k. Such people as did not flee are not being guarded.
l. Whoever has not fled will not be guarded.

B) Circumstantial participles never have the article and are never equivalent to restrictive relative clauses.[3] They are divided into different types equivalent to a wide range of different subordinate clauses. The negative for these participles is always οὐ except for the conditional ones, which take μή.

1) Most types of circumstantial participle agree with a word elsewhere in the sentence, or with the understood subject of a verb.

a) **Temporal** participles indicate the time of an action and may be accompanied by the adverbs ἅμα, μεταξύ, εὐθύς, or ἄρτι.[4]

---

[3] They are, however, occasionally equivalent to non-restrictive relative clauses.

[4] Because circumstantial participles never act as nouns, they can only be modified by adverbs, never adjectives, nor can they be the objects of prepositions; even when a participle is modified by a word that would in another context be a preposition, that word acts like an adverb because of the presence of the participle (e.g. ἅμα cannot take an object when modifying a participle).

ηὗρε τὸν ἀδελφὸν ἅμα γράφοντα.   She found her brother as he was writing.

ηὗρε τὸν ἀδελφὸν ἄρτι γεγραφότα.   She found her brother when he had just written.

b) **Final** participles express purpose and are always in the future tense; they may take ὡς.

ἀπέπεμψα τὸν δοῦλον γράψοντα.   I sent the slave away to write.

ἔγραψα ὡς σώσων τὸν δοῦλον.   I wrote in order to save the slave.

c) **Causal** participles indicate the reason for an action and are often preceded by ἅτε, οἷα, or ὡς (see E 3).

διδάσκει τὸν δοῦλον ἅτε οὐ γράψαντα.   She is teaching the slave because he did not write.

ἔφυγεν οἷα τυπτόμενος.   He fled because he was being beaten.

d) **Concessive** participles are equivalent to English clauses with "although" and are usually accompanied by καίπερ or καί with the participle or by ὅμως with the main verb.

διδάσκει τὸν δοῦλον καίπερ γράψαντα.   She is teaching the slave although he wrote.

διδασκόμενος ὅμως οὐκ ἔγραψεν ὁ   Although he was being taught, δοῦλος.   nevertheless the slave did not write.

e) **Comparative** participles are accompanied by ὥσπερ and are equivalent to an English clause with "as if."

τύπτει τὸν ἵππον ὥσπερ φυγόντα.   She is beating the horse as if it had fled.

ὁ ἵππος ἔφυγεν ὥσπερ τυπτόμενος.   The horse fled as if it were being beaten.

f) **Conditional** participles are equivalent to the protasis of a conditional sentence and therefore to an English "if"-clause. They do not have any characteristic adverbs and are therefore ambiguous unless determined by context, or unless they are negative, in which case they are identifiable by their use of μή. The main clause of a sentence containing a conditional participle follows the rules for the apodoses of conditions (see chapter VII); this means that contrafactual sentences have apodoses with a past tense of the indicative and ἄν.

τυπτόμενος φεύξεται.	If (or when) he is beaten, he will flee.
μὴ τυπτόμενος οὐ φεύξεται.	If he is not beaten, he will not flee.
(= ἐὰν μὴ τύπτηται οὐ φεύξεται.)	
μὴ πληγεὶς οὐκ ἂν ἔφυγεν.	If he had not been beaten, he would not
(= εἰ μὴ ἐπλήγη οὐκ ἂν ἔφυγεν.)	have fled.

g) Participles expressing **manner** or **means**.

παρήλαυνον τεταγμένοι.	They marched past in order.

h) Ἄγων and ἔχων = "with," for military leaders etc. (cf. chapter IV C4).

ἦλθεν ἔχων ἑκατὸν ἄνδρας.	He came with a hundred men.

> **Preliminary exercise 2 (on B 1).** Translate into Greek using participles, the adverbs listed above, and the following vocabulary: δοῦλος, -ου, ὁ "slave"; φεύγω, φεύξομαι, ἔφυγον, πέφευγα "flee"; φυλάττω, φυλάξω, ἐφύλαξα, πεφύλαχα, πεφύλαγμαι, ἐφυλάχθην "guard."
>
> a. The slave fled while he was being guarded (use present participle).
> b. The slave did not flee, because he was guarded (use present participle).
> c. The slave fled although he was guarded (use present participle).
> d. The slave fled as if he were not being guarded (use present participle).
> e. If he is not guarded, the slave will flee.
> f. The slaves are being guarded although they have not fled.
> g. As soon as they had fled, the slaves were guarded.
> h. If they do not flee (use aorist participle), the slaves will not be guarded.
> i. The slaves are being guarded as if they had fled.
> j. The slaves were guarded because they had fled.

2) Two types of circumstantial participles are absolute; i.e. they form units outside the grammatical structure of the rest of the sentence.

a) The usual type of absolute construction is the **genitive absolute**, which normally consists of a participle in the genitive agreeing with a noun in the genitive that functions as its subject.

γράφοντος τοῦ δεσπότου ἔφυγεν ὁ δοῦλος.	"The slave fled while his master was writing."

When translating into Greek, it is important to distinguish between sentences that require an ordinary circumstantial participle and those that require a genitive absolute:

if the subject of the English subordinate clause is also part of the main clause, an ordinary circumstantial participle must be used, but if the subordinate clause has a subject that is not in the main clause, the absolute construction is a good choice. The situation is tricky because often words that belong to the main clause in Greek appear in the subordinate clause in English (cf. E 2 below). Thus "When the slave fled we pursued him" does not become a genitive absolute but rather φεύγοντα τὸν δοῦλον ἐδιώξαμεν, but "When we pursued the slave he fled" becomes ἡμῶν διωκόντων ἔφυγεν ὁ δοῦλος, because although the slave appears in both clauses, he is not the subject of the subordinate clause.

b) There is also an **accusative absolute**, which works like the genitive absolute except that the participle is in the accusative and there is no noun with it. This construction is used only with impersonal verbs; see chapter XVII.

A genitive (or accusative) absolute is not always temporal; in principle any of the meanings of circumstantial participles given above can be found in a genitive absolute. But because absolute participles are less likely to be accompanied by the adverbs that indicate the type of circumstance, there are some practical limitations to their usage to avoid ambiguity.

γράφοντος τοῦ δεσπότου ἔφυγεν ὁ δοῦλος.	The slave fled since/although/because/ when his master was writing.

The negative is οὐ unless the participle is conditional, in which case it is μή.

οὐ φυλαττομένου τοῦ δεσπότου φεύξομαι.	Since my master is not on guard, I shall flee.
μὴ φυλαττομένου τοῦ δεσπότου φεύξομαι.	If my master is not on guard, I shall flee.

> **Preliminary exercise 3 (on B 2).** Each underlined verb could be translated into Greek with a participle (though if actually translating this passage one might not want to make them all participles, for stylistic reasons); indicate what case each participle would be and why.
>
> When the messenger <u>arrived</u>, the servants who <u>were</u> off duty were sitting in the courtyard, which <u>was</u> the coolest part of the palace. They were surprised to see him <u>covered</u> with dust and <u>panting</u>, since messengers rarely <u>arrived</u> in that condition. If he <u>had given</u> them a chance, they would have surrounded him to <u>ask</u> lots of questions, but as it was, although they <u>moved</u> as fast as they could, they hardly had time to get up from the benches before he had entered the king's apartments, though these <u>were</u> on the other side of the courtyard, which <u>was</u> exceptionally wide. Once he <u>disappeared</u>, they

all wanted to follow him, although normally they <u>were</u> not very enthusiastic about going into the king's apartments, which <u>were</u> so full of precious and fragile objects that you had to be very careful not to brush against anything, especially if the weather <u>was</u> not good. (When the weather <u>was</u> bad all the servants used to get very muddy, because the courtyard floor <u>was</u> made of earth and so <u>were</u> most of the palace walls, and although they <u>tried</u> hard to get the mud off they were never completely successful. And when someone <u>got</u> mud on a gold statue, the king used to have that person whipped.) But when they <u>tried</u> to enter, the guard kept them out, <u>saying</u> that the king, although he did not normally <u>grant</u> private audiences, was giving one to the messenger who <u>had come</u> with such urgency. When they <u>heard</u> this the servants were very frustrated; although the sun <u>was shining</u> and the birds <u>were singing</u> and the day <u>was</u> a perfect one, they were miserable.

Preliminary exercise 4 (on B 2). Translate into Greek using participles and the following vocabulary: δεσπότης, -ου, ὁ "master"; δοῦλος, -ου, ὁ "slave"; ἀποπέμπω, ἀποπέμψω, ἀπέπεμψα, ἀποπέπομφα, ἀποπέπεμμαι, ἀπεπέμφθην "send away"; εὔχομαι, εὔξομαι, ηὐξάμην, ηὖγμαι "pray"; θύω, θύσω, ἔθυσα, τέθυκα, τέθυμαι, ἐτύθην "sacrifice"; φεύγω, φεύξομαι, ἔφυγον, πέφευγα "flee"; φυλάττω, φυλάξω, ἐφύλαξα, πεφύλαχα, πεφύλαγμαι, ἐφυλάχθην "guard."

a.   The slaves were sent away while their masters were sacrificing (use present participle).

b.   The slaves were sent away while being guarded.

c.   We guarded the slaves while they were being sent away (use present participle).

d.   We guarded the slaves while their masters were sacrificing (use present participle).

e.   While the slaves were praying (use present participle), they were guarded.

f.   While the slaves were praying (use present participle), their masters sacrificed.

g.   When the slaves have fled, their masters will sacrifice.

h.   The slaves will pray when they are sent away.

i.   The slaves will pray while their masters sacrifice.

j.   The slaves fled while their masters were praying (use present participle).

k.   The masters sacrificed while their slaves prayed.

l.   The masters sacrificed after sending away their slaves.

m.   The slaves will be guarded while their masters pray.

n.   The slaves will be guarded while being sent away.

o.   If their masters do not sacrifice (use aorist participle), the slaves will flee.

p.   If the slaves are not sent away (use aorist participle), they will flee.

q.   If the slaves are not sent away (use aorist participle), their masters will guard them.

r.   If the slaves are not sent away (use aorist participle), their masters will not sacrifice.

C) **Supplementary** participles are used with certain verbs.

1) **Χαίρω, ἥδομαι, διατελέω**, and **λήγω** have meanings that require a present participle to complete the sense (though they can also be used absolutely in other meanings); the participle agrees with the subject of the verb that triggers it.

χαίρει γράφων.	He enjoys writing. / He likes to write.
ἥδεται γράφων.	He enjoys writing. / He likes to write.
διατελεῖ γράφουσα.	She continues writing. / She continues to write.
λήγουσι γράφοντες.	They stop writing. / They cease to write.

2) **Παύομαι** in the middle voice is used like the verbs in C 1, but the active **παύω** takes an accusative object and a participle agreeing with that object. In either case the participle is in the present tense.

παύεται γράφων.	He stops writing. / He ceases to write.
παύει με γράφοντα.	He stops me (from) writing.

3) **Φαίνομαι** and **αἰσχύνομαι** can take either a participle (present in the case of φαίνομαι, aorist in the case of αἰσχύνομαι) or an infinitive, but the two constructions mean different things.[5]

φαίνεται γράφων.	He is clearly writing.
φαίνεται γράφειν.	He seems to be writing.
(mnemonic hexameter: φαίνομαι ὢν *quod sum, quod non sum* φαίνομαι εἶναι)	
αἰσχύνεται γράψας.	He is ashamed to have written. (when he has written)
αἰσχύνεται γράφειν.	He is (too) ashamed to write. (when he does not write)

---

[5] In some authors a similar distinction is observed with ἄρχομαι: ἄρχεται γράφων "he begins by writing," but ἄρχεται γράφειν "he begins writing" / "he begins to write." In other authors the infinitive is used for both meanings.

4) **Τυγχάνω** in its meaning "happen to" can take either a present or an aorist participle, with a complex difference in meaning as follows:

τυγχάνει γράφων.	He happens to be writing.
τυγχάνει γράψας.	He happens to have written.
ἔτυχε γράφων.	He happened to be writing.
ἔτυχε γράψας.	He happened to write. / He happened to have written.
	(i.e. this one can be either aspectual or temporal)

5) **Λανθάνω** and **φθάνω** take participles that have no good equivalents in English. The participle is present with a primary tense of the verb, or aorist with a secondary tense of the verb. These verbs can also use a reverse construction whereby they become participles and the supplementary participles become finite verbs; there is no difference in meaning between the normal and reverse constructions.

ἔλαθεν αὐτοὺς γράψας.	He wrote without their notice. / He escaped their notice writing. / They did not notice him writing.
λαθὼν αὐτοὺς ἔγραψεν.	He wrote without their notice. / He escaped their notice writing. / They did not notice him writing.
ἔλαθεν ἑαυτὸν γράψας.	He wrote unawares. / He wrote without knowing it.
φθάνει αὐτοὺς γράφων.	He beats them to writing. / He writes before they do.
φθάνων αὐτοὺς γράφει.	He beats them to writing. / He writes before they do.

> **Preliminary exercise 5 (on C).** Translate into Greek using participles and the following vocabulary: δεσπότης, -ου, ὁ "master"; δοῦλος, -ου, ὁ "slave"; εὔχομαι, εὔξομαι, ηὐξάμην, –, ηὖγμαι, – "pray"; θύω, θύσω, ἔθυσα, τέθυκα, τέθυμαι, ἐτύθην "sacrifice."
>
> a. The master enjoys sacrificing. (2 ways)
> b. The master continues to sacrifice.
> c. The master ceases to sacrifice. (2 ways)
> d. We stopped the master from sacrificing.
> e. The master is clearly sacrificing.
> f. The master seems to be sacrificing.
> g. The master is not ashamed to have sacrificed.
> h. The master is ashamed to sacrifice.
> i. The master happens to be sacrificing.
> j. The master happens to have sacrificed.
> k. The master happened to be sacrificing.
> l. The master happened to sacrifice.
> m. The master sacrificed without the slaves noticing. (2 ways)

    n.   The master sacrificed without knowing it.

    o.   The master beats the slaves to sacrificing. (2 ways)

    p.   The slaves pray before their masters do. (2 ways)

    q.   The master did not notice the slaves praying. (2 ways)

    r.   The slaves prayed without knowing it.

    s.   The slaves are clearly praying.

    t.   The slaves continue to pray.

    u.   The master will stop the slaves from praying.

    v.   The slaves seem to be praying.

    w.   The slaves do not like to pray. (2 ways)

    x.   The slaves cease praying. (2 ways)

    y.   The slaves are ashamed to have prayed.

    z.   The slaves happened to be praying.

D) Participles are also used in **indirect statement** after verbs of knowing and perceiving; see chapter x.

E) Additional complications

1) The **tenses** of attributive and circumstantial participles usually express time, though sometimes, particularly in the aorist, a participle's tense indicates aspect only.[6] The time indicated by a participle is always **time relative to the main verb**; since English has a system of sequence of tenses after main verbs in the past, the tense of a participle accompanying a verb in a past tense is often different from the tense of its proper English equivalent.[7]

ηὖρον τὸν γράφοντα δοῦλον.	I found the slave who was writing.
	(present participle = English imperfect)
ηὖρον τὸν γράψαντα δοῦλον.	I found the slave who had written.
	(aorist participle = English pluperfect. Notice that Greek does not use the perfect here.)
ηὖρον τὸν γράψοντα δοῦλον.	I found the slave who was going to write.
	(future participle)
but	
εὑρίσκω τὸν γράψαντα δοῦλον.	I find the slave who wrote.
	(No change because main verb is not past)

---

[6] When the finite-verb equivalent of a participle would be a subjunctive or optative, for example in the protases of future more vivid and future less vivid conditions, the tense of the participle normally indicates aspect. In other situations aspect is sometimes, but less predictably, a factor.

[7] See chapter x for more information on English sequence of tenses and how it relates to Greek.

Often English uses a simple past tense in a subordinate clause; when translating such sentences into Greek one must consider exactly how the action of the subordinate clause relates to that of the main clause in order to decide what tense of participle to use. Thus "When they fled, they carried the money" requires a present participle (φεύγοντες τὸ ἀργύριον ἤνεγκον), because the carrying and the fleeing must have been simultaneous, but "When they escaped to Athens, they sacrificed" requires an aorist participle (Ἀθήναζε φυγόντες ἔθυσαν), because the subjects must have escaped before they sacrificed.

> **Preliminary exercise 6 (on E 1).** For each underlined verb in preliminary exercise 3, give the tense of the resulting participle in Greek.

2) When a subordinate clause begins a sentence and contains words that are also used in the main clause, English tends to give those words in full in the subordinate clause and replace them by pronouns in the main clause. In Greek the shared words will normally be found in the main clause and can be understood without any pronoun in the participial phrase, even if the participle begins the sentence. Thus "When the slaves were released they fled" becomes λυθέντες ἔφυγον οἱ δοῦλοι, and "When he pursued the slaves they fled" becomes διώκοντος αὐτοῦ ἔφυγον οἱ δοῦλοι.

3) The **adverb ὡς** has a special use with causal participles. It indicates that the cause is in the mind of the subject of the sentence (or of some other person in the sentence, if the context makes that clear), and that the speaker of the sentence assumes no responsibility for it. Sometimes there is an implication that the attribution of cause is false, but often there is no such implication; the ὡς construction is much weaker than English "allegedly" and is often used in situations where the author cannot actually be intending to cast doubt on the assertion.[8]

ἀπῆλθον ὡς νικήσαντες.	They departed as if victorious / on the grounds that they had been victorious. (The writer of the sentence does not indicate whether or not they were actually victorious but tells us that they thought or said that they were victorious.)
ἀπῆλθον νικήσαντες.	They departed victorious. (The writer of the sentence positively asserts that they were victorious.)

---

[8] It is debated whether ὡς can have this meaning with final participles as well. What is certain is that the doubting force is far less common when a participle indicates purpose; normally future participles take ὡς without casting any doubt on the genuineness of the purpose.

4) Participles retain the characteristics of a verb while assuming those of an adjective, so they can take **objects** in the case appropriate to that verb, as well as adverbs, prepositional phrases, and even dependent clauses. The use of such material with participles is very common in Greek and allows participles to be used instead of subordinate clauses even for long and complex expressions.

> γραψαμένη τὸν νεανίαν τὸν σφόδρα ἄδικον τῆς ἐκ τοῦ νεὼ κλοπῆς καὶ βουλομένη ζημιοῦν αὐτόν, ἐξαίφνης ὑπὸ τῶν θεῶν ἀπέθανεν.
> "When she had indicted the very unjust young man for the theft from the temple and was wanting to punish him, she was suddenly killed by the gods."

5) Participles connect themselves to verbs, so conjunctions can never be used to attach a participle to a finite verb. The only time conjunctions are used with participles is when a co-ordinating conjunction joins two parallel participles to each other. (When used with concessive participles καί is an adverb, not a conjunction; the same is true of ὡς with participles.)

> **Preliminary exercise 7 (on A, B, C, and E).** Translate into Greek using participles for all subordinate clauses and the following vocabulary: φιλόσοφος, -ου, ὁ "philosopher"; ἀποπέμπω, ἀποπέμψω, ἀπέπεμψα, ἀποπέπομφα, ἀποπέπεμμαι, ἀπεπέμφθην "send away"; ἀφικνέομαι, ἀφίξομαι, ἀφικόμην, –, ἀφῖγμαι, – "arrive"; διδάσκω, διδάξω, ἐδίδαξα, δεδίδαχα, δεδίδαγμαι, ἐδιδάχθην "teach."
>
> a.   Philosophers enjoy teaching. (2 ways)
> b.   The philosophers stopped teaching.
> c.   The philosophers were sent away because they arrived while we were teaching.
> d.   The philosophers were sent away on the grounds that they arrived while we were teaching.
> e.   Whoever does not teach will be sent away.
> f.   The philosophers who do not teach will be sent away.
> g.   If the philosophers do not stop teaching, we shall send them away.
> h.   If the philosophers do not teach, we shall be sent away.
> i.   If the philosophers do not teach, they will be sent away.
> j.   We did not notice the philosophers teaching. (2 ways)
> k.   The philosophers happened to be teaching while we were arriving.
> l.   The philosophers arrived in order to teach.
> m.   The philosophers arrived before we did. (2 ways)

n. Philosophers do not like to be taught. (2 ways)
o. The philosophers continued to teach while we were arriving.
p. When we arrive, we shall stop the philosophers from teaching.
q. The philosophers are clearly teaching.
r. The philosophers stopped teaching as soon as we arrived.
s. The philosophers were not ashamed to be teaching while we were being sent away.
t. Philosophers teach without knowing it. (2 ways)
u. We were sent away on the grounds that we had not taught.
v. The philosophers who taught were sent away.
w. We arrived while the philosophers were teaching.
x. The philosophers happen to be teaching.
y. The philosophers will not be sent away although they arrived while we were teaching.
z. If the philosophers do not stop teaching, they will be sent away.
aa. The philosophers sent us away as if we had not taught.
bb. When we arrived, he stopped the philosophers from teaching.
cc. When he arrived, he stopped the philosophers from teaching.
dd. When the philosophers arrived, he stopped them from teaching.
ee. The philosophers seem to be teaching although they are being sent away.
ff. The philosophers are not ashamed to have taught us.

Sentences

Translate into Greek using only words and constructions so far covered and using participles for all subordinate clauses.

1. When mortals sacrifice, the immortals rejoice.
2. When these citizens arrived at the assembly, they began to sacrifice to the gods.
3. The people who were fleeing turned away from the road without their pursuers seeing them.[9]
4. The philosopher happens to have found the young men (as they were) in the middle of seizing the thief.
5. People who have not been educated do not enjoy writing.
6. Although we arrived at the forest, we did not find wild animals.
7. This prostitute was too ashamed to send her lover into the forest to carry wood.

---

[9] I.e. escaped the notice of the men who were pursuing them as they turned away from the road.

8. When the noble philosopher had fallen into the river, a clever sophist saved him.
9. The strong man is obviously beating his little slaves.
10. That sophist indicted the beautiful prostitute for theft because (he said) she had received money from the unjust thieves.
11. If the courageous sailor does not find weapons, he will not save his cowardly comrades.
12. When the young man who had been nourished by wild animals turned the terrible bandits away from the mainland, the citizens rejoiced.
13. The men who had been released stopped seizing the things that had been left and began eating.
14. The assembly accepted the young man's advice as if he had already become a hoplite.
15. This cowardly bandit left his comrades on the island so that he might (himself) escape to the mainland.
16. Although the little thief had seized the silver, nevertheless the philosopher did not beat him.
17. Such men as did not take pleasure in money ransomed the hoplites who were suffering bad things.
18. The man who rules the island indicted his sister for theft because he had found in his house the crown that had been taken from the shrine.
19. The terrible bandits seized the offerings when they (i.e. the offerings) had just been saved from the shrine that was burning.
20. When the sophist showed the crown that had been sent by those wishing to find wisdom, the spectators were ashamed of not having been educated.
21. People who seem to be praying in the white temple often take the offerings.
22. If these wild animals do not escape to the forest, the men who throw stones will continue to harm them.
23. In order to find money, bandits burned the beautiful little shrine.
24. He (i.e. the general) happened to escape to Athens with a few hoplites after the battle.
25. While the young man burned the tree sacred to the immortals, his comrades threw the offerings into a river.
26. In (the) beginning the council prayed to the gods as if it (i.e. the council) had killed the spectators justly.
27. The slaves who were stopped by the spectator were obviously fleeing.
28. While he was teaching young men, the good philosopher fell in a river without noticing.[10]

---

[10] I.e. escaped the notice of himself (ἑαυτόν).

29. The woman who stopped the council from accepting the silver is capable of increasing the citizens' rule.

30. Mortals, even if they become wise, are not equal to the immortals.

Analysis

Translate into English as literally as is possible without being incomprehensible and explain what the construction of each participle is, what it agrees with, and why it has the tense and modifiers it does.

1. ἀλλ᾽, ὦ μακάριε, ἄμεινον σκόπει, μή σε λανθάνω οὐδὲν ὤν.

   (Plato, *Symposium* 219a; σκοπέω "consider")

2. ...τοῖς γὰρ μὴ ἔχουσι χρήματα διδόναι οὐκ ἤθελον διαλέγεσθαι.

   (Xenophon, *Memorabilia* 1.2.60–1)

3. καὶ ὅσα ἄρα τὸ πᾶν πλῆθος κρατοῦν τῶν τὰ χρήματα ἐχόντων γράφει μὴ πεῖσαν, βία μᾶλλον ἢ νόμος ἂν εἴη;

   (Xenophon, *Memorabilia* 1.2.45, Alcibiades questioning Pericles on the difference between legitimately passed laws and lawless force; πλῆθος "populace," κρατέω + gen. "have power over," γράφω "pass as law," the understood object of πείθω is rich men)

4. φημὶ γὰρ δὴ ὁμοιότατον αὐτὸν εἶναι τοῖς σιληνοῖς τούτοις τοῖς ἐν τοῖς ἑρμογλυφείοις καθημένοις, οὕστινας ἐργάζονται οἱ δημιουργοὶ σύριγγας ἢ αὐλοὺς ἔχοντας, οἳ διχάδε διοιχθέντες φαίνονται ἔνδοθεν ἀγάλματα ἔχοντες θεῶν.

   (Plato, *Symposium* 215a–b, Alcibiades speaking about Socrates; σιληνός "figure of Silenus," ἑρμογλυφεῖον "statue shop," δημιουργός "craftsman," σύριγξ "Panpipe," διχάδε "apart," διοίγνυμι "open, split," ἄγαλμα "image")

5. ταῦτα διανοηθεὶς ἔφευγον, ἐκείνων ἐπὶ τῇ αὐλείῳ θύρᾳ τὴν φυλακὴν ποιουμένων· τριῶν δὲ θυρῶν οὐσῶν, ἃς ἔδει με διελθεῖν, ἅπασαι ἀνεῳγμέναι ἔτυχον. ἀφικόμενος δὲ εἰς Ἀρχένεω τοῦ ναυκλήρου ἐκεῖνον πέμπω εἰς ἄστυ, πευσόμενον περὶ τοῦ ἀδελφοῦ· ἥκων δὲ ἔλεγεν ὅτι Ἐρατοσθένης αὐτὸν ἐν τῇ ὁδῷ λαβὼν εἰς τὸ δεσμωτήριον ἀπαγάγοι.

   (Lysias, *Oration* 12.16, the tale of the speaker's escape from the thirty tyrants and the loss of his brother; ἔφευγον "I began to flee," αὔλειος "of the courtyard" (here a two-termination adjective), Ἀρχένεω is genitive, ναύκληρος "shipmaster," δεσμωτήριον "prison")

6.   πρὸς δὲ αὖ τὰς τοῦ χειμῶνος καρτερήσεις – δεινοὶ γὰρ αὐτόθι χειμῶνες –
     θαυμάσια ἠργάζετο τά τε ἄλλα, καὶ ποτε ὄντος πάγου οἵου δεινοτάτου, καὶ
     πάντων ἢ οὐκ ἐξιόντων ἔνδοθεν, ἢ εἴ τις ἐξίοι, ἠμφιεσμένων τε θαυμαστὰ δὴ
     ὅσα καὶ ὑποδεδεμένων καὶ ἐνειλιγμένων τοὺς πόδας εἰς πίλους καὶ ἀρνακίδας,
     οὗτος δ᾽ ἐν τούτοις ἐξῇει ἔχων ἱμάτιον μὲν τοιοῦτον οἷόνπερ καὶ πρότερον εἰώθει
     φορεῖν, ἀνυπόδητος δὲ διὰ τοῦ κρυστάλλου ῥᾷον ἐπορεύετο ἢ οἱ ἄλλοι ὑποδ-
     εδεμένοι, οἱ δὲ στρατιῶται ὑπέβλεπον αὐτὸν ὡς καταφρονοῦντα σφῶν.

     (Plato, *Symposium* 220 a–b, Alcibiades on Socrates' tolerance of the cold;
     καρτέρησις "endurance," πάγος "frost," οἵου "so," ἀμφιέννυμι "put around,"
     ὑποδέω "put shoes on," ἀνελίσσω "wrap up," πῖλος "felt," ἀρνακίς "sheepskin,"
     φορέω "wear," ἀνυπόδητος "barefoot," κρύσταλλος "ice," ὑποβλέπω "regard
     with suspicion," καταφρονέω "look down on")

7.   δι᾽ ὃ καὶ τοὺς υἱεῖς οἱ πατέρες, κἂν ὦσι σώφρονες, ὅμως ἀπὸ τῶν πονηρῶν
     ἀνθρώπων εἴργουσιν, ὡς τὴν μὲν τῶν χρηστῶν ὁμιλίαν ἄσκησιν οὖσαν τῆς
     ἀρετῆς, τὴν δὲ τῶν πονηρῶν κατάλυσιν.

     (Xenophon, *Memorabilia* 1.2.20; ἄσκησις "exercise," κατάλυσις "destruction";
     how does this sentence violate the rules given in this chapter, and why do you
     think Xenophon wanted to break the rules here?)

8.   καὶ πρῶτον μὲν ὅσοι ἐξ ἄστεώς ἐστε, σκέψασθε ὅτι ὑπὸ τούτων οὕτω σφόδρα
     ἤρχεσθε, ὥστε ἀδελφοῖς καὶ ὑέσι καὶ πολίταις ἠναγκάζεσθε πολεμεῖν τοιοῦτον
     πόλεμον, ἐν ᾧ ἡττηθέντες μὲν τοῖς νικήσασι τὸ ἴσον ἔχετε, νικήσαντες δ᾽ ἂν τού-
     τοις ἐδουλεύετε.

     (Lysias, *Oration* 12.92; ἄστυ refers to Athens here, σκέπτομαι "consider," τούτων
     i.e. the thirty tyrants (same is true of τούτοις), σφόδρα "harshly," ἄρχομαι "be
     ruled," ἀναγκάζω "force," ἡττάομαι "be defeated," τὸ ἴσον ἔχω "be on equal
     terms with")

VI | The structure of a Greek sentence: word order and connection

Material to learn before using this chapter: third declension, μέγας and πολύς (Smyth §256–9, 311); Vocabulary 6 and associated principal parts

Recommended grammar reading: Smyth §240–61, 311–12

Recommended syntax reading: Smyth §2769–3003

A) A Greek sentence has a skeleton composed of verbs and connectives; most sentences, and indeed paragraphs, can be analyzed solely on the basis of such words.

1) The relationship of one verb to another is normally specified in Greek by conjunctions and/or by the form of the verb: if the verbs are co-ordinated (either two main verbs or two parallel subordinates), a co-ordinating conjunction is essential, but if one is subordinated, connection may be made by a subordinating conjunction, by a relative pronoun, or by a participle or infinitive.

> ὅτε τοίνυν τοῦθ᾽ οὕτως ἔχει, προσήκει προθύμως ἐθέλειν ἀκούειν τῶν βουλομένων συμβουλεύειν· οὐ γὰρ μόνον εἴ τι χρήσιμον ἐσκεμμένος ἥκει τις, τοῦτ᾽ ἂν ἀκούσαντες λάβοιτε, ἀλλὰ καὶ τῆς ὑμετέρας τύχης ὑπολαμβάνω πολλὰ τῶν δεόντων ἐκ τοῦ παραχρῆμ᾽ ἐνίοις ἂν ἐπελθεῖν εἰπεῖν, ὥστ᾽ ἐξ ἁπάντων ῥᾳδίαν τὴν τοῦ συμφέροντος ὑμῖν αἵρεσιν γενέσθαι. (Demosthenes, *Olynthiac* 1.1)

This sentence can be analyzed as follows into units with one verb form in each; all infinitives and participles, except attributive participles, count for this purpose as verb forms. The numeration and indentation indicate the structure; notice the roles of the underlined words.

     1.1 <u>ὅτε</u> τοίνυν τοῦθ᾽ οὕτως <u>ἔχει</u> "Since moreover this is so"

1 προσήκει "it befits (you)"

     1.2 προθύμως <u>ἐθέλειν</u> "eagerly to wish"

          1.2.1 <u>ἀκούειν</u> τῶν βουλομένων "to hear those who wish"

               1.2.1.1 <u>συμβουλεύειν</u> "to advise (you)"

2 οὐ <u>γὰρ</u> μόνον . . . τοῦτ᾽ ἂν <u>λάβοιτε</u> "for not only would you accept this"

2.1 ἀκούσαντες "when you heard (it)"

2.2 εἴ . . . ἥκει τις "if someone comes"

2.2.1 τι χρήσιμον ἐσκεμμένος "with a useful idea"

3 ἀλλὰ καὶ τῆς ὑμετέρας τύχης ὑπολαμβάνω "but also I count (as part) of your (good) fortune"

3.1 ἐκ τοῦ παραχρῆμ᾽ ἐνίοις ἂν ἐπελθεῖν "(that) it may come to several (speakers), from the on-the-spot"

3.1.1 πολλὰ τῶν δεόντων εἰπεῖν "to say many of the things that are necessary"

3.2 ὥστ᾽ ἐξ ἁπάντων ῥᾳδίαν τὴν τοῦ συμφέροντος ὑμῖν αἵρεσιν γενέσθαι "so as for the choice out of all of them of the one that is expedient for you to become easy."

2) Finite verbs are usually joined together by conjunctions or connective particles. Greeks of the Classical period had no punctuation, so neither conjunction usage nor any other feature of Greek structure is linked to punctuation. Notice the different levels of acceptability of these Greek sentences and their English equivalents, as the punctuation makes a difference in English but not in Greek:

Comma:	ἡ βουλὴ ἐβουλεύετο, ἡ δ᾽ ἐκκλησία οὔ. (good)
	The council deliberated, and the assembly did not. (good)
	ἡ βουλὴ ἐβουλεύετο, ἡ ἐκκλησία οὔ. (poor)
	The council deliberated, the assembly did not. (poor)
Semicolon:	ἡ βουλὴ ἐβουλεύετο· ἡ δ᾽ ἐκκλησία οὔ. (good)
	The council deliberated; and the assembly did not. (poor)
	ἡ βουλὴ ἐβουλεύετο· ἡ ἐκκλησία οὔ. (poor)
	The council deliberated; the assembly did not. (good)
Period/full stop:	ἡ βουλὴ ἐβουλεύετο. ἡ δ᾽ ἐκκλησία οὔ. (good)
	The council deliberated. And the assembly did not. (poor)
	ἡ βουλὴ ἐβουλεύετο. ἡ ἐκκλησία οὔ. (poor)
	The council deliberated. The assembly did not. (acceptable)

(The best way to express this sentence in Greek would be to use μέν as well as δέ, with any type of punctuation: ἡ μὲν βουλὴ ἐβουλεύετο· ἡ δ᾽ ἐκκλησία οὔ.)

3) Even the intervention of a period (full stop) makes no difference to the need for connection: almost every sentence in a work of Greek prose is connected to the preceding sentence by a conjunction or other connecting word, just as each clause within a sentence is connected. Words commonly used this way include **δέ, καί, ἀλλά, γάρ**, and **οὖν**; when translating into Greek it is a good idea to use one of these near the start of every

sentence in a connected passage, except the first. (Note that μέν cannot be used to connect a sentence to its predecessor, since it looks forward: a sentence that opens with μέν needs another connective too.) Notice how Plato often connects sentences even over a change of speaker:

> ΣΩΚΡΑΤΗΣ: . . . ταῦτα οὐχὶ καλῶς λέγεται; ". . . aren't these things well said?"
> ΚΡΙΤΩΝ: καλῶς. "(They are) well (said)."
> ΣΩΚΡΑΤΗΣ: οὐκοῦν τὰς μὲν χρηστὰς τιμᾶν, τὰς δὲ πονηρὰς μή; "Therefore (is it necessary) to honor the best (opinions) and not the bad ones?"
> ΚΡΙΤΩΝ: ναί. "Yes."
> ΣΩΚΡΑΤΗΣ: χρησταὶ δὲ οὐχ αἱ τῶν φρονίμων, πονηραὶ δὲ αἱ τῶν ἀφρόνων; "And are not the best (opinions) those of prudent men, and the bad (opinions) those of foolish men?"
> ΚΡΙΤΩΝ: πῶς δ᾽ οὔ; "And how not?"   (Plato, *Crito* 47a)

Therefore when translating into Greek one often needs to add conjunctions not present in the English; if translating a passage containing more than one sentence one *usually* needs to add conjunctions.

4) Although the conjunctions join the verbs, they are not normally placed next to the verbs; conjunctions normally come as the first or second word of the unit to which their verb belongs.

> **Preliminary exercise 1 (on A).** Indicate where in the passage below additional conjunctions (beyond those already present in English) would be needed if it were to be translated fairly literally into Greek, and suggest which conjunction(s) would be most appropriate in each place. Take into account the probable translations of the conjunctions already present, to avoid repeating the same one too many times in a row.
>
> Alcibiades was not a model citizen. He got drunk at parties, smashed up other people's property, and seduced their wives. Eventually things came to a head when he mutilated a group of sacred statues: this was thought to have annoyed the gods and thus to have jeopardized the success of a military expedition. The citizens decided to put Alcibiades in jail, but he ran off to Sparta. The Spartan king was delighted to welcome him, and Alcibiades had a wonderful time, particularly as he found the king's wife very charming. Unfortunately, when the king found out what Alcibiades was up to with his wife, Alcibiades had to leave very suddenly.

Preliminary exercise 2 (on A). Find the verbs (including infinitives and participles except attributive participles) and conjunctions in this sentence.

Οὐ μόνον δὲ δεῖ ταῦτα γιγνώσκειν, οὐδὲ τοῖς ἔργοις ἐκεῖνον ἀμύνεσθαι τοῖς τοῦ πολέμου, ἀλλὰ καὶ τῷ λογισμῷ καὶ τῇ διανοίᾳ τοὺς παρ' ὑμῖν ὑπὲρ αὐτοῦ λέγοντας μισῆσαι, ἐνθυμουμένους ὅτι οὐκ ἔνεστι τῶν τῆς πόλεως ἐχθρῶν κρατῆσαι, πρὶν ἂν τοὺς ἐν αὐτῇ τῇ πόλει κολάσηθ' ὑπηρετοῦντας ἐκείνοις. (Demosthenes, *Philippics* 3.53)

It is necessary not only to know these things and not (only) to resist him with the deeds of war, but also with both reasoning and purpose to hate those who speak among you on his behalf, considering that it is not possible to overcome the enemies of the city before you punish those in the city itself who serve them.

B) On the skeleton composed of the verbs and connectives hangs the muscle structure of the nouns, adjectives, adverbs, prepositions, etc. These tend to be grouped around their verbs, and when there are many verbs in a sentence, it is important to be able to tell which verb each other word is attached to. This is usually facilitated by opening each clause or phrase with a distinctive opening word; such a word is one that (a) cannot, at least in context, belong to the preceding phrase or clause, and (b) indicates that a particular sort of word is following. Any words that occur between the opening word and the word to which it points can be assumed to be part of the same unit, unless another opening word intervenes, in which case the reader is alerted to nesting units. Conjunctions are opening words, usually pointing to a verb, and so are relative pronouns and relative adjectives. Smaller units may be opened by prepositions, which point to objects in a particular case, or by articles (see chapter II G).

Περὶ πολλοῦ ἂν ποιησαίμην, ὦ ἄνδρες, τὸ τοιούτους ὑμᾶς ἐμοὶ δικαστὰς περὶ τούτου τοῦ πράγματος γενέσθαι, οἷοίπερ ἂν ὑμῖν αὐτοῖς εἴητε τοιαῦτα πεπονθότες· εὖ γὰρ οἶδ' ὅτι, εἰ τὴν αὐτὴν γνώμην περὶ τῶν ἄλλων ἔχοιτε, ἥνπερ περὶ ὑμῶν αὐτῶν, οὐκ ἂν εἴη ὅστις οὐκ ἐπὶ τοῖς γεγενημένοις ἀγανακτοίη, ἀλλὰ πάντες ἂν περὶ τῶν τὰ τοιαῦτα ἐπιτηδευόντων τὰς ζημίας μικρὰς ἡγοῖσθε. (Lysias 1.1)

This sentence can be analyzed into units with one verb (or, in the case of 2.1.1.1, understood verb) in each; notice the roles of the underlined words in the analysis below. Most units open with a clear opening word and close with the word pointed to by that opener; those that lack a marker at one end or the other come next to other units that mark those boundaries clearly. Note that unit 2.1.1 comes before the unit on which it depends, 2.1; this is possible because the ὅτι just before the start of 2.1.1 makes it clear that a new main verb is expected, while the εἰ at the start of 2.1.1 makes it clear that the main verb is postponed until after the subordinate clause.

1   Περὶ πολλοῦ ἂν ποιησαίμην, ὦ ἄνδρες, "I would count it of great importance,
           gentlemen,"
   1.1   τὸ τοιούτους ὑμᾶς ἐμοὶ δικαστὰς περὶ τούτου τοῦ πράγματος γενέσθαι "for
              you to become such judges for me about this affair"
      1.1.1   οἷοίπερ ἂν ὑμῖν αὐτοῖς εἴητε "as you would be for yourselves"
          1.1.1.1   τοιαῦτα πεπονθότες· "if you had suffered such things;"
2   εὖ γὰρ οἶδ᾽ ὅτι, "for I know well that,"
      2.1.1   εἰ τὴν αὐτὴν γνώμην περὶ τῶν ἄλλων ἔχοιτε "if you should have the
              same opinion about the others"
          2.1.1.1   ἥνπερ περὶ ὑμῶν αὐτῶν, "as (you have) about yourselves"
   2.1   οὐκ ἂν εἴη "there would not be"
      2.1.2   ὅστις οὐκ ἐπὶ τοῖς γεγενημένοις ἀγανακτοίη, "anyone who would not
              be indignant at the things that have happened,"
   2.2   ἀλλὰ πάντες ἂν περὶ τῶν τὰ τοιαῦτα ἐπιτηδευόντων τὰς ζημίας μικρὰς
              ἡγοῖσθε. "but you would all consider the punishments (to be)
              small for those who practice such things."

> **Preliminary exercise 3 (on B).** Take the sentence of Demosthenes given in Preliminary exercise 2 and analyze it according to the model given above. That is, break up the sentence into one-verb units (counting as verbs both infinitives and participles, except attributive participles) and indicate the relationship between units with indentation and numbering as above. There is one unit that nests inside another unit. If you have difficulty, consult Appendix C.

C) **Word order within units** is more flexible, but by no means random. The position before the verb tends to be given to the word on which the unit is focused. Adverbs and negatives normally go directly in front of the words to which they apply; an adverb or negative that applies to the sentence as a whole tends to be put in front of the verb. (Thus "He has come home again" becomes οἴκαδε πάλιν ἥκει, not *ἥκει οἴκαδε πάλιν.) The particle ἄν changes its position according to the type of clause in which it occurs: ἄν in a subordinate clause tends to follow the opening word very closely (hence the fused forms ἐάν, ὅταν, etc.), but ἄν in a main clause tends to be near the verb; if the main clause contains οὐ, the ἄν normally follows the οὐ.

D) Additional complications

1) Many opening words are **postpositive particles**. These normally come second in their clauses, but because they are always postpositive they are still effective markers of a clause boundary and signal that the clause began with the word preceding the postpositive particle. To make their position consistent and therefore the clause boundaries clear, postpositive particles may be inserted into otherwise inviolable groupings that would not normally tolerate extraneous material (e.g. ἡ δὲ βουλή).

2) All **enclitics** are postpositive; they tend to come immediately after the word to which they relate and should never begin a sentence, clause, or other unit. Thus "Some man has come" can be ἥκει ἄνθρωπός τις or ἄνθρωπός τις ἥκει, but not *τις ἄνθρωπος ἥκει.

3) The use of **μέν . . . δέ** is harder than it looks. These words are common, for Greek writers use them frequently to connect and stress the balance of parallel clauses, phrases, or sentences. However, μέν . . . δέ can only be used when the two things to be connected are exactly parallel grammatically, not when one element is in any way subordinated to the other. Thus "The first slave fled, but the second one stayed" can be well translated with ὁ μὲν πρῶτος δοῦλος ἔφυγεν, ὁ δὲ δεύτερος ἔμενεν, but "When the first slave fled, the second one stayed" requires a subordinate construction (e.g. φεύγοντος τοῦ πρώτου, ἔμενεν ὁ δεύτερος δοῦλος). This limitation does not mean that μέν . . . δέ cannot be used with participles; it is often so used, but only to connect one participle to another, not to connect either to the main verb. Thus ἔμενεν ὁ νεανίας τῶν μὲν δούλων φευγόντων, τῶν δὲ λῃστῶν ἀφικνουμένων "The young man stayed when the slaves fled and when the bandits arrived."

In addition to being parallel grammatically, units to which μέν and δέ are attached must be balanced in sense. Thus "The slave was afraid, and he fled" would not be a good candidate for μέν . . . δέ, as there is a causal relationship between the clauses that would be better expressed by a conjunction like οὖν (e.g. ἐφοβεῖτο ὁ δοῦλος· ἔφυγεν οὖν) or better still by subordination (e.g. φοβούμενος ὁ δοῦλος ἔφυγεν).

Lastly, μέν and δέ (which are both postpositive and therefore normally appear as the second words of their clauses) must immediately follow the words or phrases that provide the specific points of contrast between the clauses; if there are no specific words or phrases in which the contrast can be embodied, it is not normally practical to use μέν . . . δέ. Thus "The philosopher often arrives late, but today he's early" could use μέν . . . δέ, but only if the words are arranged so that each clause begins with one of the key words that are contrasted: πολλάκις μὲν ὀψὲ ἀφικνεῖται ὁ φιλόσοφος, τήμερον δὲ πρώ.

Preliminary exercise 4 (on D 3). For each of the following sentences, indicate whether it could be translated with μέν . . . δέ in Greek, and if so, which words the μέν and the δέ should follow and how the English should be reordered to make that possible.

a.   In appearance he was fair, and in his heart he was foul.
b.   This poor Spartan returned from battle without his shield and was beaten by his mother.
c.   When Demosthenes was young, he was incapable of public speaking, but after lots of practice he became one of the greatest orators of all time.
d.   My father is not a citizen; my mother is.
e.   Philosophers love to talk, but there's no point in listening to them.
f.   The husband looked under the bed and found Alcibiades hiding there.
g.   The husband looked under the bed, and Alcibiades slipped out the window.
h.   The husband looked under the bed, but he did not see Alcibiades, who had rolled himself up in a rug.
i.   Socrates was ugly, but people loved him anyway.
j.   Socrates was ugly in body but beautiful in soul.
k.   Socrates was ugly and wildly irritating, but that didn't justify executing him.
l.   Humans domesticated dogs, and cats domesticated humans.

4) **Τε** is a complex particle with many different uses. In Attic prose it is most often found with καί: two words or phrases are connected by placing τε after the first word (or the first word of the first phrase) and καί before the start of the second. The resulting connective cannot be translated in English in a way that distinguishes it from καί without τε; English "both . . . and" is really καί . . . καί rather than τε . . . καί. Thus ὅ τε πρῶτος δοῦλος καὶ ὁ δεύτερος ἔφυγον means "The first slave and the second one fled."[1]

Preliminary exercise 5 (on A–D). The following passage might be translated into Greek grammatically but infelicitously using the words below. Improve this translation, without changing any of the words in it, by adding conjunctions (including a μέν . . . δέ pair) and rearranging the words.

Perhaps it might seem strange that I indeed, going around, give this advice in private and poke my nose into other people's business, but I don't dare

---

[1] The use of τε alone, without καί, to mean "and" (ἄνθρωποι ἵπποι τε "men and horses") is common in poetry but not in prose.

to advise the state publicly, coming before the assembly. The cause of this
is that which you yourselves have often heard me saying in many places,
that there exists for me something divine and supernatural, which indeed
Meletos made fun of in his indictment of me. (Plato, *Apology* 31c)

ἴσως ἂν δόξειεν εἶναι ἄτοπον, ὅτι δὴ ἐγὼ συμβουλεύω ταῦτα ἰδίᾳ περιιὼν καὶ πολυπραγμονῶ, οὐ τολμῶ συμβουλεύειν τῇ πόλει δημοσίᾳ,
ἀναβαίνων εἰς τὸ πλῆθος τὸ ὑμέτερον. αἴτιον τούτου ἐστιν ὃ ὑμεῖς
ἀκηκόατε πολλάκις ἐμοῦ λέγοντος πολλαχοῦ, ὅτι γίγνεταί μοί τι θεῖον καὶ
δαιμόνιον, ὃ δὴ καὶ Μέλητος ἐπικωμῳδῶν ἐγράψατο ἐν τῇ γραφῇ.

Sentences

Translate into Greek using only words and constructions so far covered, adding connectives as appropriate and paying particular attention to word order.

1–2.   The famine killed the children, and the plague killed the women. The few men
who were left have gone, weeping, away from Greece.

3–4.   The assembly voted to send an expedition against the inhabitants of the high
mountain immediately. The shepherds there were treating the citizens' wives
with violence often.

5–6.   During the day many men guard the harbor, but at night, when the guards have
gone to the camp, savage bandits exist there. Today the guards are camping
around the harbor, in order to be roused by the bandits when they go beyond
the boundary.

7–8.   Since the birds arrived in the sacred forest again together with the spring, the
Greeks there rejoiced and sang immediately. Spring is dear to women, and birds
are dear to children.

9–10.   The orator's speeches are beautiful, and the soldiers' deeds are noble. We do not
take pleasure in these things (i.e. the speeches and the deeds): the enemy caught
many miserable prisoners yesterday while an unjust herald was gathering the
citizens.

11–12.   We have gratitude when we have received gifts, and hope when we have not yet
received gifts. This miserable old man no longer has comrades;[2] he has neither
much hope nor much gratitude.

13–15.   Hollow trees are not often empty; many wild animals exist in trees. Trees do
not grow hollow; old trees often become hollow. If we do not wish to harm
wild animals, we shall not burn the forest that has many old trees.

---

[2] Use dative of possession here ("are" = εἰσί).

16.   When the assembly was deliberating, some men were lying, and others were not; because the orator showed (i.e. revealed) this, the citizens stopped deliberating and have now gone home.

17–21.   The general who had obtained the expedition by lot marched to the harbor with a thousand soldiers. There he found an ancient temple; instead of burning this (i.e. the temple), the army made camp there in order to receive their allies. But they (i.e. the allies) arrived at the harbor without the soldiers' noticing them, for the harbor (is) big, and made camp beyond the river. They wished to make camp immediately, on the grounds that the enemy was not far away.[3] On the second day the general accepted hostages from the allies and killed the traitor who was found in the army.

22–3.   When the old man dies, his body will become a corpse. If it is not burned, birds and wild animals will eat the corpse.

24–5.   If the army marches through this forest during the night, wild animals will wound many soldiers. The land here produces big and savage wild animals.

26–7.   Such things as are not common are often new. This man, because he takes pleasure in things that are not common, wishes to find new things.[4]

28–30.   Treating women with violence is not funny. The noble guard will wound such men as do not stop harming women. This man (i.e. the guard) wishes to teach the soldiers excellence.

Analysis

Analyze according to the models given above. That is, break up the sentence into one-verb units, put each on a new line so that there is only one verb form per line (infinitives and participles, except attributive participles, count as verb forms), and indicate the relationship between units (subordination or co-ordination) by the system of indentation and numbering used above. (Therefore, only a main verb can receive a number like 1, 2, or 3; a finite verb governed by a subordinating conjunction such as εἰ or ὅτι, and any participle or infinitive, must receive a number indicating what it is subordinate to, such as 1.2 or, if it is subordinate to a clause that is itself subordinate, such as 1.1.2.) Remember that subordinate units may come before those on which they depend, and that units may nest within one another. Translate each unit into English as literally as is possible without being incomprehensible, explain the use of connectives, and indicate each unit-opening word and the word it points to. If you have difficulty, consult Appendix C.

---

[3] I.e. was not much (neuter) away.   [4] This last adjective would be better without an article.

1. κατὰ γὰρ τοὺς νόμους, ἐάν τις φανερὸς γένηται κλέπτων ἢ λωποδυτῶν ἢ βαλ-
αντιοτομῶν ἢ τοιχωρυχῶν ἢ ἀνδραποδιζόμενος ἢ ἱεροσυλῶν, τούτοις θάνατός
ἐστιν ἡ ζημία· ὧν ἐκεῖνος πάντων ἀνθρώπων πλεῖστον ἀπεῖχεν.

(Xenophon, *Memorabilia* 1.2.62, on Socrates' innocence of capital crimes;
λωποδυτέω "steal clothes," βαλαντιοτομέω "cut purses," τοιχωρυχέω
"burgle," ἀνδραποδίζομαι "enslave people," ἱεροσυλέω "rob temples," ζημία
"punishment")

2. ὁ τοίνυν Φίλιππος ἐξ ἀρχῆς, ἄρτι τῆς εἰρήνης γεγονυίας, οὔπω Διοπείθους
στρατηγοῦντος οὐδὲ τῶν ὄντων ἐν Χερρονήσῳ νῦν ἀπεσταλμένων, Σέρριον καὶ
Δορίσκον ἐλάμβανε καὶ τοὺς ἐκ Σερρείου τείχους καὶ Ἱεροῦ ὄρους στρατιώτας
ἐξέβαλλεν, οὓς ὁ ὑμέτερος στρατηγὸς κατέστησεν.

(Demosthenes, *Philippics* 3.15; ἀποστέλλω "send off")

3. ἀλλὰ Κρίτων τε Σωκράτους ἦν ὁμιλητής, καὶ Χαιρεφῶν, καὶ Χαιρεκράτης, καὶ
Ἑρμογένης, καὶ Σιμίας, καὶ Κέβης, καὶ Φαιδώνδας, καὶ ἄλλοι, οἳ ἐκείνῳ συνῆσαν,
οὐχ ἵνα δημηγορικοὶ ἢ δικανικοὶ γένοιντο, ἀλλ᾽ ἵνα, καλοί τε κἀγαθοὶ γενόμενοι,
καὶ οἴκῳ καὶ οἰκέταις καὶ οἰκείοις καὶ φίλοις καὶ πόλει καὶ πολίταις δύναιντο
καλῶς χρῆσθαι· καὶ τούτων οὐδείς, οὔτε νεώτερος οὔτε πρεσβύτερος ὤν, οὔτ᾽
ἐποίησε κακὸν οὐδέν, οὔτ᾽ αἰτίαν ἔσχεν.

(Xenophon, *Memorabilia* 1.2.48; ὁμιλητής "disciple," δημηγορικός "qualified to
speak in public," δικανικός "skilled in pleading lawsuits")

4. ἀλλὰ Σωκράτης γε τἀναντία τούτων φανερὸς ἦν καὶ δημοτικὸς καὶ φιλάνθρω-
πος ὤν· ἐκεῖνος γὰρ πολλοὺς ἐπιθυμητὰς καὶ ἀστοὺς καὶ ξένους λαβὼν οὐδένα
πώποτε μισθὸν τῆς συνουσίας ἐπράξατο, ἀλλὰ πᾶσιν ἀφθόνως ἐπήρκει τῶν
ἑαυτοῦ· ὧν τινες μικρὰ μέρη παρ᾽ ἐκείνου προῖκα λαβόντες πολλοῦ τοῖς ἄλλοις
ἐπώλουν, καὶ οὐκ ἦσαν ὥσπερ ἐκεῖνος δημοτικοί· τοῖς γὰρ μὴ ἔχουσι χρήματα
διδόναι οὐκ ἤθελον διαλέγεσθαι.

(Xenophon, *Memorabilia* 1.2.60; τἀναντία "the opposite," δημοτικός "kind to the
people," ἐπιθυμητής "disciple," ἀστός "citizen," πράττομαι "charge," ἐπαρκέω
"help," the antecedent of ὧν is πᾶσιν, μέρη i.e. parts of his knowledge, προῖκα
"freely," πωλέω "sell," ἔχω + infinitive "be able to")

5. ὑμεῖς δὲ δείξατε ἥντινα γνώμην ἔχετε περὶ τῶν πραγμάτων· εἰ μὲν γὰρ τούτου
καταψηφιεῖσθε, δῆλοι ἔσεσθε ὡς ὀργιζόμενοι τοῖς πεπραγμένοις· εἰ δὲ ἀποψη-
φιεῖσθε, ὀφθήσεσθε τῶν αὐτῶν ἔργων ἐπιθυμηταὶ τούτοις ὄντες, καὶ οὐχ ἕξετε
λέγειν ὅτι τὰ ὑπὸ τῶν τριάκοντα προσταχθέντα ἐποιεῖτε· νυνὶ μὲν γὰρ οὐδεὶς
ὑμᾶς ἀναγκάζει παρὰ τὴν ὑμετέραν γνώμην ψηφίζεσθαι.

(Lysias, *Oration* 12.90, an exhortation to a jury to condemn someone associated
with the thirty tyrants (τούτοις, which is dative after τῶν αὐτῶν); καταψηφίζω

"vote to condemn," ἀποψηφίζω "vote to acquit," ἔχω + infinitive "be able to," λέγειν i.e. to use as an excuse, προστάττω "order," παρά "contrary to")

6. ἔφη δέ, ἐπειδὴ οὗ ἐκβῆναι τὴν ψυχήν, πορεύεσθαι μετὰ πολλῶν, καὶ ἀφικνεῖσθαι σφᾶς εἰς τόπον τινὰ δαιμόνιον, ἐν ᾧ τῆς τε γῆς δύ’ εἶναι χάσματα ἐχομένω ἀλλήλοιν καὶ τοῦ οὐρανοῦ αὖ ἐν τῷ ἄνω ἄλλα καταντικρύ· δικαστὰς δὲ μεταξὺ τούτων καθῆσθαι, οὕς, ἐπειδὴ διαδικάσειαν, τοὺς μὲν δικαίους κελεύειν πορεύεσθαι τὴν εἰς δεξιάν τε καὶ ἄνω διὰ τοῦ οὐρανοῦ, σημεῖα περιάψαντας τῶν δεδικασμένων ἐν τῷ πρόσθεν, τοὺς δὲ ἀδίκους τὴν εἰς ἀριστεράν τε καὶ κάτω, ἔχοντας καὶ τούτους ἐν τῷ ὄπισθεν σημεῖα πάντων ὧν ἔπραξαν.

(Plato, *Republic* 614b–c, beginning of the myth of Er; οὗ is the genitive of ἕ ("from himself"), χάσμα "opening," ἐχομένω "next to" (dual), αὖ i.e. two other openings, καταντικρύ "opposite," κάθημαι "sit," διαδικάζω "judge thoroughly," περιάπτω "fasten around")

7. τὸ δ’ οὖν κεφάλαιον ἔφη τόδε εἶναι, ὅσα πώποτέ τινα ἠδίκησαν καὶ ὅσους ἕκαστοι, ὑπὲρ ἁπάντων δίκην δεδωκέναι ἐν μέρει, ὑπὲρ ἑκάστου δεκάκις, τοῦτο δ’ εἶναι κατὰ ἑκατονταετηρίδα ἑκάστην, ὡς βίου ὄντος τοσούτου τοῦ ἀνθρωπίνου, ἵνα δεκαπλάσιον τὸ ἔκτισμα τοῦ ἀδικήματος ἐκτίνοιεν· καὶ οἷον εἴ τινες πολλῶν θανάτων ἦσαν αἴτιοι, ἢ πόλεις προδόντες ἢ στρατόπεδα καὶ εἰς δουλείας ἐμβεβληκότες, ἢ τινος ἄλλης κακουχίας μεταίτιοι, πάντων τούτων δεκαπλασίας ἀλγηδόνας ὑπὲρ ἑκάστου κομίσαιντο, καὶ αὖ εἴ τινας εὐεργεσίας εὐεργετηκότες καὶ δίκαιοι καὶ ὅσιοι γεγονότες εἶεν, κατὰ ταὐτὰ τὴν ἀξίαν κομίζοιντο.

(Plato, *Republic* 615a–c; κεφάλαιον "summary," ἐν μέρει "in turn," κατὰ ἑκατονταετηρίδα i.e. "by 100-year periods," δεκαπλάσιος "tenfold," ἔκτισμα "payment," ἐκτίνω "pay," οἷον i.e. "for example," ἐμβάλλω "cast (people) into," κακουχία "bad conduct," μεταίτιος "participant, jointly guilty of," ἀλγηδών "pain," κομίζομαι "get")

8. πολλάκις ἐθαύμασα τῶν τὰς πανηγύρεις συναγαγόντων καὶ τοὺς γυμνικοὺς ἀγῶνας καταστησάντων, ὅτι τὰς μὲν τῶν σωμάτων εὐτυχίας οὕτω μεγάλων δωρεῶν ἠξίωσαν, τοῖς δ’ ὑπὲρ τῶν κοινῶν ἰδίᾳ πονήσασι καὶ τὰς αὑτῶν ψυχὰς οὕτω παρασκευάσασιν ὥστε καὶ τοὺς ἄλλους ὠφελεῖν δύνασθαι, τούτοις δ’ οὐδεμίαν τιμὴν ἀπένειμαν, ὧν εἰκὸς ἦν αὐτοὺς μᾶλλον ποιήσασθαι πρόνοιαν· τῶν μὲν γὰρ ἀθλητῶν δὶς τοσαύτην ῥώμην λαβόντων οὐδὲν ἂν πλέον γένοιτο τοῖς ἄλλοις, ἑνὸς δ’ ἀνδρὸς εὖ φρονήσαντος ἅπαντες ἂν ἀπολαύσειαν οἱ βουλόμενοι κοινωνεῖν τῆς ἐκείνου διανοίας.

(Isocrates, *Panegyricus* 1; πανήγυρις "festival," συνάγω i.e. "set up," γυμνικός "gymnastic," καθίστημι "establish," εὐτυχία i.e. "chance advantage," δωρεά "gift," ἀξιόω "consider worthy of," κοινόν i.e. "common good," ἰδίᾳ "personally," ἀπονέμω "assign" (the subject is still the founders of the games), εἰκός i.e. it would have been expected, πρόνοια "attention," ἀθλητής "athlete," ῥώμη "strength," γένοιτο i.e. it would be an advantage, ἀπολαύω "enjoy benefits")

9.   For additional practice, the passages given for analysis in chapters I–V can be analyzed using this system.

Review exercises 1

Translate into Greek, using only words and constructions in chapters I–VI and adding connecting words as appropriate.

1. When the four sailors arrived at the mainland on the third day, they found the old man who had written about the bandits who had seized their children. Instead of treating this man with violence, they wept in order to persuade (him) to show (them) those bandits' houses. When this man did not obey, however, they did not continue weeping but went home in silence as if they were ashamed of having wept. Now they are obviously about to leave the bandits and be gone; if we do not stop them, we shall never cease suffering at the hands of the gods. Therefore today some of us (ἡμῶν) will pursue the bandits who have camped in the temple a hundred feet long, and others will guard the children at the edge of the temple, so that we may save the sailors' children.

2. On the first day, such men as had not been seized marched across a plain nine stades wide and arrived at Athens before the enemy did. Today, the general has come here with the five hundred Greeks who escaped to the temple; since the temple did not burn, the Greeks stopped fleeing there, in order to find animals. Indeed, animals worth fifty talents were killed during the night, and at dawn the soldiers were ashamed: humans' treating animals with violence is not funny. If an army does not obtain dead animals, however, it will not continue to eat well, so the general, when he became a spectator of the corpses, sang as if he were rejoicing.

3. It is shameful for a young man not to be educated (= a young man's not being educated is shameful). Those who have been educated at Athens do not always become wise, for if they do not enjoy learning, they will not obtain wisdom. So today, when the citizens were deliberating in a road twenty feet wide, seven sophists there were obviously eating the fruit (plural) that had been sacrificed by prostitutes, although it had become sacred to the gods. The men in the road suddenly stopped deliberating in order to send the sophists home.

4. The temple sacred to the gods of the forest is twenty stades distant from Athens, near a river fifty feet wide. Since the offerings there have often been seized

by bandits during the day, yesterday at dawn guards arrived to stop thieves from taking the gold and silver. However, the men who do not take pleasure in peace and freedom dragged the prizes out of the temple without the guards noticing. By the citizens' immediately pursuing the thieves the offerings were found.

VII | Conditional, concessive, and potential clauses

Material to learn before using this chapter: ω-verbs, remainder (Smyth
§383–4: remainder); Vocabulary 7 and associated principal parts
Recommended grammar reading: Smyth §423–701
Recommended syntax reading: Smyth §1784–94, 1824–34, 2280–2382

Note: successful translation of conditional clauses into and out of English requires a clear understanding of the meanings of conditional clauses in formal written English; because these conditional clauses are rarely used in ordinary conversation they are unfamiliar to many native speakers. For example, in order to understand Greek conditionals it is necessary to know the difference between "if it isn't raining" and "if it weren't raining," and between "if I should do that" and "if I were doing that." Readers who do not feel completely confident of their grasp of such distinctions are advised to consult Appendix D, where they will find a full explanation and exercises, before proceeding further with this chapter.

A) Conditional sentences are those expressing the dependence of one action on another for its fulfillment, in other words those containing an expressed or implied εἰ "if."[1] All conditionals are composed of a protasis (the subordinate clause, which has the εἰ if there is one) and an apodosis (the main clause); although for clarity of explanation the protasis is conventionally presented first in grammatical discussions, either clause may come first in naturally produced sentences. The terminology used to describe conditionals varies widely; a conversion chart between the system used in this book and some of the others is given in Appendix E. The negative for all types of condition is μή in the protasis but οὐ in the apodosis.[2] Conditionals can be divided into four main types:[3]

---

[1] If followed by a subjunctive, the εἰ is combined with ἄν to produce ἐάν, which can contract to either ἄν or ἤν; care must be taken to identify it under these circumstances.

[2] The apodosis may, however, use the negative μή if it includes a construction that requires μή, such as a command (e.g. in the second example in section 4 below).

[3] These are only the most common types of conditional clause; there are many other possibilities, some of which should not be considered exceptions but rather ways of expressing thoughts that less often need to be expressed. Often such conditionals are formed by mixing a protasis of one type with an apodosis of another type.

1) **Simple conditions** describe specific actions in the present or past and normally indicate complete neutrality about whether or not the action described in the protasis actually takes place. They have present or past indicatives in both clauses.[4]

Present simple: protasis with εἰ + present indicative, then apodosis with present
indicative

εἰ τρέχει, νικᾷ.   If he is running (now), he is winning (this race).

Past simple: εἰ + past indicative, then past indicative

εἰ ἔδραμεν, ἐνίκησεν.   If he ran (yesterday), he won (that race).

Mixed simple: εἰ + past indicative, then present indicative, or εἰ + present indicative,
then past indicative

εἰ ἔδραμεν, νικᾷ.   If he ran (yesterday for training), he is winning (this
                                           race now).

εἰ μὴ νικᾷ, οὐκ ἔδραμεν.   If he is not winning (this race now), he did not run
                                           (yesterday for training).

2) **General conditions** describe general truths or customary or repeated actions in the present or past, without implications about whether the action of the protasis actually takes place. They have present or imperfect indicatives in the apodosis and subjunctives[5] or optatives in the protasis. Because their use of moods is determined by sequence, general conditions cannot be mixed.

Present general: ἐάν + subjunctive, then present indicative

ἐὰν τρέχῃ, νικᾷ.   If (ever) he runs (in a race), he (always) wins.

Past general: εἰ + optative, then imperfect indicative

εἰ τρέχοι, ἐνίκα.   If (ever) he ran (in a race), he (always) won.

3) **Contrafactual conditions** describe specific or general actions and assert that the action described in the protasis does not or did not take place. They have past indicatives in both clauses[6] and ἄν in the apodosis.[7]

---

[4] Occasionally other moods are used in the apodosis, for example ἀπολοίμην, Ξανθίαν εἰ μὴ φιλῶ "may I die if I do not love Xanthias" (Ar. *Ran.* 579).

[5] It is a general rule of conditional clauses that whenever the protasis has the subjunctive, ἐάν (εἰ + ἄν) is used instead of εἰ.

[6] The imperfect usually refers to present time but can also be used for repeated action in the past.

[7] Occasionally ἄν is omitted, when the apodosis contains a verb like ἔδει "should have" that conveys the unreality of the consequence.

Present contrafactual: εἰ + imperfect indicative, then imperfect indicative + ἄν

εἰ ἔτρεχεν, ἐνίκα ἄν.   If he were running (now), he would be winning (now – but he is not).

Past contrafactual: εἰ + aorist indicative, then aorist indicative + ἄν

εἰ ἔδραμεν, ἐνίκησεν ἄν.   If he had run (yesterday), he would have won (yesterday – but he did not).

Mixed contrafactual: εἰ + aorist indicative, then imperfect indicative + ἄν, or εἰ + imperfect indicative, then aorist indicative + ἄν

εἰ ἔδραμεν, ἐνίκα ἄν.   If he had run (yesterday), he would be winning (now – but he is not).

εἰ μὴ ἀγαθὸς ἦν, οὐκ ἂν ἐνίκησεν.   If he were not good, he would not have won (– but he is good, so he did win).

4) **Future conditions** describe specific or general actions and use different moods to express varying degrees of likelihood of their fulfillment. The subjunctive is the most common and indicates either neutrality about the outcome or an opinion that the condition will probably be fulfilled, the optative asserts that it is unlikely to be fulfilled, and the indicative in the protasis is normally reserved for threats and warnings.

Future more vivid: ἐάν + subjunctive, then future indicative, imperative, deliberative subjunctive, etc.[8]

ἐὰν δράμῃ, νικήσει.   If he runs, he will win (and this may well happen).

ἐὰν δράμῃ, παῦσον αὐτόν.   If he runs, stop him!

Future less vivid: εἰ + optative, then optative + ἄν

εἰ δράμοι, νικήσαι ἄν.   If he should run, he would win (but it is not likely). / If he were to run, he would win (but it is not likely). / If he ran, he would win (but it is not likely).

Future most vivid: εἰ + future indicative, then future indicative

εἰ μὴ νικήσει, ἀποκτενῶ αὐτόν.   If he does not win, I shall kill him.

---

[8] Any verb form that indicates future action can appear here, including the optative of wish, potential optative, hortatory subjunctive, or prohibitive subjunctive; other tenses of the indicative may also occur.

Summary of conditional types

	Present	Past
Simple	εἰ + pres. indic., then pres. indic.	εἰ + past indic., then past indic.
General	ἐάν + subjunctive, then pres. indic.	εἰ + optative, then impf. indic.
Contrafactual	εἰ + impf. indic., then impf. indic. + ἄν	εἰ + aor. indic., then aor. indic. + ἄν

	Future
More vivid	ἐάν + subjunctive, then fut. indic. etc.
Less vivid	εἰ + optative, then optative + ἄν
Most vivid	εἰ + fut. indic., then fut. indic.

Many conditional sentences can also be expressed with the participle (see chapter v); in these the protasis becomes the participle and the apodosis remains unchanged. The negative is still μή in the protasis and οὐ in the apodosis.

Preliminary exercise 1 (on A). For each sentence, give the formula (conjunction, mood, and tense of each verb, and ἄν if necessary) that it would require in Greek.

a. If I had been Menelaus, I would not have bothered to pursue Helen.

b. If Greek heroes were insulted, they got extremely angry.

c. I would be paying more attention if these sentences weren't so silly.

d. If this thing is your coat, you need a new one.

e. I shall get a job as a cowherd in the Alps if I don't make it as a Classicist.

f. We would not be doing this exercise if we had all died yesterday.

g. If we should do these sentences for the next two hours, we would all fall asleep.

h. Mary was allowed to vote in last November's election only if she registered before September.

i. If swimmers go into these waters, they get eaten by sharks.

j. If Jimmy goes into the water, get him out quickly!

k. You will be eaten by a shark if you try to swim here.

l. I would be amazed if she should fail the exam.

m. If people were rude to Roman emperors, they were executed.

n. If that fire was caused by the match you tossed, you ought to be ashamed of yourself.

o. If he learns these rules well, he will pass the quiz.

p. What would happen if we should all fall asleep in class?

q. I would not have done that if I were you.

r.   If ever she is sick, she does her Greek homework in bed.

s.   If ever a man rendered great services to the Athenians, they banished him.

t.   If Ariadne thinks Theseus will make her happy, she's making a big mistake.

u.   If she asks us for advice, we shall send her to you.

v.   We would be able to learn Trojan as well as Greek if Agamemnon had been more civilized.

w.   If a person gets his head chopped off, he dies.

x.   If we get our heads chopped off, our parents will sue.

y.   I would not have been so cold this morning if I were in Egypt.

z.   If Aeneas escapes from Troy, Juno will be very sad.

aa.   If Jane was in Athens yesterday, she is probably still there.

bb.   We would have no place to learn Greek if this building should collapse.

cc.   They would not have drowned if they had learned to swim.

dd.   If someone is a citizen, he or she is entitled to vote.

ee.   If I opened the door, the cat always tried to get out.

ff.   If John isn't here yet, he overslept.

gg.   If we should be asked to translate these sentences into Greek, we would have trouble.

hh.   If we were Athenians, we would have learned these constructions as children.

ii.   If Helen tries to run off with Paris, stop her!

jj.   If Zeus wanted a woman's love, he had to disguise himself to get it.

kk.   The Greek heroes would not have had such entertaining adventures if their gods had been more sensible.

ll.   If we were ancient Greeks, we would know Homer's poetry by heart.

mm.   If your dog made that mess, you ought to clean it up.

nn.   I shall kill you if you touch my Greek book.

B) Concessive clauses are conditionals with a καί next to the ἐάν or εἰ; they carry the meaning "even if."[9]

ἐτιμήθη ἂν καὶ εἰ μὴ ἐνίκησεν.   He would have been honored even if he had not won. (past contrafactual)

---

[9] Sometimes a simple condition introduced by εἰ καί means "although," i.e. concedes that the action of the protasis definitely takes place, but usually a participle with καίπερ is preferred for this meaning.

εἰ καὶ νικήσαιμεν οὐκ ἂν τιμῴμεθα.	Even if we should win, we would not be honored. (future less vivid)
γελᾷ καὶ ἐάν τι μὴ γελοῖον ᾖ.	He laughs even if something is not funny. (present general)

C) Potential clauses are the apodoses of contrafactual or future less vivid conditions, without the protases. They always take ἄν, and their negative is οὐ.

1) Potential optatives consist of an optative with ἄν and indicate future possibility, usually translated with "would," "could," "might," or "may"[10] in English.

γράψαι ἄν	he would write
οὐκ ἂν γραφείη	it could not be written
ἅπαντες ἂν ὁμολογήσειαν	all would agree

2) Potential indicatives consist of the imperfect (for present time) or aorist (for past time) indicative with ἄν and indicate that something is contrary to fact, was potential in the past, or (less often) was repeated or customary in the past. They thus convey nearly all the meanings of English "would have" and some of English "would," "might," and "used to."

ἔγραψεν ἄν	he would have written
οὐκ ἂν ἐγράφη	it would not have been written
οὐκ ἂν ἔγραφεν	he would not be writing
ἐγράφετο ἄν	it would be being written
ἔγνω ἄν τις	one might/would have known
διηρώτων ἄν	I would be asking / I used to ask

> **Preliminary exercise 2 (on C).** The underlined verbs could all be translated into Greek as potentials; indicate what mood and tense they would have.
>
> a.   It might snow next week.
> b.   This could never have been done without Martin.
> c.   Normally we wouldn't still be here at this hour, but we have an urgent deadline to meet.
> d.   Normally I would not have tried to intervene in a dispute between brothers, but this time someone might have been killed.

---

[10] English "may" is only an equivalent of the Greek potential optative when it indicates potentiality (when "he may write" means "perhaps he will write"), not when it indicates permission (when "he may write" means "he is allowed to write").

e. Please don't drop that, for it <u>would make</u> a dreadful mess.
f. Without the compass we <u>might have gotten</u> seriously lost.
g. Without a compass we <u>would now be wandering</u> around in circles.
h. If we're lucky this event <u>could be</u> a great success, but if we aren't it <u>might be</u> a disaster.
i. We <u>would not be</u> here today without the hard work of many people.
j. Careful with those wires – they <u>could kill</u> you.
k. This <u>would never have happened</u> without Bob.
l. You're going to win without even having to fight – no-one <u>would want</u> to challenge you.
m. This <u>might not have been accomplished</u> without Jenny's help.
n. This is an emergency – otherwise I <u>would not be bothering</u> you.
o. It <u>could rain</u> tomorrow.
p. Without your bright ideas, we <u>would never have ended</u> up in this mess.
q. Without your bright ideas, we <u>would not be</u> in this mess now.
r. Without your bright ideas, we <u>might not have ended</u> up in this mess.
s. Next year <u>could be</u> our last in these premises.
t. Everything <u>might have gone</u> horribly wrong, but by some miracle it didn't.
u. I don't advise wearing that to the party; people <u>would make</u> nasty remarks about it.
v. I <u>wouldn't be using</u> this office except that mine has been flooded.
w. It's not a good idea to do that, because people <u>would really hate you</u>.
x. Everything <u>would have gone</u> horribly wrong, but Mary saved the day.
y. Don't steal the church crucifix – you <u>would get</u> in loads of trouble!
z. They <u>might stay</u> for dinner, but they haven't yet decided.

Sentences

Translate into Greek using only words and constructions so far covered. Where two possibilities are indicated, give the protasis both as a participle and as a clause with a finite verb.

1. If you bring water home, we shall drink while we eat.
2. If I had not heard the immortal poem about truth then, I would be a slave to my body now. (2 ways)
3. If the child should perceive danger there, we would hear a shout immediately.
4–5. Guilty men would never have kindled a fire there; they would have hidden a fire in the forest. These shepherds are not responsible for the theft of the offerings.

6. If the shepherd's wife is fighting with that guard now, the shepherd is fighting too.

7. Even if I had learned the letters twice, I would not remember (them) today.

8. If a Greek stole money, he was not well spoken of: good Greeks never stole.

9. A good general would not abandon wounded soldiers instead of bringing (them) to a camp.

10. You would in no way be following rich men if you were not a slave to wealth. (2 ways)

11. The little child would not have stolen the money if the old man had hidden it (= them) elsewhere.

12. If he forgets his sister's name again, remind (him of it) privately.

13. Even if they were stationed in danger for many days, courageous Greeks never ran away.[11]

14–15. A prudent young man would be learning many arts privately during the winter too. This man, although he is well spoken of, is not prudent.

16. If a general has good fortune, the soldiers' spears strike only the enemy and do not miss often.

17–18. If you (pl.) do not stop running away, the army will be scattered and no-one will be saved. No-one will then bury the corpses of the soldiers who erred: only wild animals will find them (= these).

19. If the Greeks were not being persuaded by that clever orator, they would not be forgetting their reputation. (2 ways)

20–1. Stop your brother from stealing the possessions of the gods! The man responsible for that theft would be hated by many people.

22. If in truth the general, having forgotten, did not summon the allies yesterday, the citizens are reproaching him (= this man) justly.

23–4. If a just man were to judge these unjust bandits, many would be killed. They (= these men) do not have[12] honor, only violence.

25–6. Storms are hated by sailors. If a storm arrives when sailors have not[13] found land, many difficulties exist on the sea.

27. In his right hand the soldier has a spear, and in his left he has a book: this amazing man would never have left his book at home.

28. Many necessities exist in life, but neither things nor affairs will harm a young man if he becomes a philosopher.

---

[11] Run away = ἀπό + τρέχω.   [12] Use dative of possession here.

[13] Use μή here: in a protasis, even subordinate constructions tend to take μή.

29.　This philosopher alone never errs: if a herald brings writings from this man, obey immediately!

30.　Even if we learned this art well, we would not become rich: not because of possessions is art dear to good men.

Analysis

Analyze according to the model given in chapter VI, breaking up the sentence into units with one verb form in each and showing subordination by indentation and numbering. Translate each unit into English as literally as is possible without being incomprehensible and fully identify all conditional and potential clauses.

1.　τίς δὲ πατήρ, ἐὰν ὁ παῖς αὐτοῦ συνδιατρίβων τῳ σώφρων ᾖ, ὕστερον δὲ ἄλλῳ τῳ συγγενόμενος πονηρὸς γένηται, τὸν πρόσθεν αἰτιᾶται;

(Xenophon, *Memorabilia* 1.2.27; συνδιατρίβω "spend time with," τῳ = τινι)

2.　ἴσως οὖν εἴποιεν ἂν πολλοὶ τῶν φασκόντων φιλοσοφεῖν, ὅτι οὐκ ἂν ποτε ὁ δίκαιος ἄδικος γένοιτο, οὐδὲ ὁ σώφρων ὑβριστής, οὐδὲ ἄλλο οὐδέν, ὧν μάθησίς ἐστιν, ὁ μαθὼν ἀνεπιστήμων ἂν ποτε γένοιτο.

(Xenophon, *Memorabilia* 1.2.19; ἀνεπιστήμων "ignorant")

3.　ἀλλ᾽ εἰ καὶ μηδὲν αὐτὸς πονηρὸν ποιῶν ἐκείνους φαῦλα πράττοντας ὁρῶν ἐπῄνει, δικαίως ἂν ἐπετιμᾶτο.

(Xenophon, *Memorabilia* 1.2.29; ἐκείνους refers to the young men with whom Socrates associated, φαῦλος "bad," ἐπαινέω "praise," ἐπιτιμάω "censure")

4.　εἰ δὲ ἐδυστυχήσατε καὶ τούτων ἡμάρτετε, αὐτοὶ μὲν ἂν δείσαντες ἐφεύγετε μὴ πάθητε τοιαῦτα οἷα καὶ πρότερον, καὶ οὔτ᾽ ἂν ἱερὰ οὔτε βωμοὶ ὑμᾶς ἀδικουμένους διὰ τοὺς τούτων τρόπους ὠφέλησαν, ἃ καὶ τοῖς ἀδικοῦσι σωτηρία γίγνεται· οἱ δὲ παῖδες ὑμῶν, ὅσοι μὲν ἐνθάδε ἦσαν, ὑπὸ τούτων ἂν ὑβρίζοντο, οἱ δ᾽ ἐπὶ ξένης μικρῶν ἂν ἕνεκα συμβολαίων ἐδούλευον ἐρημίᾳ τῶν ἐπικουρησόντων.

(Lysias, *Oration* 12.98; the first τούτων refers to successes mentioned in a previous sentence and the others refer to the thirty tyrants; ἐπὶ ξένης "abroad," συμβόλαιον "debt contract," ἐρημίᾳ i.e. "out of reach of," ἐπικουρέω "help")

5.　ἐπερρώσθη δ᾽ ἄν τις κἀκεῖνο ἰδών, Ἀγησίλαον μὲν πρῶτον, ἔπειτα δὲ καὶ τοὺς ἄλλους στρατιώτας ἐστεφανωμένους ἀπὸ τῶν γυμνασίων ἀπιόντας καὶ ἀνατιθέντας τοὺς στεφάνους τῇ Ἀρτέμιδι.

(Xenophon, *Hellenica* 3.4.18; ἐπιρρώννυμι "encourage," ἀνατίθημι "dedicate")

6. ταῦτ' οὖν ἐγὼ μὲν ἔτι καὶ νῦν περιιὼν ζητῶ καὶ ἐρευνῶ κατὰ τὸν θεόν, καὶ τῶν ἀστῶν καὶ ξένων ἄν τινα οἴωμαι σοφὸν εἶναι· καὶ ἐπειδάν μοι μὴ δοκῇ, τῷ θεῷ βοηθῶν ἐνδείκνυμαι ὅτι οὔκ ἐστι σοφός.

    (Plato, *Apology* 23b, Socrates' description of his labors after hearing the oracular pronouncement that none was wiser than he; ἐρευνῶ "inquire after," ἀστός "citizen," ἄν = ἐάν)

7. μὰ τὸν Ποσειδῶ, εἰπεῖν τὸν Ἀλκιβιάδην, μηδὲν λέγε πρὸς ταῦτα, ὡς ἐγὼ οὐδ' ἂν ἕνα ἄλλον ἐπαινέσαιμι σοῦ παρόντος.

    (Plato, *Symposium* 214d, Alcibiades speaking to Socrates (omit the parenthetical εἰπεῖν τὸν Ἀλκιβιάδην from the analysis); πρός "against")

8. μέχρι μὲν οὖν δὴ δεῦρο τοῦ λόγου καλῶς ἂν ἔχοι καὶ πρὸς ὁντινοῦν λέγειν· τὸ δ' ἐντεῦθεν οὐκ ἄν μου ἠκούσατε λέγοντος, εἰ μὴ πρῶτον μέν, τὸ λεγόμενον, οἶνος ἄνευ τε παίδων καὶ μετὰ παίδων ἦν ἀληθής, ἔπειτα ἀφανίσαι Σωκράτους ἔργον ὑπερήφανον εἰς ἔπαινον ἐλθόντα ἄδικόν μοι φαίνεται.

    (Plato, *Symposium* 217e; ἀφανίζω "conceal," ὑπερήφανος "haughty, splendid," understand με as the subject of ἀφανίσαι. How does this sentence violate the rules given in this chapter?)

VIII | Relative clauses

Material to learn before using this chapter: contract verbs and relative
     pronoun (Smyth §338, 385, 395, 397); Vocabulary 8 and associated
     principal parts
Recommended grammar reading: Smyth §340, 346, 385–99
Recommended syntax reading: Smyth §2462–2573

A) Basic principles: a relative clause normally begins with a relative pronoun (ὅς, ἥ, ὅ "who," "which," or "that") and contains a finite verb. The pronoun takes its gender and number from its antecedent and its case from its use in its own clause; the verb is usually indicative, and the negative is usually οὐ.

εἶδον τὴν γυναῖκα ἣ ἐνίκησεν.   I saw the woman who won.

> **Preliminary exercise 1 (on A).** For each of the following English sentences, find where each relative clause begins and ends; then identify the relative pronoun and its antecedent. Give the gender, number, and case that the relative pronoun would have in Greek.
>
> a. The boy who is over there is my brother.
> b. The man that you saw is a dentist.
> c. The mountains (τὰ ὄρη) that we climbed are very high.
> d. The girls who attend this school are very happy.
> e. The person whose book you stole is my best friend!
> f. Some trees (δένδρα) that grow here live to be thousands of years old.
> g. The women to whom we gave the money are not actually poor.
> h. I know the man who found it.
> i. Is the girl whom we saw a friend of yours?
> j. The men who saved him have received medals.
> k. Did you see the girls who stole the money?
> l. Martha never heard the soprano (= female singer) whose voice she's trying to imitate.
> m. We love the boys to whom we will give these mittens.
> n. We didn't know the women whose husbands we rescued.
> o. He was attacked by a lioness that had previously killed three men.

p.   Will you give it to the boy who rescued me?

q.   We were talking with girls whom we didn't know.

r.   Who saw the man who stole that car?

Preliminary exercise 2 (on A). Translate into Greek using the following vocabulary: βοηθέω (+ dat.) "help"; νικάω "win, conquer"; στρατηγός, -οῦ, ὁ "general."

a.   We helped the general who won.

b.   The generals who were conquered helped us.

c.   They helped the general whom we conquered.

d.   The generals whom he conquered helped us.

e.   The general who helped us won.

f.   He conquered the generals who helped us.

g.   The general whom we helped was conquered.

h.   They conquered the generals whom we helped.

There are also a number of other ways that Greek relative clauses can be constructed. Although such variations are not usually mandatory, if one's purpose is to be fully comfortable with the constructions commonly used by Attic prose writers, it is useful to learn the variations of relative clause construction, as they are very frequent in Greek written by native speakers.[1]

B) Attraction (also known as assimilation) is a situation in which a relative pronoun takes the case of its antecedent rather than the one its own construction would seem to require. Attraction is normally found in restrictive relative clauses (i.e. those not preceded by a comma in English)[2] when the antecedent is genitive or dative and the relative pronoun should be accusative.

---

[1]   There are also a number of others not discussed here, including relative clauses of purpose (see chapter XII), causal relative clauses (these take the indicative, e.g. Σωκράτην φιλῶ ὃς ἀγαθός ἐστιν "I like Socrates because he is good"), and relative clauses of result (with indicative, e.g. τίς τοσοῦτο μαίνεται ὅστις Σωκράτην οὐ φιλεῖ; "Who is insane to such a degree that he does not like Socrates?").

[2]   A restrictive (or "defining") relative clause is one that defines the antecedent in a way essential to the meaning of the sentence, whereas a non-restrictive relative clause is parenthetical; that is why it is set off by commas. Additional clues to distinguishing types of relative clause are that restrictive clauses may use the relative pronoun "that" in English, or may omit the relative pronoun entirely, whereas non-restrictive ones must have "who," "whom," or "which." Examples:

Restrictive:	"I see the man they mentioned." / "I see the man that they mentioned." / "I see the man whom they mentioned." (The relative clause indicates which man I see, and therefore there is no comma.)
Non-restrictive:	"I see Socrates, whom they mentioned." (The relative clause does not indicate which man I see, but adds more information about him; therefore it is preceded by a comma.)

ἀντὶ τῶν ἀγαθῶν ὧν ἔχομεν   instead of the good things that we have (ὧν for ἅ)

τῷ χρυσῷ ᾧ ηὗρες   by means of the gold that you found (ᾧ for ὅν)

but

σὺν τῷ φύλακι, ὃν φιλοῦμεν   with the guard, whom we like (non-restrictive clause)

Preliminary exercise 3 (on B). For each of the following sentences, state whether the relative clause is restrictive, what cases the relative pronoun and the antecedent would be in without attraction, and whether attraction of the relative pronoun is possible. Assume that the verbs "love" and "accuse" take objects in the genitive, that "help" and "blame" take objects in the dative, and that all other verbs take objects in the accusative.

a.   I love Mary, who is an amazing cook.
b.   They blamed the man whom they had seen in the shop.
c.   I love Jane, whom we saw at the theatre.
d.   They blamed the man whom I love.
e.   He helped everyone whom he met.
f.   Don't accuse Jim, whom you know to be innocent.
g.   Jack saw the people whom you helped.
h.   Don't accuse the man whom you rescued.
i.   He helped me, whom he didn't even know.
j.   The man whom I love was accused of shoplifting.
k.   I love the girl whom we saw at the festival.
l.   Don't accuse a man who is innocent.
m.   Yesterday I saw the man whom I love.
n.   He helped people who had never helped him.
o.   They blamed a stranger who had acted suspiciously.
p.   They blamed Mark, whom they had seen entering the shop.
q.   We saw the person whom they blamed running from the shop.

Preliminary exercise 4 (on B). Translate each sentence into Greek; if attraction is possible, translate it twice, once without and once with attraction. Use the following vocabulary: βοηθέω (+ dat.) "help"; νικάω "win, conquer"; φιλέω "like"; κατηγορέω (+ gen.) "accuse"; μέμφομαι, μέμψομαι, ἐμεμψάμην, –, –, – (+ dat.) "blame"; ἐράω (+ gen.) "love"; στρατηγός, -οῦ, ὁ "general."

a.   He accused the general whom you like.
b.   We shall accuse the general, whom we do not like.
c.   She loves the general whom we conquered.

    d.   I love the general who was conquered.

    e.   We shall help the general whom they conquered.

    f.   He will help the general, whom he likes.

    g.   They blamed the general whom I conquered.

    h.   They blamed the general who was conquered.

C) Incorporation is a word order in which the antecedent appears inside the relative clause instead of in the main clause. Incorporation can occur only when the relative clause is restrictive and the antecedent could have taken an article; nevertheless no article is used. When incorporation is used, attraction must also be used if it is possible. An incorporated antecedent must be in the same case as the relative pronoun (whether that is the attracted case or the "ordinary" one); if antecedent and relative pronoun are in different cases and cannot be brought into the same case by attraction, incorporation is not possible.

ηὗρε τὸν λίθον ὃν ἀπέβαλες.	He found the stone you threw away.
becomes ηὗρεν ὃν ἀπέβαλες λίθον.	
σὺν τοῖς ἑταίροις οὓς ηὗρεν ἦλθεν.	He came with the comrades he found.
becomes σὺν οἷς ηὗρεν ἑταίροις ἦλθεν.	
αἱ πόλεις αἷς φόρος ἐτάχθη βοῦν ἀπάγουσιν.	The cities for which tribute was
becomes αἷς πόλεσι φόρος ἐτάχθη βοῦν	determined are sending off an ox.
ἀπάγουσιν.	

Preliminary exercise 5 (on C). Translate each sentence into Greek; if incorporation is possible, translate twice, once normally and once with incorporation. Apply attraction whenever possible. Use the following vocabulary: βοηθέω (+ dat.) "help"; νικάω "win, conquer"; κατηγορέω (+ gen.) "accuse"; μέμφομαι, μέμψομαι, ἐμεμψάμην, –, –, – (+ dat.) "blame"; ἐράω (+ gen.) "love"; στρατηγός, -οῦ, ὁ "general."

    a.   He accused the general whom you conquered.

    b.   We shall accuse the general whom she loves.

    c.   We shall accuse that general, whom she loves.

    d.   She loves the general whom we conquered.

    e.   I love the general who was conquered.

    f.   We shall help the general whom they conquered.

    g.   He conquered the general whom we conquered.

    h.   They blamed the general whom I conquered.

    i.   The general who was conquered blamed us.

    j.   The generals whom we love did not conquer.

D) Omission of the antecedent is frequent in restrictive relative clauses when the antecedent is a word easy to infer from the gender and number of the relative pronoun, such as "things" or "man." It is normally accompanied by attraction of the relative to the case of the omitted antecedent if the usual conditions for attraction are present; this is useful for making clear the role of the relative clause in the sentence. If the omitted antecedent would have been the object of a verb or preposition, the relative clause becomes that object.

ὃν οἱ θεοὶ φιλοῦσιν ἀποθνῄσκει νέος.	He whom the gods love dies young.
(for οὗτος ὃν οἱ θεοὶ φιλοῦσιν ἀποθνῄσκει νέος)	
ἔλαβεν ἃ ἐβούλετο.	He took what he wanted.
(for ἔλαβεν ταῦτα ἃ ἐβούλετο)	
ἔπειθεν οὓς ἐδύνατο.	He persuaded those whom he could (persuade).
(for ἔπειθε τούτους οὓς ἐδύνατο)	
ἔμαθεν ἀφ᾽ ὧν εἶπες.	He learned from what you said.
(for ἔμαθεν ἀπὸ τούτων ἃ εἶπες)	
ἐδήλωσε τοῦτο οἷς ἔπραττε.	He revealed this by what he did.
(for ἐδήλωσε τοῦτο ἐκείνοις ἃ ἔπραττε)	

> **Preliminary exercise 6 (on D).** Translate into Greek twice, once with the antecedent present and once with the antecedent omitted; in the second version apply attraction if possible. Use the following vocabulary: φιλέω "like"; ἀπιστέω (+ dat.) "distrust"; εὖ δράω "treat well."
>
> a. I distrust those whom I do not like.
> b. I like what you like. (use plural for "what")
> c. He is liked by those whom he likes.
> d. We do not like those whom we distrust.
> e. We shall distrust those whom you do not like.
> f. He treated well those whom he liked.
> g. We are well treated by those whom we like.

E) Correlatives occur when the relative clause precedes the main clause and is then picked up and echoed by a demonstrative pronoun at the start of the main clause. If a noun is needed to specify more precisely what the relative pronoun refers to, that noun may be found either in the relative clause or in the main clause. It is usually difficult to produce a similar construction in English, so Greek relative-correlative sentences are often translated into English by inverting the order of the clauses. When translating from English to Greek it is therefore advisable to reorder the English before attempting to translate it.

ἃ εὗρον, ταῦτα ὑμῖν ἔδωκα.	I gave you what I found. (literally "What things I found, those things I gave you.")
οἷς πιστεύομεν πολίταις, τούτοις ἀπιστοῦσιν.	They distrust the citizens whom we trust. (literally "What citizens we trust, those (citizens) they distrust.")
ἃ πάλαι μεγάλα ἦν, ταῦτα μικρὰ γέγονεν.	The ones that once were large have become small. (literally "What ones once were large, those have become small.")
οἳ δ' Ὀρχομενὸν οἰκοῦσι, τούτων ἄρχει Ἀσκάλαφος.	And Ascalaphos leads those who inhabit Orchomenos. (literally "And who inhabit Orchomenos, those (men) Ascalaphos leads.")

Preliminary exercise 7 (on E). Without translating, restructure the following English sentences into relative-correlative word order, adding a correlative pronoun if necessary. For example, a sentence like "They distrust the citizens whom we trust" would become "What citizens we trust, those (citizens) they distrust."

a. We gave away what we had.
b. The people who used to be young are now old.
c. I saw the men who saw me.
d. I know the things that you did.
e. The things that used to be in fashion are now out of fashion.
f. Don't bite the hand that feeds you!
g. I gave money to the people to whom you gave money.
h. The men whose sons are dead will lack honor in old age.
i. They laughed at the people whom they saw.
j. The daughters of men whose wives are beautiful will also be beautiful.
k. The men to whom I gave money showed no gratitude.

Preliminary exercise 8 (on E). Translate the sentences in Preliminary exercise 6 into Greek using the relative-correlative construction; do not use attraction.

F) Conditional relative clauses have the same range of meanings as conditions (see chapter VII) and follow the same patterns in terms of the mood and tense of the verbs in subordinate and main clauses, the choice of negatives (μή in the relative clause and οὐ in the main clause), and in the way that ἄν is used. When ἄν appears in the main clause of the corresponding conditional sentence, ἄν appears in the main clause of a conditional relative sentence; when ἐάν appears in the protasis of the corresponding conditional, ἄν appears directly after the relative pronoun in a conditional relative sentence. The relative pronoun itself takes the place of εἰ (or the ἐ in ἐάν). Conditional relatives often have an omitted or incorporated antecedent or a correlative pronoun. Although conditional relatives can follow the pattern of any of the types of conditional sentence discussed in chapter VII,[3] the most common are the future more vivid and the present and past general. These latter two are normally translatable using English sentences with "whoever"[4] or "whichever."

Present general:

οὓς ἂν αἱρῶμεν λύομεν.	We release whoever we capture.
cf. ἐάν τινας αἱρῶμεν, λύομεν.	If (ever) we capture some people, we release (them).

Past general:

οὓς αἱροῖμεν ἐλύομεν.	We used to release whoever we captured.
cf. εἴ τινας αἱροῖμεν, ἐλύομεν.	If (ever) we captured any people, we used to release (them).

Future more vivid:

οὓς ἂν μὴ ἕλωμεν οὐ λύσομεν.	We shall not release (people) whom we do not capture.
cf. ἐὰν μή τινας ἕλωμεν, οὐ λύσομεν.	If we do not capture any (people), we shall not release (them).

The similarity between the general relative clauses and the general conditionals is a manifestation of a broader principle within Greek (one that also applies to temporal clauses, see chapter XVI): a subordinate clause uses the indicative to refer to a specific act in the past or present, and the subjunctive (with ἄν) or the optative (without ἄν), according to sequence,[5] to indicate a generalization in the past or present. The term

---

[3] For example, past contrafactual οὓς εἵλομεν ἐλύσαμεν ἄν "We would have released whoever/anyone we had captured (but we didn't capture anyone)" (cf. εἴ τινας εἵλομεν ἐλύσαμεν ἄν "If we had captured anyone, we would have released (them)"); future less vivid οὓς ἕλοιμεν, λύσαιμεν ἄν "We would release anyone/whoever we captured (but it is unlikely that we shall capture anyone)" (cf. εἴ τινας ἕλοιμεν, λύσαιμεν ἄν "If we should capture anyone, we would release (them)").

[4] English "whoever" has no plural, but its Greek equivalent has both singular and plural, so sometimes the English singular will be equivalent to a Greek plural. In Greek the plural is used when the entity designated with "whoever" may include more than one person; the singular is reserved for a "whoever" that can be only one person at a time. For example, "Whoever comes first will get the prize" needs a singular in Greek, but "He praised whoever he saw marching in good order" needs a plural.

[5] In Greek, primary sequence occurs in sentences whose main verb is present, future, or perfect; secondary (historic) sequence involves main verbs in the imperfect, aorist, or pluperfect.

"indefinite construction" is sometimes used as a cover term for subordinate clauses of this type and can provide a useful shortcut for understanding them in sentences where the main clause is atypical or absent: if a clause referring to the present or past has the indefinite construction in Greek, it will normally have the word "ever" in English, and vice versa. This generalization does not apply to the future, however, as there ἄν + subjunctive is regularly used both for generalizations and for specific acts.

εἰδέναι ὅ τι ἂν λέγῃ ἢ πράττῃ   to know whatever he says or does (Plato, *Symposium* 172c)

> **Preliminary exercise 9 (on F).** Translate into Greek using conditional relative clauses and the following vocabulary: εὑρίσκω, εὑρήσω, ηὗρον/εὗρον, ηὕρηκα/εὕρηκα, εὕρημαι, εὑρέθην "find"; ἁρπάζω, ἁρπάσομαι, ἥρπασα, ἥρπακα, ἥρπασμαι, ἡρπάσθην "seize"; ἕπομαι, ἕψομαι, ἑσπόμην, –, –, – (+ dat.) "follow"; λῃστής, -οῦ, ὁ "bandit." Translate each sentence twice, once with the antecedent omitted and attraction if possible, and once with the relative-correlative construction and no attraction.
>
> a.   Bandits seize whatever (plural) they find.
> b.   Whoever (singular) the bandits followed was seized.
> c.   They will follow the person (singular) whom they find.
> d.   Whoever (singular) the bandits follow is seized.
> e.   He used to seize whatever (singular) he found.
> f.   I will seize what (plural) I find.
> g.   He used to follow whoever (plural) he found.
> h.   Whoever (plural) the bandits follow will be seized.
> i.   She follows whoever (singular) she finds.

G) Other relative words can also be used with the constructions above: the "usual" relative pronoun ὅς is only one member of a large group. Most of the relative words belong to sets consisting of a "specific relative," an "indefinite relative," and a correlative. The "indefinite" relatives are translated with "-ever" in English, like the "indefinite construction" just discussed, but their meaning is not precisely the same.[6] While the "indefinite construction" generalizes about things that happen on more than one occasion, "indefinite relatives" like ὅστις indicate that the group so designated is to be understood in the widest possible sense. So if the Thebans proclaim that whoever gets rid of the Sphinx will become king of Thebes, and what they mean is that absolutely anyone no matter

---

[6] I owe the information in this paragraph to P. Probert, *Early Greek Relative Clauses* (Oxford 2015), sections 5.3.2–3.

how undesirable is eligible for the reward, they would use ὅστις for "whoever" in the proclamation. If on the other hand the Athenians decree that whoever wins a competition at the Panathenaic games gets a special amphora of oil, year in and year out, they would use ἄν + subjunctive for "whoever." It is of course possible to use both constructions in the same relative clause, if both meanings are present (for example if the Sphinx were a recurrent problem in Thebes and the citizens issued a proclamation emphasizing that on a permanent basis there were no limits on who could become king by getting rid of her for a while). Some of the more common relative words are given below.[7]

Specific relative	Indefinite relative	Correlative
ὅς "who, which"	ὅστις "whoever, whichever"	οὗτος "this man"
ὅσος "as much, as many"	ὁπόσος "however much, however many"	τοσοῦτος "so much, so many"
οἷος "of what sort"	ὁποῖος "of whatever sort"	τοιοῦτος "of this sort"
οὗ "where"	ὅπου "wherever"	ἐκεῖ "there"
ὅθεν "from where"	ὁπόθεν "from wherever"	ἐκεῖθεν "from there"
οἷ "(to) where"	ὅποι "(to) wherever"	ἐκεῖσε "(to) there"
ὡς "how"	ὅπως "how(ever)"	οὕτω(ς) "in this way"

Examples:

ὅσα ἂν εὕρῃ, κομίσει.	He will bring as many as he finds. (conditional)
ὅσους ἂν εὕρῃς, τοσούτους σώσει.	He will save as many men as you find. (correlation, conditional)
ὡς ἐθέλω, οὕτω πράττω.	I do as I wish. (correlation)
ὅποι ἂν τρέχῃ, διώκεται.	Wherever he runs, he is pursued. (conditional)
ὅποι ἂν ἴῃς, ἐκεῖσε ἴμεν.	We shall go wherever you go. (correlation, conditional)
οἷόν ἐστι τὸ τῶν φύλλων γένος, τοιοῦτόν ἐστι καὶ τὸ τῶν ἀνδρῶν.	The race of men is like the race of leaves. (correlation)
ἔτλην δ' οἷ' οὔ πώ τις ἐπιχθόνιος βροτὸς ἄλλος. (*Iliad* 24.505)	I have dared such things as no other mortal man has yet dared.

As with regular correlatives, correlative sentences with these words are best translated via a two-step process: first one restructures the English so that the relative comes first and the corresponding correlative is inserted at the beginning of the main clause, and then one translates it. Thus when faced with "I shall read as many books as you write,"

---

[7] This table is a simplification with many omissions; a fuller version can be found in the vocabulary for this chapter.

one first restructures the English to "As many books as you write, so many shall I read" and then translates that into ὅσα ἂν βιβλία γράψῃς, τοσαῦτα ἀναγνώσομαι. Similarly "He went wherever I did" would become "Wherever I went, there he went" and then ὅποι ἴοιμι, ἐκεῖσε ᾔει οὗτος.

Sentences 1 (correlation only)

Translate into Greek using the relative-correlative construction and indicative relative clauses.

1. As many soldiers distrust this general as trust him.[8]
2. This doctor did as many bad things as the bandits did.
3. The allies did not help as many foreigners as we did.
4. The Greeks conquered as many men as the foreigners did.
5. This philosopher loves as many boys as the general does.
6. The wretched man does not have as big a house as I do.
7. The poems are like the poets.[9]
8. The slaves are not like their masters.
9. The doctor loves a woman like the one you love.
10. This general is the kind that soldiers disobey.
11. This man made clear the sort of affairs that we made clear.
12. As many soldiers distrust their generals as trust them.
13. The child did as I did.
14. The sailor won in the same way that the sophist did.
15. We brought what you asked for.
16. The crowd liked what I made.
17. The allies attacked the men we attacked.
18. The soldiers marched where the men who were generals marched.
19. The water (is) bitter where the army is making camp.
20. The fearful men sailed from where the sailors did.

Sentences 2 (correlation and conditional relatives)

Translate into Greek using conditional relatives with correlatives.

1. The crowd likes whatever I make.
2. The citizens vote however their wives wish.
3. The allies will not help as many foreigners as we will.

---

[8] I.e. as many soldiers as trust the general, so many distrust (him).
[9] I.e. of what sort the poets (are), of this sort (are) the poems.

4.   Greeks used to capture (= take) as many men as foreigners did.
5.   They used to bring what we did not ask for.
6.   Whatever he asks for, the wretched man will not obtain it.
7.   Soldiers march wherever the men who are generals march.
8.   Someone whom you (plural) do not treat well will not fare well.
9.   The child did whatever I did.
10. The soldiers will obey whoever is general of the army.
11. The allies attacked whoever we attacked.
12. The soldiers will find bitter water wherever the army wishes to make camp.
13. The fearful men used to sail from wherever the sailors did.

Sentences 3 (attraction, incorporation and omission)[10]

Translate the following into English, then rewrite them in Greek with "normal" (unattracted, antecedents expressed) relative clauses.

1.   χρώμεθα τοῖς ἀγαθοῖς οἷς ἔχομεν.
2.   τῷ ἡγεμόνι πιστεύσομεν ᾧ ἂν Κῦρος διδῷ.
3.   ἄξιοί ἐστε τῆς ἐλευθερίας ἧς κέκτησθε.
4.   τῶν παίδων ὧν ἔθρεψα οὗτός ἐστι μωρότατος.
5.   ἐπορεύετο σὺν ᾗ εἶχε δυνάμει.
6.   ἀμαθέστατοί ἐστε ὧν ἐγὼ οἶδα Ἑλλήνων.
7.   ἃ μὴ οἶδα οὐδὲ οἴομαι εἰδέναι.
8.   ἦλθες σὺν οἷς μάλιστα φιλεῖς.
9.   ἀμελῶ ὧν με δεῖ πράττειν.
10. ἐπιλανθάνεται ὧν ἂν ἀκούῃ.

Sentences 4 (attraction, incorporation, and omission)

Translate each of the following into Greek twice, once "normally" (with correlatives if necessary) and once with antecedents omitted or incorporated and relative pronouns attracted whenever possible. Use ordinary or conditional relative clauses as appropriate.

1.   We do not consider this man worthy of the contests he wishes to win today.
2.   The doctor inquired about these things from the children we sent.
3.   The doctor used to inquire about these things from whoever we sent.
4.   The jurors will not condemn the wives whom you abandoned.

---

[10] Sentence groups 3 and 4 may be skipped without impairing one's ability to do the exercises in later chapters.

5. The jurors will condemn whoever you abandon.
6. We shall use whatever you bring.
7. This man treats the woman he loves badly.
8. The wretched man accuses (use κατηγορέω) whoever he wants to harm.
9. The doctor accused (use κατηγορέω) the child whom we had nourished.
10. The doctor accused (use κατηγορέω) that child, whom we had nourished.

Analysis

Analyze according to the model given in chapter VI, breaking up the sentence into units with one verb form in each and showing subordination by indentation and numbering. Translate each unit into English as literally as is possible without being incomprehensible and explain all relative clauses.

1. ἐπεὶ τοίνυν τάχιστα τῶν πολιτευομένων ὑπέλαβον κρείττονες εἶναι, Σωκράτει μὲν οὐκέτι προσῇσαν· οὔτε γὰρ αὐτοῖς ἄλλως ἤρεσκεν, εἴ τε προσέλθοιεν, ὑπὲρ ὧν ἡμάρτανον ἐλεγχόμενοι ἤχθοντο· τὰ δὲ τῆς πόλεως ἔπραττον, ὧνπερ ἕνεκεν καὶ Σωκράτει προσῆλθον.

   (Xenophon, *Memorabilia* 1.2.47, on Alcibiades and his comrades; ἐπεὶ τάχιστα "as soon as," πολιτευόμενοι i.e. "the people running the city," ὑπολαμβάνω "suspect that," προσέρχομαι "visit," ἄχθομαι "be grieved," ὧνπερ ἕνεκεν i.e. originally)

2. ἀλλ᾽, ἔφη, τοῦτό γ᾽ εὖ λέγεις· ἐν γὰρ τῷ ἐπιόντι χρόνῳ βουλευόμενοι πράξομεν ὃ ἂν φαίνηται νῷν περί τε τούτων καὶ περὶ τῶν ἄλλων ἄριστον.

   (Plato, *Symposium* 219a–b; ἐπιών "future," νῷν is dual dative of ἡμεῖς; ἔφη is parenthetical and so can be ignored for purposes of analysis)

3. τίνα γὰρ εἰκὸς ἦν ἧττον ταῦτα ὑπηρετῆσαι ἢ τὸν ἀντειπόντα οἷς ἐκεῖνοι ἐβούλοντο πραχθῆναι;

   (Lysias, *Oration* 12.27; ἧττον "less well," ὑπηρετέω "serve," ἀντιλέγω + dat. "speak against")

4. ἀλλὰ τί ποιῶμεν; ὅτι ἂν σὺ κελεύῃς.

   (Plato, *Symposium* 214b)

5. ἀλλ᾽ οὐχ᾽ ὅσῳ ἂν παρὰ τῷ ὑστέρῳ χείρων φαίνηται, τοσούτῳ μᾶλλον ἐπαινεῖ τὸν πρότερον;

   (Xenophon, *Memorabilia* 1.2.27, on how a father judges the teachers of his son if the boy is good while with one and then bad when with the next)

6. οἱ μὲν οὖν ἄλλοι πάντες ἡμεῖς εἰρήκαμεν· σὺ δ’ ἐπειδὴ οὐκ εἴρηκας καὶ ἐκπέπ-
    ωκας, δίκαιος εἶ εἰπεῖν, εἰπὼν δὲ ἐπιτάξαι Σωκράτει ὅτι ἂν βούλῃ, καὶ τοῦτον
    τῷ ἐπὶ δεξιὰ καὶ οὕτω τοὺς ἄλλους.

    (Plato, *Symposium* 214c, Eryximachus’ explanation to Alcibiades of the
    rules of the symposium; δίκαιος εἶ i.e. “it is just for you,” ἐπὶ δεξιά “on his
    right”)

7. σπουδάσαντος δὲ αὐτοῦ καὶ ἀνοιχθέντος οὐκ οἶδα εἴ τις ἑώρακεν τὰ ἐντὸς
    ἀγάλματα· ἀλλ’ ἐγὼ ἤδη ποτ’ εἶδον, καί μοι ἔδοξεν οὕτω θεῖα καὶ χρυσᾶ
    εἶναι καὶ πάγκαλα καὶ θαυμαστά, ὥστε ποιητέον εἶναι ἔμβραχυ ὅτι κελεύοι
    Σωκράτης.

    (Plato, *Symposium* 216e–217a, Alcibiades comparing Socrates to a hollow statue
    with golden images inside it; σπουδάζω “be in earnest”)

8. πρῶτον μέν, ὦ ἄνδρες Ἀθηναῖοι, τοῖς θεοῖς εὔχομαι πᾶσι καὶ πάσαις, ὅσην
    εὔνοιαν ἔχων ἐγὼ διατελῶ τῇ τε πόλει καὶ πᾶσιν ὑμῖν, τοσαύτην ὑπάρξαι
    μοι παρ’ ὑμῶν εἰς τουτονὶ τὸν ἀγῶνα, ἔπειθ’ ὅπερ ἐστὶ μάλισθ’ ὑπὲρ ὑμῶν
    καὶ τῆς ὑμετέρας εὐσεβείας τε καὶ δόξης, τοῦτο παραστῆσαι τοὺς θεοὺς ὑμῖν,
    μὴ τὸν ἀντίδικον σύμβουλον ποιήσασθαι περὶ τοῦ πῶς ἀκούειν ὑμᾶς ἐμοῦ
    δεῖ (σχέτλιον γὰρ ἂν εἴη τοῦτό γε), ἀλλὰ τοὺς νόμους καὶ τὸν ὅρκον, ἐν
    ᾧ πρὸς ἅπασι τοῖς ἄλλοις δικαίοις καὶ τοῦτο γέγραπται, τὸ ὁμοίως ἀμφοῖν
    ἀκροάσασθαι.

    (Demosthenes, *De corona* 1; εὔνοια + dat. “good will,” ἔπειθ’ supply a second
    εὔχομαι here, εὐσέβεια i.e. standing with the gods, δόξα i.e. reputation among
    mortals, παρίστημι “be present” (the subject is τοὺς θεούς), the μή clause is an
    explanation of τοῦτο, ἀντίδικος “opponent,” σύμβουλος “advisor,” πρός “in addi-
    tion to,” δίκαιον i.e. fair provision, ἀκροάομαι “listen to”)

9. πρὸς γὰρ ἀντιβολίαν καὶ ὀλοφυρμὸν τραπόμενοι ἐς ἀπορίαν καθίστασαν, ἄγειν
    τε σφᾶς ἀξιοῦντες καὶ ἕνα ἕκαστον ἐπιβοώμενοι, εἴ τινά πού τις ἴδοι ἢ ἑταίρων
    ἢ οἰκείων, τῶν τε ξυσκήνων ἤδη ἀπιόντων ἐκκρεμαννύμενοι καὶ ἐπακολουθοῦν-
    τες ἐς ὅσον δύναιντο, εἴ τῳ δὲ προλίποι ἡ ῥώμη καὶ τὸ σῶμα, οὐκ ἄνευ πολ-
    λῶν ἐπιθειασμῶν καὶ οἰμωγῆς ὑπολειπόμενοι, ὥστε δάκρυσι πᾶν τὸ στράτευμα
    πλησθὲν καὶ ἀπορίᾳ τοιαύτῃ μὴ ῥᾳδίως ἀφορμᾶσθαι, καίπερ ἐκ πολεμίας τε καὶ
    μείζω ἢ κατὰ δάκρυα τὰ μὲν πεπονθότας ἤδη, τὰ δὲ περὶ τῶν ἐν ἀφανεῖ δεδιότας
    μὴ πάθωσιν.

    (Thucydides 7.75.4, the departure of the defeated Athenians from Syracuse; ἀντι-
    βολία “entreaty,” ὀλοφυρμός “lamentation,” καθίστασαν “put into” (understood
    subject is the wounded soldiers and understood object the departing ones), ἀξιόω

"ask," ἐπιβοάομαι "call to help," σύσκηνος "tent-mate," ἐκκρεμάννυμι "cling to," ἐπακολουθέω "follow after," ῥώμη "strength," ἐπιθειασμός "appeal to the gods," οἰμωγή "lamentation," ἐκ πολεμίας: understand ἀφορμωμένους, πολεμία "enemy territory," κατὰ "suitable for," ἀφανές "the future")

IX | Pronouns

Material to learn before using this chapter: pronouns, adverbs (Smyth §325, 327, 329, 331, 333–4, 339); Vocabulary 9 and associated principal parts
Recommended grammar reading: Smyth §325–40
Recommended syntax reading: Smyth §1184–5, 1190–1278

A) Αὐτός has three distinct meanings.

1) "Him," "her," "it," "them" when used alone (i.e. as a pronoun) in cases *other than the nominative*.

ἔβαλον αὐτόν.   They hit him.

2) "Self" (in the intensifying, not the reflexive, sense) when used adjectivally in predicate position, adjectivally without the article, or pronominally (i.e. alone) in the nominative.[1]

ὁ βασιλεὺς αὐτὸς θύσει.   The king himself will sacrifice.
βασιλεῖς αὐτοὶ ἐκεῖ ἔθυον.   Kings used to sacrifice there themselves.
αὐτὴ τὸν υἱὸν ἐδίδαξεν.   She taught her son herself.

3) "Same" when used with an article, in attributive position.

ὁ αὐτὸς βασιλεὺς θύσει.   The same king will sacrifice.

Therefore: αὐτὸς αὐτὸν ἐν τῷ αὐτῷ οἴκῳ εἶδον σὺν αὐτῷ τῷ βασιλεῖ.
     I myself saw him in the same house with the king himself.

---

[1] When translating English "myself," "yourself," "himself," etc. care is sometimes needed to distinguish between reflexive uses, which require Greek reflexives (or, very occasionally, the middle voice), and intensifying uses, which require αὐτός. Reflexives can only be objects (so if the word in question belongs in the nominative case, it should be αὐτός) and are always freestanding pronouns (so if the word in question is attached to anything, it should be αὐτός). Therefore "The priestess herself sacrificed to Apollo," "The priestess sacrificed to Apollo herself," and "The priestess sacrificed to Apollo himself" require forms of αὐτός, but "The priestess sacrificed herself to Apollo" needs a reflexive.

Preliminary exercise 1 (on A). Translate into Greek using forms of αὐτός and the following vocabulary: ἑταῖρος, -ου, ὁ "comrade"; γράφω, γράψω, ἔγραψα, γέγραφα, γέγραμμαι, ἐγράφην "write"; εὑρίσκω, εὑρήσω, ηὗρον/εὗρον, ηὕρηκα/εὕρηκα, εὕρημαι, εὑρέθην "find."

a. The same comrades will write.
b. The comrades themselves will write.
c. They will write the same things.
d. We ourselves shall write.
e. He found them.
f. They found the same man.
g. He himself found them.
h. The same man found him.
i. They found him.
j. I found him myself.

B) Reflexive pronouns are of two types.

1) Direct reflexives (ἐμαυτόν, ἡμᾶς αὐτούς, σεαυτόν, ὑμᾶς αὐτούς, ἑαυτόν, ἑαυτούς, and equivalent forms in the feminine, genitive, and dative) are used as the object of a verb when that object is the same person as the subject.[2]

ἐμαυτὴν εἶδον.	I saw myself. (fem.)
ἑαυτοὺς εἶδον.	They saw themselves.

2) Indirect reflexives (ἕ, σφᾶς, and their genitive and dative forms) occur in subordinate clauses, as the object of a verb when that object is the same as the subject, not of that verb, but of another verb on which that verb depends. For the indirect reflexives of the first and second person, the non-reflexive personal pronouns are used.

ἐκέλευσεν αὐτοὺς πείθεσθαι οἷ.	He told them to obey him. (same person)
ἐκέλευσεν αὐτοὺς πείθεσθαι αὐτῷ.	He told them to obey him. (different person)
ἐκέλευσεν αὐτοὺς πείθεσθαι ἑαυτοῖς.	He told them to obey themselves. (direct reflexive)
ἐκελεύσαμεν αὐτοὺς πείθεσθαι ἡμῖν.	We told them to obey us.

---

[2] Sometimes direct reflexives are also used for indirect reflexives.

Preliminary exercise 2 (on B). For each underlined pronoun, indicate whether it would be translated into Greek with a direct reflexive, an indirect reflexive, another pronoun, or nothing.

Euthyphro considered <u>himself</u> to be a very pious man. <u>He</u> prayed to the gods each morning, and <u>he</u> always washed <u>himself</u> before praying. <u>He</u> led the household prayers <u>himself</u>, rather than telling the steward to do it for <u>him</u>. <u>He</u> asked all his family to imitate <u>him</u> in piety, but his father found this a bit much. Euthyphro's father thought as highly of <u>himself</u> as Euthyphro did, so <u>he</u> ordered Euthyphro to leave <u>him</u> in peace and go preach somewhere else.

C) Demonstratives οὗτος ("this" or "that"), ὅδε ("this"), and ἐκεῖνος ("that") can be used in pairs with special meanings. (Both these meanings are based on the fact that οὗτος tends to refer back to a recently mentioned item.)

1) Οὗτος and ὅδε: "the preceding" and "the following".

> Σωκράτης μὲν ταῦτα εἶπεν, Ἀριστοφάνης δὲ τάδε ἀπεκρίνατο "Socrates said the preceding, and Aristophanes answered the following" (often found between two passages of reported speech).

> NB also the adverbial variant: Σωκράτης μὲν οὕτως εἶπεν, Ἀριστοφάνης δὲ ὧδε ἀπεκρίνατο "Socrates spoke in the way we have just described, and Aristophanes answered as follows."

2) Οὗτος and ἐκεῖνος: "the latter" and "the former".

> καὶ τὸν ἀδελφὸν καὶ τὴν ἀδελφὴν εἶδον, ἀλλ' ἐκεῖνος μέν μ' εἶδεν, αὕτη δ' οὔ. "I saw both my brother and my sister, but the former saw me and the latter did not." (i.e. "he saw me and she did not")

D) Possession can be expressed either with a possessive adjective (ἐμός, σός, ἡμέτερος, ὑμέτερος) or with the genitive of a pronoun. Unemphatic possession is expressed by the article alone when the context makes it clear (see chapter 1), but even in such contexts possessives (especially reflexive ones) may be used for emphasis (e.g. to translate "my own"). Possessive adjectives and pronouns *always* take an article in Greek prose.[3]

---

[3] This preference is so consistent and so striking that it gave rise to the Greek word for possessives, σύναρθροι ἀντωνυμίαι "pronouns with the article."

1) The **adjectives** all take attributive position.

ὁ ἐμὸς οἶκος   my house
αἱ ὑμέτεραι γυναῖκες   your wives

2) The genitives also take the article, but prefer different positions.

a) **Genitives of personal pronouns** (ἐμοῦ, μου, σοῦ, σου, ἡμῶν, ὑμῶν) and of αὐτός take the predicate position. As with other uses of the personal pronouns, the enclitic forms are usual; in forms for which an enclitic variant exists, the accented one is emphatic.

ὁ οἶκός μου   my house
ὁ οἶκος ἐμοῦ   *my* house
αἱ γυναῖκες ὑμῶν   your wives
ὁ οἶκος αὐτῆς   her house

b) **Genitives of reflexives** (ἐμαυτοῦ, etc.) and demonstratives (τούτου, ἐκείνου, etc.) take the attributive position.[4] Reflexive possessives are only used in situations in which a reflexive pronoun could be used, i.e. the possessor is the subject of the sentence.

εἶδον τὸν ἐμαυτοῦ οἶκον.   I saw my own house.
ὁ ταύτης οἶκος   her house

3) Therefore the English phrase "my friend," when it is the object of a verb, could have any of these Greek translations, only a few of which are equivalent: τὸν φίλον, τὸν ἐμὸν φίλον, τὸν φίλον μου, τὸν φίλον ἐμοῦ, τὸν ἐμαυτοῦ φίλον, τὸν ἐμαυτῆς φίλον, τὴν φίλην, τὴν ἐμὴν φίλην, τὴν φίλην μου, τὴν φίλην ἐμοῦ, τὴν ἐμαυτοῦ φίλην, τὴν ἐμαυτῆς φίλην.

> **Preliminary exercise 3 (on D).** Translate the underlined phrases into Greek; the nouns have been supplied in the appropriate case, with an indication of their genders. If there is more than one likely translation of a phrase, give them all.
>
> Euthyphro was angry at his father (πατρί, masculine), so he called his wife (γυναῖκα, feminine) to his room (δωμάτιον, neuter) and said, "Wife, my

---

[4] The plural reflexives also have an interesting periphrastic construction in which the possessive adjectives ἡμέτερος, ὑμέτερος, and σφέτερος are followed by αὐτῶν; thus εἴδομεν τὸν ἡμέτερον αὐτῶν οἶκον "We saw our own house" and εἶδον τὸν σφέτερον αὐτῶν οἶκον "They saw their own house." Frequently, however, the adjectives are used without the αὐτῶν, so that no difference is made between reflexive and non-reflexive possession in the plural.

father (πατήρ, masculine) has insulted me. He humiliated me, <u>his own</u>
<u>son</u> (υἱόν, masculine), in front of <u>our slaves</u> (δούλοις, masculine)." <u>His wife</u>
(γυνή, feminine) replied, "To insult <u>my husband</u> (ἄνδρα, masculine) is to
insult me as well. Besides, <u>my father-in-law</u> (κηδεστής, masculine) insults
me directly too, and you should see how he abuses <u>your sister</u> (ἀδελφήν,
feminine). Without <u>my husband's</u> (ἀνδρός, masculine) question I would not
have mentioned how he treats <u>his own daughter</u> (θυγατέρα, feminine) but
it's a disgrace, and you should protect <u>your siblings</u> (ἀδελφοῖς, masculine)."
When he heard <u>his wife</u> (γυναικός, feminine) say this, Euthyphro was very
angry. He brought a court case against <u>his own father</u> (πατρός, masculine),
and <u>his case</u> (δίκη, feminine) was the talk of all Athens.

E) Ἄλλος and adverbs related to it can be used in pairs, like Latin *alius*, to mean the
equivalent of English "one . . . another" or (in the plural) "some . . . others."

ἄλλος ἄλλα φέρει	One bears some things, another bears other things. / They bear different things.
ἄλλοι ἄλλοθεν ἦλθον.	Some came from one place, others from another. / They came from different places.

Two other constructions are easily confused with this one.

1) The reciprocal pronoun **ἀλλήλους** means "each other" and describes mutual
interaction.

ἀλλήλους εἶδον. versus	They saw each other. (e.g. of two people meeting unexpectedly)
ἄλλος ἄλλον εἶδεν.	One saw one, and another saw another. (e.g. of a group of people looking for horses, in which each person sees a different horse)

2) The **ὁ μέν . . . ὁ δέ** construction (see chapter 1 section B4a) is used when
"some . . . others" occurs only once in the sentence, with both words in the same case;
if two pairs and/or different cases are involved, only ἄλλος can be used.

οἱ μὲν ἀπῆλθον, οἱ δὲ οὔ. versus	Some departed, but the others did not.
ἄλλοι ἄλλας ἔγημαν.	Some men married some women, and others married other women. (not *οἱ μὲν τὰς μὲν ἔγημαν, οἱ δὲ τὰς δέ.)

Preliminary exercise 4 (on E). Translate into Greek using the following vocabulary: ἄλλος, -η, -ο "(an)other"; ἀλλήλους, -ας, -α "each other"; ὁ μέν "one/some"; τιμάω "honor"; φιλέω "like."

a. Some people honored one man, and others honored another.
b. Some (masculine) were honored, but others were not.
c. They (masculine) will honor each other.
d. One man is honored by some people, and another is honored by other people.
e. They will be honored by each other.
f. We honored some (masculine) but not others.
g. They (feminine) like each other.
h. One person likes some things, and another likes other things.
i. I like one man but not the other.
j. Some people like one thing, and others like another thing.
k. They are liked by each other.
l. Some (feminine) are liked, and others are not.

Sentences

Translate into Greek using only words and constructions so far covered. Translate all non-reflexive first- and second-person possessives twice, once with an adjective and once with a pronoun, and where possible translate third-person possessives twice, once with αὐτός and once with οὗτος.

1. When we conquered the enemy their allies fled, some to one place, others to other places.
2. Their brother always buys the same thing; our brother never buys the same thing twice.
3. We do not honor his slaves: they married their own sisters.
4. The one gave me the preceding advice, and the other advised the following.
5. You do not treat yourselves well; consult some doctor.
6. I shall take vengeance on whoever makes speeches against me: enemies do not forgive each other.
7. Your sister and my sister both married yesterday; the latter married a rich man and the former some shepherd.
8. The allies desired to consult each other in order to take vengeance on the foreigners.

9. When we summoned (them), our comrades arrived to avenge us on our enemies, some from one place and others from other places.
10. In order to sell the slave for much money, we taught him ourselves, but he did not listen.
11. I desire to forgive myself, but that is impossible.
12. Whoever conquers himself will conquer others too.
13. Some men, because they do not value peace, always desire to avenge something; but we forgive whatever our enemies do.
14. Their friend never stops giving advice; I myself listened to him for two days.
15. Some gods married their own sisters; we do not envy them.
16. Your (pl.) sons will forgive the (private) enemies who treated them badly, but they (i.e. the sons) will not honor them.
17. When the former men took vengeance on the latter, one attacked one man, another another man.
18. Their master would not spare his own sister.
19. If you desire a wife, I shall marry you myself.
20. My son and my brother are both generals; the former marches with his soldiers himself, and the latter does not.
21. Our allies used to take vengeance on whoever harmed them, not sparing their own sons; now they desire to buy peace with our money.
22. Some accused me of the preceding things, others of the following things.
23. Each of the (two) shepherds obtained a horse; now neither desires another horse.
24. These women became capable of killing many men, for they valued freedom; however the same women will spare as many men as love them.
25. Our slaves attacked the same man who had attacked them.
26. When we hurt someone, we blamed ourselves.
27. Each of these three women envies the others.
28. Their sister married the same man again.
29. Even rich men often envy others, but neither of these (two) rich men envied the other.
30. Her brother would not be envying his own son for his (i.e. the son's) money.

Analysis

Analyze according to the model given in chapter VI, breaking up the sentence into units with one verb form in each and showing subordination by indentation and numbering. Translate each unit into English as literally as is possible without being incomprehensible and explain all underlined words.

1. ὅ τι μὲν ὑμεῖς, ὦ ἄνδρες Ἀθηναῖοι, πεπόνθατε ὑπὸ τῶν ἐμῶν κατηγόρων, οὐκ οἶδα· ἐγὼ δ' οὖν καὶ αὐτὸς ὑπ' αὐτῶν ὀλίγου ἐμαυτοῦ ἐπελαθόμην, οὕτω πιθανῶς ἔλεγον.

    (Plato, *Apology* 17a; κατήγορος "accuser," ὀλίγου "almost," πιθανῶς "persuasively")

2. ἐπειδὴ τοίνυν ταῦτα ἡμῖν συνδοκεῖ, μετὰ ταῦτα τάδε σκοπῶμεν· εἰ μέλλει, φαμέν, καλῶς κεῖσθαι τὸ ὄνομα, τὰ προσήκοντα δεῖ αὐτὸ γράμματα ἔχειν;

    (Plato, *Cratylus* 433b; συνδοκέω i.e. "be agreed by," σκοπέω "consider," μέλλω would be expected to take a future infinitive here, καλῶς κεῖσθαι "be well made," προσήκων i.e. "appropriate")

3. τοῖς ἄλλοις δὴ τοῦ ἑνὸς συμβαίνει ἐκ μὲν τοῦ ἑνὸς καὶ ἐξ ἑαυτῶν κοινωνησάντων, ὡς ἔοικεν, ἕτερόν τι γίγνεσθαι ἐν ἑαυτοῖς, ὃ δὴ πέρας παρέσχε πρὸς ἄλληλα· ἡ δ' ἑαυτῶν φύσις καθ' ἑαυτὰ ἀπειρίαν.

    (Plato, *Parmenides* 158d; ἄλλος τοῦ ἑνός i.e. not single, συμβαίνω "happen," κοινωνέω "interact," πέρας πρός "limitation as regards," ἀπειρία "limitlessness," supply παρέσχε again at the end)

4. λόγον ὃν αὐτὴ πρὸς αὑτὴν ἡ ψυχὴ διεξέρχεται περὶ ὧν ἂν σκοπῇ. ὥς γε μὴ εἰδώς σοι ἀποφαίνομαι. τοῦτο γάρ μοι ἰνδάλλεται διανοουμένη οὐκ ἄλλο τι ἢ διαλέγεσθαι, αὐτὴ ἑαυτὴν ἐρωτῶσα καὶ ἀποκρινομένη, καὶ φάσκουσα καὶ οὐ φάσκουσα. ὅταν δὲ ὁρίσασα, εἴτε βραδύτερον εἴτε καὶ ὀξύτερον ἐπᾴξασα, τὸ αὐτὸ ἤδη φῇ καὶ μὴ διστάζῃ, δόξαν ταύτην τίθεμεν αὐτῆς.

    (Plato, *Theaetetus* 189e–190a; at the very beginning supply καλῶ τὸ διανοεῖσθαι "I call thinking"; διεξέρχομαι "relate," σκοπέω "consider," ἰνδάλλομαι "appear like," φάσκω "affirm," οὐ φάσκω "deny," ὁρίζω "determine," βραδύς "slow," ἐπᾴσσω "rush," διστάζω "be in doubt," δόξα "opinion," τίθημι i.e. "call")

5. ἀλλὰ μέντοι δεῖ γε πρὸς μὲν τοὺς οἰκείους πρᾴους αὐτοὺς εἶναι, πρὸς δὲ τοὺς πολεμίους χαλεπούς· εἰ δὲ μή, οὐ περιμενοῦσιν ἄλλους σφᾶς διολέσαι, ἀλλ' αὐτοὶ φθήσονται αὐτὸ δράσαντες.

    (Plato, *Republic* 375c; πρᾶος "gentle," περιμένω "wait for," διόλλυμι "destroy")

6. ἱκανῶς γάρ μέ φασι πεπύσθαι καὶ ἐπιχειροῦσιν, βουλόμενοι ἀποπιμπλάναι με, ἄλλος ἄλλα ἤδη λέγειν, καὶ οὐκέτι συμφωνοῦσιν.

    (Plato, *Cratylus* 413b; ἐπιχειρέω "attempt," ἀποπίμπλημι "satisfy," συμφωνέω "agree")

7. ἐμοῦ γὰρ πολλοὶ κατήγοροι γεγόνασι πρὸς ὑμᾶς καὶ πάλαι πολλὰ ἤδη ἔτη καὶ οὐδὲν ἀληθὲς λέγοντες, οὓς ἐγὼ μᾶλλον φοβοῦμαι ἢ τοὺς ἀμφὶ Ἄνυτον, καίπερ ὄντας καὶ τούτους δεινούς· ἀλλ' ἐκεῖνοι δεινότεροι, ὦ ἄνδρες, οἳ ὑμῶν τοὺς

πολλοὺς ἐκ παίδων παραλαμβάνοντες ἔπειθόν τε καὶ κατηγόρουν ἐμοῦ μᾶλλον οὐδὲν ἀληθές . . .

(Plato, *Apology* 18b; κατήγορος "accuser," ἔτος "year")

8.   καὶ περὶ τῶν ἄλλων δὴ ὀργάνων ὁ αὐτὸς τρόπος· τὸ φύσει ἑκάστῳ πεφυκὸς ὄργανον ἐξευρόντα δεῖ ἀποδοῦναι εἰς ἐκεῖνο ἐξ οὗ ἂν ποιῇ τὸ ἔργον, οὐχ οἷον ἂν αὐτὸς βουληθῇ, ἀλλ᾽ οἷον ἐπεφύκει.

(Plato, *Cratylus* 389c; ὄργανον "tool," φύσει i.e. "naturally," ἐξευρίσκω "invent," ἀποδίδωμι i.e. "provide," ἐξ i.e. "by means of," φύω i.e. "be made by nature")

X | Indirect statement

Material to learn before using this chapter: φημί, οἶδα, long-vowel aorists
  (Smyth §682–7, 783, 794); Vocabulary 10 and associated principal
  parts
Recommended grammar reading: Smyth §783–8, 794–821
Recommended syntax reading: Smyth §1862–3, 1866–71, 1874, 2016–24,
  2100, 2106–45, 2574–2616

A) Indirect statement is used to indicate that a declarative sentence (not a question or command) is attributed to a certain source. The introductory verb need not be a verb of saying; "he saw that," "we thought that," "it appeared that," "she hoped that," and "I am ashamed that" are all introductions that would take indirect statement in Greek. Indirect statement can be expressed by means of five different constructions, of which each introductory verb normally takes only one or two.

Much of the difficulty English speakers have with Greek indirect statement comes from the fact that in Greek the tense of the original direct statement is normally preserved in the indirect version, while in (written) English the verb of the subordinate clause is normally shifted into the past if the introductory verb is in a past tense. So if the introductory verb is in the past, the first step in translating into Greek is to change the tenses back to those of the original direct statement. Although this tense change does not always take place in English, it will normally occur in the type of writing in which most Greek indirect statements occur (e.g. historical narrative), so in translating an English indirect statement into Greek one should assume the tenses have been changed unless there is positive evidence to the contrary.[1]

Original sentence	Indirect speech after present verb	Indirect speech after past verb
I ate a fish.	He says he ate a fish.	He said he had eaten a fish.
I eat fish.	He says he eats fish.	He said he ate fish.
I am eating a fish.	He says he is eating a fish.	He said he was eating a fish.
I shall eat a fish.	He says he will eat a fish.	He said he would eat a fish.

[1] This chapter only covers sentences in which the original statement was a simple indicative; situations in which sentences with subordinate clauses and non-indicative moods become indirect are reserved for chapter XVIII. It follows from this that any apparent ambiguity in the English sentences about whether "would" represents an original "will" or an original "would" should be resolved in favor of "will."

Preliminary exercise 1 (on A). In English, give the (probable) original direct version of each of the statements reported indirectly below; you may need to change both person and tense.

a.   He said he was a vegetarian.
b.   He said he had been a vegetarian for twenty years.
c.   He said he would start being a vegetarian soon.
d.   She said the goose had laid a golden egg.
e.   She said the goose was laying a golden egg.
f.   She said the goose laid golden eggs.
g.   She said the goose would lay a golden egg tomorrow.
h.   Did you say that you had seen that goose?
i.   I said that that goose's name was Priscilla.
j.   I said that that goose's name had been Priscilla.
k.   Priscilla said that her eggs would hatch.
l.   Priscilla said that her eggs were hatching.
m.   Priscilla said that her eggs had hatched.
n.   Priscilla said that her eggs always hatched.

B) Ὅτι + indicative (or optative after a main verb in a secondary[2] tense; ὡς may be used instead of ὅτι). Whether the verb is indicative or optative, the tense is that of the original direct statement;[3] the negative is οὐ. This construction is used after verbs of saying, except φημί/φάσκω: that is, after λέγω, φράζω, ἀποκρίνομαι, and ἀγγέλλω.

εἶπεν ὅτι φάγοι/ἔφαγεν. (aorist)	He said (that) he had eaten. (pluperfect)
εἶπεν ὅτι ἐσθίοι/ἐσθίει. (present)	He said (that) he was eating. (imperfect)
εἶπεν ὅτι ἔδοιτο/ἔδεται. (future)	He said (that) he would eat.
εἶπεν ὅτι σοφοὶ γενήσοιντο/γενήσονται.	He said that they would become wise.

Preliminary exercise 2 (on B). Translate into Greek using this vocabulary: λέγω, ἐρῶ, εἶπον, εἴρηκα, εἴρημαι, ἐρρήθην "say"; θύω, θύσω, ἔθυσα, τέθυκα, τέθυμαι, ἐτύθην "sacrifice"; καλός, -ή, -όν "beautiful." When both indicative and optative possibilities are available, give both.

a.   He says that he did not sacrifice.
b.   He said that he had not sacrificed.

---

[2] Greek primary tenses are present, future, and perfect; secondary (historic) tenses are imperfect, aorist, and pluperfect.

[3] Verbs that would have been imperfect or pluperfect in the direct version are not normally changed to the optative, but occasionally the present optative represents the imperfect.

    c.   He says that he does not sacrifice.

    d.   He said that he did not sacrifice.

    e.   He says that he will not sacrifice.

    f.   He said that he would not sacrifice.

    g.   He says that she is beautiful.

    h.   He said that he was beautiful.

C) Accusative and infinitive. The tense of the infinitive is the same as in the direct statement (one can also think of it as being a tense relative to the time of the main verb).[4] If the subject of the infinitive is the same as the subject of the main verb, it is not normally expressed; if needed, it is put in the nominative. The negative is οὐ. This construction is used after φημί/φάσκω and verbs of thinking: νομίζω, οἴομαι, ἡγέομαι, ὁμολογέω "admit," δοκέω "believe," ὑπολαμβάνω, ὑποπτεύω.

ἐνόμιζεν αὐτοὺς οὐ σοφοὺς εἶναι.	He thought that they were not wise.
ἔφη ἐλθεῖν.	He said that he (himself) had come.
ὡμολόγησαν σοφοὶ οὐ γενήσεσθαι.	They admitted that they (themselves) would not become wise.

If a sentence introduced by φημί/φάσκω is negative, the negative goes with φημί rather than with the infinitive: English "say . . . not" is Greek οὔ φημι, not φημί . . . οὐ (cf. *dico* and *nego* in Latin, and English "I don't think that's wise," which really means "I think that's not wise").

οὐκ ἔφη σοφὸς εἶναι.	He said that he (himself) was not wise.

> **Preliminary exercise 3 (on C).** Translate into Greek using this vocabulary: φημί (imperfect ἔφην normally used in past) "say"; θύω, θύσω, ἔθυσα, τέθυκα, τέθυμαι, ἐτύθην "sacrifice"; καλός, -ή, -όν "beautiful." Remember not to begin a sentence with an enclitic (present-tense) form of φημί: if you need to use such a form, put it second in the sentence.
>
> a.   He says that she is beautiful.
>
> b.   He said that he (same person) was beautiful.
>
> c.   He said that they would be beautiful.
>
> d.   He says that they did not sacrifice.
>
> e.   He said that he (same person) had not sacrificed.
>
> f.   He says that he (different person) does not sacrifice.

---

[4] Verbs that would have been imperfect or pluperfect in the direct version become present or perfect infinitives respectively.

g. He said that she did not sacrifice.
h. He says that he (same person) will not sacrifice.
i. He said that they would not sacrifice.

D) Future infinitive. A few verbs take the future infinitive even in cases where we would expect another tense; in other respects they follow the rules given under C, except that the negative is μή. This construction is used after verbs of hoping, promising, threatening, and swearing: ἐλπίζω, ὑπισχνέομαι, ἀπειλέω, ὄμνυμι, ὁμολογέω "agree to," προσδέχομαι.

ἤλπιζε θύσειν.	He hoped to sacrifice. / He hoped that he would sacrifice.
ἐλπίζω αὐτοὺς μὴ θύσειν.	I hope they don't sacrifice. / I hope that they won't sacrifice.

Preliminary exercise 4 (on D). Translate into Greek using the following vocabulary: ἀπειλέω "threaten"; ἀποκτείνω, ἀποκτενῶ, ἀπέκτεινα, ἀπέκτονα, –, – "kill."

a. He threatened to kill them.
b. They threatened that he would kill me.
c. They are threatening not to kill him.
d. She is threatening that they will kill us.
e. She will threaten not to kill them.

E) Participle. The tense of the participle and case of its subject are determined as for infinitives (see C); the negative is οὐ. The participle must also agree with its subject in gender, number, and case. This construction is used after verbs of knowing and perceiving (οἶδα, αἰσθάνομαι, μανθάνω, γιγνώσκω, πυνθάνομαι, ἀκούω, ὁράω, εὑρίσκω, μέμνημαι, ἐπιλανθάνομαι, ἐπίσταμαι "know," οὐκ ἀγνοῶ "know") and often after ἀγγέλλω and verbs of showing (δείκνυμι, δηλόω, φαίνω).

εἶδεν αὐτοὺς ἀποθανόντας.	He saw that they (masc.) had died.
ᾔδει οὐ σοφὸς ὤν.	He knew that he (himself) was not wise.

Σύνοιδα and συγγιγνώσκω take the dative instead of the accusative or nominative, and the participle may agree with the dative when we would otherwise expect a nominative.

σύνοιδα αὐτῇ σοφῇ οὔσῃ.	I am conscious that she is wise.
συνῄδει ἑαυτῷ νικήσαντι/νικήσας.	He was conscious that he (himself) had won.

Ἀκούω takes the accusative for indirect statement even in situations where it would otherwise take the genitive.

ἤκουσεν αὐτοὺς ᾄδοντας.	He heard that they were singing. (i.e. he did not hear the song himself but was informed about it later by someone else)
ἤκουσεν αὐτῶν ᾀδόντων.	He heard them singing. (i.e. he heard the song in person)

> **Preliminary exercise 5 (on E).** Translate into Greek using the examples above and the following vocabulary: ἀκούω, ἀκούσομαι, ἤκουσα, ἀκήκοα, –, ἠκούσθην "hear"; ἀφικνέομαι, ἀφίξομαι, ἀφικόμην, –, ἀφῖγμαι "arrive"; δειλός, -ή, -όν "cowardly."
>
> a. I hear that he is cowardly.
> b. I am conscious that I (masculine) am cowardly. (2 ways)
> c. He was conscious that I (feminine) am cowardly.
> d. I hear that I (masculine) am cowardly.
> e. He heard that they (masculine) had arrived.
> f. They heard that we (feminine) would arrive.
> g. She heard that they (feminine) were arriving.
> h. She heard them (masculine) arriving.

F) Εἰ + indicative (or optative after secondary main verb). The tense is that of the original direct statement; the negative is usually μή. This construction is used after verbs of emotion: θαυμάζω, αἰσχύνομαι, ἀγανακτέω "be annoyed," ἀγαπάω "be content," δεινὸν ποιοῦμαι "resent."

ἐθαύμασα εἰ μὴ ἔλθοι/ἦλθεν.	I was amazed that he had not come.
αἰσχύνεται εἰ μὴ σοφός ἐστιν.	He's ashamed that he is not wise.

> **Preliminary exercise 6 (on F).** Translate into Greek using the following vocabulary: αἰσχύνομαι, αἰσχυνοῦμαι, –, –, –, ᾐσχύνθην "be ashamed"; θαυμάζω, θαυμάσομαι, ἐθαύμασα, τεθαύμακα, τεθαύμασμαι, ἐθαυμάσθην "be amazed"; ἄδικος, -ον "unjust." When both indicative and optative possibilities are available, give both.
>
> a. I was amazed that he was not ashamed.
> b. He was ashamed that they were unjust.
> c. We are amazed that he is unjust.
> d. I am amazed that you are not amazed.
> e. She is ashamed that we are amazed.

Sentences

Translate into Greek using only words and constructions so far covered; whenever both indicative and optative forms are possible, whenever a verb of saying can be translated both with φημί and with λέγω, and whenever two constructions are possible with a single verb, give both.

1. My sister said that she would not go down to the harbor. (3 ways)
2. My wife agreed to stop spending my money.
3. We believe we will become beautiful: the woman who gave birth to us is beautiful.
4. Your son knew he would never find the prison; he did not suspect that we would find it.
5. I am ashamed that you heard me; I did not know that you had stayed here.
6. We answered that the others were still waiting for the leader. (2 ways)
7. Your wife is conscious of having promised to swim through the river. (2 ways)
8. The prostitutes heard us agree not to spend your silver.
9. The foreigners said he had not been caught. (3 ways)
10. We swore that the democracy would not be harmed.
11. The clever woman knew that we had been seen, but that she herself had not been seen.
12. The archon was surprised that you admitted it; he expected you to lie. (2 ways)
13. Their friends were silent when they heard that we had been caught.
14. The herald reported that others had spent our money. (3 ways)
15. We are conscious of having erred. (2 ways)
16. The doctor expected the dog to go down to his master.
17. The children denied that they had heard the dog.
18. My son supposed he (i.e. my son) had not become clever.
19. The traitor is ashamed of having gone down there. (2 ways)
20. I heard you threatening our leader and saying that he would not live three days. (2 ways)
21. The archon is too ashamed to go down to the lawcourt.
22. The clever sophist explained to the soldiers that nothing was capable of cutting these tents, but they did not believe that such tents existed.
23. We hear that many dogs ran from the large wild animal.
24. Our savior asserts that he saw the prison and released the prisoners himself.
25. The bandit was conscious that he would be seen carrying the money. (2 ways)
26. Your (pl.) leader will someday (= ever) get to know that many people are surprised because of his bitter words.
27. Their leader hopes we will not toil to stop their army; we think we shall start today.

28. The gods see whoever is born in this land; some they expect to help, and others they will harm.
29. Some of these children hope to become soldiers, and others (hope) to become bandits; we think they will enjoy fighting.
30. Their archons saw that you were toiling but did not desire to help you.

Analysis

Analyze according to the model given in chapter VI, breaking up the sentence into units with one verb form in each and showing subordination by indentation and numbering. Translate each unit into English as literally as is possible without being incomprehensible and identify each indirect statement, explaining the moods and tenses of the indirect verbs and the cases of their subjects. Give the original direct form of each indirect statement.

1. ἃ μὴ οἶδα οὐδ' οἴομαι εἰδέναι.

   (Plato, *Apology* 21d)

2. κἄπειτα ἐπειρώμην αὐτῷ δεικνύναι ὅτι οἴοιτο μὲν εἶναι σοφός, εἴη δ' οὔ.

   (Plato, *Apology* 21c)

3. σύνοιδα γὰρ ἐμαυτῷ ἀντιλέγειν μὲν οὐ δυναμένῳ ὡς οὐ δεῖ ποιεῖν ἃ οὗτος κελεύει, ἐπειδὰν δὲ ἀπέλθω, ἡττημένῳ τῆς τιμῆς τῆς ὑπὸ τῶν πολλῶν.

   (Plato, *Symposium* 216b, Alcibiades on Socrates' effect on him; ἡττάομαι + gen. "be defeated by")

4. οἶδα δὲ καὶ Σωκράτην δεικνύντα τοῖς ξυνοῦσιν ἑαυτὸν καλὸν κἀγαθὸν ὄντα, καὶ διαλεγόμενον κάλλιστα περὶ ἀρετῆς καὶ τῶν ἄλλων ἀνθρωπίνων.

   (Xenophon, *Memorabilia* 1.2.18; ἀνθρώπινος "human")

5. μεταπέμπεσθαι δ' ἐκέλευεν αὐτόν· αὐτὸς δ' οὐκ ἔφη ἰέναι.

   (Xenophon, *Anabasis* 1.3.8; μεταπέμπομαι "summon")

6. Ἀβροκόμας δὲ οὐ τοῦτ' ἐποίησεν, ἀλλ' ἐπεὶ ἤκουσε Κῦρον ἐν Κιλικίᾳ ὄντα, ἀναστρέψας ἐκ Φοινίκης παρὰ βασιλέα ἀπήλαυνεν, ἔχων, ὡς ἐλέγετο, τριάκοντα μυριάδας στρατιᾶς.

   (Xenophon, *Anabasis* 1.4.5; ἀπελαύνω "march away," μυριάς "ten thousand")

7. ἐθαύμαζε δ', εἴ τις ἀρετὴν ἐπαγγελλόμενος ἀργύριον πράττοιτο, καὶ μὴ νομίζοι τὸ μέγιστον κέρδος ἕξειν φίλον ἀγαθὸν κτησάμενος, ἀλλὰ φοβοῖτο, μὴ ὁ γενόμενος καλὸς κἀγαθὸς τῷ τὰ μέγιστα εὐεργετήσαντι μὴ τὴν μεγίστην χάριν ἔξοι.

(Xenophon, *Memorabilia* 1.2.7; ἐπαγγέλλομαι "promise," πράττομαι i.e. "make"; εὐεργετέω "benefit"; the last μή should be οὐ, cf. Goodwin §1364)

8. ἐπεὶ γὰρ οἱ τριάκοντα πολλοὺς μὲν τῶν πολιτῶν καὶ οὐ τοὺς χειρίστους ἀπέκτεινον, πολλοὺς δὲ προετρέποντο ἀδικεῖν, εἶπέ που ὁ Σωκράτης, ὅτι θαυμαστόν οἱ δοκοίη εἶναι, εἴ τις γενόμενος βοῶν ἀγέλης νομεὺς καὶ τὰς βοῦς ἐλάττους τε καὶ χείρους ποιῶν μὴ ὁμολογοίη κακὸς βουκόλος εἶναι· ἔτι δὲ θαυμαστότερον, εἴ τις προστάτης γενόμενος πόλεως καὶ ποιῶν τοὺς πολίτας ἐλάττους καὶ χείρους μὴ αἰσχύνεται, μηδ᾽ οἴεται κακὸς εἶναι προστάτης τῆς πόλεως.

(Xenophon, *Memorabilia* 1.2.32; προτρέπομαι "incite," ἀγέλη "herd," νομεύς "herdsman," προστάτης "leader")

9. ὧν ἀμφοτέρων ἄξιον ἐπιμεληθῆναι, ἐνθυμουμένους ὅτι οὔτ᾽ ἂν ἐκεῖνα ἐδύναντο ποιεῖν μὴ ἑτέρων συμπραττόντων οὔτ᾽ ἂν νῦν ἐπεχείρησαν ἐλθεῖν μὴ ὑπὸ τῶν αὐτῶν οἰόμενοι σωθήσεσθαι, οἳ οὐ τούτοις ἥκουσι βοηθήσοντες, ἀλλὰ ἡγούμενοι πολλὴν ἄδειαν σφίσιν ἔσεσθαι τῶν τε πεπραγμένων καὶ τοῦ λοιποῦ ποιεῖν ὅ τι ἂν βούλωνται, εἰ τοὺς μεγίστων κακῶν αἰτίους λαβόντες ἀφήσετε.

(Lysias, *Oration* 12.85, on the importance of punishing the thirty tyrants; ἄξιον i.e. "you should," ἐπιμελέομαι "watch out for," ἐνθυμουμένους "considering" agrees with the ὑμᾶς that is the implied subject of ἐπιμεληθῆναι, ἐλθεῖν i.e. come to court, οὐ goes primarily with βοηθήσοντες, τούτοις i.e. the thirty tyrants, ἄδεια "immunity" (with infinitive of what they have immunity to do), τοῦ λοιποῦ "in the future"; the sentence is technically all one relative clause with no main verb; see how many constructions from chapters I–X you can find)

XI | Questions

Material to learn before using this chapter: εἰμί, εἶμι (Smyth §768, 773);
  Vocabulary 11 and associated principal parts
Recommended grammar reading: Smyth §768–76
Recommended syntax reading: Smyth §1805–9, 2636–80

A) Introductory words

1) Interrogative pronouns, adjectives, and adverbs (words meaning "who," "where," "why," etc.) are used in Greek as in English; that is, for all questions except yes-no questions. Direct questions use direct interrogatives, and indirect questions may use either direct or indirect interrogatives. A full list of these interrogatives is given in the correlatives chart in the chapter VIII vocabulary; the most important forms are:

Direct interrogative	Indirect interrogative
τίς "who?"	ὅστις
τί "what?" "why?"	ὅ τι
πόσος "how many?"	ὁπόσος
ποῖος "what sort of?"	ὁποῖος
ποῦ "where?" (if no motion involved)	ὅπου
πόθεν "from where?"	ὁπόθεν
ποῖ "where?" (with motion toward)	ὅποι
πότε "when?"	ὁπότε
πῶς "how?"	ὅπως

Examples:

τίς γράφει;	Who is writing?
ἐρωτᾷ ὅστις/τίς γράφει.	She asks who is writing.
ποῦ ἐστιν;	Where is he?
ἐρωτᾷ ὅπου/ποῦ ἐστίν.	She asks where he is.

2) The interrogative particle ἆρα is normally used for yes-no questions; it is possible to have a question without any introductory word to signal it, but because Greek does not change word order in questions some introductory word is usually needed. If the speaker does not indicate which answer he expects, ἆρα is used alone; if he expects the

answer "yes," ἆρ' οὐ is used, and if he expects the answer "no," ἆρα μή is used. When a yes-no question is indirect, it is introduced by εἰ "whether, if."

ἆρα γράφει;	Is he writing?
ἆρ' οὐ γράφει;	He's writing, isn't he?
ἆρα μὴ γράφει;	He isn't writing, is he?
ἐρωτᾷ εἰ γράφει.	She asks whether/if he is writing.

3) Questions offering two **alternatives** (direct or indirect) are introduced by πότερον . . . ἤ "whether . . . or." If they are indirect, they may also use εἴτε . . . εἴτε.

πότερον γράφει ἢ λέγει;	Is he writing or speaking?
ἐρωτᾷ πότερον γράφει ἢ λέγει.	She asks whether he is writing or speaking.
πότερον γράφει ἢ οὔ;	Is he writing or not?
ἐρωτᾷ πότερον γράφει ἢ οὔ/μή.[1]	She asks whether he is writing or not.

> **Preliminary exercise 1 (on A).** Translate into Greek using the following vocabulary: ἔρχομαι, εἶμι, ἦλθον, ἐλήλυθα, –, – "go, come"; ἐρωτάω, ἐρή-σομαι, ἠρόμην, ἠρώτηκα, ἠρώτημαι, ἠρωτήθην "ask." When there are two possibilities, give both.
>
> a. Who is coming?
> b. Where is he going?
> c. He's coming, isn't he?
> d. They aren't coming, are they?
> e. Is he coming or not?
> f. They are asking who is coming.
> g. They are asking where he is.
> h. He is asking whether they are coming.
> i. We're asking whether he is coming or not.
> j. Are you asking where he is coming from?

B) Moods

1) Ordinary direct questions take the indicative, or any other construction as appropriate.

τίς ἔγραψεν;	Who wrote?
ἆρα γράψαι ἄν;	Would he write?

---

[1] "Or not," when it stands by itself at the end of a question, is normally ἢ οὔ in direct questions but can be either ἢ οὔ or ἢ μή in indirect questions.

2) **Deliberative** questions are questions in the first person asking what the speaker is to do, i.e. those dealing with future actions that are within the speaker's control.[2] They take the subjunctive.

ἆρα εἴπω;	Shall I speak? / Am I to speak?
ἆρα γράψωμεν;	Shall we write? / Are we to write?

3) **Indirect** questions use essentially the ὅτι construction of indirect statement, except that ὅτι is replaced by the appropriate interrogative word. Therefore, the verb remains the same as the direct speech version if the main verb is primary, and can be changed to the optative of the original tense if the main verb is secondary.[3] An indirect deliberative question can either remain in the subjunctive or, after a secondary main verb, change to the corresponding tense of the optative.

ἤρετο ὅστις/τίς γράψαι/ἔγραψεν.	She asked who had written. (direct: "Who wrote?")
ἤρετο εἰ γράφοιεν/γράφουσιν.	She asked whether they were writing. (direct: "Are they writing?")
ἤρετο ὁπόσα/πόσα γράψοιεν/ γράψουσιν.	She asked how much they would write. (direct: "How much will they write?")
ἤρετο εἰ γράψῃ (γράψαι also possible but less likely here).	She asked whether she should write. (direct: "Shall I write / Am I to write?")

> **Preliminary exercise 2 (on B).** First, identify which of the sentences below contain deliberative questions (direct or indirect). Second, identify which contain indirect questions, and for each of those give the (probable) original direct question form in English. Third, translate all the sentences into Greek using the following vocabulary: καλέω, καλῶ, ἐκάλεσα, κέκληκα, κέκλημαι, ἐκλήθην "call"; ἐρωτάω, ἐρήσομαι, ἠρόμην, ἠρώτηκα, ἠρώτημαι, ἠρωτήθην "ask." Where there is more than one possibility, give them all.
>
> a.   Shall we call him?
> b.   I asked how many they had called.
> c.   He asked when he should call.

---

[2]   It is sometimes stated that all first-person questions in the future tense should be translated into Greek as deliberative subjunctives, but this is not quite true. If the Eleven are debating when to execute Socrates, and they say "Shall we execute him today?," the question is deliberative; but if Socrates then asks them "Am I going to die today?," the question is not deliberative, because Socrates does not participate in this decision.

[3]   As in indirect statement, English usually shifts the tenses after a secondary main verb (see chapter x A above), so it is necessary to shift them back in order to get the correct tense for the Greek translation.

    d.   They asked who was calling.

    e.   I shall ask where he is.

    f.   Am I to call them?

    g.   They asked whom we would call.

    h.   He asked how many were being called.

    i.   They asked whom they should call.

    j.   Shall we ask him whom he is calling?

    k.   Did she ask who would be called?

    l.   Am I to ask them whether they are calling?

    m.   Did they ask when we had called?

    n.   They are asking what sort of people they should call.

C) Indirect questions occur not only after verbs of asking, but also after those of knowing, learning, discovering, telling, wondering, etc. It is important to distinguish indirect questions from indirect statements and relative clauses when translating into Greek. The traditional method for doing this is to see whether the dependent clause can easily be transformed into a direct question; this is not foolproof, however, because with enough determination nearly anything can be transformed into a direct question. The following hints may help one get started with the process of learning to identify indirect questions, but they should not be used mechanically: only if treated as an aid to understanding the underlying differences in meaning will they be helpful in the long run.

1) An English indirect question begins with "if" or with an interrogative word (usually beginning with *wh-*); if a clause is introduced by "that" or does not have an introductory word, it is not an indirect question.

2) If a clause is introduced by a word beginning with *wh-* but that word has an antecedent in the main clause, the subordinate is a relative clause, not an indirect question.

She told me how she had written it. (indirect question)	εἶπέ μοι ὅπως αὐτὸ γράψαι.
She knew which child I had sent. (indirect question)	ᾔδει ὅντινα παῖδα πέμψαιμι.
She knew the child (that) I had sent. (relative clause)	ᾔδει τὸν παῖδα ὃν ἔπεμψα.
She knew (that) I had sent the child. (indirect statement)	ᾔδει με πέμψαντα τὸν παῖδα.

Preliminary exercise 3 (on C). Indicate whether these sentences should be translated into Greek with indirect questions, indirect statements, or relative clauses.

    a.   He discovered which room we were in.
    b.   He discovered a formula which we use every day.
    c.   He knew the song I was singing.
    d.   He knew I was singing a song.
    e.   He knew which song I was singing.
    f.   He knew where I was.
    g.   He knows the house where we used to live.
    h.   He knows where we live.
    i.   He knows we live there.
    j.   He told me who had come.
    k.   He told me the names of the people who had come.
    l.   He told me no-one had come.
    m.   He asked for the money which I had promised.
    n.   He learned who would recite.
    o.   He learned the poem he would recite.

Sentences

Translate into Greek using only words and constructions so far covered; put an introductory word at the start of every question and give both versions when two moods or two types of interrogative are possible.

    1.   Shall I invite him too?
    2.   She asked the men on the ramparts where you were, but they did not know. (3 ways)
    3.   We do not know whether you think their tower is useful or whether you desire to destroy it and take the stones to use elsewhere. (2 ways)
    4.   The men on foot asked when they should retreat.[4] (3 ways)
    5.   My teacher did not know whether you had gone to the festival or to the ramparts. (3 ways)
    6.   Peace would be beneficial, wouldn't it?

---

[4] I.e. they asked, "When shall we retreat?"

7. Only the men in the prison asked whether we were despondent about the lack of bread. (2 ways)

8. When, then, did they banish their leader?

9. You asked where you should retreat to, didn't you? (3 ways)

10. Did his guards arrest the fugitives or not?

11. Are we too to retreat to the tower?

12. Only the shepherd had not learned whether he would be banished. (2 ways)

13. When they desired to send someone to Athens, they did not know whom they should choose. (3 ways)

14. Does the ten-foot-wide river flow toward the harbor or toward the ramparts?

15. Their leader is not accustomed to be annoyed by children belonging to someone else, is he?

16. Our master expects slavery to be beneficial for us, doesn't he?

17. What witnesses shall we call to speak about the things that were done contrary to the laws?

18. If the young men should be corrupted by their own teacher, what sort of man could save them?

19. When this strife also threatens the woman who possesses us, where will we go?

20. We too are in perplexity about the same letter: where did it come from? How did you acquire it? How many people saw it? What will you do about it?

21. Do old men enjoy hearing stories about love and desire, or are they eager to forget such things?

22. When the dream came to me, I asked how much need of bread (there) would be during the winter. (3 ways)

23. Even if those witnesses should come to the lawcourt, how would you speak in the defense?

24. We did not know whether we should raise the stones to the top of the mountain. (2 ways)

25. Her teacher didn't say that perplexity is beneficial, did he?

26. If, having been banished, we become fugitives, where shall we go? We do not know how fugitives live, nor how many people will desire to arrest us! (2 ways)

27–8. What sort of person would have chosen strife instead of love? – The sort of person we used to see fighting in the marketplace would always choose strife instead of something else.

29. The temple is bare, isn't it? Did bandits come?

30. Will the leader arrest the men who destroyed our house? We hope he will be eager for (εἰς) this!

Analysis

Analyze according to the model given in chapter VI, breaking up the sentence into units with one verb form in each and showing subordination by indentation and numbering. Translate each unit into English as literally as is possible without being incomprehensible and explain all questions, giving the original form of indirect questions.

1. ὥστ' οὐκ οἶδ' ὅ τι δεῖ πολλὰ κατηγορεῖν τοιούτων ἀνδρῶν, οἳ οὐδ' ὑπὲρ ἑνὸς ἑκάστου τῶν πεπραγμένων δὶς ἀποθανόντες δίκην δοῦναι δύναιντ' ἂν ἀξίαν.

   (Lysias, *Oration* 12.37; the whole sentence is a result clause)

2. ἆρα μή, ἦν δ' ἐγώ, ὦ Μενέξενε, τὸ παράπαν οὐκ ὀρθῶς ἐζητοῦμεν;

   (Plato, *Lysis* 213d; ignore ἦν δ' ἐγώ for purposes of analysis; τὸ παράπαν "absolutely")

3. καὶ τοὺς μὲν θορύβους τοὺς ἐν τῷ πράγματι γενομένους καὶ τὰς κραυγὰς καὶ τὰς παρακελεύσεις, ἃ κοινὰ πάντων ἐστὶ τῶν ναυμαχούντων, οὐκ οἶδ' ὅ τι δεῖ λέγοντα διατρίβειν.

   (Isocrates, *Panegyricus* 97, description of a naval battle; κραυγή "cry," παρακέλευσις "exhortation," διατρίβω "waste time")

4. ὅσα δὲ οἱ ὀλίγοι τοὺς πολλοὺς μὴ πείσαντες, ἀλλὰ κρατοῦντες γράφουσι, πότερον βίαν φῶμεν, ἢ μὴ φῶμεν εἶναι;

   (Xenophon, *Memorabilia* 1.2.45, on the difference between properly enacted laws and force)

5. γελοῖον, ὦ Σώκρατες, ὅτι οἴει τι διαφέρειν εἴτε ἀλλότριος εἴτε οἰκεῖος ὁ τεθνεώς, ἀλλ' οὐ τοῦτο μόνον δεῖν φυλάττειν, εἴτε ἐν δίκῃ ἔκτεινεν ὁ κτείνας εἴτε μή, καὶ εἰ μὲν ἐν δίκῃ, ἐᾶν, εἰ δὲ μή, ἐπεξιέναι, ἐάνπερ ὁ κτείνας συνέστιός σοι καὶ ὁμοτράπεζος ᾖ.

   (Plato, *Euthyphro* 4b; διαφέρει "it makes a difference," ἐπέξειμι "proceed against (the killer)," συνέστιος i.e. "member of one's household," ὁμοτράπεζος i.e. "sharer of one's meals")

6. ὁ δὲ Σωκράτης ἐπήρετο αὐτώ, εἰ ἐξείη πυνθάνεσθαι, εἴ τι ἀγνοοῖτο τῶν προαγορευμένων.

   (Xenophon, *Memorabilia* 1.2.33; αὐτώ is a dual form and refers to Critias and Charicles; ἀγνοέομαι "not understand," προαγορεύω "proclaim")

7. ἐν δὲ τῇ πόλει οὐ συνελάμβανον αὐτόν, ὅτι τὸ πρᾶγμα οὐκ ᾔδεσαν ὁπόσον τὸ μέγεθος εἴη, καὶ ἀκοῦσαι πρῶτον ἐβούλοντο τοῦ Κινάδωνος οἵτινες εἶεν οἱ συμπράττοντες, πρὶν αἰσθέσθαι αὐτοὺς ὅτι μεμήνυνται, ἵνα μὴ ἀποδρῶσιν.

   (Xenophon, *Hellenica* 3.3.10; μηνύω "denounce," ἀποδιδράσκω "run away")

8. ἐγὼ γὰρ οὐ δύναμαι μαθεῖν πότερον λέγεις διδάσκειν με νομίζειν εἶναί τινας
    θεούς – καὶ αὐτὸς ἄρα νομίζω εἶναι θεοὺς καὶ οὐκ εἰμὶ τὸ παράπαν ἄθεος οὐδὲ
    ταύτῃ ἀδικῶ – οὐ μέντοι οὕσπερ γε ἡ πόλις ἀλλὰ ἑτέρους, καὶ τοῦτ' ἔστιν ὅ μοι
    ἐγκαλεῖς, ὅτι ἑτέρους, ἢ παντάπασί με φῂς οὔτε αὐτὸν νομίζειν θεοὺς τούς τε
    ἄλλους ταῦτα διδάσκειν.

    (Plato, *Apology* 26c; treat the parenthetical clauses as new main verbs in the anal-
    ysis; τὸ παράπαν "absolutely," ἐγκαλέω "bring as an accusation against")

Review exercises 2

Translate into Greek using only words and constructions covered so far. Add connecting words as appropriate.

1. COMPANION: O friend, what are you doing?

    TIMON: Didn't you agree not to ask what I was doing?

    COMPANION: But, O good man, I thought that no-one wanted to stay alone with-out talking. Whoever lives alone has need[1] of friends.

    TIMON: Some things annoy some people, others annoy other people. Being silent (annoys) you, and my companions (annoy) me.

    COMPANION: But if (ever) people know that they have friends, they rejoice. Who would not like the man who liked him?

    TIMON: I.

    COMPANION: I am surprised that you are always the same. Another man, even if he distrusted me, would not thus have condemned me.

    TIMON: If you don't want to be badly treated, go away.[2]

    COMPANION: What am I to say?

    TIMON: Say that you will not annoy me for many days.

2. Some people desired to destroy the old house, and others hoped to save it. The former, who were not ashamed that they did not value the house, said that they (same people) would become rich by doing what they (same people) wanted, but the latter said (use φημί) that they would not. I myself (feminine), being the general of the latter people, used to assert: "I spent my own money, although I do not have much, and I shall give (δώσω) myself to save the house, even if I die doing that. I shall fight whoever wants to treat it badly. But I don't know how I should fight; I shouldn't do bad things to not-responsible people, should I?" Those men, her enemies, would have burned the house, but her allies sent guards there. Now we hear that those evil men and the women who hope to stop them will go to a lawcourt within seven days, and (go back to direct speech here) one will say some things and another other things, and then both will say the same things again, but we do not know whether the house will be saved there.

---

[1] I.e., "to that man is a need of."   [2] "Away" = ἀπο-.

3. Although our army had not yet marched to that forest, the wretched inhabitants there were already weeping bitterly, for they knew that many of our soldiers had become savage and would spare no-one. Some of them swore never to flee, and others fled immediately; their leader honored the former and blamed the latter, and he consulted with whoever he saw, but no-one would have advised him well. He then said that he himself would speak to our general. Perhaps he would not have fared badly if he had not gone alone, but he left his soldiers at home because he hoped that they would not be harmed there. But they followed him secretly (= escaped his notice following him), some from one place and others from other places, in order to save their own leader from our men.

XII | Purpose, fear, and effort

Material to learn before using this chapter: irregular third declension,
δέδοικα (Smyth §262, 264, 267–8, 275, 703); Vocabulary 12 and
associated principal parts
Recommended grammar reading: Smyth §262–85, 702–16
Recommended syntax reading: Smyth §2065, 2086, 2193–2239, 2554

A) Purpose ("so that," "in order that," "in order to," or bare infinitive in English)
can be expressed in three ways; the first is always usable, but the other two have
restrictions.

1) A clause introduced by ἵνα, ὡς, or ὅπως[1] with the subjunctive in primary sequence
and the optative in secondary sequence; the subjunctive may also be retained in secondary sequence. The negative is μή.

ἦλθεν ἵνα ἡμᾶς σώσαι/σώσῃ.	He came to save us. / He came in order to save us.
ἦλθεν ἵνα σωθεῖμεν/σωθῶμεν.	He came so that we would be saved. / He came in order that we might be saved.
βοηθεῖτε, ὅπως μὴ ἀποθάνωμεν.	Help (us), so that we do not die! / Help (us) lest we die!

2) A future participle (normally usable only when the subject of the purpose clause is
in the main sentence, so that the participle has something to agree with). The negative
is οὐ, and ὡς may be used (see chapter v b1b and chapter v note 8).

ἦλθεν (ὡς) σώσων ἡμᾶς.	He came to save us. / He came in order to save us.

3) A relative clause introduced by a form of ὅς, ὅστις, or any other relative, with a verb in
the future indicative. This construction is the least common of the three and is generally
limited to situations in which the subject of the purpose clause (i.e. the antecedent of
the relative) is the object of the verb in the main clause and is not overly defined already
(i.e. the relative clause must be restrictive). The negative is μή.

---

[1] Negative purpose clauses sometimes omit these introductory words and are introduced by μή alone.

πέμψον τιν' ὅστις σώσει ἡμᾶς.   Send someone to save us.

ᾐτήσαμεν ἡγεμόνα ὃς ἄξει ἡμᾶς.   We asked for a guide to lead us.

οὔκ ἐστι μοι χρήματα, ὁπόθεν   I have no money to pay the fine.
    ἐκτείσω.

> **Preliminary exercise 1 (on A).** Translate into Greek in as many different ways as possible, using the following vocabulary: πέμπω, πέμψω, ἔπεμψα, πέπομφα, πέπεμμαι, ἐπέμφθην "send"; ἔρχομαι, εἶμι, ἦλθον, ἐλήλυθα, –, – "come"; τέρπω, τέρψω, ἔτερψα, –, –, ἐτέρφθην "amuse"; διαβάλλω, δια-βαλῶ, διέβαλον, διαβέβληκα, διαβέβλημαι, διεβλήθην "slander."
>
> a. We came in order to be amused.
> b. He sent us to amuse you.
> c. He sent us so that you would be amused.
> d. They will send slaves to amuse us.
> e. She came in order not to be slandered.
> f. He will send someone to slander us.
> g. They are coming to slander me.
> h. I will send a slave so that you will not be slandered.

B) Fear clauses are found with verbs of fearing, expressions of danger like κίνδυνός ἐστιν, and sometimes with related expressions like ὑποπτεύω. The three constructions below are not interchangeable.

1) Fear for the future is expressed by a clause introduced by μή with the subjunctive in primary sequence and the optative in secondary sequence; the subjunctive may also be retained in secondary sequence. The negative is οὐ.

φοβεῖται μὴ ἔλθωσιν.	He fears that they will come. / He fears lest they (should) come.
φοβεῖται μὴ οὐκ ἔλθωσιν.	He fears that they will not come. / He fears lest they (should) not come.
ἐφοβοῦντο μὴ ἔλθοι/ἔλθῃ.	They feared that he would come. / They feared lest he (should) come.

2) Fear for the present or past is expressed by μή with the indicative. The negative is οὐ.

φοβοῦμαι μὴ ἦλθεν.	I'm afraid that he came.
φοβοῦμαι μὴ ἀληθές ἐστιν.	I fear that it is true.
ἐφοβούμην μὴ οὐκ ἦλθεν.	I was afraid that he had not come.

3) When English uses an infinitive after a verb of fearing, Greek does the same. The negative is μή.

φοβούμεθα ἐλθεῖν.	We are afraid to come.
ἐφοβούμεθα μὴ ἐλθεῖν.	We were afraid not to come.

Note that English "lest" can introduce either a positive fear clause or a negative purpose clause:

ἐφοβεῖτο μὴ ἀποθάνοι. (fear)	He feared lest he (should) be killed.
ἔφυγεν ἵνα μὴ ἀποθάνοι. (purpose)	He fled lest he (should) be killed.

Preliminary exercise 2 (on B). Translate into Greek using the following vocabulary: φοβέομαι, φοβήσομαι, –, –, πεφόβημαι, ἐφοβήθην "fear"; συλλαμβάνω, συλλήψομαι, συνέλαβον, συνείληφα, συνείλημμαι, συνελήφθην "arrest"; ἐκπίπτω, ἐκπεσοῦμαι, ἐξέπεσον, ἐκπέπτωκα, –, – "be banished."

    a. We fear that we will be arrested.
    b. We are afraid to arrest them.
    c. We feared that you had been banished.
    d. I fear that he will not be arrested.
    e. I'm afraid that he is being arrested.
    f. I was afraid not to arrest him.
    g. They were afraid that they would be banished.
    h. He was afraid that we had not been banished.
    i. You are afraid to arrest me!
    j. We were afraid that they would not be banished.

C) Clauses of effort or precaution are found after expressions meaning "take care that," "bring it about," etc.;[2] the subordinate clause functions as the direct object of the verb, and therefore the introductory verb cannot have another direct object. These clauses are introduced by ὅπως and always take the future indicative; their negative is μή.

εὐλαβοῦμαι ὅπως μὴ ταῦτα ποιήσει.	I take care that he (will) not do this.
ἐμηχανήσατο ὅπως ταῦτα ποιήσομεν.	He contrived that we (would) do this.

Sometimes such clauses occur alone, with the main verb omitted; this occurs when the main verb would be an imperative and the subject of the two clauses is the same.

ὅπως οὖν ἔσεσθε ἄνδρες ἄξιοι.	Therefore (see to it that you) be worthy men.

---

[2] Many other constructions are also possible with these verbs.

Preliminary exercise 3 (on C). Translate into Greek using the following vocabulary: εὐλαβέομαι, εὐλαβήσομαι, –, –, –, ηὐλαβήθην "take care"; μηχανάομαι "contrive"; πράττω, πράξω, ἔπραξα, πέπραχα, πέπραγμαι, ἐπράχθην "bring it about that"; ἀπέρχομαι, ἄπειμι, ἀπῆλθον, ἀπελήλυθα, –, – "depart."

a. They contrived that he depart.
b. We shall bring it about that she does not depart.
c. (See to it that) you (pl.) do not depart.
d. I took care that we would not depart.
e. He will contrive that she not depart.

Sentences

Translate into Greek using only words and constructions so far covered. When multiple constructions for expressing purpose are possible, and when both optative and retained subjunctive are possible in fear clauses, give all possibilities.

1. I am afraid that my father drank the wine in order to save you from it; he thinks wine is not good for you. (2 ways)
2. The state's first legislator brought it about that graves are not in town but beyond the walls; in this way he contrived that disease be absent from the city.
3. Your king brought it about that horsemen were not afraid to use ships; he made an agreement with (in Greek "towards") the sailors about horses.
4. Their legislator chose men to rule the state well. (4 ways)
5. The seer's daughter feared that the cows sacred to Zeus would eat the flowers. (2 ways)
6. See to it that you do not fear to attack the tyrant; only those who do not fear will win.
7. The old woman will be absent in order not to be annoyed by the oxen. (2 ways)
8. The tyrant's mother fears that her son's character is not good: he contrives that many individuals are killed.
9. The seer is choosing mothers and sisters and daughters to bring flowers to the graves of the dead horsemen. (3 ways)
10. You don't fear that the memory of our family will not always exist, do you?
11. O children, see to it that you obey your fathers now and be prudent when you become men.
12. The general departed with twenty triremes to attack the hero's town. (3 ways)
13. Even the priests fear that the oxen will not swim though a river twenty feet wide.
14. Good fathers and mothers take care that their children not be harmed by swords and spears falling at home.

15.   The king will send someone to stop the ships from departing. (3 ways)
16.   Your mother is drinking the wine herself lest the old women find it.
17.   If someone should contrive that a human be capable of breathing when he has his head under water, he would be honored in many places.
18.   The suppliants stayed in the acropolis for many years because they were afraid to depart.
19.   See to it that you consider the form of the land well when you choose the place for (= of) your new city.
20.   The men in this city do not slander each other, in order that factional strife may not exist there.
21.   Some of the old women were afraid that their husbands would slander them, but others desired to slander their husbands themselves. (2 ways)
22.   Many slaves toiled for many years to make these ships. (3 ways)
23.   Their tyrant enjoyed stretching out on the walls the corpses of those who slandered their own fathers or mothers; thus he brought it about that no-one slandered his own family.
24.   The priest even sent his own daughter to amuse the king. (3 ways)
25.   The hero feared that his words had not been well chosen.
26.   My husband said (use φημί) that our first legislator was not courageous; he brought it about that swords and spears and missiles be absent from our city.
27.   My father cut the wood himself so that the old woman's husband would not toil. (2 ways)
28.   The seer was afraid to be absent from the city, on the grounds that the king had threatened him.
29.   The suppliants are waiting here today in order to see the king early. (2 ways)
30.   Whoever we amuse does not fear that he will have bad dreams.

Analysis

Analyze according to the model given in chapter VI, breaking up the sentence into units with one verb form in each and showing subordination by indentation and numbering. Translate each unit into English as literally as is possible without being incomprehensible and explain each construction covered in this chapter.

1.   ἀλλ᾽, ὦ φίλε Ἀγάθων, μηδὲν πλέον αὐτῷ γένηται, ἀλλὰ παρασκευάζου ὅπως ἐμὲ καὶ σὲ μηδεὶς διαβαλεῖ.

      (Plato, *Symposium* 222d; αὐτῷ i.e. "to his advantage")

2.   ἐπεμέλετο δὲ καὶ τούτου ὁ Κῦρος ὅπως μήποτε ἀνίδρωτοι γενόμενοι ἐπὶ τὸ ἄρισ-τον καὶ τὸ δεῖπνον εἰσίοιεν.

(Xenophon, *Cyropaedia* 2.1.29; ἐπιμέλομαι + gen. "watch out for," ἀνίδρωτος "without having sweated," ἄριστον "lunch")

3. ὡς δ' ἑώρων αὐτὸν οἰκείως τοῖς ἄρχουσι συνόντα, φοβηθέντες μὴ διαπράξαιτο ἃ βούλεται, παρεκινδύνευσάν τινες καὶ ἀποσφάττουσιν ἐν τῇ ἀκροπόλει τὸν Εὔφρονα, τῶν τε ἀρχόντων καὶ τῆς βουλῆς συγκαθημένων.

   (Xenophon, *Hellenica* 7.3.5; διαπράττω "accomplish," παρακινδυνεύω "make a rash venture," ἀποσφάττω "cut the throat of," συγκάθημαι "have a meeting")

4. ὁ δ' ὡς ἀπῆλθε κινδυνεύσας καὶ ἀτιμασθείς, βουλεύεται ὅπως μήποτε ἔτι ἔσται ἐπὶ τῷ ἀδελφῷ, ἀλλά, ἢν δύνηται, βασιλεύσει ἀντ' ἐκείνου.

   (Xenophon, *Anabasis* 1.1.4; ἐπί "in the power of")

5. ὡς δὲ ταῦτα ἀπηγγέλθη πρός τε τὸ κοινὸν τῶν Ἀρκάδων καὶ κατὰ πόλεις, ἐκ τούτου ἀνελογίζοντο Μαντινεῖς τε καὶ τῶν ἄλλων Ἀρκάδων οἱ κηδόμενοι τῆς Πελοποννήσου, ὡσαύτως δὲ καὶ Ἠλεῖοι καὶ Ἀχαιοί, ὅτι οἱ Θηβαῖοι δῆλοι εἶεν βουλόμενοι ὡς ἀσθενεστάτην τὴν Πελοπόννησον εἶναι, ὅπως ὡς ῥᾷστα αὐτὴν καταδουλώσαιντο.

   (Xenophon, *Hellenica* 7.5.1; ἀναλογίζομαι "consider," κήδομαι + gen. "be troubled for")

6. διὰ γὰρ τὸ φοβεῖσθαι μή, εἴ που κατασταίη, κυκλωθεὶς πολιορκοῖτο, ἄλλοτε ἄλλῃ τῆς χώρας ἐπῄει, ὥσπερ οἱ νομάδες, καὶ μάλα ἀφανίζων τὰς στρατοπεδεύσεις.

   (Xenophon, *Hellenica* 4.1.25; ἀφανίζω "remove traces of" (i.e. after they left), στρατοπέδευσις "encampment")

7. ταῦτ' οὖν ἔλεγεν οὐ τὸν μὲν πατέρα ζῶντα κατορύττειν διδάσκων, ἑαυτὸν δὲ κατατέμνειν· ἀλλ' ἐπιδεικνύων, ὅτι τὸ ἄφρον ἄτιμόν ἐστι, παρεκάλει ἐπιμελεῖσ-θαι τοῦ ὡς φρονιμώτατον εἶναι καὶ ὠφελιμώτατον, ὅπως, ἐάν τε ὑπὸ πατρός, ἐάν τε ὑπὸ ἀδελφοῦ, ἐάν τε ὑπὸ ἄλλου τινὸς βούληται τιμᾶσθαι, μὴ τῷ οἰκεῖος εἶναι πιστεύων ἀμελῇ, ἀλλὰ πειρᾶται, ὑφ' ὧν ἂν βούληται τιμᾶσθαι, τούτοις ὠφέλιμος εἶναι.

   (Xenophon, *Memorabilia* 1.2.55, explanation of Socrates' teachings about burying one's father and cutting one's hair and nails; κατορύττω "bury," κατατέμνω "cut up," ἄφρων "foolish")

8. οἶδα δὲ κἀκείνω σωφρονοῦντε, ἔστε Σωκράτει συνήστην, οὐ φοβουμένω μὴ ζημιοῖντο ἢ παίοιντο ὑπὸ Σωκράτους, ἀλλ' οἰομένω τότε κράτιστον εἶναι τοῦτο πράττειν.

   (Xenophon, *Memorabilia* 1.2.18; the duals and the plurals refer to the same people; ἔστε "while," συνήστην is imperfect dual of σύνειμι "be with"; can you explain the optatives?)

9. ἔστι δὴ τά γ᾽ ἐμοὶ δοκοῦντα, ψηφίσασθαι μὲν ἤδη τὴν βοήθειαν, καὶ παρασκευάσασθαι τὴν ταχίστην ὅπως ἐνθένδε βοηθήσετε, καὶ μὴ πάθητε ταὐτὸν ὅπερ καὶ πρότερον, πρεσβείαν δὲ πέμπειν, ἥτις ταῦτ᾽ ἐρεῖ καὶ παρέσται τοῖς πράγμασιν· ὡς ἔστι μάλιστα τοῦτο δέος, μὴ πανοῦργος ὢν καὶ δεινὸς ἄνθρωπος πράγμασι χρῆσθαι, τὰ μὲν εἴκων, ἡνίκ᾽ ἂν τύχῃ, τὰ δ᾽ ἀπειλῶν (ἀξιόπιστος δ᾽ ἂν εἰκότως φαίνοιτο), τὰ δ᾽ ἡμᾶς διαβάλλων καὶ τὴν ἀπουσίαν τὴν ἡμετέραν, τρέψηται καὶ παρασπάσηταί τι τῶν ὅλων πραγμάτων.

(Demosthenes, *Olynthiac* 1.2–3; βοήθεια "relief expedition," τὴν ταχίστην (ὁδόν) "as fast as possible," πρεσβεία "embassy," πρᾶγμα i.e. important political affair, ἄνθρωπος (NB crasis) refers to Philip of Macedon, εἴκω "yield," τυγχάνω i.e. be useful for his purpose, ἀξιόπιστος "worthy of belief," εἰκότως "reasonably," ἀπουσία i.e. the fact that our army is not already there, τρέπομαι "turn to his own advantage," παρασπάομαι "wrest aside for his own advantage")

XIII | Cause, result, and "on condition that"

> Material to learn before using this chapter: irregular adjectives (Smyth §290, 292–3, 297–9); Vocabulary 13 and associated principal parts
> Recommended grammar reading: Smyth §286–99
> Recommended syntax reading: Smyth §2240–79, 2555–9

A) **Cause** can be expressed in two ways.[1]

1) A clause introduced by ὅτι, ὡς, ἐπεί, etc.[2] with the verb in an appropriate tense of the indicative. The negative is οὐ.

ἦλθεν ὅτι ἤθελεν ἡμᾶς σῶσαι.	He came because he wanted to save us.
ἐπειδὴ ἤθελεν ἡμᾶς σῶσαι, ἦλθεν.	Since he wanted to save us, he came.
ἀπῆλθεν ὅτι οὐκ ἀφικόμεθα.	He left because we had not come. (note tenses)

2) A circumstantial participle, often accompanied by ἅτε, οἷα, or ὡς (see chapter v B1c, E3). The negative is οὐ.

ἦλθεν ἅτε ἐθέλων ἡμᾶς σῶσαι.	He came because he wanted to save us.
ἀπῆλθεν οἷα ἡμῶν οὐκ ἀφικομένων.	He left because we had not come.

To indicate alleged cause, one asserted by the subject of the sentence but not positively confirmed by the author, a causal clause can have an optative verb in secondary sequence. This construction is in "virtual indirect statement," so the tense of the optative indicates time, not aspect. The same idea can be conveyed by using ὡς with a causal participle (see chapter v E3).

---

[1] There are also other possibilities, including an ordinary relative clause (e.g. δόξας ἀμαθέα εἶναι, ὅς . . . ἐκέλευε "thinking that he was ignorant, because he ordered," Hdt. 1.33) and an articular infinitive governed by διά "on account of" (see chapter II E); "because" followed by a noun in English is the equivalent of διά (+ acc.) or ἕνεκα (+ gen.) in Greek.

[2] Generally ὅτι and διότι are used only in clauses that explain something already stated; causal clauses at the beginning of a sentence tend to use ἐπεί and forms related to it. This distinction is traditionally indicated by using "because" for ὅτι and "since" for ἐπεί and observing the same distinction in position with these English conjunctions.

ἦλθεν ὅτι ἐθέλοι ἡμᾶς σῶσαι.	He came on the grounds that he wanted to save us. / He came because, as he said, he wanted to save us.
ἦλθεν ὡς ἐθέλων ἡμᾶς σῶσαι.	He came on the grounds that he wanted to save us. / He came because, as he said, he wanted to save us.
ἀπῆλθεν ὅτι οὐκ ἀφικοίμεθα.	He left on the grounds that we had not come. / He left because, as he said, we had not come.

Preliminary exercise 1 (on A). Translate each sentence into Greek twice, once with a finite verb and once with a participle. Use the following vocabulary: κάμνω, καμοῦμαι, ἔκαμον, κέκμηκα, –, – "toil"; χαίρω, χαιρήσω, ἐχάρην, κεχάρηκα, –, – "rejoice"; οἰκτίρω, –, ᾤκτιρα, –, –, – "pity."

a.   Since he had toiled, we pitied him.
b.   We pitied him on the grounds that he had toiled.
c.   We pitied him on the grounds that he was toiling.
d.   We pitied him because he was toiling.
e.   He rejoices because he does not toil.
f.   Since he had not toiled, he did not rejoice.
g.   He rejoiced because he had toiled.
h.   He rejoiced on the grounds that he had toiled.

B) Result clauses are of two main types, of which the first is notably more common than the second.

1) Clauses of natural result are introduced by ὥστε and have their verbs in the infinitive (change of subject in accusative); the negative is μή. They are often preceded by οὕτω(ς), τοιοῦτος, or τοσοῦτος.

οὕτω θρασὺς ἦν ὥστε μηδέποτε φοβεῖσθαι.	He was so bold as never to be afraid.
τοσούτους ἐξέβαλον ὥστε μηδένα μένειν.	They banished so many that no-one was left.

2) Clauses of actual result are also introduced by ὥστε but have their verbs in the indicative; the negative is οὐ. They put stress on the fact that a result actually occurred.

οὕτω θρασὺς ἦν ὥστε οὐδέποτε ἐφοβεῖτο.	He was so bold that he was (actually) never afraid.
τοσούτους ἐξέβαλον ὥστε οὐδεὶς ἔμενεν.	They banished so many that (actually) no-one was left.

Note that although natural and actual result clauses often have the same English translation, they do not mean exactly the same thing. Some English sentences can be translated either way, but others cannot: English "so . . . as" + infinitive is a natural result clause, and English "so that" preceded by a comma is an actual result clause.

οὕτως ἄφρων ἦν ὥστε λίθον βαλεῖν.　　He was so foolish as to throw a stone.

ὁ λίθος γυναῖκα ἔβαλεν, ὥστε　　　　 The stone hit a woman, so that she died / so
　ἀπέθανεν.　　　　　　　　　　　　 that she was killed.

> **Preliminary exercise 2 (on B).** Translate each sentence into Greek twice,
> once with each type of result clause. Use the following vocabulary: ἐπαινέω,
> ἐπαινέσομαι, ἐπῄνεσα, ἐπῄνεκα, ἐπῄνημαι, ἐπῃνέθην "praise"; μανθάνω,
> μαθήσομαι, ἔμαθον, μεμάθηκα, –, – "learn"; τρέχω, δραμοῦμαι, ἔδραμον,
> -δεδράμηκα, –, – "run"; ταχέως "swiftly."
>
> a.　He learned so much that he was praised.
> b.　He will run so swiftly that you (plural) praise him.
> c.　He is learning such things that he is not praised.
> d.　He runs so swiftly that we praise him.
> e.　He ran so swiftly that he was praised.

C) Expressions meaning "on condition that" (ἐφ' ᾧ, ἐφ' ᾧτε) can take either the
infinitive (change of subject in accusative) or the future indicative; in either case the
negative is μή. They are often correlated with an ἐπὶ τούτῳ or ἐπὶ τούτοις in the main
clause.

ἐσώθημεν ἐφ' ᾧτε μηκέτι μάχεσθαι.　　We were spared on condition that we
　　　　　　　　　　　　　　　　　　 (would) no longer fight.

ἐπὶ τούτῳ εἶπον, ἐφ' ᾧ μηδεὶς βοήσει.　They spoke on condition that no-one
　　　　　　　　　　　　　　　　　　 (would) shout.

Sentences

Translate into Greek using only words and constructions so far covered. When both
participial and finite-verb possibilities exist for a causal clause, both natural and actual
result are possible for a result clause, or both infinitive and future are possible for an "on
condition that" clause, give all possibilities.

1.　　　The army that invaded was so big that no-one resisted it. (2 ways)
2.　　　We made an agreement on condition that everyone would go out of the city
　　　　willingly. (2 ways)

3. We sent a trustworthy comrade to help them, but they received him unwillingly because (as they said) he was not like them. (2 ways)
4. Are you so impious as to enter this temple without taking a bath?
5. Since he did not know which answer (of two) was correct, the ignorant man went out to learn something. (2 ways)
6. His wine is so sweet that we shall drink it all. (2 ways)
7. These three cities made (for themselves) a treaty on condition that each would have its own laws and customs. (2 ways)
8. When the enemy took the long walls the men in the city did not resist, on the grounds that they were in need of water and not healthy. (2 ways)
9. The sea is so wide that ships sail on it without the sailors' seeing the mainland. (2 ways)
10. I shall find you a black bird on condition that you do not harm it. (2 ways)
11. The fortunate bandits repented, so that they became friendly citizens.
12. The unfortunate suppliant departed unwillingly, because he feared he would be killed. (2 ways)
13. The (two) states had an agreement on condition that neither would invade the other. (2 ways)
14. The answer was so long that no-one listened to it willingly. (2 ways)
15. My enemies slandered my character, so that no-one listened to me because (as they thought) my words were not true. (2 ways)
16. Everyone will come on condition that they all be safe. (2 ways)
17. Their customs (are) so sensible as to bring it about that everyone in that land is happy.
18. The whole army was in the camp, because only the camp was safe. (2 ways)
19. We shall accomplish the whole work ourselves on condition that someone trustworthy advises us. (2 ways)
20. The foolish man did not take care to wait for his daughter, so that the unfortunate child was left behind.
21. If you (plural) desire to be safe, make (for yourself) a treaty on condition that all the other cities be safe too. (2 ways)
22. Our nation has accomplished[3] so many things as to be happy in respect to everything.
23. Even bold men feared to catch those hoplites, on the grounds that their spears were long and their swords not short. (2 ways)
24. I shall carry these heavy stones on condition that you (singular) carry all those. (2 ways)

[3] Use the aorist in Greek.

25. The river (is) so deep that only ignorant men swim in it. (2 ways)
26. We shall make (for ourselves) peace with anyone who wishes, on condition that they banish from their cities all foolish, ignorant, impious, and unfortunate people. (2 ways)
27. Horses enjoy being rubbed by humans because they are not capable of rubbing themselves. (2 ways)
28. The swift bird was so foolish as not to fly into the forest.
29–30. Who would accept a slave on condition that he not strike or beat him? Slaves toil only because they are beaten! (3 ways)

Analysis

Analyze according to the model given in chapter VI, breaking up the sentence into units with one verb form in each and showing subordination by indentation and numbering. Translate each unit into English as literally as is possible without being incomprehensible and explain each construction covered in this chapter.

1. καὶ εἰς τοσοῦτόν εἰσι τόλμης ἀφιγμένοι ὥσθ᾽ ἥκουσιν ἀπολογησόμενοι, καὶ λέγουσιν ὡς οὐδὲν κακὸν οὐδ᾽ αἰσχρὸν εἰργασμένοι εἰσίν.

   (Lysias, *Oration* 12.22; watch for periphrastic verb forms)

2. ὡς δὲ τοῖς ἄρχουσι ταῦτα λογιζομένοις ἐφαίνετο ἄπορα καὶ οὐκέτι ἔπειθεν αὐτοὺς ὁ Ἑρμοκράτης, αὐτὸς ἐπὶ τούτοις τάδε μηχανᾶται, δεδιὼς μὴ οἱ Ἀθηναῖοι καθ᾽ ἡσυχίαν προφθάσωσιν ἐν τῇ νυκτὶ διελθόντες τὰ χαλεπώτατα τῶν χωρίων.

   (Thucydides 7.73.3; λογίζομαι "calculate," ἄπορος "impracticable," ἐπὶ τούτοις "under these circumstances," καθ᾽ ἡσυχίαν "at leisure")

3. ὁ μέντοι Τιθραύστης, καταμαθεῖν δοκῶν τὸν Ἀγησίλαον καταφρονοῦντα τῶν βασιλέως πραγμάτων καὶ οὐδαμῇ διανοούμενον ἀπιέναι ἐκ τῆς Ἀσίας, ἀλλὰ μᾶλλον ἐλπίδας ἔχοντα μεγάλας αἱρήσειν βασιλέα, ἀπορῶν τί χρῷτο τοῖς πράγμασι, πέμπει Τιμοκράτην τὸν Ῥόδιον εἰς Ἑλλάδα, δοὺς χρυσίον εἰς πεντήκοντα τάλαντα ἀργυρίου, καὶ κελεύει πειρᾶσθαι πιστὰ τὰ μέγιστα λαμβάνοντα διδόναι τοῖς προεστηκόσιν ἐν ταῖς πόλεσιν ἐφ᾽ ᾧτε πόλεμον ἐξοίσειν πρὸς Λακεδαιμονίους.

   (Xenophon, *Hellenica* 3.5.1; καταμανθάνω "find out" is taking accusative and participle, διανοέομαι "intend," αἱρέω "conquer," εἰς "to the value of")

4. τοιαύταις διανοίαις χρώμενοι καὶ τοὺς νεωτέρους ἐν τοῖς τοιούτοις ἤθεσιν παιδεύοντες οὕτως ἄνδρας ἀγαθοὺς ἀπέδειξαν τοὺς πολεμήσαντας πρὸς τοὺς

ἐκ τῆς Ἀσίας ὥστε μηδένα πώποτε δυνηθῆναι περὶ αὐτῶν μήτε τῶν ποιητῶν μήτε τῶν σοφιστῶν ἀξίως τῶν ἐκείνοις πεπραγμένων εἰπεῖν.

(Isocrates, *Panegyricus* 82, on the subject of the Athenians in the sixth century BC; νεώτεροι "young men," ἀπέδειξαν i.e. "made into," "those from Asia" means the Persian armies)

5. ἢ καὶ βασιλεύειν, ἔφη ὁ Ἀντισθένης, ἐπίστασαι, ὅτι οἶσθα ἐπαινέσαντα αὐτὸν τὸν Ἀγαμέμνονα ὡς βασιλεύς τε εἴη ἀγαθὸς κρατερός τ' αἰχμητής;

(Xenophon, *Symposium* 4.6, on how much the addressee understands about different professions from knowing Homer's poetry well; ignore ἔφη ὁ Ἀντισθένης for purposes of analysis; αὐτόν i.e. Homer)

6. ἀγασθέντες δὲ αὐτοὺς οἱ Θηβαῖοι, ὅτι καίπερ ἐν κινδύνῳ ὄντες οὐκ ἤθελον τοῖς εὐεργέταις εἰς πόλεμον καθίστασθαι, συνεχώρησαν αὐτοῖς καὶ Φλειασίοις καὶ τοῖς ἐλθοῦσι μετ' αὐτῶν εἰς Θήβας τὴν εἰρήνην ἐφ' ᾧτε ἔχειν τὴν ἑαυτῶν ἑκάστους.

(Xenophon, *Hellenica* 7.4.10; ἄγαμαι "be amazed at," συγχωρέω "agree," supply γῆν before the last word of the passage)

7. ὃς εἰς τοσοῦτον ἦλθεν ὑπερηφανίας ὥστε μικρὸν μὲν ἡγησάμενος ἔργον εἶναι τὴν Ἑλλάδα χειρώσασθαι, βουληθεὶς δὲ τοιοῦτον μνημεῖον καταλιπεῖν ὃ μὴ τῆς ἀνθρωπίνης φύσεώς ἐστιν, οὐ πρότερον ἐπαύσατο πρὶν ἐξεῦρε καὶ συνηνάγκασεν ὃ πάντες θρυλοῦσιν, ὥστε τῷ στρατοπέδῳ πλεῦσαι μὲν διὰ τῆς ἠπείρου, πεζεῦσαι δὲ διὰ τῆς θαλάττης, τὸν μὲν Ἑλλήσποντον ζεύξας, τὸν δ' Ἄθω διορύξας.

(Isocrates, *Panegyricus* 89, on the ambitions of Xerxes; the whole sentence is a relative clause in which ὅς refers to Xerxes; ὑπερηφανία "arrogance," χειρόω "subdue," μνημεῖον "memorial," συναναγκάζω i.e. "do by force," θρυλέω "chatter about," πεζεύω "walk," ζεύγνυμι "yoke, bind fast," διορύττω "dig through")

8. παντί τε τρόπῳ ἀνηρέθιστο ἡ πόλις, καὶ τὸν Περικλέα ἐν ὀργῇ εἶχον, καὶ ὧν παρῄνεσε πρότερον ἐμέμνηντο οὐδέν, ἀλλ' ἐκάκιζον ὅτι στρατηγὸς ὢν οὐκ ἐπεξάγοι, αἴτιόν τε σφίσιν ἐνόμιζον πάντων ὧν ἔπασχον.

(Thucydides 2.21.3; ἀνερεθίζω "stir up, excite," παραινέω "advise," κακίζω "abuse" (verbally), ἐπεξάγω i.e. "lead the army out to fight")

9. οὐ τοίνυν, ἐπειδὴ τὰ μέγιστα συνδιέπραξεν, τῶν ἄλλων ὠλιγώρησεν, ἀλλ' ἀρχὴν μὲν ταύτην ἐποιήσατο τῶν εὐεργεσιῶν, τροφὴν τοῖς δεομένοις εὑρεῖν, ἥνπερ χρὴ τοὺς μέλλοντας καὶ περὶ τῶν ἄλλων καλῶν καλῶς διοικήσειν, ἡγουμένη δὲ τὸν βίον τὸν ἐπὶ τούτοις μόνον οὔπω τοῦ ζῆν ἐπιθυμεῖν ἀξίως ἔχειν οὕτως ἐπεμελήθη καὶ τῶν λοιπῶν ὥστε τῶν παρόντων τοῖς ἀνθρώποις

ἀγαθῶν, ὅσα μὴ παρὰ θεῶν ἔχομεν, ἀλλὰ δι' ἀλλήλους ἡμῖν γέγονεν, μηδὲν μὲν ἄνευ τῆς πόλεως τῆς ἡμετέρας εἶναι, τὰ δὲ πλεῖστα διὰ ταύτην γεγενῆσθαι.

(Isocrates, *Panegyricus* 38, on the virtues of archaic Athens; ὀλιγωρέω "neglect," εὐεργεσία "benefit," τροφὴν τοῖς δεομένοις εὑρεῖν is in apposition to ταύτην, understand ποεῖν after χρή, καλά "good things," διοικέω "live," ἐπὶ τούτοις μόνον i.e. with just the bare essentials, ἀξίως ἔχω "be worthy," ἐπιμελέομαι "take care of")

XIV | Comparison and negatives

....

Material to learn before using this chapter: comparison of adjectives,
adverbs (Smyth §313–20, 343, 345); Vocabulary 14 and associated
principal parts
Recommended grammar reading: Smyth §313–24, 341–5
Recommended syntax reading: Smyth §1063–98, 2462–87, 2688–2768

....

A) Comparatives in Greek can either be used like English comparatives (μείζων
"bigger"), in which case they must take a word showing what the subject is compared
to, or they may be used absolutely (μείζων "rather big, too big"). When used as comparatives they have two constructions.

1) Simple comparison in the nominative tends to use the genitive of comparison for
"than," but ἤ is also possible.

οὗτος μείζων ἐστὶ ἐκείνης.	He is bigger than she (is).
οὗτος μείζων ἐστὶν ἢ ἐκείνη.	He is bigger than she (is).

2) In more complex comparisons, ἤ is used for "than." The word after ἤ is in the same
case as the word to which it is being compared.

τούτῳ ἔστι μείζων οἶκος ἢ ἐκείνη.	He has a bigger house than she does.
πλείονας ἔφαγεν οὗτος ἢ ἐκείνη.	He ate more than she did.

Comparatives are also used with ἤ and a natural result clause to express the idea in
English "too . . . to":[1]

θρασύτερος ἦν ἢ ὥστε φοβεῖσθαι.	He was too bold to be afraid.
σωφρονέστερος ἦν ἢ ὥστε μὴ φοβεῖσθαι.	He was too sensible not to be afraid.
τοῦτο μεῖζόν ἐστιν ἢ ὥστε με αὐτὸ φαγεῖν.	That is too big for me to eat.

> **Preliminary exercise 1 (on A).** Translate into Greek using the following
> vocabulary: γενναῖος, -α, -ον "noble," σοφός, -ή, -όν "wise," πατήρ, πατρός,
> ὁ "father," ἀποτρέχω, ἀποδραμοῦμαι, ἀπέδραμον, ἀποδεδράμηκα, –, –
> "run away."

---

[1] Sometimes the ὥστε is omitted from such clauses, or ὡς is used instead.

a.   He is nobler than she is. (2 ways)
b.   He is rather noble.
c.   He has a nobler father than she does.
d.   He is too noble to run away.
e.   She is wiser than he is. (2 ways)
f.   She is rather wise.
g.   She has a wiser father than he does.
h.   She is too wise to run away.

B) Superlatives can either be used like English superlatives (μέγιστος "biggest"), in which case they often take a word showing what the subject is compared to, or they may be used absolutely (μέγιστος "very big").

1) When compared to something, superlatives take a partitive genitive.

μέγιστός ἐστι τῶν παίδων.   He is the biggest of the boys.

2) Superlatives with ὡς (or ὅτι) translate English "as . . . as possible".

ὡς μέγιστός ἐστιν.   He is as big as possible.
ὅτι τάχιστα ἔδραμεν.   He ran as fast as possible.

Comparative and superlative constructions can take a dative of degree of difference, or (only in the case of certain words) an adverbial accusative.

οὗτος πολλῷ μείζων ἐστὶν ἐκείνης.   He is much bigger than she (is).
οὗτος μακρῷ μείζων ἐστὶν ἐκείνης.   He is far bigger than she (is).
οὗτος πολὺ μείζων ἐστὶν ἐκείνης.   He is much bigger than she (is).

Preliminary exercise 2 (on B). Translate into Greek using the following vocabulary: ἀρχαῖος, -α, -ον "ancient"; μακρός, -ά, -όν "long"; οἶκος, -ου, ὁ "house"; *νύξ, νυκτός, ἡ* "night."

a.   This is the most ancient of the houses.
b.   The house is as ancient as possible.
c.   This house is much more ancient than that one.
d.   This house is far more ancient than that one.
e.   This is the longest of the nights.
f.   The night is as long as possible.
g.   This night is much longer than that one.
h.   This night is far longer than that one.

C) Multiple negatives are common in Greek. As in English, negatives do not affect one another unless they apply to the same word or phrase; like the usage in colloquial English, but unlike usage in written English, Greek negatives may strengthen one another instead of cancelling. Multiple negatives in Greek cancel each other only if the last negative is a simple οὐ or a simple μή; if the last negative is compound, they strengthen each other.

οὐδεὶς οὐκ οἶδεν.	No-one does not know. / Everyone knows. (cancelling)
οὐκ οἶδεν οὐδείς.	No-one at all knows. / *No-one* knows. (strengthening)
οὐδεὶς εἶπεν ὅτι πιστὸς οὐκ εἴη.	No-one said he was not trustworthy. (neither cancelling nor strengthening, since the two negatives apply to different words; note that this sentence does not mean "Everyone said he was trustworthy.")
εἰ μὴ εἶδε μηδέποτε . . .	If he had *never* seen . . . (strengthening with μή)

Either a single compound negative or multiple confirming negatives may be used to translate English clauses in which words like "any" or "ever" replace words like "some" after a negative; Greek indefinites like τις are not used in such contexts.

He does not know anything.	οὐδὲν οἶδεν. / οὐκ οἶδεν οὐδέν.
I did not see anyone.	οὐδένα εἶδον. / οὐκ εἶδον οὐδένα.
I don't see any children.	οὐδένα παῖδα ὁρῶ. / οὐχ ὁρῶ παῖδα οὐδένα. / παῖδας οὐχ ὁρῶ.
I never see anyone.	οὐδέποτε ὁρῶ οὐδένα.
if he doesn't ever come	ἐὰν μηδέποτε ἔλθῃ / ἐὰν μὴ ἔλθῃ μηδέποτε

> **Preliminary exercise 3 (on C).** Translate into Greek using at least one negative per sentence and the following vocabulary: κλέπτω, κλέψω, ἔκλεψα, κέκλοφα, κέκλεμμαι, ἐκλάπην "steal"; ἐσθίω, ἔδομαι, ἔφαγον, –, –, – "eat."
>
> a. No-one stole anything.
> b. I did not steal anything. (2 ways)
> c. Everyone steals.
> d. They never steal. (2 ways)
> e. No-one said that they never steal.
> f. He will never steal anything.
> g. Everyone eats.

      h.   No-one ate anything.

      i.   He is not eating anything. (2 ways)

      j.   Everyone ate.

Sentences 1

Translate into Greek with double negatives, using only words and constructions so far covered.

1. No-one ever neglects his own anger.
2. He disturbed everyone.
3. They will not read any poems.
4. Everyone has abilities.
5. I did not plot against any good-for-nothing man.
6. No-one will oppose me.
7. Trivial things befall everyone.
8. He did not deceive anyone, although he tried.
9. My daughter is not yet skilled in any art.
10. Everyone reads these easy writings.
11. There is nothing clear or precise in his writings.
12. Everyone is disappointed.
13. No-one gets by lot a share of courage.
14. Everyone stands by his own people.
15. No-one is ever present when I try my strength.
16. He did not have a share of any abilities.
17. Everything (is) legitimate in this state.
18. No-one is present any longer in the town.

Sentences 2

Translate into Greek using only words and constructions so far covered.

1. Is reading clearly easier than writing correctly?
2. That device was much too conspicuous not to be seen swiftly.
3. Love is by far the sharpest of desires.
4. The very wicked children disturb many more people than they deceive.
5. I shall try to read as clearly as possible.
6. Those wicked men are too experienced to be easily disappointed.
7. These rather trivial women foolishly believe that the rule of a king is far more legitimate than that of a tyrant.

8.   The wicked man's anger was as great as possible.
9.   Too many things came next for me to remember them all precisely.
10. The men who agree with us are much dearer to me than those who wickedly plot against us.
11. If you read as fast as possible, you will not enjoy reading.
12. We obey you eagerly because your strength is much greater than ours.
13. Even men as experienced as possible are sometimes deceived.
14. The old woman is much too good to neglect her daughter.
15. It is much easier to deceive a populace than a king.
16. The wretched children foolishly disturbed as many old women as possible.
17. That very good man nobly stands by more friends than he opposes.
18. Since they were in want of all things, the good men came out later.

Analysis

Analyze according to the model given in chapter VI, breaking up the sentence into units with one verb form in each and showing subordination by indentation and numbering. Translate each unit into English as literally as is possible without being incomprehensible and explain each construction covered in this chapter.

1.   ἐμοὶ μὲν γὰρ οὐδέν ἐστι πρεσβύτερον τοῦ ὡς ὅτι βέλτιστον ἐμὲ γενέσθαι, τούτου δὲ οἶμαί μοι συλλήπτορα οὐδένα κυριώτερον εἶναι σοῦ.

     (Plato, *Symposium* 218d; πρεσβύτερος "more important," συλλήπτωρ "partner," κυριώτερος i.e. "more capable")

2.   ἔπειτα δ' ὕστερον καὶ πρὸς τοὺς ἄλλους ἅπαντας τοὺς μετὰ Δημοσθένους ὁμολογία γίγνεται ὥστε ὅπλα τε παραδοῦναι καὶ μὴ ἀποθανεῖν μηδένα μήτε βιαίως μήτε δεσμοῖς μήτε τῆς ἀναγκαιοτάτης ἐνδείᾳ διαίτης.

     (Thucydides 7.82.2; ὁμολογία i.e. "surrender agreement," δίαιτα i.e. "means of living")

3.   φαίην δ' ἂν ἔγωγε μηδενὶ μηδεμίαν εἶναι παίδευσιν παρὰ τοῦ μὴ ἀρέσκοντος.

     (Xenophon, *Memorabilia* 1.2.39; παίδευσις "education," παρά i.e. "if he is taught by"; what rule from an earlier chapter does this sentence violate?)

4.   οἱ δ' αὖ Λακεδαιμόνιοι ἐπεὶ ᾔσθοντο αὐτὸν ἐλάττω ἔχοντα δύναμιν ἢ ὥστε τοὺς φίλους ὠφελεῖν, ἐκέλευσαν τὸν Τελευτίαν σὺν ταῖς δώδεκα ναυσὶν αἷς εἶχεν ἐν τῷ περὶ Ἀχαΐαν καὶ Λέχαιον κόλπῳ περιπλεῖν πρὸς τὸν Ἔκδικον, κἀκεῖνον μὲν ἀποπέμψαι, αὐτὸν δὲ τῶν τε βουλομένων φίλων εἶναι ἐπιμελεῖσθαι καὶ τοὺς πολεμίους ὅ τι δύναιτο κακὸν ποιεῖν.

     (Xenophon, *Hellenica* 4.8.23; κόλπος "gulf," ἐπιμελέομαι + gen. "take care of")

5.　ζητεῖν γάρ μοι δοκεῖς τοιοῦτόν τι τὸ καλὸν ἀποκρίνασθαι, ὃ μηδέποτε αἰσχρὸν μηδαμοῦ μηδενὶ φανεῖται.

(Plato, *Hippias Major* 291d; understand εἶναι before ἀποκρίνασθαι)

6.　καὶ ἐγὼ μέν, ὦ Σώκρατες, καὶ τότε ἐκέλευον σοὶ διδόναι τἀριστεῖα τοὺς στρατηγούς, καὶ τοῦτό γέ μοι οὔτε μέμψῃ οὔτε ἐρεῖς ὅτι ψεύδομαι· ἀλλὰ γὰρ τῶν στρατηγῶν πρὸς τὸ ἐμὸν ἀξίωμα ἀποβλεπόντων καὶ βουλομένων ἐμοὶ διδόναι τἀριστεῖα, αὐτὸς προθυμότερος ἐγένου τῶν στρατηγῶν ἐμὲ λαβεῖν ἢ σαυτόν.

(Plato, *Symposium* 220e, Alcibiades on Socrates' bravery and modesty; ἀριστεῖα "prize," ἀξίωμα "rank")

7.　εἰ δὲ μήτ' ἔστι μήτ' ἦν μήτ' ἂν εἰπεῖν ἔχοι μηδεὶς μηδέπω καὶ τήμερον, τί τὸν σύμβουλον ἐχρῆν ποιεῖν;

(Demosthenes, *De corona* 190; εἰπεῖν ἔχω i.e. have something to say in response to Demosthenes' offer to admit his advice was wrong if anyone can suggest something that would have been better)

8.　οὐδ' αὖ φαντασθήσεται αὐτῷ τὸ καλὸν οἷον πρόσωπόν τι οὐδὲ χεῖρες οὐδὲ ἄλλο οὐδὲν ὧν σῶμα μετέχει, οὐδέ τις λόγος οὐδέ τις ἐπιστήμη, οὐδέ που ὂν ἐν ἑτέρῳ τινι, οἷον ἐν ζῴῳ ἢ ἐν γῇ ἢ ἐν οὐρανῷ ἢ ἔν τῳ ἄλλῳ, ἀλλ' αὐτὸ καθ' αὑτὸ μεθ' αὑτοῦ μονοειδὲς ἀεὶ ὄν, τὰ δὲ ἄλλα πάντα καλὰ ἐκείνου μετέχοντα τρόπον τινὰ τοιοῦτον, οἷον γιγνομένων τε τῶν ἄλλων καὶ ἀπολλυμένων μηδὲν ἐκεῖνο μήτε τι πλέον μήτε ἔλαττον γίγνεσθαι μηδὲ πάσχειν μηδέν.

(Plato, *Symposium* 211b, Diotima on the Form of the Beautiful; φαντάζομαι "appear," οἷον "like," μονοειδής "uniform"; why is this sentence hard to analyze?)

XV | Commands, wishes, and prevention

Material to learn before using this chapter: μι-verbs: present system (Smyth §416, pages 135–7 only); Vocabulary 15 and associated principal parts
Recommended grammar reading: Smyth §412–16
Recommended syntax reading: Smyth §1780–2, 1797–1800, 1814–20, 1835–44, 2038, 2155–6, 2681–7, 2739–44

A) Commands

1) **Direct** commands are expressed by the imperative or subjunctive as follows:

Continuous Action	**Single Action**
1st person	
Present **subjunctive** (negative μή)	Aorist **subjunctive** (negative μή)
(μὴ) γράφωμεν "Let us (not) write."	(μὴ) γράψωμεν "Let us (not) write."
2nd person	
Positive: present **imperative**	Positive: aorist **imperative**
γράφετε "Write!" (all day)	γράψατε "Write!" (this letter)
Negative: μή + present **imperative**	Negative: μή + aorist **subjunctive**
μὴ γράφετε "Don't be writing!"	μὴ γράψητε "Don't write!"
3rd person	
Positive: present **imperative**	Positive: aorist **imperative** (rare)
γραφόντων "Let them write."	γραψάντων "Let them write."
Negative: μή + present **imperative**	Negative: μή + aorist **subjunctive**
μὴ γραφόντων "Let them not be writing."	μὴ γράψωσι "Let them not write."

2) **Indirect** commands are expressed by the infinitive (present or aorist according to aspect); the negative is μή.

ἐκέλευσεν αὐτοὺς μὴ γράφειν.   He ordered them not to write (continuously/ever).
ἐκέλευσεν αὐτοὺς γράψαι.   He ordered them to write (once).

Verbs taking an indirect command include λέγω, κελεύω, παρακελεύομαι, ἀξιόω "ask," δέομαι "ask," αἰτέω, οὐκ ἐάω, and κωλύω.

> **Preliminary exercise 1 (on A).** Translate into Greek using the following vocabulary: γαμέω, γαμῶ, ἔγημα, γεγάμηκα, γεγάμημαι, – "marry" (take this to be an inherently one-time action and assume male subjects); σιγάω, σιγήσομαι, ἐσίγησα, σεσίγηκα, σεσίγημαι, ἐσιγήθην "be silent" (take this to be an inherently continuous action).

> a. Be silent!
> b. Don't marry!
> c. Let's marry!
> d. Let them be silent!
> e. They ordered us not to marry.
> f. Don't be silent!
> g. Let's not be silent!
> h. Let them marry!
> i. Marry!
> j. I order you to be silent.

B) Certain verbs of preventing, forbidding, and denying, including ἀπαγορεύω, εἴργω, and ἀπαρνέομαι,[1] take an infinitive preceded by an untranslatable μή. But other verbs with similar meanings, including οὐκ ἐάω, κωλύω, and οὐ φημί, take an infinitive without μή.

εἴρξει ἡμᾶς μὴ εἰσελθεῖν.	He will prevent us from entering.
ἀπεῖπέ μοι μὴ ἀπελθεῖν.	He forbade me to go away.
οὐκ εἴασε με ἀπελθεῖν.	He forbade me to go away.

The introductory μή becomes μὴ οὐ if the governing verb has a negative,[2] but none of these negatives makes the subordinate negative: subordinate clauses of this type are *never* themselves negative (i.e. one cannot prevent someone from not doing something using one of these verbs).

οὐκ ἀπεῖπέ μοι μὴ οὐκ ἀπελθεῖν.	He did not forbid me to go away.
οὐδεὶς εἴρξει ἡμᾶς μὴ οὐκ εἰσελθεῖν.	No-one will prevent us from entering.

---

[1] See Smyth §2740–1 for a list of other verbs that can take this construction.
[2] Also often if the governing verb is a "virtual negative," a question expecting a negative answer: τίς ἀπείποι ἂν μοι μὴ οὐκ ἀπελθεῖν; "Who would forbid me to go away?"

Preliminary exercise 2 (on B). Translate into Greek using the following vocabulary: ἀπαγορεύω, ἀπερῶ, ἀπεῖπον, ἀπείρηκα, ἀπείρημαι, ἀπερρήθην (+ dat.) "forbid"; οὐκ ἐάω, ἐάσω, εἴασα, εἴακα, εἴαμαι, εἰάθην "forbid"; εἴργω, εἴρξω, εἶρξα, –, εἴργμαι, εἴρχθην "prevent"; κωλύω "prevent"; ἀπαρνέομαι "deny"; οὐ φημί, φήσω, ἔφησα, –, –, – "deny"; ἕπομαι, ἕψομαι, ἑσπόμην, –, –, – "follow"; ἀκούω, ἀκούσομαι, ἤκουσα, ἀκήκοα, –, ἠκούσθην "hear."

a.   He forbids me to follow. (2 ways)
b.   They did not forbid us to follow.
c.   She prevented him from following. (2 ways)
d.   Nothing prevents you from following. (2 ways).
e.   We deny that we followed. (2 ways)
f.   No-one denies that we followed.
g.   They forbade us to hear. (2 ways)
h.   He does not forbid me to hear.
i.   They are preventing us from hearing. (2 ways)
j.   No-one prevented you from hearing. (2 ways)
k.   I deny that I heard. (2 ways)
l.   No-one denies that you heard.

C) Wishes are of four types.

1) Wishes for the future use the optative (present or aorist) with or without εἴθε or εἰ γάρ; the negative is μή.

εἴθε γράψαιεν.	May they write!
μὴ γράφοι.	May he not be writing!

2) Wishes for the present use the imperfect indicative, always with εἴθε or εἰ γάρ; the negative is μή.

εἴθε μὴ ἔγραφεν.	If only he were not writing! / Would that he were not writing!

3) Wishes for the past use the aorist indicative, always with εἴθε or εἰ γάρ; the negative is μή.

εἴθε ἔγραψαν.	If only they had written! / Would that they had written!

4) Present and past wishes are also expressed by ὤφελον and an appropriate tense of the infinitive, with or without εἴθε/εἰ γάρ; the negative is μή.

εἴθε ὤφελε μὴ γράφειν.   If only he were not writing! / Would that he were not writing!
(= He should not be writing.)

ὤφελον γράψαι.   If only they had written! / Would that they had written!
(= They should have written.)

> **Preliminary exercise 3 (on C).** Translate into Greek using the following vocabulary: ᾄδω, ᾄσομαι, ᾖσα, –, ᾖσμαι, ᾔσθην "sing"; φεύγω, φεύξομαι, ἔφυγον, πέφευγα, –, – "flee."
>
> a. May they not sing! (3 ways)
> b. If only they were not singing! (5 ways)
> c. If only they had not sung! (5 ways)
> d. May he not flee! (3 ways)
> e. If only he were not fleeing! (5 ways)
> f. If only he had not fled! (5 ways)

Sentences

Translate into Greek using only words and constructions so far covered. When two verbs with different constructions could be used for an expression of forbidding or preventing, or when both ὤφελον and the indicative are possible for wishes, give both.

1. If only the archer were not deriving benefit from returning to this country! (2 ways)
2. Let us never owe anything to anyone.
3. No-one forbade us to show you the wider field.
4. Do not destroy the poison on the table immediately; let the witnesses see it.
5. May your father never allow you to return safely to his house!
6. Never stay in a position in which you will perish!
7. Your daughter's husband denied that he had opened the tent later. (2 ways)
8. Would that they had not perished badly because of (use ἕνεκα) profit! (2 ways)
9. Let us always, in a friendly fashion, give some part of our profit to the gods.
10. Always stay in your (plural) positions!
11. Let the soldiers never be absent from the camp.
12. No-one will prevent you from helping your own father and mother. (2 ways)
13. If only that old woman were not encouraging the enemy to set up a trophy! (2 ways)

14.   Everyone encouraged us as clearly as possible to show them our country.

15.   Let that slave not set up a tent in the middle of this field.

16.   Would that he had not wickedly destroyed the altars sacred to the gods! (2 ways)

17.   Let us prevent the archer from shutting those men in the prison. (2 ways)

18.   May we always know how to make (use τίθημι) good laws!

19.   Let the archer return to his own country swiftly with much bronze.

20.   Do not (repeatedly) give prayers to those newer gods; they do not know how to benefit us.

21.   If only we had returned to the bank more swiftly! (2 ways)

22.   I shall never allow his very wicked outrageous behavior to perish from my memory.

23.   Do not return to Athens; your very wretched enemies there will easily put an end to (= of) your freedom.

24.   Would that they were able to benefit us very conspicuously! (2 ways)

25.   The tyrant ordered the citizens to be shut in the acropolis as swiftly as possible.

26.   We shall encourage our rather unfortunate children not to destroy the profits of others.

27.   Do you know precisely how to prevent legislators from making (use τίθημι) bad laws? (2 ways)

28.   Do not owe money to the men around the banks; they will destroy you very swiftly if they are able.

29.   May no-one ever deny that the Greeks first showed democracy to human beings.

30.   Let the orators, since they are able to speak very clearly, forbid the archers to put (repeatedly) anything on the altars. (2 ways)

Analysis

Analyze according to the model given in chapter vi, breaking up the sentence into units with one verb form in each and showing subordination by indentation and numbering. Translate each unit into English as literally as is possible without being incomprehensible and explain each construction covered in this chapter.

1.   εἴθε σοι, ὦ Περίκλεις, τότε συνεγενόμην, ὅτε δεινότατος σαυτοῦ ταῦτα ἦσθα.

    (Xenophon, *Memorabilia* 1.2.46; δεινότατος σαυτοῦ i.e. cleverer than you are now, ταῦτα "about such things")

2.   ἐν δὲ τούτῳ ἀφικόμενος Ἀρίσταρχος ὁ ἐκ Βυζαντίου ἁρμοστής, ἔχων δύο τριήρεις, πεπεισμένος ὑπὸ Φαρναβάζου τοῖς τε ναυκλήροις ἀπεῖπε μὴ διάγειν ἐλθών τε ἐπὶ τὸ στράτευμα τοῖς στρατιώταις εἶπε μὴ περαιοῦσθαι εἰς τὴν Ἀσίαν.

(Xenophon, *Anabasis* 7.2.12; ἁρμοστής "governor," ναύκληρος "ship-master," διάγω "continue," περαιόομαι "cross")

3. Κλέαρχος δὲ τάδε εἶπεν· ἀλλ᾽ ὤφελε μὲν Κῦρος ζῆν· ἐπεὶ δὲ τετελεύτηκεν, ἀπαγγέλλετε Ἀριαίῳ ὅτι ἡμεῖς νικῶμέν τε βασιλέα καί, ὡς ὁρᾶτε, οὐδεὶς ἔτι ἡμῖν μάχεται, καί, εἰ μὴ ὑμεῖς ἤλθετε, ἐπορευόμεθα ἂν ἐπὶ βασιλέα.

(Xenophon, *Anabasis* 2.1.4; τελευτάω "die")

4. ἀπαγγελθέντος δὲ αὐτοῖς τούτου, καλέσαντες ὅ τε Κριτίας καὶ ὁ Χαρικλῆς τὸν Σωκράτην τόν τε νόμον ἐδεικνύτην αὐτῷ καὶ τοῖς νέοις ἀπειπέτην μὴ διαλέγεσθαι.

(Xenophon, *Memorabilia* 1.2.33, on a law banning Socrates from talking to young men)

5. εἰ γὰρ ὤφελον, ὦ Κρίτων, οἷοί τ᾽ εἶναι οἱ πολλοὶ τὰ μέγιστα κακὰ ἐργάζεσθαι, ἵνα οἷοί τ᾽ ἦσαν καὶ ἀγαθὰ τὰ μέγιστα, καὶ καλῶς ἂν εἶχεν.

(Plato, *Crito* 44d)

6. ἐν δὲ τῇ Σπάρτῃ ὁ Λυκοῦργος τοῖς ἐλευθέροις τῶν μὲν ἀμφὶ χρηματισμὸν ἀπεῖπε μηδενὸς ἅπτεσθαι, ὅσα δὲ ἐλευθερίαν ταῖς πόλεσι παρασκευάζει, ταῦτα ἔταξε μόνα ἔργα αὐτῶν νομίζειν.

(Xenophon, *Respublica Lacedaemoniorum* 7.2; χρηματισμόν "money-making")

7. πέμπει τῶν ἑταίρων τινὰς τῶν ἑαυτοῦ μετὰ ἱππέων πρὸς τὸ τῶν Ἀθηναίων στρατόπεδον, ἡνίκα ξυνεσκόταζεν· οἳ προσελάσαντες ἐξ ὅσου τις ἔμελλεν ἀκούσεσθαι καὶ ἀνακαλεσάμενοί τινας ὡς ὄντες τῶν Ἀθηναίων ἐπιτήδειοι (ἦσαν γάρ τινες τῷ Νικίᾳ διάγγελοι τῶν ἔνδοθεν) ἐκέλευον φράζειν Νικίᾳ μὴ ἀπάγειν τῆς νυκτὸς τὸ στράτευμα ὡς Συρακοσίων τὰς ὁδοὺς φυλασσόντων, ἀλλὰ καθ᾽ ἡσυχίαν τῆς ἡμέρας παρασκευασάμενον ἀποχωρεῖν.

(Thucydides 7.73.3–74.1, on the enemies' deceptive message to the Athenian army; ἡνίκα "when," συσκοτάζω "get dark," προσελάσαντες understand εἰς τοσοῦτον, ἀνακαλέομαι "summon," ἐπιτήδειοι i.e. from the pro-Athenian faction in Syracuse, διάγγελος "informant," ἔνδοθεν i.e. in Syracuse, καθ᾽ ἡσυχίαν "at leisure"; what does the use of ὡς tell us?)

8. ἢ οἴει, ὅτι Γοργίας ᾐσχύνθη σοι μὴ προσομολογῆσαι τὸν ῥητορικὸν ἄνδρα μὴ οὐχὶ καὶ τὰ δίκαια εἰδέναι καὶ τὰ καλὰ καὶ τὰ ἀγαθά, καὶ ἐὰν μὴ ἔλθῃ ταῦτα εἰδὼς παρ᾽ αὐτόν, αὐτὸς διδάξειν, ἔπειτα ἐκ ταύτης ἴσως τῆς ὁμολογίας ἐναντίον τι συνέβη ἐν τοῖς λόγοις – τοῦτο ὃ δὴ ἀγαπᾷς, αὐτὸς ἀγαγὼν ἐπὶ τοιαῦτα ἐρωτήματα – ἐπεὶ τίνα οἴει ἀπαρνήσεσθαι μὴ οὐχὶ καὶ αὐτὸν ἐπίστασθαι τὰ δίκαια καὶ ἄλλους διδάξειν;

(Plato, *Gorgias* 461b–c, a complaint directed at Socrates; προσομολογέομαι "admit" (taking here the special construction of εἴργω etc.), ταῦτα εἰδώς i.e.

someone who knows this already (we might be tempted to put the μή with εἰδώς if we were writing this), ὁμολογία i.e. the admission described in the previous part of the sentence, ἐναντίον i.e. "contradiction," the rhetorical question using ἀπαρνέομαι causes it to act as if it were preceded by a negative ("virtual negative"), αὐτόν i.e. Gorgias)

XVI | Temporal clauses

....

Material to learn before using this chapter: μι-verbs: aorist and perfect
   systems, δείκνυμι (Smyth §416, pages 138–40 only); Vocabulary 16
   and associated principal parts
Recommended grammar reading: Smyth §416–22, 717–67
Recommended syntax reading: Smyth §2383–2461

....

Temporal clauses have a close relationship to relative and conditional clauses and fall
into groups very similar to those taken by such types of clause. There is, however,
the additional complication that many different conjunctions can introduce temporal
clauses, and some of these conjunctions have idiosyncratic rules of their own.

Conjunctions indicating simultaneous action: ὅτε/ὁπότε "when"; ἕως "while, as long
   as."
Conjunctions indicating prior action: ἐπεί, ἐπειδή "when, after"; ἐπειδὴ τάχιστα "as
   soon as"; ἐξ οὗ, ἀφ' οὗ "since, after, ever since"; ὡς "when, since."
Conjunctions indicating subsequent action: ἕως, μέχρι "until"; πρίν "before, until."

A) Temporal clauses of fact are those expressing a definite fact, i.e. a specific action
(either one-time or continuous) in the past or present. They use the indicative; the
negative is οὐ. (These clauses resemble the simple conditions and indicative relative
clauses.)

τοὺς ἀγγέλους εἶδεν ὅτε ἀφικνοῦντο.	He saw the messengers when they arrived. / He saw the messengers as they arrived.
τοὺς ἀγγέλους εἶδεν ἐπειδὴ ἀφίκοντο.	He saw the messengers when they arrived. / He saw the messengers when they had arrived.
τοὺς ἀγγέλους οὐκ εἶδε μέχρι ἀφίκοντο.	He did not see the messengers until they arrived. / He did not see the messengers until they had arrived.

B) General temporal clauses are those expressing indefinite or repeated action (English "whenever," or an English temporal word that could be replaced by "whenever"). They take ἄν and the subjunctive in primary sequence, and the optative (without ἄν) in secondary sequence. The ἄν comes directly after the introductory conjunction and combines with it as follows: ἐπειδή + ἄν = ἐπειδάν, ὅτε + ἄν = ὅταν, ὁπότε + ἄν = ὁπόταν. The negative is μή. (These clauses belong to the indefinite construction and so resemble the general conditions and relative clauses; see chapters VII A2 and VIII F.)

τοὺς ἀγγέλους ἑώρα ὁπότε ἀφίκοιντο.	He used to see the messengers whenever they arrived.
τοὺς ἀγγέλους ὁρᾷ ὅταν ἀφίκωνται.	He sees the messengers whenever they arrive.
ἀεὶ ἑώρα αὐτοὺς ἐπειδὴ τάχιστα ἀφίκοιντο.	He always saw them as soon as they arrived.

C) Prospective temporal clauses are those anticipating a future event. They include all temporal clauses in sentences with a future main verb, and also all temporal clauses with an "until" that indicates anticipation or purpose, regardless of the tense of the main verb. They take the subjunctive or optative as above, with μή if negative. (These clauses resemble the future more vivid conditions, except when they take the optative.)

τοὺς ἀγγέλους ὄψεται ὅταν ἀφίκωνται.	He will see the messengers when they arrive. / He will see the messengers whenever they arrive.
τοὺς ἀγγέλους οὐκ ὄψεται ἕως ἂν ἀφίκωνται.	He will not see the messengers until they arrive.
ἔμενε μέχρι οἱ ἄγγελοι ἀφίκοιντο.	He waited for the messengers to arrive. / He waited until the messengers should arrive. / He waited until the messengers arrived.

The distinction between optative and indicative in sentences like the last of these has to do with the subject's motivation. In this sentence he was waiting for the messengers; had he been waiting for his brother and given up when the messengers happened to arrive and tell him that his brother was not coming, the action would have been expressed with the indicative.

ἔμενε μέχρι οἱ ἄγγελοι ἀφίκοντο.	He waited until the messengers arrived.

Preliminary exercise 1 (on A, B, and C). Identify which type of temporal clause each of the following sentences would contain in Greek, give the mood and tense that the underlined verb would have if translated into Greek, and state which conjunction(s) could be used to introduce the temporal clause.

a.   Goats eat flowers whenever they <u>see</u> them.
b.   That goat will eat your flowers as soon as she <u>sees</u> them.
c.   The goat ate my flowers as soon as she <u>saw</u> them.
d.   We were waiting for the princess <u>to ride</u> past.
e.   We waited until the clock <u>struck</u> twelve, but she never appeared.
f.   We saw the princess when she <u>was riding</u> in her carriage.
g.   When the princess <u>appears</u> we shall wave at her.
h.   We always used to wave at the princess when she <u>was looking</u> at the crowd.
i.   We waved at the princess as long as we <u>could</u> see her.
j.   We are waiting for the princess <u>to appear</u>.
k.   We told jokes while we <u>were waiting</u>.
l.   We waited until it <u>started</u> to rain, and then we gave up.
m.   It poured rain while we <u>were waiting</u>.

D) Temporal clauses with πρίν have two constructions. In sentences without a negative in the main clause, πρίν means "before" and takes the infinitive (change of subject in accusative). But in sentences with a negative main clause, the idea "not . . . before" is equivalent to "until," and πρίν therefore acts like other conjunctions meaning "until" and takes a dependent clause following the rules given above.[1] Sentences with a positive main clause and "until" cannot be translated with πρίν but require ἕως or μέχρι.

τοὺς ἀγγέλους εἶδε πρὶν ἀφικέσθαι.	He saw the messengers before he arrived. / He saw the messengers before arriving.
τοὺς ἀγγέλους εἶδε πρὶν αὐτοὺς ἀφικέσθαι.	He saw the messengers before they arrived.
τοὺς ἀγγέλους ὄψεται πρὶν αὐτοὺς ἀφικέσθαι.	He will see the messengers before they arrive.
τοὺς ἀγγέλους οὐκ εἶδε πρὶν ἀφίκοντο.	He did not see the messengers before they arrived. / He did not see the messengers until they arrived.

---

[1] Therefore English sentences with "until" after a positive main verb can only be translated with ἕως or μέχρι, but those with "until" after a negative main verb can be translated with ἕως, μέχρι, or πρίν.

τοὺς ἀγγέλους οὐκ ὄψεται πρὶν ἂν ἀφίκωνται.	He will not see the messengers before they arrive. / He will not see the messengers until they arrive.

Preliminary exercise 2 (on D). For each of the sentences below, indicate how the underlined word would be translated in Greek (if there is more than one option, give them all) and whether it would be followed by an infinitive, indicative, or subjunctive verb.

a.   The king arrived at the castle before we saw him.
b.   The king did not stop for rest before he reached the castle.
c.   The king's attendants waited until he was ready to continue.
d.   The king made sure he was looking his best before he arrived at the castle.
e.   The queen did not see the king until he entered the courtyard.
f.   We got to the castle before the king arrived.
g.   The king will ignore everyone until he greets the queen.
h.   The king did not speak to anyone until he had greeted the queen.
i.   The queen will not have a chance to speak to the king in private before he goes to bed.
j.   The queen waited until a messenger arrived to say that the king would not come that day.
k.   The castle was scrubbed from battlements to dungeon before the king came to see it.
l.   The king will not leave the castle until he has rested.
m.   The queen arrived at the castle before the king did.
n.   The king is not going anywhere before he has had something to eat.
o.   The queen waited in the courtyard until the king arrived.

Sentences

Translate into Greek using only words and constructions so far covered; use temporal clauses instead of temporal participles, and use πρίν for "until" whenever possible.

1.   He cleansed the bronze before he sold it to us.
2.   Wanting to deceive us, the good-for-nothing man flattered us until we trusted him.
3.   Wanting to deceive us, the very wicked man flattered us until he thought we trusted him.

4. Whenever he is wronged by some enemy, a true philosopher laughs and forgets.

5. Are you waiting to embark in this ship?

6. The thief did not give me back my horse until I shouted to the guards.

7. The prostitute's beauty enslaved my son before her lies caused him to revolt.

8. They always used to revolt as soon as their king died.

9. The soldiers waited in the plain for us to break the gates.

10. The children slept until you awakened them.

11. The slaves revolted from their masters before opening the gates on behalf of the enemy.

12. Collect money until that which we have suffices.

13. You can't eat while you are laughing, can you?

14. Whenever the assembly at Athens voted for an expedition, the rich men used to equip it.

15. Do not hand over the rule to your son until he is able to manage the affairs himself.

16. When the tyrant had destroyed our town and enslaved us, he attacked you.

17. You were sleeping while the enemy was destroying our army, weren't you?

18. The corpses on the plain had all been buried before the soldiers set up a trophy to indicate the victory.

19. Will this money suffice until we go to the bank?

20. I waited two days for my father to return.

21. Before she married, my mother tended her father until he died.

22. Our mother is with us whenever we sleep.

23. As long as the king was distributing bread to the citizens and filling the crowd with wine, everyone attended him; only the end of the bread and wine caused the populace to revolt.

24. We liked the king even before you displayed the benefit he gave your city.

25. That tyrant always enslaves some citizen when a slave dies.

26–8. Let us give the hero back his wife quickly, before he destroys the city and enslaves us all! – But how would we be able to hand her over safely? – Let someone shout to the attackers while they are trying to break the wall, and encourage their leader to stand near the gates. When he is standing there, open the gates a little: when she sees her husband, the woman will go out.

29. Many people do not become experienced until they become old men.

30. This traitor filled our town with bandits whenever the citizens were voting.

Analysis

Analyze according to the model given in chapter VI, breaking up the sentence into units with one verb form in each and showing subordination by indentation and numbering. Translate each unit into English as literally as is possible without being incomprehensible and explain each temporal clause.

1. ἄρχοντα οὖν αἱροῦμαι τῆς πόσεως, ἕως ἂν ὑμεῖς ἱκανῶς πίητε, ἐμαυτόν.

    (Plato, *Symposium* 213e, Alcibiades' drinking rules; πόσις "drinking")

2. δραπετεύω οὖν αὐτὸν καὶ φεύγω, καὶ ὅταν ἴδω, αἰσχύνομαι τὰ ὡμολογημένα.

    (Plato, *Symposium* 216b; δραπετεύω "run away from")

3. λέγεται γὰρ Ἀλκιβιάδην, πρὶν εἴκοσιν ἐτῶν εἶναι, Περικλεῖ ἐπιτρόπῳ μὲν ὄντι ἑαυτοῦ, προστάτῃ δὲ τῆς πόλεως, τοιάδε διαλεχθῆναι περὶ νόμων.

    (Xenophon, *Memorabilia* 1.2.40; ἐπίτροπος "guardian," προστάτης "leader")

4. ὁ δὲ εἱστήκει μέχρι ἕως ἐγένετο καὶ ἥλιος ἀνέσχεν· ἔπειτα ᾤχετ' ἀπιὼν προσευξάμενος τῷ ἡλίῳ.

    (Plato, *Symposium* 220d, on Socrates standing and thinking; ἀνέχω "rise," προσεύχομαι "pray")

5. ἡμῖν πρὶν σὲ εἰσελθεῖν ἔδοξε χρῆναι ἐπὶ δεξιὰ ἕκαστον ἐν μέρει λόγον περὶ Ἔρωτος εἰπεῖν ὡς δύναιτο κάλλιστον, καὶ ἐγκωμιάσαι.

    (Plato, *Symposium* 214b, explanation to Alcibiades of the symposium's original rules; χρῆναι i.e. "to oblige," ἐπὶ δεξιὰ "from left to right," μέρος i.e. "turn," ἐγκωμιάζω "praise")

6. ταῦτα δὲ εἰπόντες ἀλλήλοις σπονδὰς ἐποιήσαντο, ἕως ἀπαγγελθείη τὰ λεχθέντα Δερκυλίδᾳ μὲν εἰς Λακεδαίμονα, Τισσαφέρνει δὲ ἐπὶ βασιλέα.

    (Xenophon, *Hellenica* 3.2.20)

7. περιεμένομεν οὖν ἑκάστοτε ἕως ἀνοιχθείη τὸ δεσμωτήριον, διατρίβοντες μετ' ἀλλήλων, ἀνεῴγετο γὰρ οὐ πρῴ· ἐπειδὴ δὲ ἀνοιχθείη, εἰσῇμεν παρὰ τὸν Σωκράτη καὶ τὰ πολλὰ διημερεύομεν μετ' αὐτοῦ. καὶ δὴ καὶ τότε πρωαίτερον συνελέγημεν· τῇ γὰρ προτεραίᾳ ἐπειδὴ ἐξήλθομεν ἐκ τοῦ δεσμωτηρίου ἑσπέρας, ἐπυθόμεθα ὅτι τὸ πλοῖον ἐκ Δήλου ἀφιγμένον εἴη.

    (Plato, *Phaedo* 59d–e, on how the speaker came to be with Socrates when he died; ἑκάστοτε "every time," διατρίβω "pass time," διημερεύω "spend the day," πρωαίτερον "earlier," συλλέγω "gather")

8. ἀκούσατε οὖν μου πρὸς θεῶν, καὶ ἐὰν μὲν ἐγὼ φαίνωμαι ἀδικεῖν, οὐ χρή με ἐνθένδε ἀπελθεῖν πρὶν ἂν δῶ δίκην· ἂν δ' ὑμῖν φαίνωνται ἀδικεῖν οἱ ἐμὲ διαβάλλοντες, οὕτως αὐτοῖς χρῆσθε ὥσπερ ἄξιον.

    (Xenophon, *Anabasis* 5.7.5)

9. τῶν τε γὰρ νεκρῶν ἀτάφων ὄντων, ὁπότε τις ἴδοι τινὰ τῶν ἐπιτηδείων κείμενον,
    ἐς λύπην μετὰ φόβου καθίστατο, καὶ οἱ ζῶντες καταλειπόμενοι τραυματίαι τε
    καὶ ἀσθενεῖς πολὺ τῶν τεθνεώτων τοῖς ζῶσι λυπηρότεροι ἦσαν καὶ τῶν ἀπο-
    λωλότων ἀθλιώτεροι.

    (Thucydides 7.75.3; ἄταφος "unburied," ἐπιτήδειος "friend," τραυματίας
    "wounded man")

Review exercises 3

Translate into Greek, adding connecting words as appropriate.

1. DAUGHTER: O mother, I fear that my father will not be present when we embark in order to sail to Athens. He often used to neglect us on the grounds that we know how to help ourselves, so that I am annoyed.

    MOTHER: O very wretched daughter, stop slandering your father! And do not disturb me any longer.[1] Whenever I am trying to sleep, you prevent me. Do not deny that you knowingly[2] bring it about that I never sleep!

    DAUGHTER: If only you did not always blame me! You speak so bitterly that I am afraid to be with you.

    MOTHER: I repent of the things that have been said. Let us send someone as trustworthy as possible to tell your father to return immediately, before we sail. Everyone knows where he is.

    DAUGHTER: O mother, no-one is ever truly disappointed in you with respect to anything; you are by far the best of mothers. Let Xanthias[3] go, because he is faster than the other slaves.

    MOTHER: O Xanthias, see to it that you go to my husband and tell him not to delay but to return at once.

2. When I first saw Socrates, I was afraid to speak, on the grounds that he was much too sensible to listen to a young woman. But before he had spoken long (= for much time), I knew he was by far the kindest of men, and he swiftly brought it about that I always arrived early at the agora in order to hear him. "May nothing ever prevent him from being present! Gods, give us Socrates always," I used to pray until I saw him. Now, however, I weep, "If only the wisest of our citizens had not died!" Socrates was so skilled in all arts that everyone used to derive benefit from hearing him, and no-one of us (feminine) was ever afraid that he would not amuse us. Whenever the priests sent someone to encourage him to spend (time) in the temple, he used to go up there (i.e. to the temple) only (do not use adverbial μόνον) on condition that we came too.

---

[1] See chapter XIV C: "any longer" is to "no longer" as "anyone" is to "no-one."
[2] A Greek circumstantial participle can be the equivalent of an English adverb.   [3] Ξανθίας, -ου, ὁ.

3.   PRIEST: O king, help me! I no longer have any cows to sacrifice. Send someone as fast as possible to buy a rather good cow before the altars become empty.

   KING: I'm afraid that some of my slaves are so lazy that they cannot go to the market, and others are too unjust to be sent with money. My comrades are absent – if only they were present here! When they return, I shall tell them to bring you the best of all the cows in the market.

   PRIEST: Do not deny that your daughter is present. Let her go to the market.

   KING: My daughter is afraid to be seen by the men in the market, because they used to shout to her whenever they saw her, on the grounds that she is rather beautiful. Let us send your daughter to buy the cow.

   PRIEST: Everyone knows that my daughter is by far the most sacred of the women of the town. I forbid you to send her. See to it that your daughter goes at once.

   KING: Who is the king here, I or you?

XVII | Impersonal constructions and verbal adjectives

Material to learn before using this chapter: ἵημι, κεῖμαι, κάθημαι, δέω, χρή
(Smyth §397a, 777, 790–3); Vocabulary 17 and associated principal
parts
Recommended grammar reading: Smyth §777–82, 789–93
Recommended syntax reading: Smyth §932–5, 2076–8, 2149–52

A) Impersonal verbs are ones regularly used in the third person singular with an understood "it" as subject. They often take an infinitive and/or object(s), but the exact construction depends on the particular verb involved.

δεῖ με γράψαι.	I must write. / I have to write. / It is necessary for me to write.
ἔξεστί μοι γράψαι.	It is possible for me to write.
ἔδοξέ μοι γράψαι.	It seemed best to me to write. / I decided to write.
δεῖ μοι τούτου.	I need this. / I lack this.
μεταμέλει μοι τούτου.	I repent of this. / I am sorry about this.

1) Usually when these verbs are themselves negated the negative is οὐ, but when the infinitives they govern are negated, the negative is μή. Note that οὐ χρή means "ought not to / must not," but οὐ δεῖ with an infinitive can mean either "must not" or "does not have to."

οὐκ ἔξεστί μοι γράψαι.	It is not possible for me to write.
ἔξεστί μοι μὴ γράψαι.	It is possible for me not to write.
οὐ δεῖ μοι τούτου.	I do not need this. / I do not lack this.
οὐ χρή με γράψαι.	I ought not to write. / I should not write. / I must not write.
οὐ δεῖ με γράψαι.	I do not have to write. / It is not necessary for me to write. / I must not write. / It is necessary for me not to write.
δεῖ με μὴ γράψαι.	I must not write. / It is necessary for me not to write.
ἀνάγκη οὐδεμία ἐστί μοι γράψαι.	I have no need to write. / I do not have to write. / It is not necessary for me to write.

2) When they occur in the past tense, impersonal verbs indicating obligation, propriety, necessity, or possibility usually indicate that the action of their dependent infinitives is unfulfilled. With a present infinitive the obligation etc. is present, and with an aorist infinitive it is past.[1]

ἔδει με γράφειν.	I should be writing (but I am not).
χρῆν με γράψαι.	I should have written (but I did not).
ἐξῆν μοι γράφειν.	I could be writing (but I am not).
But note:	
οὐκ ἔδει με γράψαι.	I did not have to write. / It was necessary for me not to write (but I did anyway). / I should not have written.

3) Impersonal verbs can form neuter singular participles, but those participles do not agree with anything, since the verbs have no subjects. Therefore they are always used in an absolute construction; not the genitive absolute as for all other verbs, but the accusative absolute. Note that by definition all accusative absolute constructions are in their essence one-word phrases, as opposed to the two-word phrases of genitives absolute.

ἐξὸν ἀπελθεῖν ἔμενον.	They remained when (although, since) it was possible to depart.
δέον ἀπελθεῖν ἔμενον.	They remained when (although, since) it was necessary to depart.

4) The set of words used as accusatives absolute is not exactly the same as the set of impersonal verbs. Useful participles to know, in addition to ἐξόν and δέον, are παρόν "it being possible," ἀδύνατον ὄν "it being impossible," δόξαν "it having been determined,"

---

[1] Note the distinctions among the following: χρή με γράφειν "I should write" indicates that the speaker currently has an obligation to write but does not indicate whether he is fulfilling the obligation; χρῆν με γράφειν "I should be writing" and ἐξῆν με γράφειν "I could be writing" indicate that the speaker is not fulfilling his obligation or opportunity to write; γράφοιμι ἄν "I might write," "I could write," "I would write" indicate a remote future potential for writing, but not a present obligation or opportunity; ἔγραφον ἄν "I would be writing" indicates that the speaker is not writing, but not whether the possibility is available. If one's variety of English makes these same distinctions between the different English forms used as translations, the Greek is not difficult to remember. Those whose English dialects do not provide this assistance can help themselves by remembering that in formal written English the present progressive ("be doing") is contrafactual after modal verbs, while the simple present is not: thus "should be doing," "could be doing," "would be doing," "ought to be doing" etc. generally indicate that the action is not taking place, while "should do," "could do," "would do," "ought to do", etc. have no such force.

προσῆκον "it being fitting," παρασχόν "when there was an opportunity," and εἰρημένον "it being stated."

> **Preliminary exercise 1 (on A).** Translate into Greek using the examples above and the following vocabulary: μάχομαι, μαχοῦμαι, ἐμαχεσάμην, –, μεμάχημαι, – "fight."
>
> a. We must not fight. (3 ways)
> b. when it was possible to fight (2 ways)
> c. We should have fought. (2 ways)
> d. It is possible for us not to fight.
> e. We do not need this.
> f. It seemed best to us to fight.
> g. when it was necessary to fight
> h. We did not have to fight.
> i. We are sorry for this.
> j. We have no need to fight.
> k. We could be fighting.
> l. We do not have to fight.
> m. We need this.
> n. We ought not to fight.
> o. It is possible for us to fight.
> p. We must fight. (3 ways)
> q. We should be fighting. (2 ways)
> r. when it was impossible to fight
> s. It is not possible for us to fight.

B) Verbal adjectives are used (like the Latin gerundive) to express obligation.

1) Formation. Most verbal adjectives are formed from the sixth principal part of the verb, by removing the augment and the -θην (or -ην if there is no θ) and adding -τέος.[2]

λύω . . . ἐλύθην → λυτέος   γράφω . . . ἐγράφην → γραπτέος
δίδωμι . . . ἐδόθην → δοτέος   ἄρχω . . . ἤρχθην → ἀρκτέος
στέλλω . . . ἐστάλην → σταλτέος

---

[2] If the verb stem ends in a consonant after -θην/-ην is dropped, that consonant may need to be adjusted when in contact with the τ: β and φ change to π, and γ and χ change to κ.

Some verbal adjectives are formed from what would be the sixth principal part of verbs that do not otherwise have such a part, and others are formed irregularly; note these:

βαίνω → -βατέος	εἶμι → ἰτέος	θάπτω → θαπτέος
φέρω → οἰστέος	θύω → θυτέος	κλέπτω → κλεπτέος
ἔχω → ἑκτέος, -σχετέος³	οἶδα → ἰστέος	λέγω → ῥητέος, λεκτέος
τίθημι → θετέος	ἵημι → -ἑτέος	ἀμύνω → ἀμυντέος

The verbal adjectives decline like ἄξιος: λυτέος, λυτέα, λυτέον.

2) Usage: personal construction. A verbal adjective from a transitive verb (one that takes an accusative object) can modify a noun (or pronoun) to indicate that an action must be performed on that noun. Usually this construction is found in the nominative, and the verbal adjective functions as a predicate adjective with a form of εἰμί expressed or understood. The agent, if expressed, is in the dative.

ταῦτα ποιητέα.	These things must be done. / (One) must do these things.
θαπτέος μοι ὁ ἀδελφὸς ἦν.	My brother had to be buried by me. / I had to bury my brother.
ποταμός τις ἡμῖν ἐστι διαβατέος.	A river must be crossed by us. / We must cross a river.
ὠφελητέα σοι ἡ πόλις ἐστίν.	The city must be benefitted by you. / You must benefit the city.

3) Usage: impersonal construction. A verbal adjective from any verb, whether transitive or not, can appear in the neuter nominative singular to indicate that an action must be performed; ἐστί or a similar word is expressed or understood. In this construction the verbal adjective acts like a noun and does not agree with anything; it may take an object in whatever case that verb usually takes, and an agent in the dative. An English translation cannot be literal. Note that this is the only possible construction for the verbal adjectives of intransitive verbs.

ταῦτα ποιητέον.	These things must be done. / (One) must do these things.
θαπτέον μοι τὸν ἀδελφὸν ἦν.	I had to bury my brother.

---

³ I.e. the verbal adjective of ἔχω is ἑκτέος, but that of compounds of ἔχω is σχετέος.

ἀκουστέον ἔσται ἡμῖν αὐτοῦ.	We will have to hear him.
πειστέον σοι τῷ πατρί.	You must obey your father. / Your father must obey you.
οὐχ ἁμαρτητέον τοῦ οἴκου.	(We, you, I, one) must not miss the house.

Sometimes this construction is used with the neuter plural instead of the singular.

θαπτέα μοι τὸν ἀδελφόν.	I must bury my brother.

4) With both constructions the negative is οὐ; it indicates an obligation that the action not be done ("must not").

ταῦτα οὐ ποιητέα.	These things must not be done.
ταῦτα οὐ ποιητέον ἡμῖν.	We must not do these things.
οὐκ ἀκουστέον σοι αὐτοῦ.	You must not listen to him.

Preliminary exercise 2 (on B). Translate into Greek with verbal adjectives, using the examples above and the following vocabulary: κύων, κυνός, ὁ "dog."

a. You (plural) must not release the dogs. (2 ways)
b. I must know.
c. They must not hear you (singular).
d. The dogs had to be buried. (2 ways)
e. We had to go.
f. The dog must not be sacrificed. (2 ways)
g. He must not know this.
h. I had to carry the dog. (2 ways)
i. The dog will have to be released. (2 ways)
j. They will have to speak.
k. The dogs must be carried. (2 ways)
l. One must know these things. (2 ways)
m. You must bury the dog. (2 ways)
n. You must not go.
o. They will have to sacrifice the dog. (2 ways)
p. They had to hear us.

Sentences 1

Translate into Greek using verbal adjectives; if both personal and impersonal constructions are possible, give both.

1.   You must never laugh at your mother.
2.   No-one must ever betray our tribe. (2 ways)
3.   Sometimes one must be angry with lazy house-slaves.
4.   If we resist the men who want to imprison us, they will have to let us go. (2 ways)
5.   All the enemy's soldiers must be scattered before we can attack the town.
6.   We must not despise the men of that tribe: they are the most courageous of the Greeks.
7.   We must all work if we wish to be happy.
8.   The city must set its best general over this expedition, someone who (whoever) surpasses all the others both in courage and in judgement. (2 ways)
9.   We must all defend the city against the enemy if we wish to prevail over the foreigners. (2 ways)
10. I must seat the messengers beside the middle table before my master asks where they are sitting. (2 ways)
11. Must you put bread on your head when everyone is present? (2 ways)
12. We must defend democracy and freedom by punishing the foreigners who attacked us.

Sentences 2

Translate into Greek using impersonal verbs; when more than one impersonal verb is possible, give all possibilities. Use accusatives absolute rather than temporal clauses where possible; be prepared to use words in the list of accusative absolute participles given in A4 above.

1.   You must not be angry with your mother. (3 ways)
2.   When it is possible to work, do not sit at home! (2 ways)
3.   We could have made an attempt on the tyrant, but the old men said it was not advantageous for us.
4.   It is not proper for corpses to lie in the streets; they should be buried.
5.   The assembly did not have to set this foolish man over our army. (2 ways)
6.   It is possible never to enrage anyone, but it is difficult.

7.   You should be sending missiles against the enemy, (and) not sitting at home! (2 ways)

8.   We need more ships: we beg you to return as quickly as possible.

9.   When it is necessary not to be angry, I can never prevail over myself. (2 ways)

10. You (plural) would be better off not resisting the invading army: it will not be possible for you to conquer (it).

11. He never repented of whatever he did.

12. Although it was possible not to betray us, you had to shout! (3 ways)

13. Her children did not have a share of her possessions; therefore they lacked many things, but this was not a concern to her husband, although he was their father.

14. You should not have sold your own soul. (2 ways)

15. Since it has not been decided to imprison us, perhaps they will let us go.

16. It is always necessary to be hated by some people, but it is never necessary to be hated by everyone. (2 ways)

17. It is proper for a tyrant to be hated by noble citizens.

18. Who in this city lacks bread? Is anyone begging his companions for this?

19. Although it had been decided not to defend that island, the general did not depart.

20. Children must not despise old men and old women. (3 ways)

Analysis

Analyze according to the model given in chapter VI, breaking up the sentence into units with one verb form in each and showing subordination by indentation and numbering. Translate each unit into English as literally as is possible without being incomprehensible and explain each construction covered in this chapter.

1.   οὔκουν δεῖ οὔτε ἑνὸς ἀνδρὸς ἕνεκα οὔτε δυοῖν ἡμᾶς τοὺς ἄλλους τῆς Ἑλλάδος ἀπέχεσθαι, ἀλλὰ πειστέον ὅ τι ἂν κελεύωσι· καὶ γὰρ αἱ πόλεις ἡμῶν ὅθεν ἐσμὲν πείθονται αὐτοῖς.

     (Xenophon, *Anabasis* 6.6.14, on the power of the Spartans (αὐτοῖς and subject of κελεύωσι); ἀπέχομαι "be kept away from," supply ἐστίν after πειστέον)

2.   ἐπειδὴ δὲ οὐδαμῇ ταύτῃ ἤνυτον, ἔδοξέ μοι ἐπιθετέον εἶναι τῷ ἀνδρὶ κατὰ τὸ καρτερὸν καὶ οὐκ ἀνετέον, ἐπειδήπερ ἐνεκεχειρήκη, ἀλλὰ ἰστέον ἤδη τί ἐστι τὸ πρᾶγμα.

     (Plato, *Symposium* 217c; ἀνύτω "make progress," ἀνίημι "give up," ἐγχειρέω "undertake")

3.   καὶ μὲν δὴ οὐκ ἐν τῇ οἰκίᾳ ἀλλ᾽ ἐν τῇ ὁδῷ, σῴζειν τε αὐτὸν καὶ τὰ τούτοις ἐψηφισμένα παρόν, συλλαβὼν ἀπήγαγεν.

(Lysias, *Oration* 12.30, on someone who arrested the speaker's brother (αὐτόν) rather than taking the opportunity to save him from the thirty tyrants (τούτοις); σώζω both "save" and "keep," ψηφίζω "decree")

4. ποταμὸς δ᾽ εἰ μέν τις καὶ ἄλλος ἄρα ἡμῖν ἐστι διαβατέος οὐκ οἶδα· τὸν δ᾽ οὖν Εὐφράτην ἴσμεν ὅτι ἀδύνατον διαβῆναι κωλυόντων πολεμίων.

   (Xenophon, *Anabasis* 2.4.6)

5. οὐκοῦν καὶ τῶν μὲν μαχομένων ἀπειλητικὰ τὰ ὄμματα ἀπεικαστέον, τῶν δὲ νενικηκότων εὐφραινομένων ἡ ὄψις μιμητέα;

   (Xenophon, *Memorabilia* 3.10.8; ἀπειλητικός "threatening," ἀπεικάζω "represent" (in art), εὐφραίνομαι "be happy")

6. οὐ τοσαῦτα μὲν πεδία ἃ ὑμεῖς φίλια ὄντα σὺν πολλῷ πόνῳ διαπορεύεσθε, τοσαῦτα δὲ ὄρη ὁρᾶτε ὑμῖν ὄντα πορευτέα, ἃ ἡμῖν ἔξεστι προκαταλαβοῦσιν ἄπορα ὑμῖν παρέχειν, τοσοῦτοι δ᾽ εἰσὶ ποταμοὶ ἐφ᾽ ὧν ἔξεστιν ἡμῖν ταμιεύεσθαι ὁπόσοις ἂν ὑμῶν βουλώμεθα μάχεσθαι;

   (Xenophon, *Anabasis* 2.5.18, a threatening speech from invaders to natives; φίλιος "friendly," ἄπορα παρέχω "make impassable," ταμιεύομαι "control")

7. μετὰ ταῦτα Χειρίσοφος εἶπεν· Ἀλλ᾽ εἰ μέν τινος ἄλλου δεῖ πρὸς τούτοις οἷς λέγει Ξενοφῶν, καὶ αὐτίκα ἐξέσται ποιεῖν· ἃ δὲ νῦν εἴρηκε δοκεῖ μοι ὡς τάχιστα ψηφίσασθαι ἄριστον εἶναι· καὶ ὅτῳ δοκεῖ ταῦτα, ἀνατεινάτω τὴν χεῖρα.

   (Xenophon, *Anabasis* 3.2.33; καὶ αὐτίκα i.e. "later," ποιεῖν i.e. "discuss," ἀνατείνω "hold up")

8. καὶ πολλοῖς τῶν συνόντων προηγόρευε τὰ μὲν ποιεῖν, τὰ δὲ μὴ ποιεῖν, ὡς τοῦ δαιμονίου προσημαίνοντος· καὶ τοῖς μὲν πειθομένοις αὐτῷ συνέφερε, τοῖς δὲ μὴ πειθομένοις μετέμελε.

   (Xenophon, *Memorabilia* 1.1.4, on the quality of Socrates' advice when guided by his daimon; προαγορεύω "tell beforehand")

9. ἀθύμως γὰρ ἁπάντων τῶν συμμάχων διακειμένων, καὶ Πελοποννησίων μὲν διατειχιζόντων τὸν Ἰσθμὸν καὶ ζητούντων ἰδίαν αὑτοῖς σωτηρίαν, τῶν δ᾽ ἄλλων πόλεων ὑπὸ τοῖς βαρβάροις γεγενημένων καὶ συστρατευομένων ἐκείνοις πλὴν εἴ τις διὰ μικρότητα παρημελήθη, προσπλεουσῶν δὲ τριήρων διακοσίων καὶ χιλίων καὶ πεζῆς στρατιᾶς ἀναριθμήτου μελλούσης εἰς τὴν Ἀττικὴν εἰσβάλλειν, οὐδεμιᾶς σωτηρίας αὑτοῖς ὑποφαινομένης, ἀλλ᾽ ἔρημοι συμμάχων γεγενημένοι καὶ τῶν ἐλπίδων ἁπασῶν διημαρτηκότες, ἐξὸν αὐτοῖς μὴ μόνον τοὺς παρόντας κινδύνους διαφυγεῖν, ἀλλὰ καὶ τιμὰς ἐξαιρέτους λαβεῖν ἃς αὐτοῖς ἐδίδου βασιλεὺς ἡγούμενος, εἰ τὸ τῆς πόλεως προσλάβοι ναυτικόν, παραχρῆμα

καὶ Πελοποννήσου κρατήσειν, οὐχ ὑπέμειναν τὰς παρ' ἐκείνου δωρεὰς οὐδ', ὀργισθέντες τοῖς Ἕλλησιν ὅτι προυδόθησαν, ἀσμένως ἐπὶ τὰς διαλλαγὰς τὰς πρὸς τοὺς βαρβάρους ὥρμησαν, ἀλλ' αὐτοὶ μὲν ὑπὲρ τῆς ἐλευθερίας πολεμεῖν παρεσκευάζοντο, τοῖς δ' ἄλλοις τὴν δουλείαν αἱρουμένοις συγγνώμην εἶχον.

(Isocrates, *Panegyricus* 93–5; διάκειμαι "be disposed," διατειχίζω "build a wall across," παραμελέω "pass by and disregard," ὑποφαίνομαι "appear," διαμαρτάνω "fail to obtain," ἐξαίρετος "special," ἐδίδου "was offering," πόλεως refers to Athens, προσλαμβάνω "take over," ναυτικόν "fleet," παραχρῆμα "at once," ὑπέμειναν (ὑπομένω "submit to" i.e. accept) has "the Athenians" as understood subject, ἀσμένως "gladly," διαλλαγή "reconciliation," συγγνώμην ἔχω "forgive")

XVIII | *Oratio obliqua*

Material to learn before using this chapter: remaining aorists,
consonant-stem perfects (Smyth §402, 406–7); Vocabulary 18 and
associated principal parts
Recommended grammar reading: Smyth §400–11
Recommended syntax reading: Smyth §2617–35

Oratio obliqua is extended indirect discourse and indirect discourse containing complex sentences. It involves all the rules of indirect discourse already given (indirect statement, indirect questions, and indirect commands, chapters x, xi, and xv). Moreover, when the direct version of a speech is turned into *oratio obliqua*, the following additional changes are made:

A) The **persons** of verbs and pronouns are changed as dictated by logic, usually to the third person; the changes are the same in Greek as in English.

Direct	Indirect
φιλῶ σε. I like you.	(οὗτος) ἔφη φιλεῖν αὐτήν. He said he liked her.
	(αὕτη) ἔφη φιλεῖν αὐτόν. She said she liked him.
	Also possible but much less common:
	ἔφην φιλεῖν αὐτήν (αὐτόν, σε). I said I liked her (him, you).
	ἔφησθα φιλεῖν αὐτήν (αὐτόν, με). You said you liked her (him, me).
	ἔφη φιλεῖν με (σε). He (she) said he (she) liked me (you).

Care is needed in the use of reflexives and other pronouns. Usually, ambiguity can be avoided by using direct reflexives to refer back to the subject of the original sentence, indirect reflexives to refer to the subject of the introductory verb, and words like αὐτόν or οὗτος to refer to persons not the subject of either of those verbs. Sometimes, however, other solutions are needed; this is particularly true in the case of double indirect discourse. In such cases there are no firm rules to follow; the important thing is to avoid ambiguity.

Direct	Indirect
μισεῖ ἑαυτόν. He hates himself.	ἔφασαν τοῦτον μισεῖν ἑαυτόν. They said he hated himself.
μισεῖ ἡμᾶς. He hates us.	ἔφασαν τοῦτον μισεῖν σφᾶς. They said he hated them.
μισεῖ αὐτήν. He hates her.	ἔφασαν τοῦτον μισεῖν αὐτήν. They said he hated her.

B) Words denoting **place and time** are changed to accommodate the changed perspective of the new speaker.

Direct	Indirect
νῦν δεῦρο ἔρχεται. She is coming here now.	εἶπεν ὅτι αὕτη τότε ἐκεῖσε ἴοι. He said that she was going there then.

C) A **subject pronoun** may be needed in the indirect version where none was needed in the direct version, even for finite verbs.

Direct	Indirect
βιβλίον γράφει. He is writing a book.	ἔφη τοῦτον βιβλίον γράφειν. εἶπεν ὅτι οὗτος βιβλίον γράφοι/γράφει. He said that he (different person) was writing a book.

D) All main verbs of statements that become indirect are changed according to the rules of the type of indirect statement employed (see chapter x), but the **verbs of subordinate clauses** do not follow the same rules. Subordinate verbs may always remain as in that direct version (which is often a different tense from that of the English equivalent), but in secondary sequence originally subordinate indicatives and subjunctives may be changed to the optative (tense as in the direct version), unless they were originally in past tenses of the indicative, in which case they cannot be changed.[1] This rule holds irrespective of whether the main verb of the indirect discourse is in the optative, indicative, infinitive, or participle: subordinate verbs do not become infinitives or participles because of *oratio obliqua*.

Direct	Indirect
ἔχει ἃ γράφω βιβλία. He has the books I am writing.	ἔφασαν αὐτὸν ἔχειν ἃ αὕτη γράφει/γράφοι βιβλία. They said he had the books she was writing. εἶπον ὅτι ἔχοι ἃ αὕτη γράφει/γράφοι βιβλία. They said he had the books she was writing. λέγουσιν ὅτι ἔχει ἃ αὕτη γράφει βιβλία. They say he has the books she is writing.
ἔχει ἃ ἔγραψα βιβλία. He has the books I wrote.	ἔφασαν αὐτὸν ἔχειν ἃ αὕτη ἔγραψε βιβλία. They said he had the books she had written. εἶπον ὅτι ἔχοι ἃ αὕτη ἔγραψε βιβλία. They said he had the books she had written.

---

[1] An original infinitive or participle can never be changed.

E) When a subordinate verb is dependent upon a verb that is itself dependent upon another verb, **sequence** is determined by the rule that secondary sequence always takes precedence over primary: if *any* verb in the chain of dependency is in a secondary tense (aorist, imperfect, or pluperfect), the subordinate verb is in secondary sequence. Primary-sequence forms, however, are usually still possible by the vivid/retained construction.

λέγει ὅτι ἦλθεν ἵνα γράφοι/γράφῃ.	He says he came to write.
εἶπεν ὅτι ἴοι/ἔρχεται ἵνα γράφοι/γράφῃ.	He said he was coming to write.

F) Conditional sentences (and related constructions such as conditional relatives) in *oratio obliqua* follow the above rules, with a few wrinkles of their own:

Protasis: if the verb of saying is primary, the verb of the protasis does not change. If the verb of saying is secondary, the verb of the protasis may become optative (tense unchanged), unless it is a past tense of the indicative, in which case there can be no change (i.e. protases, being subordinate clauses, follow rule D above). An original ἐάν remains unchanged unless its verb is changed to the optative; if that happens, ἐάν becomes εἰ.

Apodosis: follows the standard rules for main clauses in indirect statement (chapter x); ἄν is always retained. But in the **ὅτι construction** there is no change after a primary introductory verb; if the introductory verb is secondary, the verb of the apodosis may become optative *even if* it is a past tense of the indicative (since it is not originally a sub-ordinate clause, rule D does not apply). *But* if the apodosis has ἄν, its verb *must* remain unchanged (to avoid ambiguity between future less vivid and contrafactual clauses). Even if there is no ἄν, original imperfects and pluperfects usually do not change.[2]

In the **infinitive and participle constructions**, the verb of the apodosis *must always* be changed to the corresponding tense of the infinitive or participle (imperfects become presents and pluperfects become perfects), and the subject must be added (in the accusative) unless it is the same as the subject of the introductory verb. If there was an ἄν with the verb in the direct version, there must be an ἄν with the infinitive or participle in the indirect version.

> **Preliminary exercise 1.** Take two sentences, first "If we do anything, she sees it" and then "If we say anything, she hears it." Translate each into Greek in all the different kinds of conditions, and then put each of those conditions into indirect speech twice, once after ἔφη and once after εἶπε, to end up with three Greek sentences for each of the nine types of condition, for each of

---

[2] When they do change, they become present and perfect optatives respectively, so the reason such change is normally avoided is the danger of ambiguity between original imperfects and original presents.

the two original English sentences. Give all possibilities. Use either of the resulting two sets of possible sentences to help with exercises 2 and 3.

a. Simple condition, present: "If we do anything, she sees it." / "He said that if they did anything, she saw it."

b. Simple condition, past: "If we did anything, she saw it." / "He said that if they had done anything, she had seen it."

c. Contrafactual condition, present: "If we were doing anything, she would be seeing it." / "He said that if they were doing anything, she would be seeing it."

d. Contrafactual condition, past: "If we had done anything, she would have seen it." / "He said that if they had done anything, she would have seen it."

e. General condition, present: "If ever we do anything, she sees it." / "He said that if ever they did anything, she saw it."

f. General condition, past: "If ever we did anything, she saw it." / "He said that if ever they did anything, she saw it."

g. Future condition, more vivid: "If we do anything, she will see it." / "He said that if they did anything, she would see it."

h. Future condition, less vivid: "If we did (should do, were to do) anything, she would see it." / "He said that if they did (should do, were to do) anything, she would see it."

i. Future condition, most vivid: "If we do anything, she will see it." (as a warning) / "He said that if they did anything, she would see it." (as a warning)

j. Simple condition, present: "If we say anything, she hears it." / "He said that if they said anything, she heard it."

k. Simple condition, past: "If we said anything, she heard it." / "He said that if they had said anything, she had heard it."

l. Contrafactual condition, present: "If we were saying anything, she would be hearing it." / "He said that if they were saying anything, she would be hearing it."

m. Contrafactual condition, past: "If we had said anything, she would have heard it." / "He said that if they had said anything, she would have heard it."

n. General condition, present: "If ever we say anything, she hears it." / "He said that if ever they said anything, she heard it."

o. General condition, past: "If ever we said anything, she heard it." / "He said that if ever they said anything, she heard it."

p.　Future condition, more vivid: "If we say anything, she will hear it." / "He said that if they said anything, she would hear it."

q.　Future condition, less vivid: "If we said (should say, were to say) anything, she would hear it." / "He said that if they said (should say, were to say) anything, she would hear it.

r.　Future condition, most vivid: "If we say anything, she will hear it." (as a warning) / "He said that if they said anything, she would hear it." (as a warning)

Preliminary exercise 2.　For each sentence, translate, give the direct speech version in Greek, and name the type of condition.

a.　ἔφη εἰ ἀκοῦσαι, ἀποκρίνασθαι ἄν.

b.　ἔφη εἰ ἀκοῦσαι, ἀποκρίνεσθαι. (2 ways)

c.　ἔφη εἰ ἀκοῦσαι, ἀποκρινεῖσθαι.

d.　ἔφη εἰ ἤκουσεν, ἀποκρίνασθαι ἄν.

e.　ἔφη εἰ ἤκουσεν, ἀποκρίνασθαι.

f.　ἔφη εἰ ἤκουεν, ἀποκρίνεσθαι ἄν.

g.　ἔφη εἰ ἀκούει, ἀποκρίνεσθαι.

h.　ἔφη εἰ ἀκούσοιτο, ἀποκρινεῖσθαι.

i.　εἶπεν ὅτι εἰ ἀκοῦσαι, ἀποκρίνοιτο.

j.　εἶπεν ὅτι εἰ ἀκοῦσαι, ἀποκρινοῖτο.

k.　εἶπεν ὅτι εἰ ἀκοῦσαι, ἀπεκρίνετο.

l.　εἶπεν ὅτι εἰ ἀκοῦσαι, ἀποκρίναιτο ἄν.

m.　εἶπεν ὅτι εἰ ἤκουσεν, ἀπεκρίνατο ἄν.

n.　εἶπεν ὅτι εἰ ἤκουσεν, ἀποκρίναιτο.

o.　εἶπεν ὅτι εἰ ἀκούοι, ἀποκρίνοιτο.

p.　εἶπεν ὅτι εἰ ἤκουεν, ἀπεκρίνετο ἄν.

q.　εἶπεν ὅτι εἰ ἀκούσοιτο, ἀποκρινοῖτο.

Preliminary exercise 3.　Translate each sentence and then put each one into indirect speech twice, once with ἔφη and once with εἶπε. Give all possibilities, and name all conditions. Assume that the speaker of the new sentences was neither the speaker nor the addressee of the original ones.

a.　ἐὰν ζητῇς, εὑρίσκεις.

b.　ἐὰν ζητῇς, εὑρήσεις.

c.　εἰ ζητοίης, ηὕρισκες.

d.　εἰ ζητοίης, εὕροις ἄν.

e.　εἰ ἐζήτησας, ηὗρες ἄν.

f.   εἰ ἐζήτησας, ηὗρες.
g.   εἰ ζητεῖς, εὑρίσκεις.
h.   εἰ ἐζήτεις, ηὕρισκες ἄν.

Sentences

Translate into Greek using only words and constructions so far covered. Give all possibilities, and give the English form of the direct version.[3]

1.   My father thought his enemies would stop terrifying him if he set free all his slaves. (2 ways)
2.   Your friends promised to meet us if we wished to converse with them. (2 ways)
3.   We heard that if that king had built a temple, he would have dedicated it to Zeus.
4.   The young man was asserting that he would be studying philosophy if the enemy were not attacking our city.
5.   I believe that these philosophers used to refute whoever tried to deceive them.
6.   Those priests explained that we would not be healthy if we did not please the gods. (3 ways)
7.   The ignorant women said (use φημί) that they would be seeking truth if their teacher were not always punishing them.
8.   Did you say (use φημί) that that tyrant always treated arrogantly whoever supplicated him? (2 ways)
9.   The seer swore not to approach the temple if he did not bury his father within three days. (2 ways)
10.   Our comrades said (use φημί) that they would not associate with us if we were jealous of them. (2 ways)

Analysis

Analyze according to the model given in chapter VI, breaking up the sentence into units with one verb form in each and showing subordination by indentation and numbering. Translate each unit into English as literally as is possible without being incomprehensible and explain each construction covered in this chapter, including naming all conditions and other constructions appearing in *oratio obliqua* and giving their original direct versions.

[3] Hint: these sentences are easier to do if one produces the English direct version first and uses that to work out the Greek.

1. ἐδόκει δ' αὐτῷ βέλτιον εἶναι πρὸς Θέογνιν μνησθῆναι· ἡγεῖτο γὰρ ἅπαν ποιή-
    σειν αὐτόν, εἴ τις ἀργύριον διδοίη.

    (Lysias, *Oration* 12.14; μιμνήσκω in passive can mean "mention")

2. ἐν δὲ τούτῳ ὁ μὲν Κλεινίας τῷ Εὐθυδήμῳ ἀπεκρίνατο, ὅτι μανθάνοιεν οἱ μαν-
    θάνοντες ἃ οὐκ ἐπίσταιντο· ὁ δὲ ἤρετο αὐτὸν διὰ τῶν αὐτῶν ὧνπερ τὸ
    πρότερον.

    (Plato, *Euthydemus* 276e, responding to a question about what learners learn;
    ἐρωτάω "question"; what is important about οὐκ?)

3. ἐπεὶ δὲ οὐχ ὅσον ὡμολόγησα εἶχεν, ὦ ἄνδρες δικασταί, ἀλλὰ τρία τάλαντα
    ἀργυρίου καὶ τετρακοσίους κυζικηνοὺς καὶ ἑκατὸν δαρεικοὺς καὶ φιάλας
    ἀργυρᾶς τέτταρας, ἐδεόμην αὐτοῦ ἐφόδιά μοι δοῦναι, ὁ δ' ἀγαπήσειν με
    ἔφασκεν, εἰ τὸ σῶμα σώσω.

    (Lysias, *Oration* 12.11, on the speaker's escape from the thirty tyrants by bribery.
    The person who had come to arrest him had offered to let him go in exchange
    for one talent of money, a deal to which the speaker agreed, but when he opened
    his treasure chest to get the money, the entire contents were seized; the subject of
    εἶχεν is the treasure chest, κυζικηνός "Cyzicene stater" (a kind of coin), δαρεικός
    "Daric" (a kind of coin), φιάλη "bowl," ἐφόδια "money for a journey," ἀγαπάω
    "be content")

4. δίδαξον δὴ πρὸς τῶν θεῶν, φάναι τὸν Ἀλκιβιάδην· ὡς ἔγωγ' ἀκούων τινῶν
    ἐπαινουμένων, ὅτι νόμιμοι ἄνδρες εἰσίν, οἶμαι μὴ ἂν δικαίως τούτου τυχεῖν τοῦ
    ἐπαίνου τὸν μὴ εἰδότα, τί ἐστι νόμος.

    (Xenophon, *Memorabilia* 1.2.41; omit φάναι τὸν Ἀλκιβιάδην from the analysis;
    νόμιμος "lawful"; how does this sentence violate the normal rules for indirect
    statement?)

5. ταῦτα δὲ ὁρῶντε καὶ ὄντε οἵω προείρησθον, πότερόν τις αὐτὼ φῇ τοῦ βίου
    τοῦ Σωκράτους ἐπιθυμήσαντε καὶ τῆς σωφροσύνης, ἣν ἐκεῖνος εἶχεν, ὀρέξασθαι
    τῆς ὁμιλίας αὐτοῦ, ἢ νομίσαντε, εἰ ὁμιλησαίτην ἐκείνῳ, γενέσθαι ἂν ἱκανωτάτω
    λέγειν τε καὶ πράττειν;

    (Xenophon, *Memorabilia* 1.2.15, defending Socrates on the charge of respon-
    sibility for the sins of Critias and Alcibiades – watch for duals referring to
    them; ταῦτα refers to Socrates' temperate lifestyle, ὀρέγω "seek," ὁμιλέω "spend
    time in the company of," the mood of φῇ does not follow the rules – can you
    explain it?)

6. Σωκράτης δὲ τὸν μὲν ἀμαθίας ἕνεκα δεσμεύοντα δικαίως ἂν καὶ αὐτὸν ᾤετο
    δεδέσθαι ὑπὸ τῶν ἐπισταμένων, ἃ μὴ αὐτὸς ἐπίσταται· καὶ τῶν τοιούτων ἕνεκα
    πολλάκις ἐσκόπει, τί διαφέρει μανίας ἀμαθία· καὶ τοὺς μὲν μαινομένους ᾤετο

συμφερόντως ἂν δεδέσθαι καὶ αὐτοῖς καὶ τοῖς φίλοις, τοὺς δὲ μὴ ἐπισταμένους τὰ δέοντα δικαίως ἂν μανθάνειν παρὰ τῶν ἐπισταμένων.

(Xenophon, *Memorabilia* 1.2.50, on the treatment of ignorance like madness; δεσμεύω "put in chains")

7. γνόντες δὲ τῶν ἀρχόντων οἱ διακεχειρικότες τὰ ἱερὰ χρήματα ὅτι εἰ δώσοιεν εὐθύνας, κινδυνεύειν ἀπολέσθαι, πέμπουσιν εἰς Θήβας, καὶ διδάσκουσι τοὺς Θηβαίους ὡς εἰ μὴ στρατεύσειαν, κινδυνεύσοιεν οἱ Ἀρκάδες πάλιν λακωνίσαι.

(Xenophon, *Hellenica* 7.4.34; διαχειρίζω "administer," εὔθυνα "account," λακωνίζω "go over to the Spartans"; how does this sentence violate the rules?)

8. ἔφη δὲ καὶ περὶ τῶν φίλων αὐτὸν λέγειν, ὡς οὐδὲν ὄφελος εὔνους εἶναι, εἰ μὴ καὶ ὠφελεῖν δυνήσονται· μόνους δὲ φάσκειν αὐτὸν ἀξίους εἶναι τιμῆς τοὺς εἰδότας τὰ δέοντα καὶ ἑρμηνεῦσαι δυναμένους· ἀναπείθοντα οὖν τοὺς νέους αὐτόν, ὡς αὐτὸς εἴη σοφώτατός τε καὶ ἄλλους ἱκανώτατος ποιῆσαι σοφούς, οὕτω διατιθέναι τοὺς ἑαυτῷ συνόντας, ὥστε μηδαμοῦ παρ᾽ αὐτοῖς τοὺς ἄλλους εἶναι πρὸς ἑαυτόν.

(Xenophon, *Memorabilia* 1.2.51–2, reporting accusations against Socrates (αὐτόν); ὄφελος (n.) "help," εὔνους "well intentioned," ἑρμηνεύω "explain," ἀναπείθω "persuade," διατίθημι "influence," παρά "in the eyes of," πρός "in comparison with"; how does Xenophon violate the usual rules for conditional sentences?)

9. Σωκράτης δ᾽ οὐ ταῦτ᾽ ἔλεγε· καὶ γὰρ ἑαυτὸν οὕτω γ᾽ ἂν ᾤετο δεῖν παίεσθαι· ἀλλ᾽ ἔφη δεῖν τοὺς μήτε λόγῳ μήτ᾽ ἔργῳ ὠφελίμους ὄντας, μήτε στρατεύματι μήτε πόλει μήτε αὐτῷ τῷ δήμῳ, εἴ τι δέοι, βοηθεῖν ἱκανούς, ἄλλως τ᾽ ἐὰν πρὸς τούτῳ καὶ θρασεῖς ὦσι, πάντα τρόπον κωλύεσθαι, κἂν πάνυ πλούσιοι τυγχάνωσιν ὄντες.

(Xenophon, *Memorabilia* 1.2.59; ταῦτα refers to an assertion that common and poor people should be beaten; οὕτω i.e. if he had said that, ἄλλως τ᾽ "especially," πρὸς τούτῳ καί "in addition to this also," κωλύω "hinder"; explain ἂν ᾤετο and ἑαυτόν and discuss the difference in mood between εἴ . . . δέοι and ἐάν . . . ὦσι)

10. ὁρᾶν δὴ ταύτῃ μὲν καθ᾽ ἑκάτερον τὸ χάσμα τοῦ οὐρανοῦ τε καὶ τῆς γῆς ἀπιούσας τὰς ψυχάς, ἐπειδὴ αὐταῖς δικασθείη, κατὰ δὲ τὼ ἑτέρω ἐκ μὲν τοῦ ἀνιέναι ἐκ τῆς γῆς μεστὰς αὐχμοῦ τε καὶ κόνεως, ἐκ δὲ τοῦ ἑτέρου καταβαίνειν ἑτέρας ἐκ τοῦ οὐρανοῦ καθαράς· καὶ τὰς ἀεὶ ἀφικνουμένας ὥσπερ ἐκ πολλῆς πορείας φαίνεσθαι ἥκειν, καὶ ἀσμένας εἰς τὸν λειμῶνα ἀπιούσας οἷον ἐν πανηγύρει κατασκηνᾶσθαι, καὶ ἀσπάζεσθαί τε ἀλλήλας ὅσαι γνώριμαι, καὶ πυνθάνεσθαι τάς τε ἐκ τῆς γῆς ἡκούσας παρὰ τῶν ἑτέρων τὰ ἐκεῖ καὶ τὰς ἐκ τοῦ οὐρανοῦ τὰ παρ᾽ ἐκείναις· διηγεῖσθαι δὲ ἀλλήλαις τὰς μὲν ὀδυρομένας τε καὶ κλαιούσας, ἀναμιμνησκομένας ὅσα τε καὶ οἷα πάθοιεν καὶ ἴδοιεν ἐν τῇ ὑπὸ γῆς

πορείᾳ – εἶναι δὲ τὴν πορείαν χιλιέτη – τὰς δ᾽ αὖ ἐκ τοῦ οὐρανοῦ εὐπαθείας διηγεῖσθαι καὶ θέας ἀμηχάνους τὸ κάλλος.

(Plato, *Republic* 614d–615a, myth of Er; the whole sentence is in *oratio obliqua* after an earlier ἔφη; κατά i.e. "via," χάσμα "opening" (there are four of these, two in the earth and two in the sky, to allow recently-dead souls into and out of the judgement area of heaven), ἐκ μὲν τοῦ . . . ἐκ δὲ τοῦ ἑτέρου is a variant of the ὁ μέν . . . ὁ δέ construction with ἕτερος added to the second part for clarity, μεστός "filled," αὐχμός "squalor," κόνις "dust," καθαρός "clean," πορεία "journey," ἄσμενος "glad," λειμών "meadow," πανήγυρις "festival," κατασκηνάομαι "encamp," ἀσπάζομαι "greet," γνώριμος "known," διηγέομαι "tell long stories, tell in full," ὀδύρομαι "mourn," χιλιέτης "lasting a thousand years," θέα "sight," ἀμήχανος "inconceivable with respect to")

XIX | Summary

Material to learn before using this chapter: numbers (Smyth §347)
Recommended syntax reading: Smyth §1759–1849, 1966–2024, 2153–92

Use of the subjunctive and optative

A. Constructions using the **optative** in secondary sequence and the **indicative** in primary sequence (in all cases the indicative can be used instead of the optative by the vivid construction, but in construction 3 below this is rare); **tense is as in direct speech**:

1. Indirect statement using ὅτι construction;
2. Indirect questions, if not deliberative;
3. Causal clauses expressing an alleged reason;
4. Subordinate clauses in indirect discourse, if the subordinate verb was originally in a primary tense of the indicative;
5. Protases of present simple and future most vivid conditions in *oratio obliqua*.

B. Constructions using the **optative** in secondary sequence and the **subjunctive** in primary sequence (in constructions 1–4 the subjunctive can be used instead of the optative by the vivid construction); tense reflects **aspect**:

1. Fear clauses (fear for the future);
2. Purpose clauses using the ἵνα construction;
3. Indirect deliberative questions;
4. Protases of future more vivid and present general conditions in *oratio obliqua* (with ἄν if subjunctive);
5. Protases of general conditions not in *oratio obliqua* (with ἄν if subjunctive);
6. Indefinite clauses (with ἄν if subjunctive)
7. Temporal clauses using the general and prospective constructions (with ἄν if subjunctive).

C. Other uses of the **subjunctive**; tense reflects **aspect**:

1. Direct deliberative questions;
2. Commands in the first person plural (exhortations);
3. Prohibitions (negative commands) in the aorist;
4. Protases of future more vivid conditions (with ἄν).

D. Other uses of the **optative**; tense reflects **aspect**:

1.   Wishes for the future;
2.   Potential optative (with ἄν);
3.   Protases and apodoses of future less vivid conditions (with ἄν).

Use of the infinitive

A. Uses in which tense reflects aspect:

1.   Indirect commands;
2.   Result clauses, unless there is stress on the actuality of result (in which case the indicative is used);
3.   Some impersonal verbs;
4.   Verbs of forbidding and preventing;
5.   Verbs of fearing, when an infinitive would be used in English;
6.   In temporal clauses after πρίν "before";
7.   Articular infinitives.

B. Other uses:

1.   Indirect statement after φημί etc.: tense follows the tense of the direct statement;
2.   After verbs of hoping, promising, threatening, and swearing: tense is always future.

Use of οὐ and μή

The general rule is that the subjunctive and imperative always take μή, the infinitive takes μή except in indirect statement, and the indicative, optative, and participle can take either οὐ or μή. Specific rules:

1.   Direct statements (in indicative), potentials, and causal clauses: always οὐ.
2.   Commands (*all* types), wishes, effort clauses, and "on condition that" clauses: always μή.
3.   Conditionals and concessive clauses: always μή in the protasis and usually οὐ in the apodosis.
4.   Purpose clauses: μή unless using the future participle, in which case οὐ.
5.   Fear clauses (not including infinitives): always introduced by μή, but the negative, if any, is οὐ.
6.   Result clauses: μή with the infinitive or οὐ with the indicative.
7.   Verbs of forbidding and preventing: some take μή without being negative, adding οὐ if the main verb is negative (though this still does not make the subordinate negative).

8. Indirect statement: οὐ with the ὅτι construction, infinitive, or participle; μή with the future infinitive and with εἰ.
9. Direct questions: μή if deliberative; otherwise οὐ if expecting the answer "yes" and μή if expecting the answer "no."
10. Indirect questions: generally οὐ, but μή if deliberative; either οὐ or μή in the second half of alternative indirect questions.
11. Relative clauses: generally οὐ, but μή when conditional or expressing purpose.
12. Temporal clauses: generally οὐ, but μή when general or prospective.
13. Adjectives: generally οὐ, but μή when indefinite/general (οἱ μὴ ἀγαθοί).
14. Participles: generally οὐ, but μή when indefinite/general or conditional.

Sentences

Translate into Greek, using multiple constructions whenever possible. The indications given below of how many are possible take into account all differences in construction discussed in previous chapters, including the difference between possession expressed by possessive adjectives and by pronouns, but not differences in vocabulary only.

1. My son reported that the cows were at rest. (4 ways)
2. The suppliant did not know whether he should be silent or refute the witness' lies by explaining where he had been. (6 ways)
3. You don't fear that we won't prevail, do you?
4. That soldier told his friends who had assigned him to that position, but they did not believe (= distrusted) him. (3 ways)
5. Those very unfortunate men agreed not to betray us if we would give them back the horses we had stolen. (4 ways)
6. My slaves would never revolt from me, because they know that they could not escape my notice plotting against me. (4 ways)
7. Do not scatter gold into the sea, lest a lack of money prevent you from studying philosophy. (2 ways)
8. The council sent their best general with five hundred men to defend their allies against the enemy. (3 ways)
9. Our army attacked the foreigners on the grounds that their (the foreigners') messenger had outraged the archons by beating (them); but they (the foreigners) said that they had commanded all their own citizens to treat other cities' leaders well. (7 ways)
10. Fugitives don't want to return to wherever they came from. (2 ways)
11. The philosopher said that preventing wild animals from entering houses was far easier than driving them out[1] after they had come in. (5 ways)

---

[1] "drive out" = ἐξ-ελαύνω

12. May the gods pity us when we supplicate (them)! (2 ways)
13. Shall we help the old women in the field, or is it proper for us to wait here while they work? (2 ways)
14. Your husband believed that a bird had terrified the children who were shouting. (3 ways)
15. The juror said that we ought to work if we wanted to receive money that day. (4 ways)
16. Let us not laugh at anyone who repents of the things he did unjustly. (4 ways)
17. The king will not let the thieves go until they stop denying that they (the thieves) stole that sword. (2 ways)
18. He feared that his master would reproach him on the grounds that he had sold the bronze for little money. (3 ways)
19. If only that dog were not sitting on our table! (3 ways)
20. Do you know where my daughter went? (3 ways)
21. That hero built a house himself in order that his mother might dwell in Athens. (2 ways)
22. The brothers asked themselves where they should bury their father. (3 ways)
23. The guards said that these courageous old men always resisted whoever attacked them. (4 ways)
24. The orator said that if anyone should order him to free his slaves, he would laugh at that person. (2 ways)
25. The good-for-nothing bandits threatened to punish the priest if he did not continue to deceive the people who dwelled in that country. (3 ways)
26. Let our savior never say that I am not able to stop drinking! (2 ways)
27. The tyrant imprisoned whoever did not praise the government.
28. Since our dog allegedly bit his hand, your father indicted us on a charge of outrageous behavior. (4 ways)
29. It is necessary for the priest to cleanse the altar whenever anyone sacrifices by burning animals.
30. Your son waited many years to be able to manage his own affairs.

XX | Consolidation

A) Passages to be rewritten in Greek, making the changes specified

1. These selections come from the beginning of Plato's *Symposium*, which is in double indirect speech: Apollodorus reports the words of Aristodemus, who tells of his own encounter with Socrates. Rewrite them (i.e. everything in them: statements, questions, and orders) in direct speech, beginning Ἐμοὶ γὰρ ἐνέτυχεν Σωκράτης . . . (The bulk of the narration could end up either in the imperfect or in the historical present; the choice between these, once made, should be consistently applied.)

174a: ἔφη γὰρ οἱ Σωκράτη ἐντυχεῖν λελουμένον τε καὶ τὰς βλαύτας ὑπο-δεδεμένον, ἃ ἐκεῖνος ὀλιγάκις ἐποίει· καὶ ἐρέσθαι αὐτὸν ὅποι ἴοι οὕτω καλὸς γεγενημένος.

174d–e: τοιαῦτ' ἄττα σφᾶς ἔφη διαλεχθέντας ἰέναι. τὸν οὖν Σωκράτη ἑαυτῷ πως προσέχοντα τὸν νοῦν κατὰ τὴν ὁδὸν πορεύεσθαι ὑπολειπόμενον, καὶ περι-ιμένοντος οὗ κελεύειν προϊέναι εἰς τὸ πρόσθεν. ἐπειδὴ δὲ γενέσθαι ἐπὶ τῇ οἰκίᾳ τῇ Ἀγάθωνος, ἀνεῳγμένην καταλαμβάνειν τὴν θύραν, καὶ τι ἔφη αὐτόθι γελοῖον παθεῖν. οἳ μὲν γὰρ εὐθὺς παῖδά τινα τῶν ἔνδοθεν ἀπαν-τήσαντα ἄγειν οὗ κατέκειντο οἱ ἄλλοι, καὶ καταλαμβάνειν ἤδη μέλλοντας δειπνεῖν· εὐθὺς δ' οὖν ὡς ἰδεῖν τὸν Ἀγάθωνα, φάναι . . .

175a: καὶ ἓ μὲν ἔφη ἀπονίζειν τὸν παῖδα, ἵνα κατακέοιτο· ἄλλον δέ τινα τῶν παίδων ἥκειν ἀγγέλλοντα ὅτι Σωκράτης οὗτος ἀναχωρήσας ἐν τῷ τῶν γειτόνων προθύρῳ ἕστηκε καὶ οὗ καλοῦντος οὐκ ἐθέλει εἰσιέναι.

175c: μετὰ ταῦτα ἔφη σφᾶς μὲν δειπνεῖν, τὸν δὲ Σωκράτη οὐκ εἰσιέναι. τὸν οὖν Ἀγάθωνα πολλάκις κελεύειν μεταπέμψασθαι τὸν Σωκράτη, ἓ δὲ οὐκ ἐᾶν. ἥκειν οὖν αὐτὸν οὐ πολὺν χρόνον ὡς εἰώθει διατρίψαντα, ἀλλὰ μάλιστα σφᾶς μεσοῦν δειπνοῦντας. τὸν οὖν Ἀγάθωνα – τυγχάνειν γὰρ ἔσχατον κατακείμενον μόνον – "δεῦρ'," ἔφη φάναι . . .

212c–d: εἰπόντος δὲ ταῦτα τοῦ Σωκράτους τοὺς μὲν ἐπαινεῖν, τὸν δὲ Ἀριστοφάνη λέγειν τι ἐπιχειρεῖν, ὅτι ἐμνήσθη αὐτοῦ λέγων ὁ Σωκράτης περὶ τοῦ λόγου· καὶ ἐξαίφνης τὴν αὔλειον θύραν κρουομένην πολὺν ψόφον παρασχεῖν ὡς κωμαστῶν, καὶ αὐλητρίδος φωνὴν ἀκούειν. τὸν οὖν Ἀγάθωνα, "παῖδες," φάναι, "οὐ σκέψεσθε; καὶ ἐὰν μέν τις τῶν ἐπιτηδείων ᾖ, καλεῖτε· εἰ δὲ μή, λέγετε ὅτι οὐ πίνομεν, ἀλλὰ ἀναπαυόμεθα ἤδη." καὶ οὐ πολὺ ὕστερον Ἀλκιβιάδου τὴν φωνὴν ἀκούειν ἐν τῇ αὐλῇ σφόδρα μεθύοντος καὶ μέγα βοῶντος, ἐρωτῶντος ὅπου Ἀγάθων καὶ κελεύοντος

ἄγειν παρ' Ἀγάθωνα. ἄγειν οὖν αὐτὸν παρὰ σφᾶς τήν τε αὐλητρίδα ὑπο-
λαβοῦσαν καὶ ἄλλους τινὰς τῶν ἀκολούθων, καὶ ἐπιστῆναι ἐπὶ τὰς θύρας
ἐστεφανωμένον αὐτὸν κιττοῦ τέ τινι στεφάνῳ δασεῖ καὶ ἴων, καὶ ταινίας
ἔχοντα ἐπὶ τῆς κεφαλῆς πάνυ πολλάς, καὶ εἰπεῖν· . . .

213a–b: πάντας οὖν ἀναθορυβῆσαι καὶ κελεύειν εἰσιέναι καὶ κατακλίνεσθαι, καὶ
τὸν Ἀγάθωνα καλεῖν αὐτόν. καὶ τὸν ἰέναι ἀγόμενον ὑπὸ τῶν ἀνθρώπων,
καὶ περιαιρούμενον ἅμα τὰς ταινίας ὡς ἀναδήσοντα, ἐπίπροσθεν τῶν
ὀφθαλμῶν ἔχοντα οὐ κατιδεῖν τὸν Σωκράτη, ἀλλὰ καθίζεσθαι παρὰ τὸν
Ἀγάθωνα ἐν μέσῳ Σωκράτους τε καὶ ἐκείνου· παραχωρῆσαι γὰρ τὸν
Σωκράτη ὡς ἐκεῖνον κατιδεῖν. παρακαθεζόμενον δὲ αὐτὸν ἀσπάζεσθαί τε
τὸν Ἀγάθωνα καὶ ἀναδεῖν.

223b–d: τὸν μὲν οὖν Ἀγάθωνα ὡς κατακεισόμενον παρὰ τῷ Σωκράτει ἀνίστασ-
θαι· ἐξαίφνης δὲ κωμαστὰς ἥκειν παμπόλλους ἐπὶ τὰς θύρας, καὶ ἐπιτυχόν-
τας ἀνεῳγμέναις ἐξιόντος τινὸς εἰς τὸ ἄντικρυς πορεύεσθαι παρὰ σφᾶς
καὶ κατακλίνεσθαι, καὶ θορύβου μεστὰ πάντα εἶναι, καὶ οὐκέτι ἐν κόσμῳ
οὐδενὶ ἀναγκάζεσθαι πίνειν πάμπολυν οἶνον. τὸν μὲν οὖν Ἐρυξίμαχον καὶ
τὸν Φαῖδρον καὶ ἄλλους τινὰς ἔφη ὁ Ἀριστόδημος οἴχεσθαι ἀπιόντας, ἓ
δὲ ὕπνον λαβεῖν, καὶ καταδαρθεῖν πάνυ πολύ, ἅτε μακρῶν τῶν νυκτῶν
οὐσῶν, ἐξεγρέσθαι δὲ πρὸς ἡμέραν ἤδη ἀλεκτρυόνων ᾀδόντων, ἐξεγρό-
μενος δὲ ἰδεῖν τοὺς μὲν ἄλλους καθεύδοντας καὶ οἰχομένους, Ἀγάθωνα δὲ
καὶ Ἀριστοφάνη καὶ Σωκράτη ἔτι μόνους ἐγρηγορέναι καὶ πίνειν ἐκ φιάλης
μεγάλης ἐπὶ δεξιά. τὸν οὖν Σωκράτη αὐτοῖς διαλέγεσθαι· καὶ τὰ μὲν ἄλλα
ὁ Ἀριστόδημος οὐκ ἔφη μεμνῆσθαι τῶν λόγων· οὔτε γὰρ ἐξ ἀρχῆς παρ-
αγενέσθαι ὑπονυστάζειν τε· τὸ μέντοι κεφάλαιον, ἔφη, προσαναγκάζειν
τὸν Σωκράτη ὁμολογεῖν αὐτοὺς τοῦ αὐτοῦ ἀνδρὸς εἶναι κωμῳδίαν καὶ
τραγῳδίαν ἐπίστασθαι ποιεῖν, καὶ τὸν τέχνῃ τραγῳδιοποιὸν ὄντα καὶ
κωμῳδιοποιὸν εἶναι. ταῦτα δὴ ἀναγκαζομένους αὐτοὺς καὶ οὐ σφόδρα
ἑπομένους νυστάζειν, καὶ πρῶτον μὲν καταδαρθεῖν τὸν Ἀριστοφάνη, ἤδη
δὲ ἡμέρας γιγνομένης τὸν Ἀγάθωνα. τὸν οὖν Σωκράτη, κατακοιμήσαντ'
ἐκείνους, ἀναστάντα ἀπιέναι – καὶ ἓ ὥσπερ εἰώθει ἕπεσθαι – καὶ ἐλθόντα
εἰς Λύκειον, ἀπονιψάμενον, ὥσπερ ἄλλοτε τὴν ἄλλην ἡμέραν διατρίβειν,
καὶ οὕτω διατρίψαντα εἰς ἑσπέραν οἴκοι ἀναπαύεσθαι.

2. This is the opening of Plato's *Republic* (327a–328e), which is narrated in direct speech
by Socrates. Rewrite it in indirect speech, beginning Ἔφη ὁ Σωκράτης καταβῆναι τῇ
προτεραίᾳ . . . The direct quotes should end up in double indirect speech; look at exercise A1 above if you are unsure how to do this.

Κατέβην χθὲς εἰς Πειραιᾶ μετὰ Γλαύκωνος τοῦ Ἀρίστωνος, προσευξόμενός τε τῇ θεῷ καὶ ἅμα τὴν ἑορτὴν βουλόμενος θεάσασθαι τίνα τρόπον

ποιήσουσιν, ἅτε νῦν πρῶτον ἄγοντες. καλὴ μὲν οὖν μοι καὶ ἡ τῶν
ἐπιχωρίων πομπὴ ἔδοξεν εἶναι, οὐ μέντοι ἧττον ἐφαίνετο πρέπειν ἣν οἱ
Θρᾷκες ἔπεμπον. προσευξάμενοι δὲ καὶ θεωρήσαντες ἀπῇμεν πρὸς τὸ
ἄστυ. κατιδὼν οὖν πόρρωθεν ἡμᾶς οἴκαδε ὡρμημένους Πολέμαρχος ὁ
Κεφάλου ἐκέλευσε δραμόντα τὸν παῖδα περιμεῖναί ἑ κελεῦσαι. καί μου
ὄπισθεν ὁ παῖς λαβόμενος τοῦ ἱματίου, "κελεύει ὑμᾶς," ἔφη, "Πολέμαρχος
περιμεῖναι." καὶ ἐγὼ μετεστράφην τε καὶ ἠρόμην ὅπου αὐτὸς εἴη. "οὗτος,"
ἔφη, "ὄπισθεν προσέρχεται· ἀλλὰ περιμένετε." "ἀλλὰ περιμενοῦμεν," ἦ δ'
ὃς ὁ Γλαύκων. καὶ ὀλίγῳ ὕστερον ὅ τε Πολέμαρχος ἧκε καὶ Ἀδείμαντος ὁ
τοῦ Γλαύκωνος ἀδελφὸς καὶ Νικήρατος ὁ Νικίου καὶ ἄλλοι τινές, ὡς ἀπὸ
τῆς πομπῆς. ὁ οὖν Πολέμαρχος ἔφη "ὦ Σώκρατες, δοκεῖτέ μοι πρὸς ἄστυ
ὡρμῆσθαι ὡς ἀπιόντες." "οὐ γὰρ κακῶς δοξάζεις," ἦν δ' ἐγώ. "ὁρᾷς οὖν
ἡμᾶς," ἔφη, "ὅσοι ἐσμέν;" "πῶς γὰρ οὔ;" "ἢ τοίνυν τούτων," ἔφη, "κρείττους γένεσθε ἢ μένετ' αὐτοῦ." "οὐκοῦν," ἦν δ' ἐγώ, "ἔτι ἐλλείπεται τὸ ἢν
πείσωμεν ὑμᾶς, ὡς χρὴ ἡμᾶς ἀφεῖναι;" "ἦ καὶ δύναισθ' ἄν," ἦ δ' ὅς, "πεῖσαι
μὴ ἀκούοντας;" "οὐδαμῶς," ἔφη ὁ Γλαύκων. "ὡς τοίνυν μὴ ἀκουσομένων,
οὕτω διανοεῖσθε." καὶ ὁ Ἀδείμαντος, "ἆρά γε," ἦ δ' ὅς, "οὐδ' ἴστε ὅτι λαμπὰς ἔσται πρὸς ἑσπέραν ἀφ' ἵππων τῇ θεῷ;" "ἀφ' ἵππων;" ἦν δ' ἐγώ·
"καινόν γε τοῦτο. λαμπάδια ἔχοντες διαδώσουσιν ἀλλήλοις ἁμιλλώμενοι
τοῖς ἵπποις; ἢ πῶς λέγεις;" "οὕτως," ἔφη ὁ Πολέμαρχος· "καὶ πρός γε παννυχίδα ποιήσουσιν, ἣν ἄξιον θεάσασθαι. ἐξαναστησόμεθα γὰρ μετὰ τὸ
δεῖπνον καὶ τὴν παννυχίδα θεασόμεθα καὶ ξυνεσόμεθά τε πολλοῖς τῶν
νέων αὐτόθι καὶ διαλεξόμεθα. ἀλλὰ μένετε καὶ μὴ ἄλλως ποιεῖτε." καὶ ὁ
Γλαύκων, "ἔοικεν," ἔφη, "μενετέον εἶναι." "ἀλλ' εἰ δοκεῖ," ἦν δ' ἐγώ, "οὕτω
χρὴ ποιεῖν."

Ἦμεν οὖν οἴκαδε εἰς τοῦ Πολεμάρχου, καὶ Λυσίαν τε αὐτόθι
κατελάβομεν καὶ Εὐθύδημον, τοὺς τοῦ Πολεμάρχου ἀδελφούς, καὶ δὴ
καὶ Θρασύμαχον τὸν Χαλκηδόνιον καὶ Χαρμαντίδην τὸν Παιανιέα
καὶ Κλειτοφῶντα τὸν Ἀριστωνύμου· ἦν δ' ἔνδον καὶ ὁ πατὴρ ὁ τοῦ
Πολεμάρχου Κέφαλος. καὶ μάλα πρεσβύτης μοι ἔδοξεν εἶναι· διὰ χρόνου
γὰρ καὶ ἑωράκη αὐτόν. καθῆστο δὲ ἐστεφανωμένος ἐπί τινος προσκε-
φαλαίου τε καὶ δίφρου· τεθυκὼς γὰρ ἐτύγχανεν ἐν τῇ αὐλῇ. ἐκαθεζόμεθα
οὖν παρ' αὐτόν· ἔκειντο γὰρ δίφροι τινὲς αὐτόθι κύκλῳ. εὐθὺς οὖν με
ἰδὼν ὁ Κέφαλος ἠσπάζετό τε καὶ εἶπεν "ὦ Σώκρατες, οὐδὲ θαμίζεις
ἡμῖν καταβαίνων εἰς τὸν Πειραιᾶ· χρῆν μέντοι. εἰ μὲν γὰρ ἐγὼ ἔτι ἐν
δυνάμει ἦν τοῦ ῥᾳδίως πορεύεσθαι πρὸς τὸ ἄστυ, οὐδὲν ἄν σε ἔδει
δεῦρο ἰέναι, ἀλλ' ἡμεῖς ἂν παρὰ σὲ ἦμεν· νῦν δέ σε χρὴ πυκνότερον
δεῦρο ἰέναι· ὡς εὖ ἴσθι ὅτι ἔμοιγε, ὅσον αἱ κατὰ τὸ σῶμα ἡδοναὶ ἀπο-
μαραίνονται, τοσοῦτον αὔξονται αἱ περὶ τοὺς λόγους ἐπιθυμίαι τε καὶ
ἡδοναί. μὴ οὖν ἄλλως ποίει, ἀλλὰ τοῖσδέ τε τοῖς νεανίαις ξύνισθι καὶ δεῦρο

παρ' ἡμᾶς φοίτα ὡς παρὰ φίλους τε καὶ πάνυ οἰκείους." "καὶ μήν," ἦν δ'
ἐγώ, "ὦ Κέφαλε, χαίρω γε διαλεγόμενος τοῖς σφόδρα πρεσβύταις· δοκεῖ
γάρ μοι χρῆναι παρ' αὐτῶν πυνθάνεσθαι, ὥσπερ τινὰ ὁδὸν προεληλυ-
θότων, ἣν καὶ ἡμᾶς ἴσως δεήσει πορεύεσθαι, ποία τίς ἐστι, τραχεῖα καὶ
χαλεπή, ἢ ῥᾳδία καὶ εὔπορος· καὶ δὴ καὶ σοῦ ἡδέως ἂν πυθοίμην, ὅ τί
σοι φαίνεται τοῦτο, ἐπειδὴ ἐνταῦθα ἤδη εἶ τῆς ἡλικίας, ὃ δὴ ἐπὶ γήραος
οὐδῷ φασιν εἶναι οἱ ποιηταί, πότερον χαλεπὸν τοῦ βίου ἢ πῶς σὺ αὐτὸ
ἐξαγγέλλεις."

3. Rewrite these passages from Plato's *Euthydemus*, turning each direct quotation into
indirect speech (indirect questions, commands, or statements as appropriate: for indirect statement use φημί as the verb of saying). When there is a choice of whether to
change something to the optative/indirect form or to retain the indicative/direct version, give both possibilities. In addition, change Plato's constructions to the "correct"
form when they deviate from that standard. There are many ways to do each of these,
and more changes to the original are needed to produce an idiomatic result than in the
passages above. (Hint: in each passage there are two principal speakers. In the first passage they are Dionysodorus and Ctesippus, and in the second they are Socrates, who
narrates in the first person, and Cleinias.) Begin Ἤρετο ὁ Διονυσόδωρος τὸν Κτήσιππον πῶς (ὅπως) λέγει (λέγοι) . . .

- Πῶς λέγεις, ἔφη ὁ Διονυσόδωρος, ὦ Κτήσιππε; εἰσὶν γάρ τινες οἳ λέγουσι
  τὰ πράγματα ὡς ἔχει;
- Εἰσὶν μέντοι, ἔφη, οἱ καλοί τε κἀγαθοὶ καὶ οἱ τἀληθῆ λέγοντες.
- Τί οὖν; ἦ δ' ὅς· τἀγαθὰ οὐκ εὖ, ἔφη, ἔχει, τὰ δὲ κακὰ κακῶς;
- Συνεχώρει.
- Τοὺς δὲ καλούς τε καὶ ἀγαθοὺς ὁμολογεῖς λέγειν ὡς ἔχει τὰ πράγματα;
- Ὁμολογῶ.
- Κακῶς ἄρα, ἔφη, λέγουσιν, ὦ Κτήσιππε, οἱ ἀγαθοὶ τὰ κακά, εἴπερ ὡς
  ἔχει λέγουσιν.
- Ναὶ μὰ Δία, ἦ δ' ὅς, σφόδρα γε, τούς γοῦν κακοὺς ἀνθρώπους· ὧν σύ,
  ἐάν μοι πείθῃ, εὐλαβήσῃ εἶναι, ἵνα μή σε οἱ ἀγαθοὶ κακῶς λέγωσιν. ὡς
  εὖ ἴσθ' ὅτι κακῶς λέγουσιν οἱ ἀγαθοὶ τοὺς κακούς.
- Καὶ τοὺς μεγάλους, ἔφη ὁ Εὐθύδημος, μεγάλως λέγουσι καὶ τοὺς θερμοὺς
  θερμῶς;
- Μάλιστα δήπου, ἔφη ὁ Κτήσιππος· τούς γοῦν ψυχροὺς ψυχρῶς λέγουσί
  τε καὶ φασὶν διαλέγεσθαι.
- Σὺ μέν, ἔφη ὁ Διονυσόδωρος, λοιδορῇ, ὦ Κτήσιππε, λοιδορῇ.
- Μὰ Δί' οὐκ ἔγωγε, ἦ δ' ὅς, ὦ Διονυσόδωρε, ἐπεὶ φιλῶ σε, ἀλλὰ νου-
  θετῶ σε ὡς ἑταῖρον, καὶ πειρῶμαι πείθειν μηδέποτε ἐναντίον ἐμοῦ οὕτως

ἀγροίκως λέγειν ὅτι ἐγὼ τούτους βούλομαι ἐξολωλέναι, οὓς περὶ πλείστου ποιοῦμαι. (284d–e)

– Ἆρ' οὖν, ὦ Κλεινία, ἤδη τοῦτο ἱκανὸν πρὸς τὸ εὐδαίμονα ποιῆσαί τινα,
   τό τε κεκτῆσθαι τἀγαθὰ καὶ τὸ χρῆσθαι αὐτοῖς;
– Ἔμοιγε δοκεῖ.
– Πότερον, ἦν δ' ἐγώ, ἐὰν ὀρθῶς χρῆταί τις ἢ καὶ ἐὰν μή;
– Ἐὰν ὀρθῶς.
– Καλῶς γε, ἦν δ' ἐγώ, λέγεις. πλέον γάρ που οἶμαι θάτερόν ἐστιν, ἐάν τις
   χρῆταί ὁτῳοῦν μὴ ὀρθῶς πράγματι ἢ ἐὰν ἐᾷ· τὸ μὲν γὰρ κακόν, τὸ δὲ
   οὔτε κακὸν οὔτε ἀγαθόν. ἢ οὐχ οὕτω φαμέν;
– Συνεχώρει.
– Τί οὖν; ἐν τῇ ἐργασίᾳ τε καὶ χρήσει τῇ περὶ τὰ ξύλα μῶν ἄλλο τί ἐστιν
   τὸ ἀπεργαζόμενον ὀρθῶς χρῆσθαι ἢ ἐπιστήμη ἡ τεκτονική;
– Οὐ δῆτα, ἔφη.
– Ἀλλὰ μήν που καὶ ἐν τῇ περὶ τὰ σκεύη ἐργασίᾳ τὸ ὀρθῶς ἐπιστήμη ἐστὶν
   ἡ ἀπεργαζομένη.
– Συνέφη. (280e–281a)

4. Change these passages from Plato's *Symposium* into indirect speech, after the verbs
of saying that are already present.

193e: ἀλλὰ πείσομαί σοι, ἔφη φάναι τὸν Ἐρυξίμαχον· καὶ γάρ μοι ὁ λόγος ἡδέως
         ἐρρήθη. καὶ εἰ μὴ συνήδη Σωκράτει τε καὶ Ἀγάθωνι δεινοῖς οὖσι περὶ τὰ
         ἐρωτικά, πάνυ ἂν ἐφοβούμην μὴ ἀπορήσωσι λόγων διὰ τὸ πολλὰ καὶ παν-
         τοδαπὰ εἰρῆσθαι· νῦν δὲ ὅμως θαρρῶ.

194c: οὐ μεντἂν καλῶς ποιοίην, φάναι, ὦ Ἀγάθων, περὶ σοῦ τι ἐγὼ ἄγροικον
         δοξάζων· ἀλλ' εὖ οἶδα ὅτι εἴ τισιν ἐντύχοις οὓς ἡγοῖο σοφούς, μᾶλλον ἂν
         αὐτῶν φροντίζοις ἢ τῶν πολλῶν. ἀλλὰ μὴ οὐχ οὗτοι ἡμεῖς ὦμεν – ἡμεῖς μὲν
         γὰρ καὶ ἐκεῖ παρῆμεν καὶ ἦμεν τῶν πολλῶν – εἰ δὲ ἄλλοις ἐντύχοις σοφοῖς,
         τάχ' ἂν αἰσχύνοιο αὐτούς, εἴ τι ἴσως οἴοιο αἰσχρὸν ὂν ποιεῖν· ἢ πῶς λέγεις;

5. Rewrite the following passage of Demosthenes, *Philippics* I (35–7) in Greek so that it
is simpler and more like Plato's writings.

Καίτοι τί δήποτ', ὦ ἄνδρες Ἀθηναῖοι, νομίζετε τὴν μὲν τῶν Παναθηναίων
ἑορτὴν καὶ τὴν τῶν Διονυσίων ἀεὶ τοῦ καθήκοντος χρόνου γίγνεσθαι,
ἄν τε δεινοὶ λάχωσιν ἄν τ' ἰδιῶται οἱ τούτων ἑκατέρων ἐπιμελούμενοι,
εἰς ἃ τοσαῦτ' ἀναλίσκεται χρήματα, ὅσ' οὐδ' εἰς ἕνα τῶν ἀποστόλων,
καὶ τοσοῦτον ὄχλον καὶ παρασκευὴν ὅσην οὐκ οἶδ' εἴ τι τῶν ἁπάντων
ἔχει, τοὺς δ' ἀποστόλους πάντας ὑμῖν ὑστερίζειν τῶν καιρῶν, τὸν εἰς
Μεθώνην, τὸν εἰς Παγασάς, τὸν εἰς Ποτείδαιαν; ὅτι ἐκεῖνα μὲν ἅπαντα

νόμῳ τέτακται, καὶ πρόοιδεν ἕκαστος ὑμῶν ἐκ πολλοῦ τίς χορηγὸς ἢ γυμ-
νασίαρχος τῆς φυλῆς, πότε καὶ παρὰ τοῦ καὶ τί λαβόντα τί δεῖ ποιεῖν,
οὐδὲν ἀνεξέταστον οὐδ' ἀόριστον ἐν τούτοις ἠμέληται· ἐν δὲ τοῖς περὶ τοῦ
πολέμου καὶ τῇ τούτου παρασκευῇ ἄτακτα, ἀδιόρθωτα, ἀόρισθ' ἅπαντα.
τοιγαροῦν ἅμ' ἀκηκόαμέν τι καὶ τριηράρχους καθίσταμεν καὶ τούτοις
ἀντιδόσεις ποιούμεθα καὶ περὶ χρημάτων πόρου σκοποῦμεν, καὶ μετὰ
ταῦτ' ἐμβαίνειν τοὺς μετοίκους ἔδοξε καὶ τοὺς χωρὶς οἰκοῦντας, εἶτ' αὐτοὺς
πάλιν, εἶτ' ἀντεμβιβάζειν, εἶτ' ἐν ὅσῳ ταῦτα μέλλεται, προαπόλωλε τὸ
ἐφ' ὃ ἂν ἐκπλέωμεν· τὸν γὰρ τοῦ πράττειν χρόνον εἰς τὸ παρασκευάζεσ-
θαι ἀναλίσκομεν, οἱ δὲ τῶν πραγμάτων οὐ μένουσι καιροὶ τὴν ἡμετέραν
βραδυτῆτα καὶ εἰρωνείαν. ἃς δὲ τὸν μεταξὺ χρόνον δυνάμεις οἰόμεθ' ἡμῖν
ὑπάρχειν, οὐδὲν οἷαί τ' οὖσαι ποιεῖν ἐπ' αὐτῶν τῶν καιρῶν ἐξελέγχονται.

B) Passages translated from Greek texts, for retranslation back into Greek

Translate the following passages into Greek, sticking as closely as you can to the elements of Platonic style you have seen in earlier exercises. Words in parentheses should
not be translated, and words in square brackets should be translated instead of the more
idiomatic English they follow. Remember that English relative clauses are often best rendered by participles in Greek. (Hint: do not be tempted to look up the original Greek
before you have written your own, as seeing the original will render you incapable of
thinking out your own version. And because the natural result of correct application
of all the rules you have learned will not be precisely the same as the original, such a
shortcut will be immediately evident to anyone teaching you.)

1.   And he, having heard, burst out laughing very bitterly and said, "O Herakles," he
     said, "this is that well-known irony of Socrates, and I knew that and was predicting
     to these men that you would not want to answer, but that you would feign igno-
     rance and do everything rather than answer, if someone asked you something."
     "You are wise," I said, "O Thrasymachus; so you knew well that, if you should ask
     someone how much twelve is, and having asked you should order him in advance:
     "See to it for me, O human, that you don't say that twelve is twice six, nor that it
     is three times four, nor that it is six times two, nor that it is four times three; as I
     shall not accept (it) from you, if you talk such nonsense." It was clear, I think, to
     you that no-one would answer the person who was inquiring thus. But if he had
     said to you, "O Thrasymachus, how do you say? Am I not to answer any of the
     things which you ordered in advance? Not even, O amazing one, if it happens to
     be some one of these, but I am to say something other than the truth? Or how
     do you say?" What would you have said to him with regard to that?" "May (these
     things) be (such)," he said, "as if indeed the latter (were) similar to the former!"

Vocabulary

(to) burst out laughing	ἀνακαγχάζω	bitterly	σαρδάνιον
well-known	εἰωθώς, -υῖα, -ός	irony	εἰρωνεία, -ας, ἡ
(to) predict	προλέγω	(to) feign ignorance	εἰρωνεύομαι
(to) order in advance	προεῖπον	six times	ἑξάκις
four times	τετράκις	(to) talk nonsense	φλυαρέω
amazing one	θαυμάσιος, -ου, ὁ		

2.   "At least nothing prevents (this being the case)," I said; "and therefore even if it is not similar, but it appears similar [= it appears such] to the one who was asked, do you think that he will any the less answer what appears (correct) to him, whether we forbid him or not [= both if we forbid him and if not]?" "So," he said, "are you too going to do this [= to do thus]? Will you answer some one of the things I forbade (you to answer)?" "I would not be surprised," said I, "if when I have considered [= to me having considered] it should seem best (to do) thus." "What then," he said, "if I show you another answer contrary to all these (answers) about justice (and) better than these? What do you think worthy for (you) to suffer?" "What else," said I, "than the very thing which it is fitting for one who does not know to suffer? It is fitting, somehow, (for such a one) to learn from one who knows; so I too think (it) worthy (for me) to suffer this." "You are sweet," he said, "but in addition to the learning you must also pay money [= in addition to the learning, also pay money! (imperative)]." "Okay, when I have some [= when it is to me]," I said.

Vocabulary

similar	ὅμοιος, -α, -ον	(to) be fitting	προσήκει (impersonal)
justice	δικαιοσύνη, -ης, ἡ	(to) pay	ἀποτίνω, ἀποτείσω, ἀπέτεισα
(to) think worthy	ἀξιόω	in addition to	πρός (+ dat.)

3. – Indeed this story now speaks (to us) using truth, (namely) that however many cities not a god but some mortal rules, for them (i.e. the citizens of such cities) there is not a rest from evils nor from toils. It (i.e. the story) thinks that it is necessary for us to imitate, by every device, the life that is said (to have existed) in the time of Kronos, and (that it is necessary for us) to manage our households and our cities in obedience [= obeying], publicly and privately, to however much of immortality is in us (hint: change the order of these clauses), calling the ordering of the mind law. If one man or an oligarchy or a democracy, having a soul that yearns for pleasures and desires and needs to be filled with these things, and that is in no way continent but is gripped by an endless sickness insatiable for evils,

(if) one of such a sort indeed rules a city or some individual, trampling the laws underfoot, (then), as [= which] we were saying just now, there is no way of being saved [= there is not a device of safety]. We have to consider this story, (to decide) whether we shall obey it or what we shall do.

– Indeed I suppose we must obey (it).

– Then are you aware that some (people) say that there are as many forms of laws as (there are forms) of governments? And we have just now gone through (use the perfect here) how many (forms) of governments the many say (exist). Do not think that the current dispute is about a trivial (thing); (it is) about the greatest (thing), for (the question of) what ought to be the aim of justice and injustice [= the just and the unjust, to where (they) should look] being disputed has again come (use perfect) to us.

Vocabulary

rest	ἀνάφυξις, -εως, ἡ	(to) be continent	στέγω
toil	πόνος, -ου, ὁ	(to) grip	ξυνέχω
imitate	μιμέομαι	endless	ἀνήνυτος, -ον
in the time of	ἐπί (+ gen.)	sickness	νόσημα, -ατος, τό
Kronos	Κρόνος, -ου, ὁ	insatiable for	ἄπληστος, -ον (+ gen.)
manage	διοικέω	(to) trample underfoot	καταπατέω
household	οἴκησις, -εως, ἡ	safety	σωτηρία, -ας, ἡ
publicly	δημοσίᾳ	(to) consider	σκοπέω
ordering	διανομή, -ῆς, ἡ	I suppose	που
oligarchy	ὀλιγαρχία, -ας, ἡ	(to) be aware	ἐννοέω
(to) yearn for	ὀρέγομαι (+ gen.)	dispute	ἀμφισβήτησις, -εως, ἡ
pleasure	ἡδονή, -ῆς, ἡ	(to) look	βλέπω
(to) fill with	πληρόω (+ gen.)	(to) dispute	ἀμφισβητέω

C) Passages in which the rules of Greek syntax are not entirely followed

Each of the following passages contains at least one violation of the rules set out in this book. Identify the "errors" and explain what the "correct" form would be. In some cases there are reasons why the rules were not followed – can you explain those reasons?

1. Plato, *Lysis* 206b–e

> Ἀλλὰ διὰ ταῦτα δή σοι, ὦ Σώκρατες, ἀνακοινοῦμαι, καὶ εἴ τι ἄλλο ἔχεις, συμβούλευε τίνα ἄν τις λόγον διαλεγόμενος ἢ τί πράττων προσφιλὴς παιδικοῖς γένοιτο.
>
> Οὐ ῥᾴδιον, ἦν δ' ἐγώ, εἰπεῖν· ἀλλ' εἴ μοι ἐθελήσαις αὐτὸν ποιῆσαι εἰς λόγους ἐλθεῖν, ἴσως ἂν δυναίμην σοι ἐπιδεῖξαι ἃ χρὴ αὐτῷ διαλέγεσθαι ἀντὶ τούτων ὧν οὗτοι λέγειν τε καὶ ᾄδειν φασί σε.

Ἀλλ' οὐδέν, ἔφη, χαλεπόν. ἂν γὰρ εἰσέλθῃς μετὰ Κτησίππου τοῦδε καὶ καθεζόμενος διαλέγῃ, οἶμαι μὲν καὶ αὐτός σοι πρόσεισι – φιλήκοος γάρ, ὦ Σώκρατες, διαφερόντως ἐστίν, καὶ ἅμα, ὡς Ἑρμαῖα ἄγουσιν, ἀναμεμειγμένοι ἐν ταὐτῷ εἰσιν οἵ τε νεανίσκοι καὶ οἱ παῖδες – πρόσεισιν οὖν σοι. εἰ δὲ μή, Κτησίππῳ συνήθης ἐστὶν διὰ τὸν τούτου ἀνεψιὸν Μενέξενον· Μενεξένῳ μὲν γὰρ δὴ πάντων μάλιστα ἑταῖρος ὢν τυγχάνει. καλεσάτω οὖν οὗτος αὐτόν, ἐὰν ἄρα μὴ προσίῃ αὐτός.

Ταῦτα, ἦν δ' ἐγώ, χρὴ ποιεῖν. Καὶ ἅμα λαβὼν τὸν Κτήσιππον προσῇα εἰς τὴν παλαίστραν· οἱ δ' ἄλλοι ὕστεροι ἡμῶν ἦσαν.

2.   Plato, *Lysis* 207d–208b

Ἐπεχείρουν δὴ μετὰ τοῦτο ἐρωτᾶν ὁπότερος δικαιότερος καὶ σοφώτερος αὐτῶν εἴη. μεταξὺ οὖν τις προσελθὼν ἀνέστησε τὸν Μενέξενον, φάσκων καλεῖν τὸν παιδοτρίβην· ἐδόκει γάρ μοι ἱεροποιῶν τυγχάνειν. ἐκεῖνος μὲν οὖν ᾤχετο· ἐγὼ δὲ τὸν Λύσιν ἠρόμην,

– Ἦ που, ἦν δ' ἐγώ, ὦ Λύσι, σφόδρα φιλεῖ σε ὁ πατὴρ καὶ ἡ μήτηρ;
– Πάνυ γε, ἦ δ' ὅς.
– Οὐκοῦν βούλοιντο ἄν σε ὡς εὐδαιμονέστατον εἶναι;
– Πῶς γὰρ οὔ;
– Δοκεῖ δέ σοι εὐδαίμων εἶναι ἄνθρωπος δουλεύων τε καὶ ᾧ μηδὲν ἐξείη ποιεῖν ὧν ἐπιθυμοῖ;
– Μὰ Δί' οὐκ ἔμοιγε, ἔφη.
– Οὐκοῦν εἴ σε φιλεῖ ὁ πατὴρ καὶ ἡ μήτηρ καὶ εὐδαίμονά σε ἐπιθυμοῦσι γενέσθαι, τοῦτο παντὶ τρόπῳ δῆλον ὅτι προθυμοῦνται ὅπως ἂν εὐδαιμονοίης.
– Πῶς γὰρ οὐχί; ἔφη.
– Ἐῶσιν ἄρα σε ἃ βούλει ποιεῖν, καὶ οὐδὲν ἐπιπλήττουσιν οὐδὲ διακωλύουσι ποιεῖν ὧν ἂν ἐπιθυμῇς;
– Ναὶ μὰ Δία ἐμέ γε, ὦ Σώκρατες, καὶ μάλα γε πολλὰ κωλύουσιν.
– Πῶς λέγεις; ἦν δ' ἐγώ. βουλόμενοί σε μακάριον εἶναι διακωλύουσι τοῦτο ποιεῖν ὃ ἂν βούλῃ; ὧδε δέ μοι λέγε. ἢν ἐπιθυμήσῃς ἐπί τινος τῶν τοῦ πατρὸς ἁρμάτων ὀχεῖσθαι λαβὼν τὰς ἡνίας, ὅταν ἁμιλλᾶται, οὐκ ἂν ἐῷέν σε ἀλλὰ διακωλύοιεν;
– Μὰ Δί' οὐ μέντοι ἄν, ἔφη, ἐῷεν.
– Ἀλλὰ τίνα μήν;
– Ἔστιν τις ἡνίοχος παρὰ τοῦ πατρὸς μισθὸν φέρων.
– Πῶς λέγεις; μισθωτῷ μᾶλλον ἐπιτρέπουσιν ἢ σοὶ ποιεῖν ὅτι ἂν βούληται περὶ τοὺς ἵππους, καὶ προσέτι αὐτοῦ τούτου ἀργύριον τελοῦσιν;
– Ἀλλὰ τί μήν; ἔφη.

– Ἀλλὰ τοῦ ὀρικοῦ ζεύγους οἶμαι ἐπιτρέπουσίν σοι ἄρχειν, κἂν εἰ βούλοιο
λαβὼν τὴν μάστιγα τύπτειν, ἐῷεν ἄν.
– Πόθεν, ἦ δ’ ὅς, ἐῷεν;
– Τί δέ; ἦν δ’ ἐγώ· οὐδενὶ ἔξεστιν αὐτοὺς τύπτειν;
– Καὶ μάλα, ἔφη, τῷ ὀρεοκόμῳ.

3.   Plato, *Lysis* 209c–e

Εἶεν, ἦν δ’ ἐγώ· τί δέ; τῷ γείτονι ἆρ’ οὐχ ὁ αὐτὸς ὅρος ὅσπερ τῷ πατρὶ
περὶ σοῦ; πότερον οἴει αὐτὸν ἐπιτρέπειν σοι τὴν αὐτοῦ οἰκίαν οἰκονομεῖν,
ὅταν σε ἡγήσηται βέλτιον περὶ οἰκονομίας ἑαυτοῦ φρονεῖν, ἢ αὐτὸν ἐπισ-
τατήσειν;
– Ἐμοὶ ἐπιτρέψειν οἶμαι.
– Τί δ’; Ἀθηναίους οἴει σοι οὐκ ἐπιτρέψειν τὰ αὐτῶν, ὅταν αἰσθάνωνται
ὅτι ἱκανῶς φρονεῖς;
– Ἔγωγε.
– Πρὸς Διός, ἦν δ’ ἐγώ, τί ἄρα ὁ μέγας βασιλεύς; πότερον τῷ πρεσβυτάτῳ
ὑεῖ, οὗ ἡ τῆς Ἀσίας ἀρχὴ γίγνεται, μᾶλλον ἂν ἐπιτρέψειεν ἑψομένων
κρεῶν ἐμβάλλειν ὅτι ἂν βούληται ἐμβαλεῖν εἰς τὸν ζωμόν, ἢ ἡμῖν, εἰ ἀφικόμενοι παρ’ ἐκεῖνον ἐνδειξαίμεθα αὐτῷ ὅτι ἡμεῖς κάλλιον φρονοῦμεν ἢ ὁ
ὑὸς αὐτοῦ περὶ ὄψου σκευασίας;
– Ἡμῖν δῆλον ὅτι, ἔφη.

4.   Find a passage of any Attic prose author (Plato, Xenophon, Thucydides, Aristotle,
or an orator) that does not completely follow the rules given in this book. Your passage should be about one page long and should contain at least two deviations from
the rules. Identify all the deviations the passage contains, explain them, and give the
"correct" version of each. The goal is to find as many deviations as possible and thereby
to appreciate the extent to which the rules you have learned are an oversimplification;
therefore the way to do badly in this exercise is to fail to spot deviations in the passage
you have chosen. (Hint: if you have difficulties, one way to start is to look up a rule in
Smyth and follow up his references to the exceptions.)

D) Other exercises

1.   Translate into English and analyze without reliance on punctuation.

Καὶ ναὶ μὰ Δί’ ὦ Σώκρατες περί γε ἐπιτηδευμάτων καλῶν καὶ ἔναγχος
αὐτόθι ηὐδοκίμησα διεξιὼν ἃ χρὴ τὸν νέον ἐπιτηδεύειν ἔστι γάρ μοι
περὶ αὐτῶν παγκάλως λόγος συγκείμενος καὶ ἄλλως εὖ διακείμενος καὶ

τοῖς ὀνόμασι πρόσχημα δέ μοί ἐστι καὶ ἀρχὴ τοιάδε τις τοῦ λόγου
ἐπειδὴ ἡ Τροία ἥλω λέγει ὁ λόγος ὅτι Νεοπτόλεμος Νέστορα ἔροιτο
ποῖά ἐστι καλὰ ἐπιτηδεύματα ἃ ἄν τις ἐπιτηδεύσας νέος ὢν εὐδοκιμώ-
τατος γένοιτο μετὰ (supply δὲ here) ταῦτα δὴ λέγων ἐστὶν ὁ Νέστωρ
καὶ ὑποτιθέμενος αὐτῷ πάμπολλα νόμιμα καὶ πάγκαλα τοῦτον (supply γὰρ here) δὴ καὶ ἐκεῖ ἐπεδειξάμην καὶ ἐνθάδε μέλλω ἐπιδεικνύναι
εἰς τρίτην ἡμέραν ἐν τῷ Φειδοστράτου διδασκαλείῳ καὶ ἄλλα πολλὰ
καὶ ἄξια ἀκοῆς ἐδεήθη γάρ μου Εὔδικος ὁ Ἀπημάντου ἀλλ’ ὅπως παρέ-
σει καὶ αὐτὸς καὶ ἄλλους ἄξεις οἵτινες ἱκανοὶ ἀκούσαντες κρῖναι τὰ
λεγόμενα

Ἀλλὰ ταῦτ’ ἔσται ἂν θεὸς ἐθέλῃ ὦ Ἱππία νυνὶ μέντοι βραχύ τί μοι περὶ
αὐτοῦ ἀπόκριναι καὶ γάρ με εἰς καλὸν ὑπέμνησας ἔναγχος γάρ τις ὦ
ἄριστε εἰς ἀπορίαν με κατέβαλεν ἐν λόγοις τισὶ τὰ μὲν ψέγοντα ὡς αἰσχρὰ
τὰ δ’ ἐπαινοῦντα ὡς καλὰ οὕτω πως ἐρόμενος καὶ μάλα ὑβριστικῶς πόθεν
δέ μοι σὺ ἔφη ὦ Σώκρατες οἶσθα ὁποῖα καλὰ καὶ αἰσχρά ἐπεὶ φέρε ἔχοις ἂν
εἰπεῖν τί ἔστι τὸ καλόν καὶ ἐγὼ διὰ τὴν ἐμὴν φαυλότητα ἠπορούμην τε καὶ
οὐκ εἶχον αὐτῷ κατὰ τρόπον ἀποκρίνασθαι ἀπιὼν οὖν ἐκ τῆς συνουσίας
ἐμαυτῷ τε ὠργιζόμην καὶ ὠνείδιζον καὶ ἠπείλουν ὁπότε πρῶτον ὑμῶν τῳ
τῶν σοφῶν ἐντύχοιμι ἀκούσας καὶ μαθὼν καὶ ἐκμελετήσας ἰέναι πάλιν ἐπὶ
τὸν ἐρωτήσαντα ἀναμαχούμενος τὸν λόγον νῦν οὖν ὃ λέγω εἰς καλὸν ἥκεις
καί με δίδαξον ἱκανῶς αὐτὸ τὸ καλὸν ὅ τι ἔστι καὶ πειρῶ μοι ὅτι μάλιστα
ἀκριβῶς εἰπεῖν ἀποκρινόμενος μὴ ἐξελεγχθεὶς τὸ δεύτερον αὖθις γέλωτα
ὄφλω οἶσθα γὰρ δή που σαφῶς καὶ σμικρόν που τοῦτ’ ἂν εἴη μάθημα ὧν
σὺ τῶν πολλῶν ἐπίστασαι

(Plato, *Hippias Major* 286a–e; ἐπιτηδεύματα “practices,” ἔναγχος
“recently,” αὐτόθι i.e. in Sparta, εὐδοκιμέω “become famous,” διέξειμι
i.e. “tell,” συντίθημι “put together,” διατίθημι “arrange,” ὄνομα “word,”
πρόσχημα “plan,” ὑποτίθεμαι “suggest,” εἰς τρίτην ἡμέραν “the day
after tomorrow,” διδασκαλεῖον “school,” εἰς καλόν i.e. “of the beautiful,”
ὑπομιμνήσκω “remind,” ψέγω “blame,” οὕτω for ὧδε, φέρε “come on!”
(parenthetical), ἔχω + inf. “be able to,” κατὰ τρόπον “in a (good) manner,” ἐκμελετάω “practice,” ὅτι μάλιστα ἀκριβῶς “as precisely as possible,”
τὸ δεύτερον i.e. “again,” ὀφλισκάνω “bring on oneself,” μάθημα “piece of
knowledge,” τῶν πολλῶν is an incorporated antecedent)

2.   Compose your own paragraph in Greek on one of the topics below. Use at least one
construction from each of chapters I–XVIII, and identify them by including the chapter
number next to the construction in question.

a. How were the ancient opinions of war different from our own?
b. Is wealth now more highly valued than it was in antiquity?
c. What would Socrates say about the education system you have experienced?
d. What would you do if you could visit ancient Greece?
e. Of the people you know, who is most similar to Socrates, and why?
f. Of the people you know, who is most similar to Alcibiades, and why?

APPENDIX A
Errors in Smyth's Grammar

§227, right-hand column, dative should be Ἑρμῆ not Ἑρμῇ.

§237n., cross-reference should be to page 4A, not page 3.

§306, feminine accusative plural λυσάσας should have long marks over all three vowels.

§342, first column, Ἀθήνησι should be Ἀθήνησι.

§384, third column, third singular subjunctive should be λελοιπὼς ᾖ not λελοιπὼς ἤ.

§406, right-hand column, last form should be πεπραγμένος εἴην not πεπραγμένος εἶην.

§416, p. 135, right-hand column, third plural subjunctive should be διδῶσι not διδῶσ.

§424b, it is not true that certain second aorist imperatives are accented εἰπέτε, ἐλθέτε, etc. The plurals have recessive accentuation, and only the singulars have the irregular accent εἰπέ etc.

§668d, p. 195, 3rd line of footnotes, -αῖεν should be -αιεν.

§682, singular subjunctive should be γνῶ, γνῷς, γνῷ, not γνῶ, γνῶς, γνῶ.

§2499, first line, η should be ᾖ.

English tenses and their Greek equivalents (indicative only)

English tense	English form, active	English form, passive	Greek equivalent
Simple present	"I eat." "I do not eat." "Do I eat?"	"It is (not) eaten by me." "Is it eaten by me?"	Present[1]
Present progressive	"I am (not) eating." "Am I eating?"	"It is (not) being eaten by me." "Is it being eaten by me?"	Present[2]
Future	"I will (not) eat." "Will I eat?" "I shall (not) eat." "Shall I eat?"	"It will (not) be eaten by me." "Will it be eaten by me?" "It shall (not) be eaten by me." "Shall it be eaten by me?"	Future
Future progressive	"I will (not) be eating." "I shall (not) be eating."	"It will (not) be being eaten by me." "It shall (not) be being eaten by me."	Future
Simple past	"I ate." "I did not eat." "Did I eat?"	"It was (not) eaten by me." "Was it eaten by me?"	Aorist or imperfect[3]
Past progressive	"I was (not) eating." "Was I eating?"	"It was (not) being eaten by me." "Was it being eaten by me?"	Imperfect[4]
Past repetitive	"I used to eat."	"It used to be eaten by me."	Imperfect[5]
Perfect	"I have (not) eaten." "Have I eaten?"	"It has (not) been eaten by me." "Has it been eaten by me?"	Aorist or perfect
Perfect progressive	"I have (not) been eating." "Have I been eating?"	"It has (not) been being eaten by me." "Has it been being eaten by me?"	Present

(cont.)

[1] Or perfect in the case of certain verbs like ἵστημι.
[2] Or perfect in the case of certain verbs like ἵστημι.
[3] The imperfect is likely when the action is continuous by nature, as "live."
[4] Or pluperfect in the case of certain verbs like ἵστημι.
[5] Or pluperfect in the case of certain verbs like ἵστημι.

(*cont.*)

English tense	English form, active	English form, passive	Greek equivalent
Pluperfect	"I had (not) eaten." "Had I eaten?"	"It had (not) been eaten by me." "Had it been eaten by me?"	Usually aorist
Future perfect	"I will (not) have eaten."	"It will (not) have been eaten by me."	Future perfect
	"Will I have eaten?"	"Will it have been eaten by me?"	
	"I shall (not) have eaten."	"It shall (not) have been eaten by me."	
	"Shall I have eaten?"	"Shall it have been eaten by me?"	

NB also:

English present participle (active) "eating" = Greek present active or aorist active participle

English past participle (passive) "eaten" = Greek present passive or aorist passive participle

English perfect participle (active) "having eaten" = Greek aorist active participle

English perfect participle (passive) "having been eaten" = Greek aorist passive participle

APPENDIX C
Hints for analyzing Greek sentences

The system of analysis suggested in this book is not perfect, because it does not capture all elements of the organization of clauses. The author has, however, restrained her impulse to use a more nuanced system in the interests of providing a simple and straightforward set of rules that can be followed consistently. This appendix, being designed primarily for readers who are still having difficulty with analysis after completing chapter vi but also for those who would like to pursue analysis further, therefore offers first a more detailed step-by-step explanation of how to use the recommended system, and then suggestions for another that can be used once the basic one has been mastered.

A) **Recommended system of analysis.** The key point is the principle of division: sentences are divided so that each part has exactly one verb form. Infinitives and participles count as verb forms except for attributive participles, which count as adjectives; verbal adjectives in -τέος count as adjectives. Suppose one wishes to analyze the following sentence:

> ἐπειδὴ ἐγγὺς τοῦ στομίου ἦμεν μέλλοντες ἀνιέναι καὶ τἄλλα πάντα
> πεπονθότες, ἐκεῖνόν τε κατείδομεν ἐξαίφνης καὶ ἄλλους, σχεδόν τι αὐτῶν
> τοὺς πλείστους τυράννους· ἦσαν δὲ καὶ ἰδιῶταί τινες τῶν μεγάλα
> ἡμαρτηκότων· οὓς οἰομένους ἤδη ἀναβήσεσθαι οὐκ ἐδέχετο τὸ στόμιον,
> ἀλλ᾽ ἐμυκᾶτο, ὁπότε τις τῶν οὕτως ἀνιάτως ἐχόντων εἰς πονηρίαν ἢ μὴ
> ἱκανῶς δεδωκὼς δίκην ἐπιχειροῖ ἀνιέναι.

> (Plato, *Republic* 615d–e, the myth of Er; στόμιον "mouth" (of the afterworld); ἐκεῖνον refers to Ardiaeus, a (supposedly) famously wicked tyrant; ἰδιώτης "private citizen," ἁμαρτάνω "do wrong," μυκάομαι "bellow," ἀνιάτως ἔχω "be incorrigible," ἐπιχειρέω "attempt")

The steps of the analysis would be as follows.

1) **Identify all the verb forms**, except attributive participles. Thus:

> ἐπειδὴ ἐγγὺς τοῦ στομίου <u>ἦμεν</u> <u>μέλλοντες</u> <u>ἀνιέναι</u> καὶ τἄλλα πάντα
> <u>πεπονθότες</u>, ἐκεῖνόν τε <u>κατείδομεν</u> ἐξαίφνης καὶ ἄλλους, σχεδόν τι αὐτῶν
> τοὺς πλείστους τυράννους· <u>ἦσαν</u> δὲ καὶ ἰδιῶταί τινες τῶν μεγάλα
> ἡμαρτηκότων· οὓς <u>οἰομένους</u> ἤδη <u>ἀναβήσεσθαι</u> οὐκ <u>ἐδέχετο</u> τὸ στόμιον,

ἀλλ' ἐμυκᾶτο, ὁπότε τις τῶν οὕτως ἀνιάτως ἐχόντων εἰς πονηρίαν ἢ μὴ ἱκανῶς δεδωκὼς δίκην ἐπιχειροῖ ἀνιέναι.

Notice that ἡμαρτηκότων and ἐχόντων have not been marked, because they are attributive participles and could be identified as such by their articles.

2) **Divide the sentence** into units, each unit having one of these verb forms; the introductory words of the various clauses are the keys to correct division.

The initial ἐπειδή points to a finite verb and means that the first division comes after that verb (ἦμεν) and before the next one; therefore the only possibility is for the first unit to be ἐπειδὴ ἐγγὺς τοῦ στομίου ἦμεν. The second unit must be just μέλλοντες, as it has other verbs before and after it. The third is just ἀνιέναι, because the following καί opens a new unit. The word καί points to is πεπονθότες, and the τε two words later is a postpositive unit opener, so the unit must be καὶ τἄλλα πάντα πεπονθότες. The next opening word is the postpositive δέ after ἦσαν; therefore that unit is ἐκεῖνόν τε κατείδομεν ἐξαίφνης καὶ ἄλλους, σχεδόν τι αὐτῶν τοὺς πλείστους τυράννους. The unit attached to ἦσαν continues until the next opening word, the relative pronoun οὕς, and is therefore ἦσαν δὲ καὶ ἰδιῶταί τινες τῶν μεγάλα ἡμαρτηκότων.

With οὕς more serious difficulties start to emerge. The opener is a relative pronoun, and relative pronouns always point to finite verbs, but the next two verb forms are not finite and therefore cannot be what the opener is pointing to; therefore there are nesting units. Ignoring οὕς for the moment, identify the nesting units. There are two verb forms, οἰομένους and ἀναβήσεσθαι, with an adverb in between; since adverbs normally precede their verbs, we can be reasonably confident that the division comes before the adverb. Similarly on the other side of ἀναβήσεσθαι there is a negative and then another verb; negatives normally precede their verbs, so the division comes before the negative. Therefore the two nested units are οἰομένους and ἤδη ἀναβήσεσθαι. Now we have a finite verb that can go with οὕς, so we put them together, using ellipsis (. . .) to indicate the join,[1] and look for the end of the unit, which is signaled by the next opener, ἀλλά. So the unit is οὕς . . . οὐκ ἐδέχετο τὸ στόμιον. The end of the next unit is identified by the opener ὁπότε, so it is ἀλλ' ἐμυκᾶτο.

With ὁπότε once again we find an opener that points to a finite verb over a participle, so it is necessary to identify the nested unit centered on δεδωκώς. This must start with ἤ, which is an opener, and could in theory end either before or after δίκην. At this point

---

[1] Because ellipsis is needed for this type of situation, it is best not to use it as an efficient way to identify long units (e.g. writing ἐπειδή . . . ἦμεν for the first unit would not make it clear that there are no nesting units within this unit). Such abbreviated indications are also risky because, when one uses them, one often fails to look closely enough for nesting units and to think hard enough about exactly where divisions occur, and thus they lead to errors as well as to ambiguity. A good principle for analysis, therefore, is that every single word in a unit should be specifically indicated in the analysis; an efficient way to do this with long units is to write out their first and last words and abbreviate those in between to their first letters only.

a knowledge of idiom is needed: δίκην δίδωμι is a common phrase meaning "to pay the penalty," and no Greek would have used those two words next to each other without expecting the reader to take them together. Therefore the division comes after δίκην, and the nested unit is ἢ μὴ ἱκανῶς δεδωκὼς δίκην. That leaves the temporal clause as ὁπότε τις τῶν οὕτως ἀνιάτως ἐχόντων εἰς πονηρίαν . . . ἐπιχειροῖ, and the final unit must be just ἀνιέναι.

Now, therefore, we have the sentence divided into units as follows:

> ἐπειδὴ ἐγγὺς τοῦ στομίου ἦμεν |μέλλοντες |ἀνιέναι καὶ τᾶλλα πάντα πεπονθότες, |ἐκεῖνόν τε κατείδομεν ἐξαίφνης καὶ ἄλλους, σχεδόν τι αὐτῶν τοὺς πλείστους τυράννους· |ἦσαν δὲ καὶ ἰδιῶταί τινες τῶν μεγάλα ἡμαρτηκότων· |οὓς . . . |οἰομένους |ἤδη ἀναβήσεσθαι | . . . οὐκ ἐδέχετο τὸ στόμιον, |ἀλλ᾽ ἐμυκᾶτο, |ὁπότε τις τῶν οὕτως ἀνιάτως ἐχόντων εἰς πονηρίαν . . . |ἢ μὴ ἱκανῶς δεδωκὼς δίκην | . . . ἐπιχειροῖ |ἀνιέναι.

3) **Work out** how the units relate to one another. Is the first unit a main verb? If so, it would get the number 1, but since it is opened by the subordinating conjunction ἐπειδή it is not a main verb. None of the next three verbs can be the main verb either, since they are not finite,[2] so the first main verb, which gets the number 1, must be κατείδομεν. Everything before that main verb must depend on it, and the ἐπειδή tells us that the first unit can depend directly on the main verb, so the first unit gets the number 1.1 to indicate that it is the first unit dependent on the first main verb. Now there follow three non-finite verb forms, which in theory could depend either directly on the main verb or on the temporal clause 1.1. However, there is a general rule that Greek subordinates of all kinds are assumed to go with what precedes unless there is some indication that they do not,[3] and no such indication is given here for μέλλοντες, which therefore must depend on ἦσαν and so be numbered 1.1.1. Now μέλλω takes a future infinitive, so it is fairly obvious that the following unit, ἀνιέναι, must depend on μέλλοντες and be numbered 1.1.1.1. Next, the καί makes it clear that the following unit is not another level of subordination, but parallel to something already stated. As the verb of the unit is a

---

[2] Main verbs are always finite except in *oratio obliqua* (with a few rare exceptions), and they are usually indicative; they can be subjunctive or optative only if using one of the few constructions that require such a mood in the main verb, such as the deliberative subjunctive or the potential optative.

[3] Such indication usually comes in the form of a co-ordinating and a subordinating conjunction used together. Thus when a subordinate clause that comes between two main clauses begins with εἰ or ὅτε, it goes with the main clause that precedes it, but if it begins with εἰ δέ or ὅτι γάρ, it goes with the one that follows; in that case the subordinating conjunction (εἰ or ὅτι) belongs to the unit at hand, and the co-ordinating conjunction belongs to the main verb that comes later, being used to attach it to a previous main verb. Similarly an infinitive or participle attaches itself to a preceding verb without any conjunction; if a participle is accompanied by a co-ordinating conjunction, it depends on the following verb, and the conjunction joins that verb to a previous finite verb.

participle, the parallel unit must be one with a participle, i.e. μέλλοντες. Therefore this unit depends directly on the initial temporal clause and so receives the number 1.1.2 (i.e. the second unit depending on the first unit that depends on the first main verb). So the beginning of the sentence can be analyzed as follows, indenting once for each level of subordination:

> 1.1 ἐπειδὴ ἐγγὺς τοῦ στομίου ἦμεν
>> 1.1.1 μέλλοντες
>>> 1.1.1.1 ἀνιέναι
>> 1.1.2 καὶ τἄλλα πάντα πεπονθότες,
> 1 ἐκεῖνόν τε κατείδομεν ἐξαίφνης καὶ ἄλλους, σχεδόν τι αὐτῶν τοὺς πλείστους τυράννους·

Now we have a co-ordinating conjunction, δέ, that connects parallel units; the unit to which it belongs has a finite verb and therefore needs to be connected to the previous finite verb. That verb is the first main verb, κατείδομεν, and therefore this clause is the second main verb and receives the number 2. It is followed by a relative clause, which must be directly subordinate to it since there is no indication to the contrary, so the relative clause gets the number 2.1. The units nested inside the relative clause must be subordinate to that clause; οἰομένους is a participle and therefore can easily attach itself directly to any verb, whereas ἀναβήσεσθαι is an infinitive and so can only be attached to certain verbs,[4] of which οἶμαι is one but δέχομαι is not, and therefore οἰομένους must depend directly on the relative clause while ἀναβήσεσθαι depends on οἰομένους. So this section must work as follows:

> 2 ἦσαν δὲ καὶ ἰδιῶταί τινες τῶν μεγάλα ἡμαρτηκότων·
>> 2.1 οὕς . . . οὐκ ἐδέχετο τὸ στόμιον,
>>> 2.1.1 οἰομένους
>>>> 2.1.1.1 ἤδη ἀναβήσεσθαι

One could arrange these differently without changing the numbering, by putting the relative clause on the last line on the grounds that its verb comes after the other verbs. However, there are distinct advantages to ordering the units by the order of appearance of the first words of those units: this is the order in which the author wanted the reader to be aware of the existence of those clauses, so it is usually easier to understand and to translate them in that order.

The next unit opens with a co-ordinating conjunction followed by a finite verb, which must therefore be parallel to the preceding finite verb (unless there is some indication

---

[4] Some verbs that take infinitives, including οἶμαι, do so because of indirect statement and are listed in chapter x. Many others, like ἐθέλω, take an infinitive that is not considered to be indirect statement; most of these are obvious to English speakers because their English equivalents also take infinitives, but when in doubt one can consult LSJ, where the constructions of individual verbs are given.

that one should look further back, but there is none here). So ἐμυκᾶτο must be a second verb in the relative clause and therefore ultimately dependent on ἦσαν, and it therefore receives the number 2.2. The following temporal clause should be dependent on what precedes it, in this case ἐμυκᾶτο, and therefore gets the number 2.2.1. The unit nested inside the temporal clause must be dependent on it and therefore can be numbered 2.2.1.1, meaning that the final unit, which must also be dependent on the temporal clause since ἐπιχειρέω takes an infinitive, gets 2.2.1.2. The remainder of the sentence would therefore be analyzed as:

> 2.2 ἀλλ᾽ ἐμυκᾶτο,
>> 2.2.1 ὁπότε τις τῶν οὕτως ἀνιάτως ἐχόντων εἰς πονηρίαν . . . ἐπιχειροῖ
>>> 2.2.1.1 ἢ μὴ ἱκανῶς δεδωκὼς δίκην
>>> 2.2.1.2 ἀνιέναι.

Notice that the last two units are not in any real sense parallel to one another. Numbering of the type they have does not necessarily indicate parallelism (though parallel clauses often get such numbering), but rather dependence on the same unit. Notice also that unit 2.2.1.1 is problematic, because the τις in 2.2.1 has two modifiers, the first of which is a partitive genitive composed of an attributive participle and the second is a circumstantial participle; these are fundamentally parallel constructions and are linked by the co-ordinating conjunction ἤ, so it is unfortunate that this system of analysis forces us to make one dependent on the other.[5]

4) **Translate** the sentence. Of course, one could translate the sentence earlier, and it is certainly a good idea to find the meanings of unfamiliar words before starting so that one knows what type of constructions they are likely to take, but after becoming familiar with the process of analysis one finds that it is much easier to translate afterwards. The results for this sentence are:

> 1.1 ἐπειδὴ ἐγγὺς τοῦ στομίου ἦμεν "When we were near the mouth (of the afterworld),"
>> 1.1.1 μέλλοντες "when we were about"
>>> 1.1.1.1 ἀνιέναι "to go up (out of it),"
>> 1.1.2 καὶ τἆλλα πάντα πεπονθότες, "and when we had experienced all the other things,"
> 1 ἐκεῖνόν τε κατείδομεν ἐξαίφνης καὶ ἄλλους, σχεδόν τι αὐτῶν τοὺς πλείστους τυράννους· "we suddenly saw him and others, almost most of them tyrants;"

---

[5] It would of course be possible to change the rules of this system of analysis so that attributive participles counted as separate verb forms; such a change would solve the difficulty in this sentence, but it would create similar problems in many other sentences, since attributive participles are more likely to be paired with adjectives than with circumstantial participles.

2 ἦσαν δὲ καὶ ἰδιῶταί τινες τῶν μεγάλα ἡμαρτηκότων· "and there were also some private citizens (i.e. non-tyrants), from among those who had done the greatest wrongs,"

   2.1 οὕς . . . οὐκ ἐδέχετο τὸ στόμιον, "whom the mouth did not receive"

      2.1.1 οἰομένους "when they thought"

         2.1.1.1 ἤδη ἀναβήσεσθαι "that they were now going to go up,"

   2.2 ἀλλ' ἐμυκᾶτο, "but it bellowed,"

      2.2.1 ὁπότε τις τῶν οὕτως ἀνιάτως ἐχόντων εἰς πονηρίαν . . . ἐπιχειροῖ "whenever one of those who were incorrigible with respect to wickedness . . . tried"

         2.2.1.1 ἢ μὴ ἱκανῶς δεδωκὼς δίκην "or had not sufficiently paid the penalty"

         2.2.1.2 ἀνιέναι. "to go up." (i.e. "whenever one of those who were incorrigible with respect to wickedness or had not sufficiently paid the penalty tried to go up.")

Notice that until the end, the English translation is perfectly intelligible in the order of the analyzed clauses; this is usually the case. The only problem occurs at the point where an insufficiently nuanced analysis system has been unable to capture exactly what is going on in the Greek.

5) **Comment** on the particular features of the sentence that relate to the chapter in question. If this sentence were being analyzed for chapter vi, where the topic is word order and connection, one would mark the verb forms and the opening words and indicate how we know what is parallel and what is subordinate to what (see the discussion above). If on the other hand this sentence were being analyzed for chapter xvi, on temporal clauses, one would comment only on unit 1.1, which one would identify as being a simple temporal clause taking the indicative because it refers to a specific act in the past, and unit 2.2.1, which one would identify as being a general temporal clause taking the optative because it refers to a repeated action and is in secondary sequence; one would also comment on the different conjunctions used, ἐπειδή and ὁπότε.

B) **More nuanced systems of analysis.** Here the goal is to make it perfectly obvious what depends on what and what is parallel to what, without violating word order by moving things around and using ellipsis as in the basic system. It is also important to break up the sentence into units that its author would have recognized as units; this is particularly valuable in analyzing sentences from the orators, where one may need to find the orator's own cola in order to see the rhetorical devices he used. No hard-and-fast set of rules will allow one to do this successfully, so considerable flexibility is required. For example, some infinitives and participles act like verbs and need to be treated as their own units, while others work like nouns or adjectives and should not be separated from their surroundings; though circumstantial participles are more likely to belong to the former group and attributive ones to the latter, exceptions occur in both directions. Often words that are not verbs need to be given their own lines to make it clear that they belong to more than one unit. And once such words have their own lines, the distinction between what is and what is not a separate unit becomes blurred, making it difficult or impossible to number the units; numbering is in any case inadequate to capture some situations, such as those in which one subordinate depends on two main clauses. As a result, the entire force of the analysis must be carried by the indentations.

The sentence we have been analyzing, for example, could also be handled as follows:

    ἐπειδὴ ἐγγὺς τοῦ στομίου ἦμεν

        μέλλοντες

            ἀνιέναι

        καὶ τἆλλα πάντα πεπονθότες,

  ἐκεῖνόν τε κατείδομεν ἐξαίφνης καὶ ἄλλους, σχεδόν τι αὐτῶν τοὺς πλείστους

                                  τυράννους·

  ἦσαν δὲ καὶ ἰδιῶταί τινες τῶν μεγάλα ἡμαρτηκότων·

    οὓς

        οἰομένους

            ἤδη ἀναβήσεσθαι

      οὐκ ἐδέχετο τὸ στόμιον,

      ἀλλ' ἐμυκᾶτο,

        ὁπότε

           τις

              τῶν οὕτως ἀνιάτως ἐχόντων εἰς πονηρίαν

              ἢ μὴ ἱκανῶς δεδωκὼς δίκην

         ἐπιχειροῖ

           ἀνιέναι.

Notice that the beginning of the sentence, which was relatively straightforward, has not changed apart from deletion of the numbers; the alterations are only in the more complex clauses. The relative is handled by making οὓς a unit by itself, so that the parallel way that the two verbs of the relative clause go back to the relative can be more clearly demonstrated. The temporal clause at the end is broken up so that the verb depends directly on the introductory conjunction, and the two modifiers that qualify τις are also separated in a way that shows their relationship to τις and to each other. This version has divided the sentence into more units than the basic system, and that will nearly always be the case if one uses the more nuanced system properly: it is frequently the case that something which is not a verb form would be better off having its own line, but it is almost never the case that two verbs really belong on the same line.

The advantages of using a more nuanced system with rhetorical works can be illustrated from the following sentence of Isocrates (*Panegyricus* 47–9), where rhymes and other echoes in sound have been marked; notice how the rhymes often link parallel units, and also how often parallel units are approximately the same length:

φιλοσοφίαν τοίνυν,

ἢ

πάντα ταῦτα

συνεξεῦρε

καὶ συγκατεσκεύασεν

καὶ πρός τε τὰς πράξεις ἡμᾶς ἐπαίδευσεν

καὶ πρὸς ἀλλήλους ἐπράϋνε

καὶ τῶν συμφορῶν

τάς τε δι᾽ ἀμαθίαν

καὶ τὰς ἐξ ἀνάγκης γιγνομένας

διεῖλεν

καὶ

τὰς μὲν φυλάξασθαι,

τὰς δὲ καλῶς ἐνεγκεῖν

ἐδίδαξεν,

ἡ πόλις ἡμῶν κατέδειξεν,

καὶ λόγους ἐτίμησεν,

ὧν

πάντες μὲν ἐπιθυμοῦσιν,

τοῖς δ᾽ ἐπισταμένοις φθονοῦσιν,

συνειδυῖα μὲν

ὅτι τοῦτο μόνον ἐξ ἁπάντων τῶν ζῴων ἴδιον ἔφυμεν ἔχοντες

καὶ διότι τούτῳ πλεονεκτήσαντες καὶ τοῖς ἄλλοις ἅπασιν αὐτῶν

διηνέγκαμεν,

ὁρῶσα δὲ

περὶ μὲν τὰς ἄλλας πράξεις οὕτω ταραχώδεις οὔσας τὰς τύχας

ὥστε

πολλάκις ἐν αὐταῖς

καὶ τοὺς φρονίμους ἀτυχεῖν

καὶ τοὺς ἀνοήτους κατορθοῦν,

τῶν δὲ λόγων τῶν καλῶς καὶ τεχνικῶς ἐχόντων οὐ μετὸν τοῖς
φαύλοις,

ἀλλὰ ψυχῆς εὖ φρονούσης ἔργον ὄντας,

καὶ τούς τε σοφοὺς καὶ τοὺς ἀμαθεῖς δοκοῦντας εἶναι ταύτῃ
πλεῖστον ἀλλήλων διαφέροντας,

ἔτι δὲ τοὺς εὐθὺς ἐξ ἀρχῆς ἐλευθέρως τεθραμμένους

ἐκ μὲν ἀνδρίας καὶ πλούτου καὶ τῶν τοιούτων ἀγαθῶν οὐ
γιγνωσκομένους,

ἐκ δὲ τῶν λεγομένων μάλιστα καταφανεῖς γιγνομένους,

καὶ τοῦτο σύμβολον τῆς παιδεύσεως ἡμῶν ἑκάστου πιστότατον
ἀποδεδειγμένον,

καὶ τοὺς λόγῳ καλῶς χρωμένους

οὐ μόνον ἐν ταῖς αὑτῶν δυναμένους,

ἀλλὰ καὶ παρὰ τοῖς ἄλλοις ἐντίμους ὄντας.

Those who are having difficulty with the basic system are sometimes tempted to attribute those difficulties to the system's own shortcomings and to move on to a more nuanced system before they have thoroughly mastered the basic one. In doing so they may be attracted not only by its greater accuracy but also by a feeling that if the system has no hard and fast rules it must be easier, since one's decisions about whether to give a specific participle, relative pronoun, or infinitive its own line or not cannot be wrong. Unfortunately, this is not the case. With a more nuanced system it is easy to be wrong; for example in the sentence we have been examining it would be wrong not to separate the τῶν οὕτως ἀνιάτως ἐχόντων εἰς πονηρίαν from the τις, because doing so is the only way to enable oneself to reflect the parallelism of ἢ μὴ ἱκανῶς δεδωκὼς δίκην accurately. But it would have been impossible to predict the necessity for this separation, since it is very rare that a partitive genitive would need to be separated from the word on which it depends. In other words, the more flexible system has many more ways to be actually wrong than does the basic system, but without rules there is no way of predicting in advance what will be wrong. Those wishing to use this system are strongly advised first to master the basic one and then, when moving on to this one, to keep the basic one in mind and be sure never to end up with a unit containing more than one verb form.

Many people find the process of sentence analysis intimidating at first, but this problem usually disappears after a few weeks, since in the vast majority of cases, difficulties with sentence analysis are simply due to inexperience and unfamiliarity with the process. The only way to overcome such problems is to practice, using as simple a system as possible until one is thoroughly comfortable with the underlying principles and ready to move on to more advanced work. The author herself required a considerable amount of such practice and therefore urges others not to be discouraged about their ability to master analysis until they have tried it extensively.

English conditional clauses

The meanings of the English formulae conventionally used to translate the main types of Greek conditional sentence are as follows. (NB that the "protasis" is the if-clause of a conditional and the "apodosis" is the main clause; despite those names, the clauses can come in either order.)

Simple conditions

No information is conveyed about whether the situation envisioned in the protasis is real or how often it occurs. The verbs are indicative, any type of past or present, and the tenses of the two verbs need not match.

> "If he <u>is</u> on the phone, he's <u>talking</u> to Maria." (We do not know whether he is on the phone.)

> "If there's a message, someone <u>called</u> while we were out." (We do not know whether there is a message.)

General conditions

These are formed just like simple conditions in English, except that the two verbs will normally share the same tense and sometimes "if ever" is used to make the generality more obvious when translating into or out of Greek. In a natural English sentence "if ever" is rare, and the only difference between simple and general is one of meaning: the general conditions envision a situation that by its nature is repeated or general.

> "If it <u>rains</u>, class picnics <u>are</u> cancelled." (At this school, whenever it rains the picnics are cancelled.)

> "If he <u>is</u> late, she <u>gets</u> upset." (Whenever he is late, she gets upset.)

> "If Romans <u>wanted</u> to live long lives, they <u>did</u> not <u>make</u> rude gestures at the Emperor." (A general statement about all Romans.)

Present contrafactual conditions

The situation envisioned in the protasis is stated not to be the case at the time the sentence is uttered. The verb of the protasis is "were" if it is a form of the verb "be";

otherwise it is "were" plus a present participle. The verb of the apodosis is "would be" if it is a form of the verb "be"; otherwise it is "would be" plus a present participle.

> "If I <u>were</u> you, I <u>would be filing</u> for divorce this minute." (I am not you.)

> "If he <u>were</u> here, everything <u>would be</u> okay." (He is not here.)

> "If they <u>were cooking</u> dinner, they <u>would be making</u> a mess." (They are not cooking dinner.)

> "If you <u>were learning</u> Chinese, you <u>would</u> not <u>be worrying</u> about this kind of problem." (You are not learning Chinese.)

Past contrafactual conditions

The situation envisioned in the protasis is stated not to have been the case in the past. The verb of the protasis is pluperfect ("had" plus a past participle). The verb of the apodosis is "would have" plus a past participle.

> "If I <u>had been</u> in your position, I <u>would have filed</u> for divorce at once." (I was not in your position.)

> "If he <u>had been</u> here, everything <u>would have been</u> okay." (He was not here.)

> "If they <u>had cooked</u> dinner, they <u>would have made</u> a mess." (They did not cook dinner.)

> "If you <u>had learned</u> Chinese, you <u>would</u> not <u>have worried</u> about this kind of problem." (You did not learn Chinese.)

Contrafactual conditions can freely be mixed, with a protasis of one type and an apodosis of the other.

> "If I <u>were</u> you, I <u>would</u> not <u>have done</u> that." (present + past)

> "If you <u>had learned</u> this last year, you <u>would</u> not <u>be learning</u> it now." (past + present)

Future more vivid conditions

The situation envisioned in the protasis may or may not occur in the future; no information is offered as to its likelihood. The verb of the protasis is in the present, and the verb of the apodosis is in the future.

"If it <u>rains</u>, we <u>shall postpone</u> the picnic." (We do not know whether it will rain.)

"If he <u>comes</u>, there <u>will be</u> trouble." (We do not know whether he will come.)

"If they <u>are</u> late, she <u>will get</u> upset." (We do not know whether they will be late.)

The Greek future most vivid is also translated with a future more vivid in English.

Future less vivid conditions

The situation envisioned in the protasis might occur in the future, but the speaker wishes to represent it as not very likely. The verb of the protasis can have a variety of different forms ("should" plus infinitive, "were to" plus infinitive, simple past), but the verb of the apodosis is almost always "would" plus infinitive (NB not "would be" plus participle: that is the present contrafactual, which is easily confused with the future less vivid).

"If it <u>should rain</u>, we <u>would postpone</u> the picnic." (The speaker does not think it will rain.)

"If it <u>were to rain</u>, we <u>would postpone</u> the picnic." (The speaker does not think it will rain.)

"If it <u>rained</u>, we <u>would postpone</u> the picnic." (The speaker does not think it will rain.)

"If he <u>should be</u> late, there <u>would be</u> trouble." (The speaker does not think he will be late.)

"If he <u>were to be</u> late, there <u>would be</u> trouble." (The speaker does not think he will be late.)

Exercise

Take the following sentences and change their tenses to those of the type of conditional indicated, which should express the circumstances indicated after it. Example: given the sentence "If Mary is there, she is protesting" and asked to change it to the past simple, in other words the past when we do not know whether Mary was there, one would say "If Mary was there, she was protesting" or "If Mary was there, she protested"; if asked to change it to the past contrafactual, in other words the past when we know that Mary was not there, one would say "If Mary had been there, she would have protested." One of the results in each group will be identical to the original sentence, and sometimes two of the results may be identical to each other: with these sentences it is not possible to distinguish between simple and general conditions in English. A complete key for this exercise can be found at the end of Appendix G.

"If Jim is in charge everything is going well."

a. past simple (i.e. we do not know whether Jim was in charge)
b. past contrafactual (i.e. Jim was not in charge)
c. present simple (i.e. we do not know whether Jim is in charge)
d. present contrafactual (i.e. Jim is not in charge)
e. future more vivid (i.e. we do not know whether Jim will be in charge)
f. future less vivid (i.e. Jim is unlikely to be in charge)

"If Jane goes to the shop she buys a paper."

g. past general (i.e. this was Jane's habitual custom)
h. past contrafactual (i.e. Jane did not go to the shop)
i. present general (i.e. this is Jane's habitual custom)
j. present contrafactual (i.e. Jane is not going to the shop)
k. future more vivid (i.e. we do not know whether Jane will go to the shop)
l. future less vivid (i.e. Jane is unlikely to go to the shop)

"If Fido sees a cat he chases it."

m. past general (i.e. every cat that Fido saw was chased)
n. past contrafactual (i.e. Fido did not see a cat yesterday)
o. present general (i.e. every cat that Fido sees is chased)
p. present contrafactual (i.e. thank goodness Fido does not see that cat)
q. future more vivid (i.e. this is what will happen if that cat comes around the corner)
r. future less vivid (i.e. Fido is going somewhere where there are no cats)
s. future most vivid (i.e. Fido's proclivities described as a warning to someone hired to walk him)

"No doubt Mark got a job if he applied for one."

t. past simple (i.e. we do not know if Mark applied)
u. past contrafactual (i.e. Mark did not apply)
v. present simple (i.e. we do not know if Mark is applying)
w. present contrafactual (i.e. Mark is not applying)
x. future more vivid (i.e. we do not know if Mark will apply)
y. future less vivid (i.e. Mark is unlikely to apply)

A selection of terminologies for describing Greek conditional sentences

This book follows the terminology of the left-hand column (Goodwin etc.).

English	Goodwin, Mastronarde, Hansen & Quinn, Chase & Phillips	Smyth	Abbott & Mansfield	Athenaze	Reading Greek	Nairn & Nairn	Oxford Grammar of Classical Greek	Greek
If he is running, he is winning	Simple Present	Simple Present	Fulfilled	Present Particular (Open)	—	Present, Open	Present Open	εἰ + pres. ind. / pres. ind.
If he was running, he was winning	Simple Past	Simple Past	Fulfilled	Past Particular (Open)	—	Past, Open	Past Open	εἰ + past ind. / past ind.
If he runs, he will win	Future More Vivid	More Vivid Future	Distinct Future (Open)	Future More Vivid (Open)	—	Future, Vivid	Future Open	ἐάν + subj. / fut. ind.
(Same, in threats and warnings)	Future Most Vivid	Emotional Future	Distinct Future (Open)	Future Particular or Minatory (Open)	—	Future, Vivid	Future Open	εἰ + fut. ind. / fut. ind.
If he should run, he would win	Future Less Vivid	Less Vivid Future	Indistinct Future (Open)	Future Remote or Less Vivid	Future Remote or Improbable	Future, Remote	Remote Future	εἰ + opt. / opt. + ἄν

(cont.)

(cont.)

English	Goodwin, Mastronarde, Hansen & Quinn, Chase & Phillips	Smyth	Abbott & Mansfield	Athenaze	Reading Greek	Nairn & Nairn	Oxford Grammar of Classical Greek	Greek
If he were running, he would be winning	Present Contrary to fact (Contrafactual)	Present Unreal	Unfulfilled	Present Contrary to fact	Present Unfulfilled	Present Unfulfilled	Present Unfulfilled	εἰ + impf. ind. / impf. ind. + ἄν
If he had run, he would have won	Past Contrary to fact (Contrafactual)	Past Unreal	Unfulfilled	Past Contrary to fact	Past Unfulfilled	Past Unfulfilled	Past Unfulfilled	εἰ + aor. ind. / aor. ind. + ἄν
If (ever) he runs, he wins	Present General	Present General	General	Present General (Open)	—	General or Indefinite	Indefinite	ἐάν + subj. / pres. indic.
If (ever) he ran, he won	Past General	Past General	General	Past General (Open)	—	General or Indefinite	Indefinite	εἰ + opt. / impf. indic.

North and Hillard, Sidgwick, and *Teach Yourself Greek* avoid the use of any terminology, but note that North and Hillard consider only the first seven of these to be conditions; they group the last two with the indefinite construction.

Short, easily confused words

Forms preceded by a hyphen occur only in compounds.

ἡ	article, feminine nominative singular
ἥ	relative pronoun, feminine nominative singular
ἥ	article, feminine nominative singular before an enclitic
ἤ	"or"; "than"; "either"
ἦ	εἰμί, imperfect indicative first person singular
ᾖ	εἰμί, present subjunctive third person singular
ᾗ	relative pronoun, feminine dative singular
-ᾗ	ἵημι, aorist active subjunctive third person singular
-ᾖ	ἵημι, aorist middle subjunctive second person singular
εἶ	εἰμί, present indicative second person singular
εἶ	εἶμι, present indicative second person singular
εἰ	"if"
ἱῇ	ἵημι, present active subjunctive third person singular
ἱῇ	ἵημι, present middle/passive subjunctive second person singular
ἵει	ἵημι, present active imperative second person singular
ἵει	ἵημι, imperfect active indicative third person singular
ὦ	vocative particle
ὦ	εἰμί, present subjunctive first person singular
-ὦ	ἵημι, aorist active subjunctive first person singular
ᾧ	relative pronoun, masculine/neuter dative singular
ἐν	"in"
ἕν	"one," neuter nominative/accusative singular
-ἕν	ἵημι, aorist active participle neuter nominative/accusative singular
ἥν	relative pronoun, feminine accusative singular
ἤν	alternative form for ἐάν
ἦν	εἰμί, imperfect indicative first person singular
ἦν	εἰμί, imperfect indicative third person singular
ᾔειν	εἶμι, imperfect indicative first person singular
ᾔει(ν)	εἶμι, imperfect indicative third person singular
εἴην	εἰμί, present optative first person singular
-εἴην	ἵημι, aorist active optative first person singular
εἶεν	εἰμί, present optative third person plural
εἶεν	"well," "quite so" (particle used in dialog)

-εῖεν	ἵημι, aorist active optative third person plural
ἱέν	ἵημι, present active participle neuter nominative/accusative singular
ἵην	ἵημι, imperfect active indicative first person singular
ἱείην	ἵημι, present active optative first person singular
ἱεῖεν	ἵημι, present active optative third person plural
εἶναι	εἰμί, present infinitive
-εῖναι	ἵημι, aorist active infinitive
ἰέναι	εἶμι, present infinitive
ἱέναι	ἵημι, present active infinitive
ἦτε	εἰμί, imperfect indicative second person plural
ἦτε	εἰμί, present subjunctive second person plural
ἦτε	εἶμι, imperfect indicative second person plural
-ῆτε	ἵημι, aorist active subjunctive second person plural
ᾖστε	οἶδα, imperfect indicative second person plural
εἶτε	εἰμί, present optative second person plural
-εῖτε	ἵημι, aorist active indicative second person plural
-εῖτε	ἵημι, aorist active optative second person plural
-ἕτε	ἵημι, aorist active imperative second person plural
ἐστέ	εἰμί, present indicative second person plural
ἔστε	εἰμί, present imperative second person plural
ἔστε	"until"
ἴτε	εἶμι, present indicative second person plural
ἴτε	εἶμι, present imperative second person plural
ἴστε	οἶδα, present indicative second person plural
ἴστε	οἶδα, present imperative second person plural
ἵετε	ἵημι, present active indicative second person plural
ἵετε	ἵημι, imperfect active indicative second person plural
ἵετε	ἵημι, present active imperative second person plural
ἱῆτε	ἵημι, present active subjunctive second person plural
ἱεῖτε	ἵημι, present active optative second person plural
ἴθι	εἶμι, present imperative second person singular
ἴσθι	εἰμί, present imperative second person singular
ἴσθι	οἶδα, present imperative second person singular
-ἕς	ἵημι, aorist active imperative second person singular
εἷς	"one," masculine nominative singular
-εἷς	ἵημι, aorist active participle masculine nominative singular
εἰς	"into"
ᾖς	εἰμί, present subjunctive second person singular
ἧς	relative pronoun, feminine genitive singular
-ῇς	ἵημι, aorist active subjunctive second person singular

ᾔεις	εἶμι, imperfect indicative second person singular
ἴῃς	εἶμι, present subjunctive second person singular
ἵης	ἵημι, present active indicative second person singular
ἱῇς	ἵημι, present active subjunctive second person singular
ἱεῖς	ἵημι, present active indicative second person singular
ἵεις	ἵημι, imperfect active indicative second person singular
ἱείς	ἵημι, present active participle masculine nominative singular
εἰσί	εἰμί, present indicative third person plural
εἶσι	εἶμι, present indicative third person singular
-εῖσι	ἵημι, aorist active participle masculine/neuter dative plural
ἱεῖσι	ἵημι, present active participle masculine/neuter dative plural
ἦσαν	εἰμί, imperfect indicative third person plural
ἦσαν	εἰμί, imperfect indicative third person plural
ἦσαν	οἶδα, imperfect indicative third person plural
ᾖσαν	ᾄδω, aorist active indicative third person plural
ᾔεσαν	εἰμί, imperfect indicative third person plural
-εῖσαν	ἵημι, aorist active indicative third person plural
εἴησαν	εἰμί, present optative third person plural
-εἵησαν	ἵημι, aorist active optative third person plural
ἵεσαν	ἵημι, imperfect active indicative third person plural
ἱείησαν	ἵημι, present active optative third person plural
ἦμεν	εἰμί, imperfect indicative first person plural
ᾖμεν	εἰμί, imperfect indicative first person plural
ᾖσμεν	οἶδα, imperfect indicative first person plural
εἶμεν	εἰμί, present optative first person plural
-εῖμεν	ἵημι, aorist active indicative first person plural
-εἶμεν	ἵημι, aorist active optative first person plural
ἐσμέν	εἰμί, present indicative first person plural
ἴμεν	εἶμι, present indicative first person plural
ἴσμεν	οἶδα, present indicative first person plural
ἵεμεν	ἵημι, present active indicative first person plural
ἵεμεν	ἵημι, imperfect active indicative first person plural
ἱεῖμεν	ἵημι, present active optative first person plural
ἴασι	εἶμι, present indicative third person plural
ἱᾶσι	ἵημι, present active indicative third person plural
ἴσασι	οἶδα, present indicative third person plural
ὦσι	εἰμί, present subjunctive third person plural
-ὦσι	ἵημι, aorist active subjunctive third person plural
ἴωσι	εἶμι, present subjunctive third person plural
ἵωσι	ἵημι, present active subjunctive third person plural

APPENDIX G
Partial answer key

Chapter I

Preliminary exercise 1
a. yes (rule A3)
b. yes (definite), no (rule A5), yes (rule A4)
c. no (indefinite), yes (definite), yes (definite)
d. yes (rule A1)
e. no (indefinite), no (rule A5)
f. yes (rule A3), yes (rule A1)
g. yes (rule A4)

Preliminary exercise 2
a. yes (rule B1), yes (definite), yes (rule B4b), no (indefinite)
b. yes (rule B3), no (rule B4b does not apply because the antecedent of "they" was not in an oblique case in the previous clause)
c. yes (rule B2), no (indefinite), yes (rule B1)
d. no (indefinite), yes (definite), yes (rule B1), yes (rule B4a), yes (rule B4a)
e. yes (rule B1), yes (rule B2)
f. yes (rule B2), yes (rule B1)

Sentences
1. ὁ ἵππος τὸν δεσπότην φέρει.
2. ὁ μὲν βιβλίον φέρει, ὁ δὲ οὔ.
3. οἱ ποιηταὶ οὐκ ἀεὶ εὖ βουλεύονται.
4. οἱ ποιηταὶ τὴν ἀνδρείαν οὐχ εὑρίσκουσι τῷ θύειν ἐν ἀγορᾷ.
5. οἱ νέοι εὖ μανθάνουσιν.
6. οἱ ἐν ἀγορᾷ ἵππον θῦσαι/θύειν ἐθέλουσιν.
7. αἱ νῦν τῷ βουλεύεσθαι μανθάνουσιν.
8. ὁ ποιητὴς μετὰ τοῦ ἀδελφοῦ βουλεύεσθαι ἐθέλει, ὁ δὲ ἐν ἀγορᾷ θύει.
9. οἱ ποιηταὶ τοὺς ἀδελφοὺς ἐπαίδευσαν.
10. ἡ ἀνδρεία οὐ κακή.

Analysis
1. Of Darius and Parysatis there are born two children, the older Artaxerxes (Ἀρταξέρξης, no article because not known to the reader) and the younger Cyrus (Κῦρος, no article because not known to the reader); and when Darius grew weak

and anticipated the end of his (τοῦ, article used for possession) life, he wanted both his (τώ, article used for possession) children to be present.

Chapter II

Preliminary exercise 1

a. δοῦλον ἀγαθόν / ἀγαθὸν δοῦλον
b. ὁ ἀγαθὸς δοῦλος / ὁ δοῦλος ὁ ἀγαθός
c. τὸν ἐν ἀγορᾷ δοῦλον / τὸν δοῦλον τὸν ἐν ἀγορᾷ
d. τῷ τοῦ ἀγαθοῦ δούλῳ / τῷ δούλῳ τῷ τοῦ ἀγαθοῦ
e. ὁ τοῦ νέου δοῦλος / ὁ δοῦλος ὁ τοῦ νέου
f. not translatable this way because it would require two identical articles in succession
g. δούλῳ νέῳ / νέῳ δούλῳ
h. τῷ νέῳ δούλῳ τῷ τῆς ἀγαθῆς / τῷ τῆς ἀγαθῆς δούλῳ τῷ νέῳ
i. τοῦ τῆς ἀγαθῆς δούλου / τοῦ δούλου τοῦ τῆς ἀγαθῆς

Preliminary exercise 2

a. ἀγαθὸς ὁ δοῦλος. / ὁ δοῦλος ἀγαθός.
b. ἀγαθὸς ὁ ἀδελφός. / ὁ ἀδελφὸς ἀγαθός.
c. ὁ ἀδελφὸς δοῦλος. / δοῦλος ὁ ἀδελφός.
d. ὁ δοῦλος ἀδελφός. / ἀδελφὸς ὁ δοῦλος.
e. οὗτος ὁ δοῦλος
f. ταῦτα
g. τούτους τοὺς λίθους
h. ταύταις
i. τούτου
j. τούτους τοὺς ἀδελφούς

Preliminary exercise 3

a. τῷ μανθάνειν
b. διὰ τὸ μανθάνειν
c. τῷ λίθους ἐσθίειν / τῷ ἐσθίειν λίθους
d. διὰ τὸ λίθους ἐσθίειν / διὰ τὸ ἐσθίειν λίθους
e. οὐκ ἀγαθὸν τὸ λίθους ἐσθίειν.
f. ἀγαθὸν τὸ λίθους μὴ ἐσθίειν. / ἀγαθὸν τὸ μὴ ἐσθίειν λίθους.
g. ἀγαθὸν τὸ (τοὺς) δούλους μανθάνειν.

Preliminary exercise 4

a. αἱ καλαὶ οὐ μανθάνουσιν. / οὐ μανθάνουσιν αἱ καλαί.
b. ἄγγελος ὁ ἐν τῇ οἰκίᾳ.

c. αἱ μὴ καλαὶ οὐ μανθάνουσιν. / οὐ μανθάνουσιν αἱ μὴ καλαί.

d. ἄγγελοι οἱ καλοί.

e. αἱ οὐ καλαὶ μανθάνουσιν. / μανθάνουσιν αἱ οὐ καλαί.

f. ἀδελφαὶ αἱ κακαί.

g. οἱ μὴ κακοὶ μανθάνουσιν. / μανθάνουσιν οἱ μὴ κακοί.

h. ἀδελφαὶ αἱ ἐν τῇ οἰκίᾳ.

Sentences

1. ἡ ἕως ἀεὶ καλή, καὶ ἐν μέσῃ τῇ ὁδῷ.

2. τῶν ἐν ταύτῃ τῇ οἰκίᾳ οἱ μὲν νοῦν ἔχουσιν, οἱ δὲ οὔ.

3. οὐδέποτε ἀγαθόν, ὦ φίλε, τὸ δεσπότας τοὺς ἵππους βάλλειν.

4. νῦν οὐ θύσουσιν οἱ μὴ ἐν τῷ νεῷ.

5. ὁ δοῦλος (ὁ) μετὰ τοῦ ποιητοῦ ἐκ τῆς οἰκίας (τῆς) ἐν (more idiomatically ἐπ') ἄκρᾳ τῇ θαλάττῃ εἰς τοῦτον τὸν καλὸν νεὼν βιβλία ἀεὶ ἔφερεν.

6. τῷ νέον ἵππον τοῖς τῆς θαλάττης θεοῖς θύειν, ὁ ἐν τῷ μέσῳ οἴκῳ τὴν τῆς ἀδελφῆς μοῖραν πάλαι ἔμαθεν.

7. οἱ ἀπὸ τῆς τῶν καλῶν ἵππων γῆς ἐν οἴκῳ παλαιῷ ἐν (more idiomatically ἐπ') ἄκρᾳ τῇ θαλάττῃ πάλιν μόνοι ἐσθίουσιν.

8. καὶ ἡ εἰρήνη, ὦ ἀγαθέ, καὶ ἡ ἐλευθερία καὶ ἡ ἀρετὴ τοῖς ἐλευθέροις φίλαι.

9. ὁ ἐν μέσοις τοῖς ἀγγέλοις τὴν τῶν θεῶν γλῶτταν εὖ μανθάνειν ἐθέλει/βούλεται.

10. οἱ καλοὶ καὶ ἀγαθοὶ ταύτην τὴν νέαν παιδεύεσθαι πολλάκις ἐβούλοντο/ἤθελον, ἡ δὲ νοῦν ἀγαθὸν οὐκ ἔχει.

Analysis

1. And Socrates, when he agreed that being a worker (τὸ μὲν ἐργάτην εἶναι is an articular infinitive with its predicate in the middle) is useful (ὠφέλιμον is predicate of the following εἶναι) for a person and good (ἀγαθόν is also predicate of εἶναι), and that being lazy (τὸ δὲ ἀργὸν (εἶναι) is an articular infinitive) is harmful (βλαβερόν is predicate of an understood εἶναι) and bad (κακόν is another predicate of the understood εἶναι), and that working (τὸ μὲν ἐργάζεσθαι, articular infinitive) is good (ἀγαθόν, predicate) and being lazy (τὸ δὲ ἀργεῖν, articular infinitive) is bad (κακόν, predicate), he said that those who do something good work and are good workers (ἐργάτας ἀγαθούς, predicate), and he called lazy those who play dice or do something else wicked and causing loss.

Chapter III

Preliminary exercise 1

a. ὁ σοφὸς τὸν ξένον ἐδίωξεν.

b. ὁ σοφὸς ὑπὸ τοῦ ξένου ἀπέθανεν.

c. διώκειν

d. ὁ ξένος ὑπὸ τοῦ σοφοῦ ἐδιώκετο.

e. ὁ σοφὸς τὸν ξένον οὐκ ἐδίωκεν ὅτι ἀπέθνῃσκεν.

f. ὁ σοφὸς ὑπὸ τοῦ ξένου ἐδιώχθη.

g. ἀποθανεῖν

h. ὁ ξένος τὸν σοφὸν διώξεται.

i. διῶξαι

Preliminary exercise 2

a. γαμεῖται

b. αἱρούμεθα

c. ψεύδεται

d. φυλάττομεν

e. φέρονται

f. τὰ ζῷα φαίνεται

g. τιμωρεῖται

h. συμβουλευόμεθα

i. γαμεῖ

Sentences

1.   μετὰ ταύτην τὴν δίκην ὁ ἀνδρεῖος δικαστὴς εὐθὺς ὑπὸ τῶν ἐχθρῶν ἀπέθανεν.

2.   (τὰ) θηρία πολλάκις κακὰ πάσχει ὑπ᾽ ἀνθρώπων.

3.   ὁ τοῦ γενναίου ἐχθρὸς μάτην ἤθελε τεθνηκέναι.

4.   τὰ ζῷα ἴσως ὑπὸ τῶν πολεμίων ἐλύθη.

5.   μετὰ τὴν νίκην οἱ μὲν τῶν πολεμίων ἐτεθνήκεσαν, οἱ δὲ ὑφ᾽ ὁπλιτῶν ἐφυλάττοντο.

6.   ὁ φρόνιμος ὁπλίτης τὸν μόνον υἱὸν ἐν τῇ μέσῃ νήσῳ φυλάττει, ὁ δὲ ἐθέλει τοὺς πολεμίους ἐκ ταύτης τῆς γῆς ἐλάσαι.

7.   ὁ ῥᾴθυμος ναύτης ἴσως ἀπέθανε τῷ εἰς μέσον τὸν ποταμὸν πεσεῖν.

8.   οἱ τοῦ ἀγαθοῦ υἱοὶ ζῷα ἤδη ἄγουσιν.

9.   τὰ θηρία ὑπ᾽ ἀνθρώπων ἡρπάσθη.

10. οὔπω τέθνηκεν ὁ ἀνάξιος ναύτης.

Analysis

1. The camels were only frightening (ἐφόβουν, imperfect for ongoing action in the past) the horses, but the horsemen on them were not being killed (κατεκαίνοντο, imperfect for ongoing action in the past), nor were the camels themselves being killed (ἀπέθνησκον, imperfect for ongoing action in the past, translated with an English passive because of the agent construction following; one could also translate this "dying at the hands of") by (ὑπό, agent construction) the horsemen; for no horse was approaching (ἐπέλαζε, imperfect for ongoing action in the past) them.

Chapter IV

Preliminary exercise 1

a. τῇ τρίτῃ ἡμέρᾳ Ἀθήναζε ἀφίξεται.

b. ἡ οἰκία τρεῖς σταδίους ἀπέχει (ἀπό) τῶν Ἀθηνῶν.

c. λίθος πέντε ποδῶν τὸ ὕψος

d. ἑπτὰ ἡμερῶν οἴκαδε ἀφίξεται.

e. πέντε ἡμέρας Ἀθήνησι μένουσιν.

f. οἰκία ἑπτὰ ποδῶν τὸ εὖρος

g. τῇ τετάρτῃ ἡμέρᾳ οἴκοθεν ἀφίξεται.

h. πέντε ἡμέρας οἴκοι μενεῖ.

Preliminary exercise 2

The general arrived with (ἄγων/ἔχων) only fifty soldiers, who were swiftly defeated by (ὑπό) the enemy. He fought with (dative, rule C5) great courage – I know, because I fought along with (μετά/σύν) him – but not with (dative, rule C5) good fortune, for he was hit by (dative, rule C2) several arrows and his horse was killed by (dative, rule C2) a spear-thrust. In the end he was captured by (ὑπό) a gigantic cavalry officer who came with (ἄγων/ἔχων) ten men when the general was already wounded. The men caught him with (dative, rule C2) a rope, which they threw around him from a distance, but once they had secured him he was, with (σύν, rule C5) justice, treated with (dative, rule C5) great respect. The other captives with (μετά/σύν) him were, in (dative, rule C5) truth, amazed at the way he endured his sufferings in (dative, rule C5) silence, while they acknowledged their own with (σύν, rule C5) lamentations.

Preliminary exercise 3

I have a statue (dative of possession) worth two talents (genitive of price and value). It was a bargain: I bought it for fifty minae (genitive of price and value). It is very beautiful, especially in its face (dative/accusative of respect), and is supposed to have been made by one of Pheidias' (genitive of possession) sons. It was formerly owned by a Spartan (dative of possession) nobleman, who was not really very Spartan with respect to his tastes (dative/accusative of respect) or his budget (dative/accusative of respect): he bought it for a talent and a half (genitive of price and value). He also had five other statues (dative of possession) that were even more beautiful; I don't know how much (genitive of price and value) they were worth, but they were all excellent in design (dative/accusative of respect), in workmanship (dative/accusative of respect), and in the quality (dative/accusative of respect) of their materials.

Sentences

1. Ἀθήνησι τοῖς μὲν ζῷα ταλάντου ἐνίοτέ ἐστι, τοῖς δὲ ζῷα δυοῖν δραχμῶν.

2. κατὰ τοῦτον τῷ ὄντι οὐκ ἀδύνατον ἐνθάδε τὸ δικαστὰς βάλλεσθαι καρποῖς.

3. τῇ δευτέρᾳ ἡμέρᾳ, ἔχων ἑκατὸν ὁπλίτας, τοὺς οἰκητὰς τρία στάδια ἐδίωξε πρὸς ποταμὸν εἴκοσι ποδῶν τὸ εὖρος.
4. ἡ τοῦ ναύτου ἀδελφή, οὐ φρόνιμος τὴν γνώμην, ἄρτι ἐνθένδε οἴκαδε ἕλκεται ὑπὸ τοῦ ἀδελφοῦ ἄνευ τῶν οἰκετῶν.
5. τοῖς παρὰ τῷ δικαστῇ ἐστὶ ξένος Μαραθῶνι.
6. τῶν ξένων οἱ ἄδικοι ἐνίοτε λίθοις ἔβαλλον τοὺς δούλους ὀργῇ, οἱ δὲ νῦν δεῦρο Ἀθήνηθεν πεφεύγασιν.
7. οἱ τῶν ναυτῶν υἱοὶ οἱ πρὸ τοῦ νεὼ οὐδέποτε ἐθέλουσιν οἴκοι τῆς ἡμέρας λούεσθαι.
8. τῇ ἀληθείᾳ οὐ φρόνιμον τὸ χρυσῷ λύεσθαι ὁπλίτας ῥαθύμους τὸν πόλεμον.
9. πρὸ τῆς μάχης τούτων τῶν πολιτῶν οἱ μὲν ἓξ ἡμέρας ἔθυον, οἱ δὲ ἑπτὰ ἡμέρας.
10. οἱ νέοι οἱ Ἀθήνησι τοῖς ἐκεῖ σοφοῖς εὖ πεπαίδευνται.

Analysis

1. Near this city (πόλιν, accusative because of preposition) was a stone pyramid, one plethron (πλέθρου, genitive because a dimension) wide (εὖρος, accusative of respect) and two plethra (πλέθρων, genitive because a dimension) high (ὕψος, accusative of respect) (literally: of one plethron with respect to width and two plethra with respect to height).

Chapter V

Preliminary exercise 1

a. οἱ δοῦλοι οἱ οὐ φυλαττόμενοι φεύξονται. / οἱ οὐ φυλαττόμενοι δοῦλοι φεύξονται.
b. οἱ δοῦλοι οἱ φυλαττόμενοι οὐκ ἔφυγον. / οἱ φυλαττόμενοι δοῦλοι οὐκ ἔφυγον.
c. οἱ φυλαττόμενοι οὐ φεύξονται.
d. οἱ οὐ φυλαττόμενοι φεύξονται.
e. οἱ μὴ φυλαττόμενοι φεύξονται.
f. οἱ μὴ φυλαττόμενοι/φυλαχθέντες ἔφυγον.

Preliminary exercise 2

a. ὁ δοῦλος ἔφυγεν ἅμα φυλαττόμενος.
b. ὁ δοῦλος οὐκ ἔφυγεν ἄτε φυλαττόμενος.
c. ὁ δοῦλος ἔφυγε καίπερ φυλαττόμενος.
d. ὁ δοῦλος ἔφυγεν ὥσπερ οὐ φυλαττόμενος.
e. μὴ φυλαττόμενος ὁ δοῦλος φεύξεται.

Preliminary exercise 3

When the messenger arrived (genitive absolute), the servants who were (nominative because it agrees with "servants," which is the subject) off duty were sitting in the courtyard, which was (dative because it agrees with "courtyard," which is dative after ἐν "in") the coolest part of the palace. They were surprised to see him covered (accusative because it agrees with "him," which is the object of "see") with dust and panting (accusative because it agrees with "him"), since messengers rarely arrived (genitive absolute) in that condition. If he had given (accusative because it agrees with "him" in next clause, which is the object of "surrounded") them a chance, they would have surrounded him to ask (nominative because it agrees with "they") lots of questions, but as it was, although they moved (nominative because it agrees with "they" in the next clause) as fast as they could, they hardly had time to get up from the benches before he had entered the king's apartments, though these were (accusative because it agrees with "apartments," which is the object of "entered") on the other side of the courtyard, which was (genitive because it agrees with "courtyard") exceptionally wide. Once he disappeared (accusative because it agrees with "him" in the next clause), they all wanted to follow him, although normally they were (nominative because it agrees with "they" in the previous clause) not very enthusiastic about going into the king's apartments, which were (accusative because it agrees with "apartments," which would be accusative after εἰς "into") so full of precious and fragile objects that you had to be very careful not to brush against anything, especially if the weather was (genitive absolute) not good.

Preliminary exercise 4

a. οἱ δοῦλοι ἀπεπέμφθησαν θυόντων τῶν δεσποτῶν.
b. οἱ δοῦλοι ἀπεπέμφθησαν φυλαττόμενοι.
c. ἐφυλάξαμεν τοὺς δούλους ἀποπεμπομένους.
d. ἐφυλάξαμεν τοὺς δούλους θυόντων τῶν δεσποτῶν.
e. εὐχόμενοι οἱ δοῦλοι ἐφυλάττοντο.
f. εὐχομένων τῶν δούλων, ἔθυσαν οἱ δεσπόται.
g. φυγόντων τῶν δούλων, θύσουσιν οἱ δεσπόται.
h. οἱ δοῦλοι εὔξονται ἀποπεμπόμενοι.
i. οἱ δοῦλοι εὔξονται τῶν δεσποτῶν θυόντων.

Preliminary exercise 5

a. ὁ δεσπότης χαίρει θύων. / ὁ δεσπότης ἥδεται θύων.
b. ὁ δεσπότης διατελεῖ θύων.
c. ὁ δεσπότης λήγει θύων. / ὁ δεσπότης παύεται θύων.
d. τὸν δεσπότην θύοντα ἐπαύσαμεν.
e. ὁ δεσπότης φαίνεται θύων.
f. ὁ δεσπότης φαίνεται θύειν.
g. ὁ δεσπότης οὐκ αἰσχύνεται θύσας.
h. ὁ δεσπότης αἰσχύνεται θύειν.
i. ὁ δεσπότης τυγχάνει θύων.
j. ὁ δεσπότης τυγχάνει θύσας.
k. ὁ δεσπότης ἔτυχε θύων.

l. ὁ δεσπότης ἔτυχε θύσας.

m. ὁ δεσπότης ἔθυσε τοὺς δούλους λαθών. / ὁ δεσπότης θύσας τοὺς δούλους ἔλαθεν.

Preliminary exercise 6

When the messenger arrived (present), the servants who were (present) off duty were sitting in the courtyard, which was (present) the coolest part of the palace. They were surprised to see him covered (present) with dust and panting (present), since messengers rarely arrived (present) in that condition. If he had given (aorist) them a chance, they would have surrounded him to ask (future) lots of questions, but as it was, although they moved (either present or aorist possible) as fast as they could, they hardly had time to get up from the benches before he had entered the king's apartments, though these were (present) on the other side of the courtyard, which was (present) exceptionally wide. Once he disappeared (aorist), they all wanted to follow him, although normally they were (present) not very enthusiastic about going into the king's apartments, which were (present) so full of precious and fragile objects that you had to be very careful not to brush against anything, especially if the weather was (present) not good.

Preliminary exercise 7

a. οἱ φιλόσοφοι χαίρουσι/ἥδονται διδάσκοντες.

b. οἱ φιλόσοφοι ἐπαύσαντο διδάσκοντες. (In prose there is no aorist of λήγω.)

c. οἱ φιλόσοφοι ἀπεπέμφθησαν ἅτε ἀφικόμενοι ἡμῶν διδασκόντων.

d. οἱ φιλόσοφοι ἀπεπέμφθησαν ὡς ἀφικόμενοι ἡμῶν διδασκόντων.

e. ὁ μὴ διδάξας (or διδάσκων) ἀποπεμφθήσεται. / οἱ μὴ διδάξαντες (or διδάσκοντες) ἀποπεμφθήσονται.

f. οἱ φιλόσοφοι οἱ οὐ διδάξαντες/διδάσκοντες ἀποπεμφθήσονται.

g. τοὺς φιλοσόφους ἀποπέμψομεν μὴ παυσαμένους διδάσκοντας.

h. ἀποπεμφθησόμεθα τῶν φιλοσόφων μὴ διδασκόντων/διδαξάντων.

i. ἀποπεμφθήσονται οἱ φιλόσοφοι μὴ διδάξαντες/διδάσκοντες.

j. οἱ φιλόσοφοι ἡμᾶς ἔλαθον διδάξαντες. / οἱ φιλόσοφοι ἡμᾶς λαθόντες ἐδίδαξαν.

k. οἱ φιλόσοφοι ἔτυχον διδάσκοντες ἡμῶν ἀφικνουμένων.

l. οἱ φιλόσοφοι ἀφίκοντο (ὡς) διδάξοντες.

m. οἱ φιλόσοφοι ἔφθασαν ἡμᾶς ἀφικόμενοι. / οἱ φιλόσοφοι φθάσαντες ἡμᾶς ἀφίκοντο.

n. οἱ φιλόσοφοι οὐ χαίρουσι/ἥδονται διδασκόμενοι.

o. οἱ φιλόσοφοι διετέλουν/διετέλεσαν διδάσκοντες ἡμῶν ἀφικνουμένων.

p. ἀφικόμενοι τοὺς φιλοσόφους παύσομεν διδάσκοντας.

Sentences

1. θυόντων τῶν θνητῶν, χαίρουσιν οἱ ἀθάνατοι.

2. εἰς τὴν ἐκκλησίαν ἀφικόμενοι, οὗτοι οἱ πολῖται ἤρχοντο τοῖς θεοῖς θύειν.

3. οἱ φεύγοντες τοὺς διώκοντας ἔλαθον ἀπὸ τῆς ὁδοῦ τραπόμενοι/στρεψάμενοι.

4. ὁ φιλόσοφος τυγχάνει εὑρὼν τοὺς νεανίας μεταξὺ τὸν κλέπτην ἁρπάζοντας.
5. οἱ μὴ πεπαιδευμένοι οὐ χαίρουσι γράφοντες.
6. καίπερ εἰς ὕλην ἀφικόμενοι, θηρία οὐχ ηὕρομεν.
7. αὕτη ἡ ἑταίρα ᾐσχύνετο εἰς ὕλην πέμψαι τὸν ἐραστὴν οἴσοντα ξύλα.
8. τὸν γενναῖον φιλόσοφον εἰς τὸν ποταμὸν πεσόντα ἔσωσε σοφιστὴς δεινός.
9. ὁ ἰσχυρὸς φαίνεται τοὺς μικροὺς δούλους τύπτων.
10. οὗτος ὁ σοφιστὴς τὴν καλὴν ἑταίραν κλοπῆς ἐγράψατο ὡς ἀργύριον παρὰ τῶν ἀδίκων κλεπτῶν δεξαμένην.

Analysis

1. But consider better, fortunate one, lest you fail to see that I am nothing (lit. lest I escape your notice being nothing). (Ὤν is supplementary participle after λανθάνω, in present tense to match tense of λανθάνω.)

Chapter VI

Preliminary exercise 1

Alcibiades was not a model citizen. He γάρ got drunk at parties, καί smashed up other people's property, and (καί) seduced their wives. Eventually οὖν things came to a head when he mutilated a group of sacred statues: this γάρ was thought to have annoyed the gods and (καί or δέ) thus jeopardized the success of a military expedition. The οὖν citizens decided to put Alcibiades in jail, but (ἀλλά or δέ) he ran off to Sparta.

Preliminary exercise 2

Conjunctions are underlined and verbs double underlined.

Οὐ μόνον δὲ δεῖ ταῦτα γιγνώσκειν, οὐδὲ τοῖς ἔργοις ἐκεῖνον ἀμύνεσθαι τοῖς τοῦ πολέμου, ἀλλὰ καὶ τῷ λογισμῷ καὶ τῇ διανοίᾳ τοὺς παρ' ὑμῖν ὑπὲρ αὐτοῦ λέγοντας μισῆσαι, ἐνθυμουμένους ὅτι οὐκ ἔνεστι τῶν τῆς πόλεως ἐχθρῶν κρατῆσαι, πρὶν ἂν τοὺς ἐν αὐτῇ τῇ πόλει κολάσηθ' ὑπηρετοῦντας ἐκείνοις.

Preliminary exercise 3

1 δὲ δεῖ "It is necessary"
- 1.1 οὐ μόνον . . . ταῦτα γιγνώσκειν "not only to know these things"
- 1.2 οὐδὲ τοῖς ἔργοις ἐκεῖνον ἀμύνεσθαι τοῖς τοῦ πολέμου "and not (only) to resist him with the deeds of war"
- 1.3 ἀλλὰ καὶ τῷ λογισμῷ καὶ τῇ διανοίᾳ τοὺς παρ' ὑμῖν ὑπὲρ αὐτοῦ λέγοντας μισῆσαι "but also with both reasoning and purpose to hate those who speak among you on his behalf,"
  - 1.3.1 ἐνθυμουμένους "considering"
    - 1.3.1.1 ὅτι οὐκ ἔνεστι "that it is not possible"

          1.3.1.1.1 τῶν τῆς πόλεως ἐχθρῶν κρατῆσαι "to overcome the enemies of the city"

          1.3.1.1.2 πρὶν ἂν τοὺς ἐν αὐτῇ τῇ πόλει κολάσηθ᾽ ὑπηρετοῦντας ἐκείνοις. "before you punish those in the city itself who serve them."

Preliminary exercise 4

The units to which μέν and δέ are attached are underlined.

a. In appearance μέν he was fair, in his heart δέ he was foul.
b. Cannot be translated with μέν ... δέ.
c. When he was young μέν, Demosthenes was incapable of public speaking; after lots of practice δέ he became one of the greatest orators of all time.
d. My father μέν is not a citizen; my mother δέ is.
e. Cannot be translated with μέν ... δέ.
f. Cannot be translated with μέν ... δέ.

Preliminary exercise 5

Words that have been moved are underlined; words that have been added have a double underline.

ἴσως ἂν οὖν δόξειεν ἄτοπον εἶναι, ὅτι δὴ ἐγὼ ἰδίᾳ μὲν ταῦτα συμβουλεύω περιιὼν καὶ πολυπραγμονῶ, δημοσίᾳ δὲ οὐ τολμῶ ἀναβαίνων εἰς τὸ πλῆθος τὸ ὑμέτερον συμβουλεύειν τῇ πόλει. τούτου δὲ αἴτιόν ἐστιν ὃ ὑμεῖς ἐμοῦ πολλάκις ἀκηκόατε πολλαχοῦ λέγοντος, ὅτι μοι θεῖόν τι καὶ δαιμόνιον γίγνεται, ὃ δὴ καὶ ἐν τῇ γραφῇ ἐπικωμῳδῶν Μέλητος ἐγράψατο.

Sentences

1–2. ὁ μὲν λιμὸς τοὺς παῖδας ἀπέκτεινεν, ὁ δὲ λοιμὸς τὰς γυναῖκας. οἱ οὖν λειφθέντες οἱ ὀλίγοι κλάοντες ᾤχοντο ἀπὸ τῆς Ἑλλάδος.

3–4. ἡ ἐκκλησία ἐψηφίσατο στρατείαν ἐπὶ τοὺς τοῦ ἄκρου ὄρους οἰκητὰς εὐθὺς πέμψαι. οἱ γὰρ ἐκεῖ ποιμένες τὰς τῶν πολιτῶν γυναῖκας πολλάκις ἐβιάζοντο.

5–6. τῆς μὲν ἡμέρας πολλοὶ τὸν λιμένα φυλάττουσιν· τῆς δὲ νυκτός, τῶν φυλάκων εἰς στρατόπεδον οἰχομένων, ἄγριοι λῃσταὶ ἐκεῖ ὑπάρχουσιν. τήμερον οὖν αὐλίζονται οἱ φύλακες περὶ τῷ λιμένι ἐγερθησόμενοι ὑπὸ τῶν λῃστῶν ὑπὲρ τὸν ὅρον πορευθέντων.

7–8. τῶν ὀρνίθων ἅμα τῷ ἦρι εἰς τὴν ἱερὰν ὕλην ἀφικομένων, οἱ ἐκεῖ Ἕλληνες εὐθὺς ἐχάρησαν καὶ ᾖσαν. τὸ μὲν γὰρ ἔαρ γυναιξὶ φίλον, οἱ δὲ ὄρνιθες παισὶ φίλοι.

9–10. οἱ μὲν τοῦ ῥήτορος λόγοι καλοί, τὰ δὲ τῶν στρατιωτῶν ἔργα γενναῖα. ἀλλὰ τούτοις οὐχ ἡδόμεθα· οἱ γὰρ πολέμιοι πολλοὺς ἀθλίους αἰχμαλώτους χθὲς κατέλαβον ἅμα κήρυκος ἀδίκου τοὺς πολίτας ἀγείροντος.

Analysis

1.   1.1 κατὰ γὰρ τοὺς νόμους, ἐάν τις φανερὸς γένηται "For according to the laws,
            if someone becomes manifest in (i.e. is shown to be)"
            1.1.1 κλέπτων "stealing"
            1.1.2 ἢ λωποδυτῶν "or stealing clothes"
            1.1.3 ἢ βαλαντιοτομῶν "or cutting purses"
            1.1.4 ἢ τοιχωρυχῶν "or burgling"
            1.1.5 ἢ ἀνδραποδιζόμενος "or enslaving people"
            1.1.6 ἢ ἱεροσυλῶν, "or robbing temples,"
        1 τούτοις θάνατός ἐστιν ἡ ζημία· "for these death is the punishment;"
            1.2 ὧν ἐκεῖνος πάντων ἀνθρώπων πλεῖστον ἀπεῖχεν. "from which things that
            man has most of all men stayed away."

Review exercises 1

1. τῇ τρίτῃ ἡμέρᾳ εἰς τὴν ἤπειρον ἀφικόμενοι οἱ τέτταρες ναῦται ηὗρον τὸν γέροντα
   τὸν γράψαντα περὶ τῶν λῃστῶν τῶν τοὺς παῖδας ἁρπασάντων. ἀντὶ δὲ τοῦ τοῦτον βιάζεσθαι, ἔκλαυσαν πείσοντες φῆναι τὰς τούτων τῶν λῃστῶν οἰκίας. τούτου μέντοι οὐ πιθομένου, οὐ διετέλεσαν/διετέλουν κλάοντες ἀλλὰ οἴκαδε σιγῇ
   ἐπορεύθησαν ὥσπερ αἰσχυνόμενοι κλαύσαντες. νῦν οὖν φαίνονται μέλλοντες τοὺς
   λῃστὰς λείψειν καὶ οἰχήσεσθαι· καὶ μὴ παύσαντες τούτους, οὐδέποτε παυσόμεθα
   πάσχοντες ὑπὸ τῶν θεῶν. τήμερον οὖν οἱ μὲν ἡμῶν διωξόμεθα τοὺς λῃστὰς τοὺς
   αὐλισθέντας ἐν τῷ νεῷ τῷ ἑκατὸν ποδῶν τὸ μῆκος, οἱ δὲ φυλάξομεν τοὺς παῖδας
   ἐν (more idiomatically ἐπ᾽) ἄκρῳ τῷ νεῷ, σώσοντες τοὺς τῶν ναυτῶν παῖδας.

Chapter VII

Preliminary exercise 1
a. εἰ + aorist indicative, aorist indicative + ἄν
b. εἰ + present optative, imperfect indicative
c. imperfect indicative + ἄν, εἰ + imperfect indicative
d. εἰ + present indicative, present indicative
e. future indicative, ἐάν + aorist subjunctive
f. imperfect indicative + ἄν, εἰ + aorist indicative
g. εἰ + present optative, aorist optative + ἄν
h. imperfect or aorist indicative, εἰ + aorist indicative
i. ἐάν + present subjunctive, present indicative
j. ἐάν + aorist subjunctive, imperative
k. future indicative, εἰ + future indicative or ἐάν + aorist subjunctive

l.   present or aorist optative + ἄν, εἰ + aorist optative
m. εἰ + present optative, imperfect indicative
n.   εἰ + aorist indicative, present indicative
o.   ἐάν + aorist or present subjunctive, future indicative
p.   aorist optative + ἄν, εἰ + aorist optative
q.   aorist indicative + ἄν, εἰ + imperfect indicative
r.   ἐάν + present subjunctive, present indicative
s.   εἰ + present optative, imperfect indicative
t.   εἰ + present indicative, present indicative

Preliminary exercise 2
a.   aorist optative
b.   aorist indicative
c.   imperfect indicative
d.   aorist indicative, aorist indicative
e.   aorist optative
f.   aorist indicative
g.   imperfect indicative
h.   present optative, present optative
i.   imperfect indicative
j.   aorist optative
k.   aorist indicative
l.   present or aorist optative
m. aorist indicative

Sentences
1.   ἐὰν ὕδωρ οἴκαδε κομίσῃς, πιόμεθα ἐσθίοντες.
2.   εἰ μὴ τὸ ἀθάνατον ποίημα περὶ τῆς ἀληθείας τότε ἤκουσα (μή . . . ἀκούσας), τῷ
      σώματι νῦν ἐδούλευον ἄν.
3.   εἰ ὁ παῖς κίνδυνον ἐκεῖ αἴσθοιτο, βοὴν εὐθὺς ἀκούσαιμεν ἄν.
4–5. (οἱ) αἴτιοι οὐδέποτε ἂν ἐκεῖ ἧψαν πῦρ· ἐν γὰρ τῇ ὕλῃ πῦρ ἔκρυψαν ἄν. οὗτοι οὖν
      οἱ ποιμένες ἀναίτιοι τῆς τῶν ἱερῶν κλοπῆς.
6.   εἰ ἡ τοῦ ποιμένος γυνὴ τούτῳ τῷ φύλακι νῦν μάχεται, μάχεται καὶ ὁ ποιμήν.
7.   καὶ εἰ τὰ γράμματα δὶς ἔμαθον, οὐκ ἂν τήμερον ἐμεμνήμην.
8.   εἰ Ἕλλην χρήματα κλέπτοι/κλέψαι, οὐ καλῶς ἤκουεν· οἱ γὰρ ἀγαθοὶ Ἕλληνες
      οὐδέποτε ἔκλεπτον/ἔκλεψαν.
9.   στρατηγὸς ἀγαθὸς στρατιώτας τρωθέντας οὐκ ἂν καταλίποι ἀντὶ τοῦ εἰς
      στρατόπεδον κομίσαι.
10. πλουσίοις οὐδαμῶς ἂν εἴποιμι εἰ μὴ τῷ πλούτῳ ἐδούλευες (μὴ . . . δουλεύων).

Analysis

1.   1 τίς δὲ πατὴρ . . . τὸν πρόσθεν αἰτιᾶται; "But what father blames the former man,"

    1.1 ἐὰν ὁ παῖς αὐτοῦ . . . σώφρων ᾖ "if his son is well-mannered"

        1.1.1 συνδιατρίβων τῳ "when he spends time with someone,"

    1.2 ὕστερον δὲ . . . πονηρὸς γένηται "and later becomes wicked"

        1.2.1 ἄλλῳ τῳ συγγενόμενος "when he is with some other man?"

Present general condition with a double protasis following the apodosis.

Chapter VIII

Preliminary exercise 1

Relative clauses are underlined, relative pronouns are double underlined, antecedents are in italics.

a. The *boy* who is over there is my brother. (masc. nom. sing.)
b. The *man* that you saw is a dentist. (masc. acc. sing.)
c. The *mountains* that we climbed are very high. (neut. acc. pl.)
d. The *girls* who attend this school are very happy. (fem. nom. pl.)
e. The *person* whose book you stole is my best friend! (masc. gen. sing.)
f. Some *trees* that grow here live to be thousands of years old. (neut. nom. pl.)
g. The *women* to whom we gave the money are not actually poor. (fem. dat. pl.)
h. I know the *man* who found it. (masc. nom. sing.)
i. Is the *girl* whom we saw a friend of yours? (fem. acc. sing.)

Preliminary exercise 2

a. ἐβοηθήσαμεν τῷ στρατηγῷ ὃς ἐνίκησεν.
b. ἐβοήθησαν ἡμῖν οἱ στρατηγοὶ οἳ ἐνικήθησαν.
c. ἐβοήθησαν τῷ στρατηγῷ ὃν ἐνικήσαμεν.
d. ἐβοήθησαν ἡμῖν οἱ στρατηγοὶ οὓς ἐνίκησεν.

Preliminary exercise 3

a. Not restrictive, so attraction not possible. Relative pronoun nominative, antecedent genitive.
b. Restrictive; relative pronoun accusative and antecedent dative: attraction possible.
c. Not restrictive, so attraction not possible. Relative pronoun accusative, antecedent genitive.
d. Restrictive; relative pronoun genitive, antecedent dative: attraction not possible.
e. Restrictive; relative pronoun accusative, antecedent dative: attraction possible.
f. Not restrictive, so attraction not possible. Relative pronoun accusative, antecedent genitive.

g. Restrictive; relative pronoun dative, antecedent accusative: attraction not possible.

h. Restrictive; relative pronoun accusative, antecedent genitive: attraction possible.

i. Not restrictive, so attraction not possible. Relative pronoun accusative, antecedent dative.

Preliminary exercise 4

a. κατηγόρησε τοῦ στρατηγοῦ ὃν φιλεῖς / οὗ φιλεῖς.

b. κατηγορήσομεν τοῦ στρατηγοῦ, ὃν οὐ φιλοῦμεν. (no attraction: non-restrictive clause)

c. ἐρᾷ τοῦ στρατηγοῦ ὃν ἐνικήσαμεν / οὗ ἐνικήσαμεν.

d. ἐρῶ τοῦ στρατηγοῦ ὃς ἐνικήθη. (no attraction: relative pronoun is not accusative)

Preliminary exercise 5

a. κατηγόρησε τοῦ στρατηγοῦ οὗ ἐνίκησας. / κατηγόρησεν οὗ ἐνίκησας στρατηγοῦ.

b. κατηγορήσομεν τοῦ στρατηγοῦ οὗ ἐρᾷ. / κατηγορήσομεν οὗ ἐρᾷ στρατηγοῦ.

c. κατηγορήσομεν τούτου τοῦ στρατηγοῦ, οὗ ἐρᾷ. (non-restrictive clause)

d. ἐρᾷ τοῦ στρατηγοῦ οὗ ἐνικήσαμεν. / ἐρᾷ οὗ ἐνικήσαμεν στρατηγοῦ.

e. ἐρῶ τοῦ στρατηγοῦ ὃς ἐνικήθη. (incorporation not possible because the case difference cannot be resolved by attraction)

Preliminary exercise 6

a. ἀπιστῶ τούτοις οὓς οὐ φιλῶ. / ἀπιστῶ οἷς οὐ φιλῶ.

b. φιλῶ ταῦτα ἃ φιλεῖς. / φιλῶ ἃ φιλεῖς.

c. φιλεῖται ὑπὸ τούτων οὓς φιλεῖ. / φιλεῖται ὑφ' ὧν φιλεῖ.

d. οὐ φιλοῦμεν τούτους οἷς ἀπιστοῦμεν. / οὐ φιλοῦμεν οἷς ἀπιστοῦμεν.

Preliminary exercise 7

a. What we had, that we gave away.

b. What people used to be young, those (people) are now old.

c. Which men saw me, those (men) I saw.

d. What things you did, those things I know.

e. What things used to be in fashion, those (things) are now out of fashion.

f. What hand feeds you, don't bite that (hand)!

Preliminary exercise 8

a. οὓς οὐ φιλῶ, τούτοις ἀπιστῶ.

b. ἃ φιλεῖς, ταῦτα φιλῶ.

c. οὓς φιλεῖ, ὑπὸ τούτων φιλεῖται.

d. οἷς ἀπιστοῦμεν, τούτους οὐ φιλοῦμεν.

Preliminary exercise 9

a. οἱ λῃσταὶ ἁρπάζουσιν ἃ ἂν εὑρίσκωσιν. / ἃ ἂν εὑρίσκωσιν, ταῦτα ἁρπάζουσιν οἱ λῃσταί.

b. ἡρπάζετο ᾧ ἕποιντο οἱ λῃσταί. / ᾧ ἕποιντο οἱ λῃσταί, οὗτος ἡρπάζετο.

c. ἕψονται ᾧ ἂν εὑρίσκωσιν. / ὃν ἂν εὑρίσκωσιν, τούτῳ ἕψονται.

d. ἁρπάζεται ᾧ ἂν ἕπωνται οἱ λῃσταί. / ᾧ ἂν ἕπωνται οἱ λῃσταί, οὗτος ἁρπάζεται.

e. ἥρπαζεν ὃ εὑρίσκοι. / ὃ εὑρίσκοι, τοῦτο ἥρπαζεν.

Sentences 1

1. ὅσοι στρατιῶται τούτῳ τῷ στρατηγῷ πιστεύουσι, τοσοῦτοι ἀπιστοῦσιν.

2. ὅσα κακὰ ἐποίησαν οἱ λῃσταί, τοσαῦτα (ἐποίησεν) οὗτος ὁ ἰατρός.

3. ὅσοις ἐβοηθήσαμεν βαρβάροις, οὐ τοσούτοις (ἐβοήθησαν) οἱ σύμμαχοι.

4. ὅσους ἐνίκησαν οἱ βάρβαροι, τοσούτους (ἐνίκησαν) οἱ Ἕλληνες.

5. ὅσων παίδων ἐρᾷ ὁ στρατηγός, τοσούτων (ἐρᾷ) οὗτος ὁ φιλόσοφος.

Sentences 2

1. ἃ/ὃ ἂν ποιῶ, ταῦτα/τοῦτο φιλεῖ ὁ ὄχλος.

2. ὡς ἂν ἐθέλωσιν αἱ γυναῖκες, οὕτως ψηφίζονται οἱ πολῖται.

3. ὅσοις ἂν βοηθήσωμεν βαρβάροις, οὐ τοσούτοις βοηθήσουσιν οἱ σύμμαχοι.

4. ὅσους λαμβάνοιεν οἱ βάρβαροι, τοσούτους ἐλάμβανον οἱ Ἕλληνες.

5. ἃ/ὃ μὴ αἰτοῖμεν, ταῦτα/τοῦτο ἐκόμιζον.

Sentences 3

1. We use the good things that we have. χρώμεθα τοῖς ἀγαθοῖς ἃ ἔχομεν.

2. We shall trust whatever leader Cyrus gives. πιστεύσομεν τῷ ἡγεμόνι ὃν ἂν Κῦρος διδῷ.

3. You are worthy of the freedom that you have obtained. ἄξιοί ἐστε τῆς ἐλευθερίας ἣν κέκτησθε.

4. This is the most foolish of the children whom I have nourished. οὗτός ἐστι μωρότατος τῶν παίδων οὓς ἔθρεψα.

5. He marched with the force that he had. ἐπορεύετο σὺν τῇ δυνάμει ἣν εἶχεν.

Sentences 4

1. τοῦτον οὐκ ἀξιοῦμεν τῶν ἀγώνων οὓς τήμερον νικᾶν ἐθέλει. / τοῦτον οὐκ ἀξιοῦμεν ὧν τήμερον νικᾶν ἐθέλει ἀγώνων.

2. ταῦτα ἐπύθετο ὁ ἰατρὸς τῶν παίδων οὓς ἐπέμψαμεν. / ταῦτα ἐπύθετο ὁ ἰατρὸς ὧν ἐπέμψαμεν παίδων.

3. ταῦτα ἐπυνθάνετο ὁ ἰατρὸς τούτων οὓς πέμποιμεν. / ταῦτα ἐπυνθάνετο ὁ ἰατρὸς ὧν πέμποιμεν.

4. τῶν γυναικῶν ἃς κατελίπετε οὐ καταγνώσονται οἱ δικασταί. / ὧν κατελίπετε γυναικῶν οὐ καταγνώσονται οἱ δικασταί.

5. καταγνώσονται οἱ δικασταὶ τούτων, οὓς ἂν καταλίπητε. / καταγνώσονται οἱ δικασταὶ ὧν ἂν καταλίπητε.

Analysis

1.
    1.1 ἐπεὶ τοίνυν τάχιστα . . . ὑπέλαβον "So as soon as they suspected"
        1.1.1 τῶν πολιτευομένων . . . κρείττονες εἶναι, "that they were stronger than the people running the city,"
    1 Σωκράτει μὲν οὐκέτι προσῇεσαν· "they no longer visited Socrates,"
    2 οὔτε γὰρ αὐτοῖς ἄλλως ἤρεσκεν, "for he was not pleasing to them in other ways"
        3.1 εἴ τε προσέλθοιεν, "and if ever they did visit him,"
        3.2.1 ὑπὲρ ὧν ἡμάρτανον "on account of the things they had done wrong" (ὧν is an attracted relative pronoun; the object of ἡμάρτανον should be accusative)
        3.2 ἐλεγχόμενοι "being refuted,"
    3 ἤχθοντο· "they were grieved;"
    4 τὰ δὲ τῆς πόλεως ἔπραττον, "rather they engaged in politics,"
        4.1 ὧνπερ ἕνεκεν καὶ Σωκράτει προσῆλθον. "on account of which they had visited Socrates in the first place." (ordinary relative clause)

Chapter IX

Preliminary exercise 1

a. οἱ αὐτοὶ ἑταῖροι γράψουσιν.

b. αὐτοὶ οἱ ἑταῖροι γράψουσιν. / οἱ ἑταῖροι αὐτοὶ γράψουσιν.

c. τὰ αὐτὰ γράψουσιν.

d. αὐτοὶ γράψομεν.

e. αὐτοὺς εὗρεν.

Preliminary exercise 2

Euthyphro considered himself (direct reflexive) to be a very pious man. He (not expressed in Greek) prayed to the gods each morning, and he (not expressed in Greek) always washed himself (direct reflexive, or nothing if middle voice used) before praying. He (not expressed in Greek) led the household prayers himself (another pronoun: αὐτός), rather than telling the steward to do it for him (indirect reflexive).

Preliminary exercise 3

Euthyphro was angry at his father (τῷ πατρί), so he called his wife (τὴν γυναῖκα) to his room (τὸ δωμάτιον) and said, "Wife, my father (ὁ πατήρ, ὁ πατήρ μου, ὁ ἐμὸς πατήρ, or perhaps ὁ πατὴρ ἐμοῦ) has insulted me. He humiliated me, his own son (τὸν ἑαυτοῦ υἱόν), in front of our slaves (τοῖς δούλοις, τοῖς ἡμετέροις δούλοις, τοῖς δούλοις ἡμῶν)." His wife (ἡ γυνή, ἡ γυνὴ αὐτοῦ, ἡ τούτου γυνή) replied, "To insult my husband (τὸν ἐμὸν ἄνδρα, τὸν ἄνδρα μου, or perhaps τὸν ἄνδρα ἐμοῦ) is to insult me as well."

Preliminary exercise 4

a. ἄλλοι ἄλλον ἐτίμησαν.
b. οἱ μὲν ἐτιμήθησαν, οἱ δὲ οὔ.
c. ἀλλήλους τιμήσουσιν.
d. ἄλλος ὑπ' ἄλλων τιμᾶται.
e. ὑπ' ἀλλήλων τιμηθήσονται.
f. τοὺς μὲν ἐτιμήσαμεν, τοὺς δὲ οὔ.

Sentences

1. ἡμῶν τοὺς πολεμίους νικώντων, οἱ τούτων σύμμαχοι (οἱ σύμμαχοι αὐτῶν) ἄλλοι ἄλλοσε ἔφυγον.
2. ὁ μὲν τούτων ἀδελφὸς (ὁ μὲν ἀδελφὸς αὐτῶν) τὸ αὐτὸ ἀεὶ ὠνεῖται, ὁ δὲ ἡμῶν (ὁ δὲ ἡμέτερος) οὐδέποτε τὸ αὐτὸ δὶς ὠνεῖται.
3. οὐ τιμῶμεν τοὺς τούτου δούλους (τοὺς δούλους αὐτοῦ)· ἔγημαν γὰρ τὰς ἑαυτῶν ἀδελφάς.
4. ὁ μὲν ταῦτα συνεβούλευσεν, ὁ δὲ τάδε.
5. οὐκ εὖ ποιεῖτε ὑμᾶς αὐτούς· ἰατρῷ τινι οὖν συμβουλεύεσθε.
6. ὃς ἂν κατ' ἐμοῦ λόγους ποιῇ, τοῦτον τιμωρήσομαι· οἱ γὰρ ἐχθροὶ ἀλλήλοις οὐ συγγιγνώσκουσιν.
7. ἡ σὴ ἀδελφή (ἡ ἀδελφὴ σοῦ) καὶ ἡ ἐμή (ἡ ἐμοῦ) ἀμφότεραι χθὲς ἐγήμαντο· ἀλλὰ αὕτη μὲν πλουσίῳ ἐγήματο, ἐκείνη δὲ ποιμένι τινί.
8. οἱ σύμμαχοι ἐπεθύμουν συμβουλεύεσθαι ἀλλήλοις τιμωρησόμενοι τοὺς βαρβάρους.
9. ἡμῶν μεταπεμψαμένων οἱ ἑταῖροι ἄλλοι ἄλλοθεν ἀφίκοντο ἡμῖν τιμωρήσοντες τοὺς ἐχθρούς.
10. τὸν δοῦλον αὐτοὶ ἐδιδάξαμεν, πωλήσοντες αὐτὸν πολλῶν χρημάτων, ὁ δὲ οὐχ ὑπήκουεν.

Analysis

1.   1.1 Ὅτι μὲν ὑμεῖς, ὦ ἄνδρες Ἀθηναῖοι, πεπόνθατε ὑπὸ τῶν ἐμῶν κατηγόρων, "Men of Athens, what you suffered at the hands of my accusers"

1 οὐκ οἶδα· "I do not know;"

2 ἐγὼ δ' οὖν καὶ αὐτὸς ὑπ' αὐτῶν ὀλίγου ἐμαυτοῦ ἐπελαθόμην, "but I myself almost forgot myself under their influence,"

3 οὕτω πιθανῶς ἔλεγον. "so persuasively were they speaking."

Ἐμῶν is a possessive adjective and therefore in attributive position.

Αὐτός is in the nominative without an article and therefore means "myself."

Αὐτῶν is not nominative and does not have an article and therefore means "them."

Ἐμαυτοῦ is a reflexive referring back to the subject of the sentence and therefore means "myself" here.

Chapter X

Preliminary exercise 1

a. I am a vegetarian. (NB *not* "I was a vegetarian": that would become "He said he had been a vegetarian.")

b. I have been a vegetarian for twenty years. / I was a vegetarian for twenty years. (NB *not* "I had been a vegetarian.")

c. I shall (will) start being a vegetarian soon.

d. The goose laid (has laid) a golden egg.

e. The goose is laying a golden egg.

f. The goose lays golden eggs.

g. The goose will lay a golden egg tomorrow.

Preliminary exercise 2

a. λέγει ὅτι οὐκ ἔθυσεν.

b. εἶπεν ὅτι οὐκ ἔθυσεν/θῦσαι.

c. λέγει ὅτι οὐ θύει.

d. εἶπεν ὅτι οὐ θύει/θύοι.

Preliminary exercise 3

a. καλήν φησι αὐτὴν εἶναι.

b. ἔφη καλὸς εἶναι.

c. ἔφη αὐτοὺς καλοὺς ἔσεσθαι.

d. οὔ φησιν αὐτοὺς θῦσαι.

e. οὐκ ἔφη θῦσαι.

Preliminary exercise 4

a. ἠπείλησεν ἀποκτενεῖν αὐτούς.

b. ἠπείλησαν αὐτὸν ἀποκτενεῖν με.

c. ἀπειλοῦσι μὴ ἀποκτενεῖν αὐτόν.

Preliminary exercise 5

a. ἀκούω αὐτὸν δειλὸν ὄντα.

b. σύνοιδα ἐμαυτῷ δειλὸς ὢν / δειλῷ ὄντι.

c. συνῄδει μοι δειλῇ οὔσῃ.

d. ἀκούω δειλὸς ὤν.

Preliminary exercise 6

a. ἐθαύμασα εἰ μὴ αἰσχύνοιτο/αἰσχύνεται.

b. ᾐσχύνθη εἰ ἄδικοι εἶεν/εἰσιν.

c. θαυμάζομεν εἰ ἄδικός ἐστιν.

Sentences

1. ἡ ἀδελφή μου (ἡ ἐμὴ ἀδελφὴ) οὐκ ἔφη πρὸς λιμένα καταβήσεσθαι. / ἡ ἀδελφή μου εἶπεν ὅτι πρὸς λιμένα οὐ καταβήσοιτο (καταβήσεται).

2. ἡ γυνή μου (ἡ ἐμὴ γυνὴ) ὡμολόγησε παύσεσθαι ἀναλίσκουσα τὰ ἐμὰ χρήματα (τὰ χρήματά μου).

3. νομίζομεν γενήσεσθαι καλοί· καλὴ γὰρ ἡ τεκοῦσα ἡμᾶς.

4. ὁ μὲν υἱός σου (ὁ μὲν σὸς υἱὸς) ᾔδει οὐδέποτε εὑρήσων τὸ δεσμωτήριον· ἡμᾶς δὲ οὐχ ὑπώπτευεν εὑρήσειν αὐτό.

5. αἰσχύνομαι εἰ ἤκουσάς μου· οὐ γὰρ ᾔδη σε ἐνθάδε μείναντα.

6. ἀπεκρινάμεθα ὅτι οἱ ἄλλοι τὸν ἡγεμόνα ἔτι μένοιεν (μένουσιν).

7. ἡ γυνή σου (ἡ σὴ γυνὴ) σύνοιδεν ἑαυτῇ ὑποσχομένη (ὑποσχομένη) διὰ τοῦ ποταμοῦ νευσεῖσθαι.

8. αἱ ἑταῖραι ἤκουσαν ἡμῶν ὁμολογούντων μὴ ἀναλώσειν τὸν ἄργυρόν σου (τὸν σὸν ἄργυρον).

9. οἱ βάρβαροι οὐκ ἔφασαν αὐτὸν ἁλῶναι. / οἱ βάρβαροι εἶπον ὅτι οὗτος οὐχ ἁλοίη (ἥλω/ἑάλω).

10. ὠμόσαμεν μὴ βλαβήσεσθαι τὴν δημοκρατίαν.

Analysis

1.   1.1 ἃ μὴ οἶδα "Whatever I do not know,"
    1 οὐδ' οἴομαι "I do not think"
        1.2 εἰδέναι. "that I know."

Indirect statement with present infinitive for an original present tense, and subject not expressed because it is the same as the subject of the main verb; the original direct statement would have been οἶδα "I know."

Chapter XI

Preliminary exercise 1
a. τίς ἔρχεται;
b. ποῖ ἔρχεται;
c. ἆρ’ οὐκ ἔρχεται;
d. ἆρα μὴ ἔρχονται;
e. πότερον ἔρχεται ἢ οὔ;

Preliminary exercise 2.1
The deliberative questions in a–g are a, c, and f.

Preliminary exercise 2.2
a. –
b. How many did they/you call? ("have called" also possible, but *not* "had called")
c. When shall I call / am I to call / should I call?
d. Who is calling? (*not* "Who was calling?")
e. Where is he?
f. –
g. Whom will you call?

Preliminary exercise 2.3
Because many forms of καλέω are ambiguous between present and future, the tenses of such forms are labeled here.
a. ἆρα καλέσωμεν αὐτόν;
b. ἠρόμην πόσους/ὁπόσους ἐκάλεσαν/καλέσαιεν.
c. ἤρετο πότε/ὁπότε καλέσῃ/καλέσαι.
d. ἤροντο τίς/ὅστις καλεῖ/καλοίη. (present)
e. ἐρήσομαι ποῦ/ὅπου ἐστίν.
f. ἆρα καλέσω αὐτούς;
g. ἤροντο τίνα/τίνας/ὅντινα/οὕστινας καλοῦμεν/καλοῖμεν. (future)

Preliminary exercise 3
a. indirect question
b. relative clause
c. relative clause
d. indirect statement
e. indirect question
f. indirect question
g. relative clause
h. indirect question

Sentences

1. ἆρα καὶ τοῦτον (αὐτόν) καλέσω;
2. τοὺς ἐπὶ τοῖς πύργοις ἤρετο ποῦ (ὅπου) εἴης (εἶ)· οἱ δὲ οὐκ ᾔδεσαν.
3. οὐκ ἴσμεν πότερον (εἴτε) νομίζεις τὸν τούτων πύργον χρήσιμον εἶναι ἢ (εἴτε) ἐπι-θυμεῖς διαφθεῖραι αὐτὸν καὶ τοὺς λίθους ἑλεῖν ἄλλοθι χρησόμενος.
4. οἱ πεζοὶ ἤροντο πότε (ὁπότε) ἀναχωρήσαιεν (ἀναχωρήσωσιν).
5. ὁ διδάσκαλός μου οὐκ ᾔδει πότερον (εἴτε) πρὸς τὴν ἑορτὴν ἢ (εἴτε) πρὸς τοὺς πύργους ἔλθοις (ἦλθες).
6. ἆρ' οὐκ ὠφέλιμος ἂν εἴη ἡ εἰρήνη;
7. μόνοι οἱ ἐν τῷ δεσμωτηρίῳ ἤροντο εἰ περὶ τῆς ἐνδείας τοῦ σίτου ἀθυμοῖμεν (ἀθυ-μοῦμεν).
8. πότε ἆρα τὸν ἡγεμόνα ἐξέβαλον;
9. ἆρ' οὐκ ἤρεσθε ποῖ (ὅποι) ἀναχωρήσαιτε (ἀναχωρήσητε);
10. πότερον οἱ τούτου φύλακες τοὺς φυγάδας συνέλαβον ἢ οὔ;

Analysis

1.   1 ὥστ' οὐκ οἶδ' "So that I do not know"
      1.1 ὅ τι δεῖ "why it is necessary"
         1.1.1 πολλὰ κατηγορεῖν τοιούτων ἀνδρῶν, "to accuse such men a lot,"
            1.1.1.1 οἳ οὐδ' . . . δύναιντ' ἂν "(men) who would not be able,"
               1.1.1.1.1.1 ὑπὲρ ἑνὸς ἑκάστου τῶν πεπραγμένων δὶς ἀποθανόντες "even if they died twice for each one of the things they did,"
            1.1.1.1.1 δίκην δοῦναι . . . ἀξίαν. "to pay a fitting penalty."

Indirect question using indirect interrogative and indicative verb in primary sequence; the original direct question was τί δεῖ;

Review exercises 2

1.   ἙΤΑΙΡΟΣ: ὦ φίλε, τί ποιεῖς;
      ΤΙΜΩΝ: ἆρ' οὐχ ὡμολόγησας μὴ ἐρωτήσειν (ἐρήσεσθαι) ὅ τι (τί) ποιοίην (ποιῶ);
      ἙΤΑΙΡΟΣ: ἀλλ', ὦ ἀγαθέ, ἐνόμιζον οὐδένα βούλεσθαι μόνον μένειν ἄνευ τοῦ λέγειν. ὅστις γὰρ ἂν μόνος ζῇ, τούτῳ ἔνδεια φίλων ἐστίν.
      ΤΙΜΩΝ: ἀλλὰ ἄλλους λυπεῖ· σὲ μὲν γὰρ τὸ σιγᾶν, ἐμὲ δὲ οἱ ἑταῖροι (οἱ ἑταῖροί μου).
      ἙΤΑΙΡΟΣ: ἀλλ' ἐάν τινες (οἳ ἂν) εἰδῶσιν ἔχοντες φίλους, χαίρουσιν. τίς γὰρ οὐκ ἂν φιλοίη τὸν φιλοῦντα ἕ; (ὃς γὰρ φιλοίη ἕ, τοῦτον τίς οὐκ ἂν φιλοίη;)
      ΤΙΜΩΝ: ἐγώ.
      ἙΤΑΙΡΟΣ: θαυμάζω εἰ ἀεὶ ὁ αὐτὸς εἶ. ἄλλος γάρ, καὶ εἰ ἠπίστει μοι, (καὶ μὴ πιστεύων μοι,) οὐκ ἂν οὕτως κατέγνω μου.

ΤΙΜΩΝ: ἐὰν μὴ βούλῃ (μὴ βουλόμενος) κακῶς δρᾶσθαι (ποιεῖσθαι), ἄπιθι.
ἙΤΑΙΡΟΣ: τί εἴπω;
ΤΙΜΩΝ: εἰπὲ ὅτι οὐ λυπήσεις (οὐ φάθι λυπήσειν) με πολλὰς ἡμέρας.

Chapter XII

Preliminary exercise 1

a. ἤλθομεν ἵνα τερπώμεθα/τερποίμεθα. / ἤλθομεν (ὡς) τερφθησόμενοι.
b. ἔπεμψεν ἡμᾶς ἵνα τέρπωμεν/τέρψωμεν/τέρποιμεν/τέρψαιμεν ὑμᾶς/σε. / ἔπεμψεν
    ἡμᾶς (ὡς) τέρψοντάς σε/ὑμᾶς. (It is better not to use a relative clause here because
    "us" is already well defined; personal pronouns rarely take restrictive relative
    clauses.)
c. ἔπεμψεν ἡμᾶς ἵνα τέρπῃ/τέρποιο/τέρπησθε/τέρποισθε.
d. πέμψουσι δούλους ἵνα τέρπωσιν/τέρψωσιν ἡμᾶς. / πέμψουσι δούλους (ὡς) τέρψ-
    οντας ἡμᾶς. / πέμψουσι δούλους οἳ/οἵτινες τέρψουσιν ἡμᾶς.

Preliminary exercise 2

a. φοβούμεθα μὴ συλληφθῶμεν.
b. φοβούμεθα συλλαβεῖν αὐτούς.
c. ἐφοβούμεθα μὴ ἐξέπεσες.
d. φοβοῦμαι μὴ οὐ συλληφθῇ.
e. φοβοῦμαι μὴ συλλαμβάνεται.

Preliminary exercise 3

a. ἐμηχανῶντο/ἐμηχανήσαντο ὅπως ἄπεισιν.
b. πράξομεν ὅπως μὴ ἄπεισιν.
c. ὅπως μὴ ἄπιτε.

Sentences

1. φοβοῦμαι μὴ ὁ πατήρ μου τὸν οἶνον ἔπιε σώσων σε ἀπὸ τούτου (ἵνα σώσαι σε
    ἀπὸ τούτου)· νομίζει γὰρ τὸν οἶνον οὐκ ἀγαθὸν σοι εἶναι.
2. ὁ τῆς πόλεως νομοθέτης ὁ πρῶτος ἔπραξεν ὅπως οἱ τάφοι μὴ ἐν ἄστει ἔσονται
    ἀλλὰ ὑπὲρ τὰ τείχη· τούτῳ οὖν τῷ τρόπῳ ἐμηχανήσατο ὅπως ἡ νόσος ἀπὸ τῆς
    πόλεως ἀπέσται.
3. ὁ βασιλεὺς ὑμῶν ἔπραξεν ὅπως ἱππεῖς μὴ φοβήσονται χρῆσθαι ναυσί· ὁμολογίαν
    γὰρ ἐποιήσατο πρὸς τοὺς ναύτας περὶ ἵππων.
4. ὁ νομοθέτης αὐτῶν ἄνδρας εἵλετο οἳ τῆς πόλεως εὖ ἄρξουσιν / ἵνα τῆς πόλεως εὖ
    ἄρχοιεν (ἄρχωσιν) / τῆς πόλεως εὖ ἄρξοντας.
5. ἡ τοῦ μάντεως θυγάτηρ ἐφοβεῖτο μὴ οἱ βόες οἱ τοῦ Διὸς ἱεροὶ τὰ ἄνθη φάγοιεν
    (φάγωσιν).

6. ὅπως μὴ φοβήσεσθε προσβαλεῖν τῷ τυράννῳ· μόνοι γὰρ οἱ μὴ φοβούμενοι νική-
σουσιν.

7. ἡ γραῦς ἀπέσται ἵνα μὴ ὑπὸ τῶν βοῶν λυπῆται / οὐ λυπηθησομένη.

8. ἡ τοῦ τυράννου μήτηρ φοβεῖται μὴ οἱ τοῦ υἱοῦ τρόποι οὐκ ἀγαθοί εἰσιν· μηχανᾶται
γὰρ ὅπως ἀποθανοῦνται πολλοὶ ἰδιῶται.

9. ὁ μάντις μητέρας καὶ ἀδελφὰς καὶ θυγατέρας αἱρεῖται αἳ ἄνθη κομιοῦσιν πρὸς τοὺς
τάφους τοὺς τῶν τεθνηκότων ἱππέων / ἵνα κομίσωσιν / κομιούσας.

10. ἆρα μὴ φοβεῖ μὴ οὐκ ἀεὶ ὑπάρχῃ ἡ τοῦ γένους ἡμῶν μνήμη;

Analysis

1. 1 ἀλλ᾽, ὦ φίλε Ἀγάθων, μηδὲν πλέον αὐτῷ γένηται, "But, dear Agathon, let nothing more happen to his advantage,"

2 ἀλλὰ παρασκευάζου "but take care"

2.1 ὅπως ἐμὲ καὶ σὲ μηδεὶς διαβαλεῖ. "that no-one slanders me and you."

The last line is an effort clause introduced by παρασκευάζου.

Chapter XIII

Preliminary exercise 1

a. ἐπεὶ ἔκαμεν, ᾠκτίραμεν αὐτόν. / ᾠκτίραμεν αὐτὸν ἅτε (οἷα) καμόντα.

b. ᾠκτίραμεν αὐτὸν ὅτι κάμοι. / ᾠκτίραμεν αὐτὸν ὡς καμόντα.

c. ᾠκτίραμεν αὐτὸν ὅτι κάμνοι. / ᾠκτίραμεν αὐτὸν ὡς κάμνοντα.

d. ᾠκτίραμεν αὐτὸν ὅτι ἔκαμεν. / ᾠκτίραμεν αὐτὸν ἅτε (οἷα) κάμνοντα.

Preliminary exercise 2

a. τοσαῦτα ἔμαθεν ὥστε ἐπαινεῖσθαι (ἐπαινεθῆναι) / ὥστε ἐπῃνέθη.

b. οὕτω ταχέως δραμεῖται ὥστε ὑμᾶς ἐπαινεῖν (ἐπαινέσαι) αὐτόν / ὥστε ἐπαινέσεσθε
αὐτόν.

c. τοιαῦτα μανθάνει ὥστε μὴ ἐπαινεῖσθαι (ἐπαινεθῆναι) / ὥστε οὐκ ἐπαινεῖται.

Sentences

1. ὁ εἰσβάλλων στρατὸς τοσοῦτος ἦν ὥστε μηδένα ὑπομεῖναι αὐτόν / ὥστε οὐδεὶς
ὑπέμεινε αὐτόν.

2. ὁμολογίαν ἐπὶ τούτῳ ἐποιησάμεθα, ἐφ᾽ ᾧτε πάντες ἑκόντες ἐκβήσονται ἐκ τῆς
πόλεως / ἐφ᾽ ᾧτε πάντας ἑκόντας ἐκβῆναι ἐκ τῆς πόλεως.

3. πιστὸν ἑταῖρον ἐπέμψαμεν βοηθήσοντα αὐτοῖς, οἱ δὲ ἄκοντες τοῦτον ἐδέξαντο ὅτι
οὐχ ὅμοιος σφίσιν εἴη / ὡς οὐχ ὅμοιον σφίσιν ὄντα.

4. ἆρα οὕτως ἀσεβὴς εἶ ὥστε τοῦτον τὸν νεὼν εἰσιέναι ἄνευ τοῦ λούεσθαι;

5. ἐπεὶ οὐκ ᾔδει (οὐκ εἰδώς) ὁποτέρα ἀπόκρισις ὀρθὴ εἴη, ὁ ἀμαθὴς ἐξέβη μαθησό-
μενός τι.

6.   ὁ οἶνος αὐτοῦ οὕτως ἡδύς ἐστι ὥστε ἡμᾶς πάντα πίνειν / ὥστε πάντα πιόμεθα.

7.   αὗται αἱ τρεῖς πόλεις σπονδὰς ἐπὶ τούτοις ἐποιήσαντο, ἐφ᾽ ᾧτε ἑκάστη ἕξει
     (ἑκάστην ἔχειν) τοὺς ἑαυτῆς νόμους καὶ ἔθη.

8.   τῶν πολεμίων τὰ μακρὰ τείχη αἱρούντων, οἱ ἐν τῇ πόλει οὐχ ὑπέμειναν, ὅτι ἐνδεεῖς
     εἶεν (ὡς ἐνδεεῖς ὄντες) ὕδατος καὶ οὐχ ὑγιεῖς.

9.   οὕτως εὐρεῖα ἡ θάλαττα ὥστε ναῦς ἐπ᾽ αὐτῇ πλεῖν (ὥστε νῆες ἐπ᾽ αὐτῇ πλέουσιν)
     ἄνευ τοῦ τοὺς ναύτας τὴν ἤπειρον ὁρᾶν.

10. ὄρνιν μέλανα ἐπὶ τούτοις εὑρήσω σοι, ἐφ᾽ ᾧτε αὐτὸν μὴ βλάψεις / ἐφ᾽ ᾧτέ σε μὴ
     βλάψαι αὐτόν.

Analysis

1.   1 καὶ εἰς τοσοῦτόν εἰσι τόλμης ἀφιγμένοι "And they have arrived at such a point
       of daring"
          1.1 ὥσθ᾽ ἥκουσιν "that they have come" (actual result clause)
               1.1.1 ἀπολογησόμενοι, "to defend themselves,"
          1.2 καὶ λέγουσιν "and that they say" (actual result clause)
               1.2.1 ὡς οὐδὲν κακὸν οὐδ᾽ αἰσχρὸν εἰργασμένοι εἰσίν. "that they have done
               nothing bad or shameful."

Chapter XIV

Preliminary exercise 1

a. (οὗτος) γενναιότερός ἐστι ταύτης. / (οὗτος) γενναιότερός ἐστιν ἢ αὕτη.

b. γενναιότερός ἐστιν.

c. τούτῳ ἐστὶν γενναιότερος πατὴρ ἢ ταύτῃ.

d. γενναιότερός ἐστιν ἢ ὥστε ἀποδραμεῖν.

Preliminary exercise 2

a. οὗτος ἀρχαιότατός ἐστιν τῶν οἴκων.

b. ὁ οἶκος ὡς/ὅτι ἀρχαιότατός ἐστιν.

c. οὗτος ὁ οἶκος πολλῷ/πολὺ ἀρχαιότερός ἐστιν ἐκείνου / ἢ ἐκεῖνος.

d. οὗτος ὁ οἶκος μακρῷ ἀρχαιότερός ἐστιν ἐκείνου / ἢ ἐκεῖνος.

Preliminary exercise 3

a. οὐδεὶς οὐδὲν ἔκλεψεν.

b. οὐδὲν ἔκλεψα. / οὐκ ἔκλεψα οὐδέν.

c. οὐδεὶς οὐ κλέπτει.

d. οὐδέποτε κλέπτουσιν. / οὐ κλέπτουσιν οὐδέποτε.

e. οὐδεὶς εἶπεν ὅτι οὐδέποτε κλέπτοιεν/κλέπτουσιν.

Sentences 1

1. οὐδεὶς οὐδέποτε ἀμελεῖ τῆς ἑαυτοῦ ὀργῆς.
2. οὐδένα οὐκ ἐκίνησεν.
3. οὐκ ἀναγνώσονται οὐδὲν ποίημα.
4. οὐδεὶς οὐκ ἔχει δυνάμεις.
5. οὐκ ἐπεβούλευσα οὐδενὶ μοχθηρῷ.

Sentences 2

1. ἆρα τὸ σαφῶς ἀναγιγνώσκειν ῥᾷον τοῦ ὀρθῶς γράφειν;
2. αὕτη ἡ μηχανὴ πολλῷ φανερωτέρα ἦν ἢ ὥστε μὴ ταχέως ὀφθῆναι.
3. μακρῷ ὀξύτατος τῶν ἐπιθυμιῶν ὁ ἔρως.
4. οἱ πανουργότατοι παῖδες πολὺ πλείονας κινοῦσιν ἢ σφάλλουσιν.
5. πειράσομαι ὡς σαφέστατα ἀναγιγνώσκειν.

Analysis

1.   1 ἐμοὶ μὲν γὰρ οὐδέν ἐστι πρεσβύτερον "For nothing is more important to me"
        1.1 τοῦ ὡς ὅτι βέλτιστον ἐμὲ γενέσθαι, "than for me to be as good as possible,"
      2 τούτου δὲ οἶμαί μοι "and I think that for me in this (project)"
        2.1 συλλήπτορα οὐδένα κυριώτερον εἶναι σοῦ. "there is no more capable part-
        ner than you."

   Πρεσβύτερον is a comparative followed by the genitive of comparison τοῦ . . . ἐμὲ
   γενέσθαι; ὅτι βέλτιστον is a superlative with ὅτι meaning "as . . . as possible";
   κυριώτερον is a comparative followed by the genitive of comparison σοῦ.

Chapter XV

Preliminary exercise 1

a. σίγα/σιγᾶτε.
b. μὴ γήμῃς/γήμητε.
c. γήμωμεν.
d. σιγώντων.
e. ἐκέλευσαν ἡμᾶς μὴ γῆμαι.

Preliminary exercise 2

a. ἀπαγορεύει μοι μὴ σπέσθαι. / οὐκ ἐᾷ με σπέσθαι.
b. οὐκ ἀπεῖπον ἡμῖν μὴ οὐχ σπέσθαι.
c. εἶρξεν αὐτὸν μὴ σπέσθαι. / ἐκώλυσεν αὐτὸν σπέσθαι.
d. οὐδὲν εἴργει σε μὴ οὐχ σπέσθαι. / οὐδὲν κωλύει σε σπέσθαι.
e. ἀπαρνούμεθα μὴ σπέσθαι. / οὔ φαμεν σπέσθαι.
f. οὐδεὶς ἀπαρνεῖται μὴ οὐχ ἡμᾶς σπέσθαι.

Preliminary exercise 3

a.　εἴθε μὴ ᾄσαιεν. / εἰ γὰρ μὴ ᾄσαιεν. / μὴ ᾄσαιεν.

b.　εἴθε μὴ ᾖδον. / εἰ γὰρ μὴ ᾖδον. / ὤφελον μὴ ᾄδειν. / εἴθε ὤφελον μὴ ᾄδειν. / εἰ γὰρ
ὤφελον μὴ ᾄδειν.

c.　εἴθε μὴ ᾖσαν. / εἰ γὰρ μὴ ᾖσαν. / ὤφελον μὴ ᾄσαι. / εἴθε ὤφελον μὴ ᾄσαι. / εἰ γὰρ
ὤφελον μὴ ᾄσαι.

Sentences

1.　εἴθε/εἰ γὰρ ὁ τοξότης μὴ ὠνίνατο ἐπανιὼν εἰς ταύτην τὴν χώραν. / (εἴθε/εἰ γὰρ)
ὤφελεν ὁ τοξότης μὴ ὀνίνασθαι . . .

2.　μηδέποτε μηδὲν μηδενὶ ὀφείλωμεν.

3.　οὐδεὶς ἀπεῖπεν ἡμῖν μὴ οὐ δεῖξαί σοι τὸν εὐρύτερον ἀγρόν.

4.　μὴ εὐθὺς ἀπολέσῃς τὸ φάρμακον τὸ ἐπὶ τῆς τραπέζης· ἰδόντων γὰρ αὐτὸ οἱ
μάρτυρες.

5.　εἴθε/εἰ γὰρ μηδέποτε ἐῴη σε ὁ πατήρ σου ἀσφαλῶς ἐπανελθεῖν εἰς τὴν ἑαυτοῦ
οἰκίαν.

6.　μηδέποτε μένε ἐν τάξει ἐν ᾗ ἀπολεῖ.

7.　ὁ ἀνὴρ ὁ τῆς θυγατρός σου ἀπηρνήθη μὴ ὕστερον ἀνοῖξαι τὴν σκηνήν. / . . . οὐκ
ἔφη ἀνοῖξαι . . .

8.　εἴθε/εἰ γὰρ μὴ κέρδους ἕνεκα κακῶς ἀπώλοντο. / (εἴθε/εἰ γὰρ) ὤφελον μὴ κακῶς
ἀπολέσθαι κέρδους ἕνεκα.

9.　τοῖς θεοῖς ἀεὶ εὐμενῶς διδῶμεν μέρος τι τοῦ κέρδους ἡμῶν.

10.　ἀεὶ μένετε ἐν ταῖς τάξεσιν ὑμῶν.

Analysis

1.　　1　εἴθε σοι, ὦ Περίκλεις, τότε συνεγενόμην, "O Pericles, if only I had known you
then,"

　　　1.1　ὅτε δεινότατος σαυτοῦ ταῦτα ἦσθα. "when you were cleverer about such
things than you are now!"

　　Wish for the past using aorist indicative.

Chapter XVI

Preliminary exercise 1

a.　General temporal clause, present subjunctive, ἐπειδάν.

b.　Prospective temporal clause, aorist subjunctive, ἐπειδάν.

c.　Temporal clause of fact, aorist indicative, ἐπεί/ἐπειδή.

d.　Prospective temporal clause, aorist optative, ἕως/μέχρι.

e.　Temporal clause of fact (or could be called a prospective temporal clause with indicative), aorist indicative, ἕως/μέχρι.

f. Temporal clause of fact, imperfect indicative, ὅτε/ὁπότε.

g. Prospective temporal clause, aorist subjunctive, ἐπειδάν.

Preliminary exercise 2

a. πρίν, infinitive

b. πρίν/ἕως/μέχρι, indicative

c. ἕως/μέχρι, optative

d. πρίν, infinitive

e. πρίν/ἕως/μέχρι, indicative

f. πρίν, infinitive

g. ἕως/μέχρι ἄν, subjunctive

h. πρίν/ἕως/μέχρι, indicative (an argument for the optative could be made)

Sentences

1. τὸν χαλκὸν ἐκάθηρε πρὶν ἀποδόσθαι αὐτὸν ἡμῖν.

2. βουλόμενος ἡμᾶς ψεύδειν, ὁ μοχθηρὸς ἐθεράπευεν ἡμᾶς ἕως πιστεύοιμεν οἷ.

3. βουλόμενος ἡμᾶς ψεύδειν, ὁ πανουργότατος ἐθεράπευεν ἡμᾶς ἕως ἐνόμισεν ἡμᾶς πιστεύειν οἷ.

4. ἐπειδὰν ἀδικῆται ὑπ' ἐχθροῦ τινος, ὁ ἀληθὴς φιλόσοφος (or, more idiomatically, ὁ ὡς ἀληθῶς φιλόσοφος) γελᾷ καὶ ἐπιλανθάνεται.

5. ἆρα μένεις ἕως ἂν εἰς ταύτην τὴν ναῦν ἀναβῇς;

6. ὁ κλέπτης τὸν ἵππον μου οὐκ ἀπέδωκέ μοι πρὶν (ἕως, μέχρι) τοὺς φύλακας ἐβόησα.

7. τὸ τῆς ἑταίρας κάλλος τὸν ἐμὸν υἱὸν ἐδούλωσε πρὶν τὰ ταύτης ψεύδη ἀποστῆσαι αὐτόν.

8. ἀεὶ ἀφίσταντο ἐπειδὴ τάχιστα ἀποθάνοι ὁ βασιλεὺς αὐτῶν.

9. οἱ στρατιῶται ἐν τῷ πεδίῳ ἔμενον ἕως τὰς πύλας ῥήξαιμεν.

10. οἱ παῖδες ἐκάθευδον ἕως ἤγειρας αὐτούς.

Analysis

1. 1 ἄρχοντα οὖν αἱροῦμαι τῆς πόσεως . . . ἐμαυτόν. "So I appoint myself leader of the drinking"

    1.1 ἕως ἂν ὑμεῖς ἱκανῶς πίητε "until you have drunk sufficiently."

Prospective temporal clause using ἕως + ἄν + subjunctive.

Review exercises 3

1. ΘΥΓΑΤΗΡ: ὦ μῆτερ, φοβοῦμαι μὴ ὁ πατὴρ οὐ παρῇ ὅταν ἀναβαίνωμεν (ἡμῶν ἀναβαινουσῶν) ἵνα πλέωμεν (πλευσόμεναι) Ἀθήναζε. πολλάκις γὰρ ἠμέλει ἡμῶν, ὅτι ἐπισταίμεθα (ὡς ἐπισταμένων) ὠφελεῖν ἡμᾶς αὐτάς, ὥστε λυποῦμαι (ὥστε με λυπεῖν is also possible but less good here).

MHTHP: ὦ μοχθηροτάτη θύγατερ, παῦσαι διαβάλλουσα τὸν πατέρα, μηδὲ κίνει με μηκέτι. ὅταν γὰρ πειρῶμαι καθεύδειν, κωλύεις με (ἀεὶ γὰρ κωλύεις με πειρωμένην καθεύδειν). μὴ οὖν ἀπαρνηθῇς μὴ οὐκ εἰδυῖα πράττειν ὅπως μηδέποτε καθευδήσω.

ΘΥΓΑΤΗΡ: εἴθε μὴ ἀεὶ ἐμέμφου μοι. (ὤφελες μὴ ἀεὶ μέμφεσθαί μοι.) οὕτω γὰρ πικρῶς λέγεις ὥστε με φοβεῖσθαι συνεῖναί σοι.

MHTHP: μεταγιγνώσκω τὰ λεχθέντα. πέμψωμεν οὖν τινα ὡς πιστότατον ὃς ἐρεῖ (ἵνα εἴπῃ, ἐροῦντα) τῷ πατρί σου εὐθὺς ἐπανελθεῖν πρὶν ἡμᾶς πλεῖν. οὐδεὶς γὰρ οὐκ οἶδεν (πάντες γὰρ ἴσασιν) ὅπου (ποῦ) ἐστίν.

ΘΥΓΑΤΗΡ: ὦ μῆτερ, οὐδεὶς οὐδέποτε ἀληθῶς σφάλλεταί σου οὐδέν. μακρῷ γὰρ ἀρίστη μητέρων εἶ. ἐλθέτω οὖν Ξανθίας, ὅτι θάττων ἐστὶ (ἅτε θάττων ὢν) τῶν ἄλλων δούλων.

MHTHP: ὦ Ξανθία, ὅπως εἶ ὡς τὸν ἄνδρα μου καὶ ἐρεῖς (ἐρῶν) αὐτῷ μὴ μέλλειν, ἀλλ᾽ εὐθὺς ἐπανελθεῖν.

Chapter XVII

Preliminary exercise 1

a. δεῖ ἡμᾶς μὴ μάχεσθαι (μαχέσασθαι). / οὐ χρὴ ἡμᾶς μάχεσθαι. / ἀνάγκη ἐστὶν ἡμῖν μὴ μάχεσθαι.

b. ἐξὸν/παρὸν μάχεσθαι/μαχέσασθαι

c. ἔδει ἡμᾶς μαχέσασθαι. / χρῆν ἡμᾶς μαχέσασθαι.

d. ἔξεστιν ἡμῖν μὴ μάχεσθαι/μαχέσασθαι.

e. οὐ δεῖ ἡμῖν τούτου.

f. ἔδοξεν ἡμῖν μάχεσθαι/μαχέσασθαι.

g. δέον μάχεσθαι/μαχέσασθαι

h. οὐκ ἔδει ἡμᾶς μάχεσθαι/μαχέσασθαι.

i. μεταμέλει ἡμῖν τούτου.

j. ἀνάγκη οὐδεμία ἐστὶν ἡμῖν μάχεσθαι/μαχέσασθαι.

Preliminary exercise 2

a. κύνες ὑμῖν οὐ λυτέοι εἰσίν. / κύνας ὑμῖν οὐ λυτέον ἐστίν.

b. ἰστέον ἐστί μοι.

c. οὐκ ἀκουστέον ἐστί σου αὐτοῖς.

d. οἱ κύνες θαπτέοι ἦσαν. / τοὺς κύνας θαπτέον ἦν.

e. ἰτέον ἦν ἡμῖν.

f. ὁ κύων οὐ θυτέος ἐστίν. / τὸν κύνα οὐ θυτέον ἐστίν.

g. τοῦτο οὐκ ἰστέον ἐστὶν αὐτῷ.

h. ὁ κύων μοι οἰστέος ἦν. / τὸν κύνα μοι οἰστέον ἦν.

Sentences 1
1. τῆς μητρὸς οὐδέποτε καταγελαστέον σοί ἐστιν.
2. ἡ φυλὴ ἡμῶν οὐδέποτε οὐδενὶ προδοτέα ἐστίν. / οὐδενὶ οὐδέποτε προδοτέον ἐστὶ τὴν ἡμετέραν φυλήν.
3. οἰκέταις ῥᾳθύμοις ἐνίοτε ὀργιστέον.
4. ἐὰν ἀμυνώμεθα τοὺς ἐθέλοντας δῆσαι ἡμᾶς, ἀφετέοι ἐσόμεθα αὐτοῖς. / . . . ἀφετέον ἡμᾶς ἔσται αὐτοῖς.
5. πάντες οἱ τῶν πολεμίων στρατιῶται σκεδαστέοι (πάντας τοὺς τῶν πολεμίων στρατιώτας σκεδαστέον) πρὶν ἡμᾶς δύνασθαι ἐπιθέσθαι τῷ ἄστει.

Sentences 2
1. οὐ χρή σε ὀργίζεσθαι τῇ μητρί. / δεῖ σε μὴ ὀργίζεσθαι τῇ μητρί. / ἀνάγκη ἐστί σοι μὴ ὀργίζεσθαι τῇ μητρί.
2. ἐξὸν/παρὸν ἐργάζεσθαι, μὴ οἴκοι κάθησο.
3. ἐξῆν ἡμῖν ἐπιχειρῆσαι τῷ τυράννῳ, ἀλλὰ οἱ γέροντες εἶπον ὅτι ἡμῖν οὐ συμφέροι/συμφέρει.
4. οὐ πρέπει τοῖς νεκροῖς ἐν ταῖς ὁδοῖς κεῖσθαι· χρὴ γὰρ αὐτοὺς ταφῆναι.
5. οὐκ ἔδει τὴν ἐκκλησίαν (ἀνάγκη οὐδεμία ἦν τῇ ἐκκλησίᾳ) τοῦτον τὸν ἄφρονα τῇ ἡμετέρᾳ στρατιᾷ ἐπιστῆσαι.

Analysis
1. 1 οὔκουν δεῖ "So it is not necessary"
    1.1 οὔτε ἑνὸς ἀνδρὸς ἕνεκα οὔτε δυοῖν ἡμᾶς τοὺς ἄλλους τῆς Ἑλλάδος ἀπέχεσθαι, "for the rest of us to be kept away from Greece, neither because of one man nor because of two,"
    2 ἀλλὰ πειστέον ἐστὶν "but we/everyone/one must obey"
    2.1 ὅ τι ἂν κελεύωσι· "whatever they order;"
    3 καὶ γὰρ αἱ πόλεις ἡμῶν . . . πείθονται αὐτοῖς. "for also our cities, the ones from which we come, obey them."
    3.1 ὅθεν ἐσμὲν

In clause 1 δεῖ with accusative and infinitive; in 2 a -τέος adjective in the impersonal neuter.

Chapter XVIII

Preliminary exercise 1
Versions in parentheses are those that are possible but less likely for reasons of aspect.
a. Simple condition, present: "If we do anything, she sees it." / "He said that if they did anything, she saw it."

Direct: εἴ τι πράττομεν, ὁρᾷ.

ἔφη εἴ τι πράττουσι/πράττοιεν, ταύτην ὁρᾶν.

εἶπεν ὅτι εἴ τι πράττουσι/πράττοιεν, αὕτη ὁρᾷ/ὁρῴη.

b. Simple condition, past: "If we did anything, she saw it." / "He said that if they had done anything, she had seen it."

Direct: εἴ τι ἐπράξαμεν, εἶδεν.

ἔφη εἴ τι ἔπραξαν, ταύτην ἰδεῖν.

εἶπεν ὅτι εἴ τι ἔπραξαν, αὕτη εἶδεν/ἴδοι.

c. Contrafactual condition, present: "If we were doing anything, she would be seeing it." / "He said that if they were doing anything, she would be seeing it."

Direct: εἴ τι ἐπράττομεν, ἑώρα ἄν.

ἔφη εἴ τι ἔπραττον, ταύτην ὁρᾶν ἄν.

εἶπεν ὅτι εἴ τι ἔπραττον, αὕτη ἑώρα ἄν.

d. Contrafactual condition, past: "If we had done anything, she would have seen it." / "He said that if they had done anything, she would have seen it."

Direct: εἴ τι ἐπράξαμεν, εἶδεν ἄν.

ἔφη εἴ τι ἔπραξαν, ταύτην ἰδεῖν ἄν.

εἶπεν ὅτι εἴ τι ἔπραξαν, αὕτη εἶδεν ἄν.

e. General condition, present: "If ever we do anything, she sees it." / "He said that if ever they did anything, she saw it."

Direct: ἐάν τι πράττωμεν/πράξωμεν, ὁρᾷ.

ἔφη ἐάν τι πράττωσι (πράξωσι) / εἴ τι πράττοιεν (πράξαιεν), ταύτην ὁρᾶν.

εἶπεν ὅτι ἐάν τι πράττωσι (πράξωσι) / εἴ τι πράττοιεν (πράξαιεν), αὕτη ὁρᾷ/ὁρῴη.

f. General condition, past: "If ever we did anything, she saw it." / "He said that if ever they did anything, she saw it."

Direct: εἴ τι πράττοιμεν/πράξαιμεν, ἑώρα.

ἔφη εἴ τι πράττοιεν/πράξαιεν, ταύτην ὁρᾶν.

εἶπεν ὅτι εἴ τι πράττοιεν/πράξαιεν, αὕτη ἑώρα.

g. Future condition, more vivid: "If we do anything, she will see it." / "He said that if they did anything, she would see it."

Direct: ἐάν τι πράξωμεν/πράττωμεν, ὄψεται.

ἔφη ἐάν τι πράξωσι (πράττωσι) / εἴ τι πράξαιεν (πράττοιεν), ταύτην ὄψεσθαι.

εἶπεν ὅτι ἐάν τι πράξωσι (πράττωσι) / εἴ τι πράξαιεν (πράττοιεν), αὕτη ὄψεται/ὄψοιτο.

h. Future condition, less vivid: "If we did (should do, were to do) anything, she would see it." / "He said that if they did (should do, were to do) anything, she would see it."

Direct: εἴ τι πράξαιμεν/πράττοιμεν, ἴδοι/ὁρῴη ἄν.

ἔφη εἴ τι πράξαιεν/πράττοιεν, ταύτην ἰδεῖν/ὁρᾶν ἄν.

εἶπεν ὅτι εἴ τι πράξαιεν/πράττοιεν, αὕτη ἴδοι/ὁρῴη ἄν.

i. Future condition, most vivid: "If we do anything, she will see it." / "He said that if they did anything, she would see it."
Direct: εἴ τι πράξομεν, ὄψεται.
ἔφη εἴ τι πράξουσι/πράξοιεν, ταύτην ὄψεσθαι.
εἶπεν ὅτι εἴ τι πράξουσι/πράξοιεν, αὕτη ὄψεται/ὄψοιτο.

Preliminary exercise 2

a. "He said that if he should hear, he would answer." εἰ ἀκούσαιμι, ἀποκριναίμην ἄν (future less vivid).
b. "He said that if he heard, he answered." ἐὰν ἀκούσω, ἀποκρίνομαι (present general) or εἰ ἀκούσαιμι, ἀπεκρινόμην (past general).
c. "He said that if he heard, he would answer." ἐὰν ἀκούσω, ἀποκρινοῦμαι (future more vivid).
d. "He said that if he had heard, he would have answered." εἰ ἤκουσα, ἀπεκρινάμην ἄν (past contrafactual).
e. "He said that if he had heard, he had answered." εἰ ἤκουσα, ἀπεκρινάμην (past simple).
f. "He said that if he were hearing, he would be answering." εἰ ἤκουον, ἀπεκρινόμην ἄν (present contrafactual).
g. "He said that if he heard, he answered." εἰ ἀκούω, ἀποκρίνομαι (present simple).
h. "He said that if he heard, he would answer." εἰ ἀκούσομαι, ἀποκρινοῦμαι (future most vivid).

Preliminary exercise 3

a. "If ever you seek, you find" (present general). ἔφη αὐτόν, ἐὰν ζητῇ (εἰ ζητοίη), εὑρίσκειν. / εἶπεν ὅτι ἐὰν ζητῇ (εἰ ζητοίη), οὗτος εὑρίσκοι (εὑρίσκει).
b. "If you seek, you will find" (future more vivid). ἔφη αὐτόν, ἐὰν ζητῇ (εἰ ζητοίη), εὑρήσειν. / εἶπεν ὅτι ἐὰν ζητῇ (εἰ ζητοίη), οὗτος εὑρήσοι (εὑρήσει).
c. "If ever you sought, you found" (past general). ἔφη αὐτόν, εἰ ζητοίη, εὑρίσκειν. / εἶπεν ὅτι εἰ ζητοίη, οὗτος ηὕρισκεν.
d. "If you should seek, you would find" (future less vivid). ἔφη αὐτόν, εἰ ζητοίη, εὑρεῖν ἄν. / εἶπεν ὅτι εἰ ζητοίη, οὗτος εὕροι ἄν.

Sentences

1. ὁ πατήρ μου ἐνόμιζε τοὺς ἐχθροὺς παύσεσθαι ἐκπλήττοντας ἓ ἐὰν τοὺς δούλους πάντας ἐλευθεροῖ (εἰ . . . ἐλευθεροίη). English direct version: "My enemies will stop terrifying me if I set free all my slaves." (future more vivid)
2. οἱ φίλοι σου ὑπέσχοντο ἀπαντήσεσθαι ἡμῖν ἐὰν βουλώμεθα (εἰ βουλοίμεθα) διαλέγεσθαι σφίσιν. English direct version: "We shall meet you if you wish to converse with us." (future more vivid)

3. ἠκούσαμεν τοῦτον τὸν βασιλέα, εἰ νεών ᾠκοδόμησεν, ἀναθέντα ἂν αὐτὸν τῷ Διί.
   English direct version: "If that king had built a temple, he would have dedicated it to
   Zeus." (past contrafactual)
4. ἔφασκεν ὁ νεανίας φιλοσοφεῖν ἂν εἰ μὴ οἱ πολέμιοι ἐπετίθεντο τῇ ἡμετέρᾳ πόλει.
   English direct version: "I would be studying philosophy if the enemy were not attack-
   ing our city." (present contrafactual)

Analysis

1.   1 ἐδόκει δ' αὐτῷ "And it seemed to him"
       1.1 βέλτιον εἶναι "to be best"
            1.1.1 πρὸς Θέογνιν μνησθῆναι· "to ask Theognis,"
      2 ἡγεῖτο γὰρ "for he thought"
       2.1 ἅπαν ποιήσειν αὐτόν, "that he (Theognis) would do everything"
            2.1.1 εἴ τις ἀργύριον διδοίη. "if someone gave him money."

Clause 1.1 is indirect statement after ἐδόκει, with accusative and infinitive; the
original direct version would have been βέλτιόν ἐστιν. Clauses 2.1 and 2.1.1 are
a future more vivid conditional sentence in indirect statement after ἡγεῖτο, with
the apodosis (2.1) using accusative and infinitive and the protasis (2.1.1) changing
an original subjunctive to optative. The original direct version of the conditional
would be ἅπαν ποιήσει ἐάν τις ἀργύριον διδῷ "he will do everything if someone
gives him money."

Chapter XIX

Sentences

1. ὁ ἐμὸς υἱὸς (ὁ υἱός μου) ἤγγειλε τὰς βοῦς ἡσυχαζούσας (ὅτι αἱ βόες ἡσυχάζουσιν /
   ὅτι αἱ βόες ἡσυχάζοιεν).
2. ὁ ἱκέτης οὐκ ᾔδει πότερον (εἴτε) σιγᾷ (σιγῴη) ἢ (εἴτε) ἐλέγξῃ (ἐλέγξαι) τὰ τοῦ
   μάρτυρος ψεύδη τῷ φράζειν ποῦ (ὅπου) ἐγένετο (γένοιτο). / . . . πότερον χρείη
   (χρὴ) σιγᾶν ἢ ἐλέγξαι . . .
3. ἆρα μὴ φοβεῖ μὴ οὐ περιγενώμεθα;
4. οὗτος ὁ στρατιώτης τοῖς φίλοις εἶπε τίς (ὅστις) προστάξαι (προσέταξεν) οἷ
   ταύτην τὴν τάξιν· οἱ δὲ ἠπίστευσαν αὐτῷ.
5. οὗτοι οἱ δυστυχέστατοι ὡμολόγησαν μὴ προδώσειν ἡμᾶς ἐὰν ἀποδῶμεν (εἰ
   ἀποδοῖμεν) σφίσι τοὺς ἵππους οὓς ἐκλέψαμεν (τοὺς κλαπέντας ὑφ' ἡμῶν ἵππους)
   (οὓς ἐκλέψαμεν ἵππους).
6. οἱ ἐμοὶ δοῦλοι (οἱ δοῦλοί μου) οὐδέποτε ἂν ἀποσταῖέν μου, ὅτι ἴσασιν (ἅτε εἰδότες)
   οὐ δυνάμενοι λανθάνειν με ἐπιβουλεύοντές μοι (λανθάνοντές με ἐπιβουλεύειν μοι).
7. μὴ σκεδάσῃς χρυσὸν εἰς τὴν θάλατταν, ἵνα μὴ ἔνδεια χρημάτων κωλύσῃ σε
   φιλοσοφεῖν (εἴρξῃ σε μὴ οὐ φιλοσοφεῖν).

8. ἡ βουλὴ ἔπεμψε τὸν ἄριστον στρατηγὸν ἄγοντα πεντακοσίους ἵνα τοῖς συμ-
    μάχοις τοὺς πολεμίους ἀμῦναι (ἀμύνῃ) / ὡς ... ἀμυνοῦντα.

9. ἡ ἡμετέρα στρατιὰ (ἡ στρατιὰ ἡμῶν) τοῖς βαρβάροις ἐπέθετο ὅτι ὑβρίσαι ὁ ἄγγε-
    λος (ὡς ὑβρίσαντος τοῦ ἀγγέλου) αὐτῶν (or τούτων in attributive position) τοὺς
    ἄρχοντας τῷ τύπτειν (ὅτι παίσας ὑβρίσαι ὁ τούτων ἄγγελος τοὺς ἄρχοντας)· οἱ
    δὲ εἶπον ὅτι ἐκέλευσαν (κελεύσαιεν) (οἱ δὲ ἔφασαν κελεῦσαι) πάντας τοὺς ἑαυτῶν
    πολίτας εὖ ποιεῖν τοὺς ἡγεμόνας τοὺς τῶν ἄλλων πόλεων.

10. ὁπόθεν ἂν ἔλθωσιν, ἐκεῖσε οἱ φυγάδες οὐκ ἐθέλουσιν ἐπανελθεῖν. / οἱ φυγάδες οὐκ
    ἐθέλουσιν ἐπανελθεῖν ὁπόθεν ἂν ἔλθωσιν.

Chapter XX

A) NB: underlined words are altered from the original; words deleted from the original
without change to the surrounding words are crossed out. Words in parentheses are
alternative possibilities to those that precede them, and words in square brackets are
non-mandatory additions.

1. 174a: ἐμοὶ γὰρ ἐνέτυχεν Σωκράτης λελουμένος τε καὶ τὰς βλαύτας ὑποδεδεμένος,
             ἃ οὗτος ὀλιγάκις ἐποίει· καὶ ἠρόμην αὐτόν, "ποῖ εἶ οὕτω καλὸς
             γεγενημένος;"

    174d–e: τοιαῦτ' ἄττα σφᾶς ἔφη διαλεχθέντες ᾖμεν. ὁ οὖν Σωκράτης ἑαυτῷ πως
             προσέχων τὸν νοῦν κατὰ τὴν ὁδὸν πορεύεται (ἐπορεύετο) ὑπολειπόμενος,
             καὶ περιμένοντος ἐμοῦ, "πρόιθι," ἔφη, "εἰς τὸ πρόσθεν." ἐπειδὴ δὲ ἐγενόμην
             ἐπὶ τῇ οἰκίᾳ τῇ Ἀγάθωνος, ἀνεῳγμένην καταλαμβάνω (κατελάμβανον)
             τὴν θύραν, καί τι ἔφη αὐτόθι γελοῖον ἔπαθον. ἐμοὶ μὲν γὰρ εὐθὺς παῖς
             τις τῶν ἔνδοθεν ἀπαντήσας ἄγει (ἦγεν) οὗ κατέκειντο οἱ ἄλλοι, καὶ
             καταλαμβάνω (κατελάμβανον) [αὐτοὺς] ἤδη μέλλοντας δειπνεῖν· εὐθὺς δ'
             οὖν ὡς εἶδέ [με] ὁ Ἀγάθων, ἔφη ...

    175a: καὶ ἐμὲ μὲν ἔφη ἀπονίζει (ἀπένιζεν) ὁ παῖς, ἵνα κατακέωμαι (κατακεοίμην)·
             ἄλλος δέ τις τῶν παίδων ἥκει (ἧκεν) ἀγγέλλων, ὅτι "Σωκράτης οὗτος
             ἀναχωρήσας ἐν τῷ τῶν γειτόνων προθύρῳ ἕστηκε καὶ ἐμοῦ καλοῦντος
             οὐκ ἐθέλει εἰσιέναι."

    175c: μετὰ ταῦτα ἔφη ἡμεῖς μὲν δειπνοῦμεν (ἐδειπνοῦμεν), ὁ δὲ Σωκράτης
             οὐκ εἰσέρχεται (εἰσῄει). ὁ οὖν Ἀγάθων πολλάκις κελεύει (ἐκέλευε),
             "μεταπέμψασθε τὸν Σωκράτη," ἐγὼ δὲ οὐκ ἐῶ (εἴων). ἧκεν (ἧκει)
             οὖν αὐτὸν οὐ πολὺν χρόνον ὡς εἰώθει διατρίψας, ἀλλὰ μάλιστα ἡμᾶς
             μεσοῦν δειπνοῦντας. ὁ οὖν Ἀγάθων – τυγχάνει (ἐτύγχανε) γὰρ ἔσχατος
             κατακείμενος μόνος – "δεῦρ'," ἔφη φάναι ...

    212c–d: εἰπόντος δὲ ταῦτα τοῦ Σωκράτους οἱ μὲν ἐπαινοῦσι (ἐπῄνουν), ὁ δὲ
             Ἀριστοφάνης λέγειν τι ἐπιχειρεῖ (ἐπεχείρει), ὅτι ἐμνήσθη αὐτοῦ λέγων

ὁ Σωκράτης περὶ τοῦ λόγου· καὶ ἐξαίφνης ἡ αὔλειος θύρα κρουομένη πολὺν ψόφον <u>παρέσχεν</u> ὡς κωμαστῶν, καὶ αὐλητρίδος φωνὴν <u>ἀκούομεν</u> (<u>ἠκούομεν</u>). ὁ οὖν Ἀγάθων, "παῖδες," ἔφη, "οὐ σκέψεσθε; καὶ ἐὰν μέν τις τῶν ἐπιτηδείων ᾖ, καλεῖτε· εἰ δὲ μή, λέγετε ~~ὅτι~~ 'οὐ <u>πίνουσιν</u>, ἀλλὰ ἀναπαύονται ἤδη.'" καὶ οὐ πολὺ ὕστερον Ἀλκιβιάδου τὴν φωνὴν <u>ἀκούομεν</u> (<u>ἠκούομεν</u>) ἐν τῇ αὐλῇ σφόδρα μεθύοντος καὶ μέγα βοῶντος, ἐρωτῶντος "<u>ποῦ</u> Ἀγάθων;" καὶ ~~κελεύοντος~~ "ἄγετέ [με] παρ' Ἀγάθωνα." <u>ἄγει</u> (ἦγε, ἄγουσι, ἦγον) οὖν αὐτὸν παρὰ <u>ἡμᾶς</u> ἥ τε <u>αὐλητρὶς</u> ὑπολαβοῦσα καὶ ἄλλοι τινὲς τῶν ἀκολούθων, καὶ <u>ἐπέστη</u> ἐπὶ τὰς θύρας ἐστεφανωμένος ~~αὐτὸν~~ κιττοῦ τέ τινι στεφάνῳ δασεῖ καὶ ἴων, καὶ ταινίας <u>ἔχων</u> ἐπὶ τῆς κεφαλῆς πάνυ πολλάς, καὶ <u>εἶπεν</u> . . .

2. Ἔφη ὁ Σωκράτης <u>καταβῆναι</u> τῇ <u>προτεραίᾳ</u> εἰς Πειραιᾶ μετὰ Γλαύκωνος τοῦ Ἀρίστ- ωνος, προσευξόμενός τε τῇ θεῷ καὶ ἅμα τὴν ἑορτὴν βουλόμενος θεάσασθαι τίνα τρόπον ποιήσουσιν (<u>ποιήσοιεν</u>), ἅτε <u>τότε</u> <u>πρῶτον</u> ἄγοντες. <u>καλὴν</u> μὲν οὖν <u>οἱ</u> καὶ <u>τὴν</u> τῶν ἐπιχωρίων <u>πομπὴν</u> δόξαι εἶναι, οὐ μέντοι ἧττον <u>φαίνεσθαι</u> πρέπειν ἣν οἱ Θρᾷκες ἔπεμπον. <u>ἔφη</u> δὲ <u>σφᾶς</u> προσευξαμένους καὶ θεωρήσαντας ἀπιέναι πρὸς τὸ ἄστυ. <u>κατιδόντα</u> οὖν πόρρωθεν <u>σφᾶς</u> οἴκαδε ὡρμημένους Πολέμαρχον <u>τὸν</u> Κεφάλου <u>κελεῦσαι</u> δραμόντα τὸν παῖδα περιμεῖναι ἓ <u>κελεῦσαι</u>. καὶ <u>οὗ</u> ὄπισ- θεν τὸν παῖδα λαβόμενον τοῦ ἱματίου φάναι Πολέμαρχον κελεύειν <u>σφᾶς</u> περι- μεῖναι (<u>εἶπεν</u> ὅτι Πολέμαρχος κελεύοι (κελεύει) <u>σφᾶς</u> περιμεῖναι). καὶ ἔφη αὐτὸς <u>μεταστραφῆναί</u> τε καὶ ἐρέσθαι ὅπου αὐτὸς εἴη. τὸν δὲ παῖδα φάναι ἐκεῖνον ὄπισ- θεν <u>προσιέναι</u> (τὸν δὲ παῖδα εἰπεῖν ὅτι ἐκεῖνος ὄπισθεν <u>προσίοι</u> (προσέρχεται)), καὶ κελεύειν σφᾶς περιμένειν. φάναι (<u>ὡμολογεῖν</u>) δὲ τὸν Γλαύκωνα σφᾶς περιμενεῖν (<u>εἰπεῖν</u> (ἀποκρίνασθαι) δὲ τὸν Γλαύκωνα ὅτι περιμενοῖεν (περιμενοῦσι)). καὶ ὀλίγῳ ὕστερον τόν τε Πολέμαρχον ἥκειν καὶ Ἀδείμαντον τὸν τοῦ Γλαύκωνος ἀδελφὸν καὶ Νικήρατον τὸν Νικίου καὶ ἄλλους τινάς, ὡς ἀπὸ τῆς πομπῆς. <u>τὸν</u> οὖν Πολέμαρχον ἔφη φάναι <u>σφᾶς</u> <u>δοκεῖν</u> (<u>εἰπεῖν</u> ὅτι δοκοῦσι/δοκοῖεν) πρὸς ἄστυ ὡρμῆσθαι ὡς ἀπιόντας. <u>οὗ</u> δὲ ὁμολογήσαντος, (<u>ἔφη</u> δὲ φάναι αὐτὸν οὐ κακῶς δοξάζειν, καὶ) ἐκεῖνον ἐρέσθαι εἰ <u>ὁρᾷ</u> (<u>ὁρώη</u>) σφᾶς, ὅσοι <u>εἰσί</u> (<u>εἶεν</u>). αὐτὸς δὲ <u>ὁμολογῆσαι</u>, καὶ (αὐτὸς δὲ <u>ἐρέσθαι</u> ὅπως οὐχ <u>ὁρᾷ</u> (<u>ὁρώη</u>), καὶ) (<u>οὗ</u> δὲ <u>ὁμολογήσαντος,</u>) ἐκεῖνον <u>κελεύειν</u> σφᾶς ἢ ~~τοίνυν~~ κρείττους ἐκείνων <u>γενέσθαι</u> ἢ μένειν ἐκεῖ. ἔφη δὲ <u>ἐρέσθαι</u> εἰ ἔτι ἐλλείπεται (<u>ἐλλείποιτο</u>) τὸ ἢν <u>πείσωσιν</u> ἐκείνους, ὡς <u>χρὴ</u> (<u>χρείη</u>) σφᾶς ἀφεῖναι, ἀλλ' ἐκεῖνον <u>ἐρέσθαι</u> εἰ καὶ <u>δύναιντο</u> ἂν πεῖσαι μὴ ἀκούοντας. τοῦ δὲ Γλαύκωνος οὐ <u>φάσκοντος,</u> (τὸν δὲ Γλαύκωνα εἰπεῖν ὅτι οὐδαμῶς, καὶ) Πολέμαρχον κελεύειν σφᾶς ὡς τοίνυν μὴ ἀκουσομένων, οὕτω <u>διανοεῖσθαι</u>. καὶ <u>τὸν</u> Ἀδείμαντον <u>ἐρέσθαι</u> εἰ <u>ἴσασι</u> (<u>εἰδεῖεν</u>) ὅτι λαμπὰς <u>ἔσται</u> (<u>λαμπάδα ἐσομένην</u>) πρὸς ἑσπέραν ἀφ' ἵππων τῇ θεῷ. <u>ἔφη</u> δὲ <u>ἐρέσθαι</u> εἰ ἀληθῶς ἀφ' ἵππων καὶ φάναι καινόν γε ἐκεῖνο, ἐρόμενος εἰ λαμπά- δια ἔχοντες <u>διαδώσουσιν</u> (<u>διαδώσοιεν</u>) ἀλλήλοις ἁμιλλώμενοι τοῖς ἵπποις, ἢ πῶς

(ὅπως) λέγει (λέγοι). ὁμολογήσαντα δὲ Πολέμαρχον φάναι καὶ πρός γε ποιήσειν αὐτοὺς παννυχίδα, ἣν ἄξιον θεάσασθαι. ἐξαναστήσεσθαι γὰρ σφᾶς μετὰ τὸ δεῖπνον καὶ τὴν παννυχίδα θεάσεσθαι καὶ ξυνέσεσθαί τε πολλοῖς τῶν νέων αὐτόθι καὶ διαλέξεσθαι. κελεύειν δὲ μένειν καὶ μὴ ἄλλως ποιεῖν. καὶ τὸν Γλαύκωνα φάναι ἐοικέναι μενετέον εἶναι. ἔφη δὲ αὐτὸς φάναι εἰ δοκεῖ (δοκοίη) οὕτω χρῆναι ποιεῖν.

3. (The range of possibilities here is so large that this is just an illustration of one thing that could be done to answer this question.) Ἤρετο ὁ Διονυσόδωρος τὸν Κτήσιππον πῶς (ὅπως) λέγει (λέγοι), εἴ εἰσίν (εἰ εἶέν) τινες οἳ λέγουσι (λέγοιεν) τὰ πράγματα ὡς ἔχει (ἔχοι)· ὁ δὲ ἔφη εἶναι τοὺς καλούς τε κἀγαθοὺς καὶ τοὺς τἀληθῆ λέγοντας. ἐρομένου οὖν ἐκείνου εἰ τἀγαθὰ εὖ ἔχει (ἔχοι), τὰ δὲ κακὰ κακῶς, καὶ εἰ ὁμολογεῖ (ὁμολογοίη) τοὺς καλούς τε καὶ ἀγαθοὺς λέγειν ὡς ἔχει (ἔχοι) τὰ πράγματα, συνεχώρει. ἐπεὶ δὲ ἔφη ὁ Διονυσόδωρος τοὺς ἄρα ἀγαθοὺς κακῶς λέγειν τὰ κακά, εἴπερ ὡς ἔχει (ἔχοι) λέγουσιν (λέγοιεν), ὁ Κτήσιππος ὁμολογῶν παρήνεσεν αὐτῷ εὐλαβεῖσθαι, ἐὰν οἳ πείθηται (εἰ οἳ πείθοιτο), τῶν ἀγαθῶν εἶναι, ἵνα μὴ αὐτὸν οἱ ἀγαθοὶ κακῶς λέγωσιν (λέγοιεν)· τοὺς γὰρ ἀγαθοὺς ἔφη σφόδρα γε κακῶς λέγειν τοὺς γοῦν κακοὺς ἀνθρώπους. ἤρετο δὲ ὁ Εὐθύδημος εἰ οἱ ἀγαθοὶ καὶ τοὺς μεγάλους μεγάλως λέγουσι (λέγοιεν) καὶ τοὺς θερμοὺς θερμῶς, καὶ ἀποκρινομένου τοῦ Κτησίππου ὅτι μάλιστα, τοὺς γοῦν ψυχροὺς ψυχρῶς λέγουσί (λέγοιέν) τε καὶ φασὶν (φαῖεν) διαλέγεσθαι, ἔφη ὁ Διονυσόδωρος τοῦτον λοιδορεῖσθαι. ὁ δὲ οὐκ ἔφη, φάσκων ἐπεὶ φιλεῖ (φιλοίη) αὐτόν, νουθετεῖν ὡς ἑταῖρον, καὶ πειρᾶσθαι πείθειν μηδέποτε ἐναντίον οὗ οὕτως ἀγροίκως λέγειν ὅτι τούτους βούλεται (βούλοιτο) ἐξολωλέναι, οὓς περὶ πλείστου ποιεῖται (ποιοίη).

B)
1. The original is Plato, *Republic* 337a–c
2. The original is Plato, *Republic* 337 c–d.
3. The original is Plato, *Laws* 713d–714b.

Appendix D

a. If Jim was in charge, everything went (was going) well.
b. If Jim had been in charge, everything would have gone well.
c. If Jim is in charge, everything is going well.
d. If Jim were in charge, everything would be going well.
e. If Jim is in charge, everything will go well.
f. If Jim should be (if Jim were to be, if Jim were) in charge, everything would go well.
g. If Jane went to the shop she bought a paper.
h. If Jane had gone to the shop she would have bought a paper.
i. If Jane goes to the shop she buys a paper.

j.　If Jane were going to the shop she would be buying a paper.

k.　If Jane goes to the shop she will buy a paper.

l.　If Jane should go (if Jane were to go, if Jane went) to the shop she would buy a paper.

m.　If Fido saw a cat, he chased it.

n.　If Fido had seen a cat, he would have chased it.

o.　If Fido sees a cat, he chases it.

p.　If Fido saw (if Fido were seeing) that cat, he would be chasing it.

q.　If Fido sees that cat, he will chase it.

r.　If Fido should see (if Fido were to see, if Fido saw) a cat, he would chase it.

s.　If Fido sees a cat, he will chase it.

t.　No doubt Mark got a job if he applied for one.

u.　No doubt Mark would have gotten a job if he had applied for one.

v.　No doubt Mark is getting a job if he is applying for one.

w.　No doubt Mark would be getting a job if he were applying for one.

x.　No doubt Mark will get a job if he applies for one.

y.　No doubt Mark would get a job if he should apply (if he were to apply, if he applied) for one.

The next step: prose composition as an art form

All the exercises in this book were written to be translated into Greek: someone who has learned the grammar and syntax will know immediately which constructions to use in translating them. English that was not written with translation into Greek in mind, however, is far more difficult to handle. Often it needs to be restructured considerably in order to produce idiomatic Greek, and that restructuring is a different skill from those practiced in the rest of this book. The exclusion of this skill from the earlier exercises is deliberate, for it is incompatible with this book's main goal of developing fluent reading skills by providing practice in active use of all the grammar and syntax: if the exercises had not made it obvious which constructions needed to be used, it would have been impossible to ensure that all were practiced.

The translation into Greek of English that was not written for that purpose is, however, also a valuable exercise, because it allows one to think more creatively about Greek idiom, to create a piece of writing that is aesthetically beautiful, and thereby to understand more fully what an author like Plato was doing when he created a beautiful piece of prose. This appendix is designed to help readers move on to this type of prose composition if they wish to. Here are some points to keep in mind.

Idiom

When translating a piece of English that was not originally written for that purpose, the first thing to remember is that one needs to translate not the words, but the *thoughts* that those words express. English is full of idiomatic expressions whose whole is not the same as the sum of their parts. For example, we use "look up" not only to mean raising the eyes to an elevated object, but also to refer to finding a word in a dictionary. In the first meaning "look up" could be translated literally into Greek, but in the second it could not: it would need to be replaced by a phrase such as "find in the lexicon." Similarly the English idiom "the king ascended the throne" means that the king began to rule; to translate this properly into Greek one would need to translate this underlying meaning, not the words that convey it, which in Greek would have no such implied meaning. Greek, of course, has idioms too, and a really good writer of Greek prose will use these wherever they are appropriate.

Vocabulary choice

Most English words have more than one meaning, and so do most Greek words, so there are almost never one-to-one vocabulary equivalences. When choosing vocabulary, especially from a large dictionary, it is important to make sure that the Greek word one plans to use is the appropriate one for the context in which one plans to use it; simply verifying that the Greek word can overlap in meaning with the English word in the passage is rarely enough once one steps beyond the world of the prose composition textbook with its specially designed vocabulary and exercises. A good rule of thumb is never to use an unfamiliar word simply on the basis of what an English-to-Greek dictionary tells you: always look it up first in LSJ (the *big* version of LSJ!) and check the fine print about its usage, to make sure it has the necessary meaning to fit the passage. In order to produce Greek at all similar to what Plato or one of his contemporaries would have written, one must also restrict oneself to words attested in classical prose: many poetic and post-classical words exist, and their inclusion in a prose composition is normally considered a serious flaw.

Abstractions

Prose composition students are usually advised to avoid abstract nouns, because most English abstract nouns are really idioms that should in Greek be replaced by the concrete ideas they represent. For example, the sentence "Alcibiades' plot was discovered" would be best rephrased in Greek to "Alcibiades was discovered plotting." Greek does, however, contain a fair number of abstractions of its own, so it is not really a good idea to eliminate them all. Rather one should avoid abstractions except for those that are common in Greek in the particular meaning desired; perusal of a good dictionary can usually help to identify these. If the acceptability of a particular abstraction cannot be verified, it is normally a good idea to use a concrete word instead.

Sentence structure

Greek writers liked long sentences, and in many types of prose they particularly liked sentences with extensive subordination. In turning idiomatic English into idiomatic Greek it is often necessary to combine several sentences into one, not simply by adding conjunctions but also by turning some main clauses into subordinate constructions. Since Greek prose makes far more use of participles than does English, a good translation usually introduces quite a few participles not present or even hinted at in the original.

Non-Greek names and modern concepts

Some English passages contain material that has no good Greek equivalent, and these can be tackled in two ways. One possibility is to replace the non-Greek words and ideas with their closest Greek equivalents; so for example a passage about Hitler's submarines might be turned into a passage about Darius' triremes. This type of replacement is only successful if the ancient equivalent fits the context reasonably well; in the example just given the suggested replacement would work in a stirring patriotic speech exhorting listeners not to fear the vessels in question, but it would be disastrous in a battle narrative where the submarines' ability to submerge was a crucial part of the story, or in a passage where specific features of Hitler's character not shared with Darius (e.g. anti-Semitism) were relevant. In order to make sure the equivalents are good ones, therefore, it is necessary to have a clear understanding both of the modern context and of the ancient one used to replace it.

The other possibility is to transliterate non-Greek names into the Greek alphabet and use periphrases or explanations for any concepts unknown to the ancients. This is in fact what most ancient writers did; the New Testament is full of names like Ἀβραάμ and Δαυίδ, and transliterations like Οὐαλέριος are frequent in discussions of Romans. So although using Ἵτλερ for Hitler looks dreadful, it has excellent ancient precedents. Likewise a submarine can be described as a ship that sails under the water (with a participle: ναῦς ὑφ' ὕδατι πλέουσα), and this is in fact what a classical Greek writer would have done if faced with the need to discuss one.

An example

The English passage below is taken from W. S. Landor's *Imaginary Conversations of Literary Men and Statesmen* (London 1829; vol. II p. 90), where it is part of a larger dialogue between Newton and Barrow. (English from the nineteenth century is often used as a basis for Greek prose composition, because its structure is often very similar to that of Greek: education at that period involved substantial training in Latin and Greek, with the result that the English produced by educated people was often directly influenced by those languages. More recent English is often harder to translate into Greek.)

> NEWTON: I had something more, sir, to say – or rather – I had something more, sir, to ask – about Friendship.
>
> BARROW: All men, but the studious above all, must beware in the formation of it. Advice or caution on this subject comes immaturely and ungracefully from the young, exhibiting a proof either of temerity or suspicion; but when you hear it from a man of my age, who has been singularly fortunate in the past, and foresees the same felicity in those springing up before him, you may accept it as the direction of a calm observer, telling you all he has remarked on the greater part of a road which he has nearly gone through, and which you have but just entered. Never take into your confidence, or admit often into your company, any man who does not know, on some important subject,

more than you do. Be his rank, be his virtues, what they may, he will be a hindrance to your pursuits, and an obstruction to your greatness. If indeed the greatness were such as courts can bestow, and such as can be laid on the shoulders of a groom and make him look like the rest of the company, my advice would be misplaced; but since all transcendent, all true and genuine greatness must be of a man's own raising, and only on the foundation that the hand of God has laid, do not let any touch it: keep them off civilly, but keep them off. Affect no Stoicism; display no indifference: let their coin pass current; but do not you exchange for it the purer ore you carry, nor think the milling pays for the alloy.

When translated into Greek this passage can easily be recast as a Platonic dialogue, a change that allows the non-Greek names Newton and Barrow to be replaced with the Platonic characters Glaucon and Thrasymachus. (Of course the first Platonic character one thinks of is Socrates, but neither of these characters is at all like Plato's Socrates, so Glaucon and Thrasymachus are more plausible.) The use of Plato as a model also results in a change of the dialogue format from one with speaker designations outside the syntax of the text to one in which it is made clear in the text itself who is speaking and to whom. The comparison of an older person to a traveller who has preceded one along a road is even specifically used in Plato (*Republic* 328e); it would therefore have been legitimate to borrow a quotation from Plato there, though that has not been done in this translation. The Greek version below was made by the Oxford Classicist M. L. West, to whom I am very grateful for permission to use it here.

Καὶ ὅς, ἤθελον δέ, ἔφη, ὦ Θρασύμαχε, ὁ Γλαύκων, καὶ ἄλλο τι λέγειν, ἢ μᾶλλον ἄλλο τι ἤθελόν σε ἐρέσθαι περὶ τῆς φιλίας. καὶ ὁ Θρασύμαχος, πάντας μέν, ἔφη, δεῖ φυλάττεσθαι αὐτὴν τίνα τρόπον ποιήσονται, τοὺς δὲ φιλομαθεῖς πάντων μάλιστα. οἱ μὲν γὰρ νεώτεροι ἐάν τι παραινῶσιν ἢ νουθετῶσι περὶ τούτου τοῦ πράγματος, ὡς πρὸ καιροῦ καὶ οὐ πρεπόντως λεγόμενον ἄν τις ἀκούοι· φανερὸς δ' ἂν εἴη ὁ νουθετῶν ἢ θράσους μεστὸς ὢν ἢ ὑποψίας. ἀλλ' ὅταν παρὰ τηλικοῦδε ἀνδρὸς ἀκούσῃς, ὑπερφυῶς τε αὐτοῦ ηὐτυχηκότος καὶ ὁμοίαν προορῶντος τὴν εὐδαιμονίαν ἐν τοῖς ἐγγὺς αὐξανομένοις, ἀποδεκτέον ὡς θεωροῦ σώφρονος ποδηγοῦντος καὶ πάντα διδάσκοντος ὅσα εἶδε κατὰ τὴν ὁδόν, ἅτε πολλὴν ἤδη πεπορευμένος καὶ ἐγγὺς ὢν τοῦ τέλους, σὺ δ' ἄρτι ὥρμησαι. μηδέποτε οὖν μηδένα ποιοῦ φίλον μηδὲ φοιτᾶν ἔα παρὰ σοί, ὅστις μὴ πλέονα σοῦ εἰδῇ σπουδαίου τινὸς πράγματος πέρι. οὐδὲν γὰρ διαφέρει οὔτε γένους οὔτ' ἀρετῶν πῶς ἔχει, ἀλλ' ἐπιτηδεύοντά σε ὁτιοῦν κωλύσει καὶ τῶν μεγάλων ἐφιεμένῳ ἐμποδὼν γενήσεται. καὶ μὴν εἰ περὶ τοιούτου μεγέθους σπουδάζοις οἷον βασιλεὺς ἂν δωροῖτο, ἢ οἷον ἂν καὶ δούλῳ περιβαλλόμενον ἐξισοῖ ἂν αὐτὸν τῷ ἄλλῳ ὁμίλῳ προσορᾶν, οὐκ ἂν εἰς καιρὸν ταῦτα παρήνουν· ἀλλ᾽ ἐπεὶ τὰ ὡς ἀληθῶς καὶ ἐτύμως ὑπερβάλλοντα μεγέθη οὐκ ἔστιν εἰ μὴ αὐτὸν ἐν ἑαυτῷ τρέφειν, μηδὲ ἐπ᾽ ἄλλων τινῶν ἢ τῶν ὑπὸ τοῦ θεοῦ τεθειμένων βάθρων, οὐδένα ἄλλον ἐατέον μετασχεῖν τοῦ πράγματος, ἀλλὰ πάντως ἀπαμυντέον, μὴ φορτικῶς ἀλλ᾽ ὅμως. καὶ μὴ προσποιοῦ αὐτάρκης τις εἶναι μηδὲ ὑπεροπτικός· τὸ ἐκείνων νόμισμα δέχου καὶ μὴ ἀποδοκίμαζε, ἀλλ᾽ ὅπως μὴ ἀνταλλάξῃ αὐτὸ τοῦ ἀπέφθου χρυσίου ὃ σὺ ἔχεις, μηδὲ τοῦ καλοῦ χαρακτῆρος ἕνεκα τὸ κίβδηλον τιμήσεις.

Principal parts

A) Regular principal parts

The six principal parts of a verb represent the first person singular indicative of the following forms: present active, future active, aorist active, perfect active, perfect middle/passive, aorist passive. Regular verbs form their principal parts like λύω:

λύω λύσω, ἔλυσα, λέλυκα, λέλυμαι, ἐλύθην

Most contract verbs are also predictable. Most -άω and all -έω contracts form principal parts like τιμάω, and -όω contracts follow δηλόω.

τιμάω τιμήσω, ἐτίμησα, τετίμηκα, τετίμημαι, ἐτιμήθην
δηλόω δηλώσω, ἐδήλωσα, δεδήλωκα, δεδήλωμαι, ἐδηλώθην

Contract verbs of the -άω type with stems ending in ι, ε, or ρ, however, form principal parts like δράω:

δράω δράσω, ἔδρασα, δέδρακα, δέδραμαι, ἐδράθην

Deponent verbs, even if they are otherwise regular, lack some principal parts. Middle deponents form their principal parts like the middle of λύω:

λύομαι λύσομαι, ἐλυσάμην, –, λέλυμαι, –

Passive deponents form their principal parts like the passive of λύω:

λύομαι –, –, –, λέλυμαι, ἐλύθην (future λυθήσομαι)

Compound verbs of which the first element is a prepositional prefix add the prefix separately to each principal part, so it may undergo different modifications each time. Most final vowels are dropped before the augment (where ἐκ- also becomes ἐξ-), and final ν changes to agree with the first letter of the verb stem but appears as itself before the augment. Note the following examples:

ἐκλύω ἐκλύσω, ἐξέλυσα, ἐκλέλυκα, ἐκλέλυμαι, ἐξελύθην
καταλύω καταλύσω, κατέλυσα, καταλέλυκα, καταλέλυμαι, κατελύθην
συλλύω συλλύσω, συνέλυσα, συλλέλυκα, συλλέλυμαι, συνελύθην
ἀφίστημι ἀποστήσω, ἀπέστησα/ἀπέστην, ἀφέστηκα, ἀφέσταμαι,
ἀπεστάθην

B) Irregular principal parts

Note the following conventions:

- Verbs beginning with vowels augment the imperfect like the aorist, and unaugmented aorist forms have the same initial vowel as the present, unless otherwise noted.
- All future contracts (i.e. verbs with futures ending in -ῶ or οῦμαι) are -έω contracts unless otherwise noted.
- A hyphen in front of a form indicates that it is found only in compounds.

ἀγγέλλω	ἀγγελῶ, ἤγγειλα, ἤγγελκα, ἤγγελμαι, ἠγγέλθην
ἀγείρω	–, ἤγειρα, –, –, –
ἄγω	ἄξω, ἤγαγον,[1] ἦχα, ἦγμαι, ἤχθην
ᾄδω	ᾄσομαι, ᾖσα, –, ᾖσμαι, ᾔσθην
αἱρέω	αἱρήσω, εἷλον,[2] ᾕρηκα, ᾕρημαι, ᾑρέθην (was chosen)
αἴρω	ἀρῶ, ἦρα, ἦρκα, ἦρμαι, ἤρθην
αἰσθάνομαι	αἰσθήσομαι, ᾐσθόμην, –, ᾔσθημαι, –
αἰσχύνομαι	αἰσχυνοῦμαι, –, –, –, ᾐσχύνθην
ἀκούω	ἀκούσομαι, ἤκουσα, ἀκήκοα, –, ἠκούσθην
ἁλίσκομαι	ἁλώσομαι, ἑάλων/ἥλων,[3] ἑάλωκα/ἥλωκα, –, –
ἁμαρτάνω	ἁμαρτήσομαι, ἥμαρτον, ἡμάρτηκα, ἡμάρτημαι, ἡμαρτήθην
ἀμύνω	ἀμυνῶ, ἤμυνα, –, –, –
ἀναλίσκω	ἀναλώσω, ἀνήλωσα, ἀνήλωκα, ἀνήλωμαι, ἀνηλώθην
ἀνοίγνυμι	ἀνοίξω, ἀνέῳξα,[4] ἀνέῳχα, ἀνέῳγμαι, ἀνεῴχθην
ἀπαγορεύω	ἀπερῶ, ἀπεῖπον, ἀπείρηκα, ἀπείρημαι, ἀπερρήθην
ἀπαντάω	ἀπαντήσομαι, ἀπήντησα, ἀπήντηκα, –, –
ἀπεχθάνομαι	ἀπεχθήσομαι, ἀπηχθόμην, –, ἀπήχθημαι, –
ἀποθνῄσκω	ἀποθανοῦμαι, ἀπέθανον, τέθνηκα, –, –
ἀποκρίνομαι	ἀποκρινοῦμαι, ἀπεκρινάμην, –, ἀποκέκριμαι, –
ἀποκτείνω[5]	ἀποκτενῶ, ἀπέκτεινα, ἀπέκτονα, –, –
ἀπόλλυμι	ἀπολῶ, ἀπώλεσα (transitive) and ἀπωλόμην (intransitive), ἀπολώλεκα (transitive) and ἀπόλωλα (intransitive), –, –
ἅπτω	ἅψω, ἧψα, –, ἧμμαι, ἤφθην
ἀρέσκω	ἀρέσω, ἤρεσα, –, –, –
ἀρκέω	ἀρκέσω, ἤρκεσα, –, –, –
ἁρπάζω	ἁρπάσομαι, ἥρπασα, ἥρπακα, ἥρπασμαι, ἡρπάσθην
ἄρχω	ἄρξω, ἦρξα, ἦρχα, ἦργμαι, ἤρχθην
αὐλίζομαι	–, ηὐλισάμην, –, –, ηὐλίσθην

[1] Unaugmented form ἀγαγ-.   [2] Unaugmented form ἑλ-.   [3] Unaugmented form ἁλ-.
[4] Unaugmented form ἀνοιξ-.   [5] In Attic prose the passive of ἀποκτείνω is ἀποθνῄσκω.

αὐξάνω	αὐξήσω, ηὔξησα, ηὔξηκα, ηὔξημαι, ηὐξήθην
ἀφικνέομαι	ἀφίξομαι, ἀφικόμην, –, ἀφῖγμαι, –
βαίνω	-βήσομαι, -έβην, βέβηκα, –, –
βάλλω	βαλῶ, ἔβαλον, βέβληκα, βέβλημαι, ἐβλήθην
βλάπτω	βλάψω, ἔβλαψα, βέβλαφα, βέβλαμμαι, ἐβλάφθην/ἐβλάβην
βούλομαι	βουλήσομαι, –, –, βεβούλημαι, ἐβουλήθην
γαμέω	γαμῶ, ἔγημα, γεγάμηκα, γεγάμημαι, –
γελάω	γελάσομαι, ἐγέλασα, –, –, ἐγελάσθην
γίγνομαι	γενήσομαι, ἐγενόμην, γέγονα, γεγένημαι, –
γιγνώσκω	γνώσομαι, ἔγνων, ἔγνωκα, ἔγνωσμαι, ἐγνώσθην
γράφω	γράψω, ἔγραψα, γέγραφα, γέγραμμαι, ἐγράφην
δάκνω	δήξομαι, ἔδακον, –, δέδηγμαι, ἐδήχθην
δεῖ[6]	δεήσει, ἐδέησε, –, –, –
δείκνυμι	δείξω, ἔδειξα, δέδειχα, δέδειγμαι, ἐδείχθην
δέομαι	δεήσομαι, –, –, δεδέημαι, ἐδεήθην
δέχομαι	δέξομαι, ἐδεξάμην, –, δέδεγμαι, –
δέω	δήσω, ἔδησα, δέδεκα, δέδεμαι, ἐδέθην
διαλέγομαι	διαλέξομαι/διαλεχθήσομαι, –, –, διείλεγμαι, διελέχθην
διαφθείρω	διαφθερῶ, διέφθειρα, διέφθαρκα (transitive) and διέφθορα (intransitive), διέφθαρμαι, διεφθάρην
διδάσκω	διδάξω, ἐδίδαξα, δεδίδαχα, δεδίδαγμαι, ἐδιδάχθην
δίδωμι	δώσω, ἔδωκα (middle ἐδόμην), δέδωκα, δέδομαι, ἐδόθην
διώκω	διώξομαι, ἐδίωξα, δεδίωχα, –, ἐδιώχθην
δοκέω	δόξω, ἔδοξα, –, δέδογμαι, –
δύναμαι	δυνήσομαι, –, –, δεδύνημαι, ἐδυνήθην
ἐάω	ἐάσω, εἴασα, εἴακα, εἴαμαι, εἰάθην
ἐγείρω	ἐγερῶ, ἤγειρα, ἐγρήγορα (intransitive), ἐγήγερμαι, ἠγέρθην
ἐθέλω	ἐθελήσω, ἠθέλησα, ἠθέληκα, –, –
εἰμί	ἔσομαι,[7] ἐγενόμην, γέγονα, –, –
εἴργω	εἴρξω, εἶρξα, –, εἴργμαι, εἴρχθην
ἐκπλήττω	ἐκπλήξω, ἐξέπληξα, –, ἐκπέπληγμαι, ἐξεπλάγην
ἐλαύνω	ἐλῶ,[8] ἤλασα, ἐλήλακα, ἐλήλαμαι, ἠλάθην
ἐλέγχω	ἐλέγξω, ἤλεγξα, –, ἐλήλεγμαι, ἠλέγχθην
ἕλκω	-έλξω, εἵλκυσα, -είλκυκα, -είλκυσμαι, -εἱλκύσθην
ἐναντιόομαι	ἐναντιώσομαι, –, –, ἠναντίωμαι, ἠναντιώθην
ἐπαινέω	ἐπαινέσομαι, ἐπῄνεσα, ἐπῄνεκα, ἐπῄνημαι, ἐπῃνέθην

---

[6] Subjunctive δέῃ, optative δέοι, infinitive δεῖν, participle δέον, imperfect ἔδει.
[7] Third person singular ἔσται.   [8] This is ἐλάω, not ἐλέω.

ἐπιλανθάνομαι   ἐπιλήσομαι, ἐπελαθόμην, –, ἐπιλέλησμαι, –

ἐπίσταμαι⁹   ἐπιστήσομαι, –, –, –, ἠπιστήθην

ἕπομαι¹⁰   ἕψομαι, ἑσπόμην,¹¹ –, –, –

ἐργάζομαι   ἐργάσομαι, εἰργασάμην/ἠργασάμην, –, εἴργασμαι,
             εἰργάσθην/ἠργάσθην

ἔρχομαι/εἶμι¹²   εἶμι, ἦλθον,¹³ ἐλήλυθα, –, –

ἐρωτάω   ἐρωτήσω/ἐρήσομαι, ἠρόμην, ἠρώτηκα, ἠρώτημαι, ἠρωτήθην

ἐσθίω¹⁴   ἔδομαι, ἔφαγον, –, –, –

εὐλαβέομαι   εὐλαβήσομαι, –, –, – ηὐλαβήθην

εὑρίσκω   εὑρήσω, ηὗρον/εὗρον, ηὕρηκα/εὕρηκα, εὕρημαι, εὑρέθην

εὔχομαι   εὔξομαι, ηὐξάμην, –, ηὖγμαι, –

ἔχω¹⁵   ἕξω/σχήσω, ἔσχον,¹⁶ ἔσχηκα, -έσχημαι, –

ζάω   βιώσομαι/ζήσω, ἐβίων, βεβίωκα, –, –

ἥδομαι   ἡσθήσομαι, –, –, –, ἥσθην

ἥκω   ἥξω, –, –, –, –

θάπτω   θάψω, ἔθαψα, –, τέθαμμαι, ἐτάφην

θαυμάζω   θαυμάσομαι, ἐθαύμασα, τεθαύμακα, τεθαύμασμαι, ἐθαυμάσθην

θύω   θύσω, ἔθυσα, τέθυκα, τέθυμαι, ἐτύθην

ἵημι   ἥσω, ἧκα (middle εἵμην), εἷκα, εἷμαι, εἵθην

ἵστημι¹⁷   στήσω, ἔστησα (transitive) and ἔστην (intransitive), ἕστηκα
           (intransitive), ἕσταμαι, ἐστάθην

καθαίρω   καθαρῶ, ἐκάθηρα, –, κεκάθαρμαι, ἐκαθάρθην

καθεύδω   καθευδήσω, –, –, –, –

κάθημαι   –, –, –, –, –

καίω   καύσω, ἔκαυσα, -κέκαυκα, κέκαυμαι, ἐκαύθην

καλέω   καλῶ, ἐκάλεσα, κέκληκα, κέκλημαι, ἐκλήθην

κάμνω   καμοῦμαι, ἔκαμον, κέκμηκα, –, –

κεῖμαι   κείσομαι, –, –, –, –

---

⁹ Imperfect ἠπιστάμην.   ¹⁰ Imperfect εἰπόμην.   ¹¹ Unaugmented form σπ-.

¹² Ἔρχομαι is used only for the present indicative in Attic prose, while εἶμι takes its place for all non-indicative present forms and the imperfect, as well as for all future forms; the future ἐλεύσομαι is poetic.

¹³ Unaugmented form ἐλθ-.   ¹⁴ Imperfect ἤσθιον.   ¹⁵ Imperfect εἶχον.   ¹⁶ Unaugmented form σχ-.

¹⁷ Meanings of different forms: in present, imperfect, and future the active forms mean "set up," the middle forms mean both "set oneself up" (i.e. get into a standing position) and "set up (something else) for oneself"; the passive forms mean "be set up." The first aorist active means "set up," the first aorist middle means "set (something else) up for oneself," the second aorist means "stood," and the aorist passive means "was set up." The perfect active means "stand," the pluperfect active means "was standing, stood," the future perfect active (ἑστήξω) means "will stand," and the perfect middle/passive means "has been stood up" and "has stood up (something) for oneself." Many compounds of ἵστημι have the same distribution of active, middle, passive, and intransitive meanings.

κελεύω	κελεύσω, ἐκέλευσα, κεκέλευκα, κεκέλευσμαι, ἐκελεύσθην
κλάω[18]	κλαιήσω/κλαήσω "shall weep" and κλαύσομαι "shall suffer for it," ἔκλαυσα, –, –, –
κλέπτω	κλέψω, ἔκλεψα, κέκλοφα, κέκλεμμαι, ἐκλάπην
κομίζω	κομιῶ, ἐκόμισα, κεκόμικα, κεκόμισμαι, ἐκομίσθην
κόπτω	κόψω, ἔκοψα, -κέκοφα, κέκομμαι, -εκόπην
κρίνω	κρινῶ, ἔκρινα, κέκρικα, κέκριμαι, ἐκρίθην
κρύπτω	κρύψω, ἔκρυψα, κέκρυφα, κέκρυμμαι, ἐκρύφθην
κτάομαι	κτήσομαι, ἐκτησάμην, –, κέκτημαι, ἐκτήθην
λαγχάνω	λήξομαι, ἔλαχον, εἴληχα, εἴλημμαι, ἐλήχθην
λαμβάνω	λήψομαι, ἔλαβον, εἴληφα, εἴλημμαι, ἐλήφθην
λανθάνω	λήσω, ἔλαθον, λέληθα, –, –
λέγω (1)	ἐρῶ/λέξω, εἶπον[19]/ἔλεξα, εἴρηκα, εἴρημαι, ἐρρήθην[20]/ἐλέχθην
λέγω (2)	-λέξω, -έλεξα, -είλοχα, -είλεγμαι/-λέλεγμαι, -ελέγην/-ελέχθην
λείπω	λείψω, ἔλιπον, λέλοιπα, λέλειμμαι, ἐλείφθην
μανθάνω	μαθήσομαι, ἔμαθον, μεμάθηκα, –, –
μάχομαι	μαχοῦμαι, ἐμαχεσάμην, –, μεμάχημαι, –
μέλει	μελήσει, ἐμέλησε, μεμέληκε, –, –
μέλλω	μελλήσω, ἐμέλλησα, –, –, –
μέμφομαι	μέμψομαι, ἐμεμψάμην, –, –, –
μένω	μενῶ, ἔμεινα, μεμένηκα, –, –
μιμνήσκω	-μνήσω, -έμνησα, –, μέμνημαι "remember," ἐμνήσθην "remembered"[21]
νέμω	νεμῶ, ἔνειμα, διανενέμηκα, νενέμημαι, ἐνεμήθην
νέω	νευσοῦμαι, -ένευσα, -νένευκα, –, –
νομίζω	νομιῶ, ἐνόμισα, νενόμικα, νενόμισμαι, ἐνομίσθην
οἶδα	εἴσομαι, –, –, –, –
οἰκτίρω	–, ᾤκτιρα, –, –, –
οἴομαι/οἶμαι[22]	οἰήσομαι, –, –, –, ᾠήθην
οἴχομαι	οἰχήσομαι, –, –, –, –
ὄμνυμι	ὀμοῦμαι, ὤμοσα, ὀμώμοκα, ὀμώμομαι/ὀμώμοσμαι, ὠμόθην/ὠμόσθην
ὀνίνημι	ὀνήσω, ὤνησα (middle ὠνήμην "received benefit"), –, –, ὠνήθην
ὁράω[23]	ὄψομαι, εἶδον,[24] ἑόρακα/ἑώρακα, ἑώραμαι/ὦμμαι, ὤφθην
ὀργίζω	ὀργιῶ, ὤργισα, –, ὤργισμαι, ὠργίσθην

---

[18] The -α- does not contract with the endings.   [19] Unaugmented form εἰπ-.
[20] Fut. pass. ῥηθήσομαι.   [21] Fut. μνησθήσομαι "shall remember."
[22] Imperfect ᾤμην, rarely ᾠόμην.   [23] Imperfect ἑώρων.   [24] Unaugmented form ἰδ-.

ὁρμάομαι	ὁρμήσομαι, –, –, ὥρμημαι, ὡρμήθην
ὀφείλω	ὀφειλήσω, ὠφείλησα/ὤφελον, ὠφείληκα, –, ὠφειλήθην
ὀφλισκάνω	ὀφλήσω, ὦφλον, ὦφληκα, ὦφλημαι, –
πάσχω	πείσομαι, ἔπαθον, πέπονθα, –, –
πείθω	πείσω, ἔπεισα (middle ἐπιθόμην), πέπεικα (transitive) and πέποιθα (intransitive), πέπεισμαι, ἐπείσθην
πέμπω	πέμψω, ἔπεμψα, πέπομφα, πέπεμμαι, ἐπέμφθην
πέτομαι	-πτήσομαι, -επτόμην, –, –, –
πίμπλημι	ἐμπλήσω, ἐνέπλησα, ἐμπέπληκα, ἐμπέπλησμαι, ἐνεπλήσθην
πίνω	πίομαι, ἔπιον, πέπωκα, -πέπομαι, -επόθην
πίπτω	πεσοῦμαι, ἔπεσον, πέπτωκα, –, –
πλέω	πλεύσομαι/πλευσοῦμαι, ἔπλευσα, πέπλευκα, πέπλευσμαι, –
-πλήττω	-πλήξω, -έπληξα, πέπληγα, πέπληγμαι, ἐπλήγην (but in compounds -επλάγην)
πνέω	-πνεύσομαι/πνευσοῦμαι, ἔπνευσα, -πέπνευκα, –, –
πράττω	πράξω, ἔπραξα, πέπραχα (transitive) and πέπραγα (intransitive, "fare"), πέπραγμαι, ἐπράχθην
πυνθάνομαι	πεύσομαι, ἐπυθόμην, –, πέπυσμαι, –
πωλέω	πωλήσω, –, πέπρακα, πέπραμαι, ἐπράθην
ῥέω	ῥυήσομαι, ἐρρύην, ἐρρύηκα, –, –
ῥήγνυμι	-ῥήξω, ἔρρηξα,[25] -έρρωγα (intransitive), –, ἐρράγην
ῥίπτω	ῥίψω, ἔρριψα, ἔρριφα, ἔρριμμαι, ἐρρίφθην
σημαίνω	σημανῶ, ἐσήμηνα, –, σεσήμασμαι, ἐσημάνθην
σιγάω	σιγήσομαι, ἐσίγησα, σεσίγηκα, σεσίγημαι, ἐσιγήθην
σιωπάω	σιωπήσομαι, ἐσιώπησα, σεσιώπηκα, –, ἐσιωπήθην
σκεδάννυμι	-σκεδῶ,[26] -εσκέδασα, –, ἐσκέδασμαι, ἐσκεδάσθην
σκοπέω[27]	σκέψομαι, ἐσκεψάμην, –, ἔσκεμμαι, –
σπείρω	σπερῶ, ἔσπειρα, –, ἔσπαρμαι, ἐσπάρην
σπένδομαι	σπείσομαι, ἐσπεισάμην, –, ἔσπεισμαι, –
σπουδάζω	σπουδάσομαι, ἐσπούδασα, ἐσπούδακα, ἐσπούδασμαι, ἐσπουδάσθην
στέλλω	στελῶ, ἔστειλα, -έσταλκα, ἔσταλμαι, ἐστάλην
στρέφω	-στρέψω, ἔστρεψα, –, ἔστραμμαι, ἐστράφην
σφάλλω	σφαλῶ, ἔσφηλα, –, ἔσφαλμαι, ἐσφάλην
σῴζω	σώσω, ἔσωσα, σέσωκα, σέσῳσμαι, ἐσώθην
ταράττω	ταράξω, ἐτάραξα, –, τετάραγμαι, ἐταράχθην

[25] Unaugmented form ῥηξ-.   [26] This is σκεδάω, not σκεδέω.
[27] Also σκέπτομαι, but σκοπέω is more usual in Attic prose.

τάττω	τάξω, ἔταξα, τέταχα, τέταγμαι, ἐτάχθην
-τείνω	τενῶ, -έτεινα, -τέτακα, τέταμαι, -ετάθην
τελέω	τελῶ, ἐτέλεσα, τετέλεκα, τετέλεσμαι, ἐτελέσθην
τέμνω	τεμῶ, ἔτεμον, -τέτμηκα, τέτμημαι, ἐτμήθην
τέρπω	τέρψω, ἔτερψα, –, –, ἐτέρφθην
τίθημι	θήσω, ἔθηκα (middle ἐθέμην), τέθηκα, κεῖμαι/τέθειμαι, ἐτέθην
τίκτω	τέξομαι, ἔτεκον, τέτοκα, –, –
τιτρώσκω	τρώσω, ἔτρωσα, –, τέτρωμαι, ἐτρώθην
τρέπω	τρέψω, ἔτρεψα (middle ἐτραπόμην), τέτροφα, τέτραμμαι, ἐτράπην
τρέφω	θρέψω, ἔθρεψα, τέτροφα, τέθραμμαι, ἐτράφην
τρέχω	δραμοῦμαι, ἔδραμον, -δεδράμηκα, –, –
τρίβω	τρίψω, ἔτριψα, τέτριφα, τέτριμμαι, ἐτρίβην
τυγχάνω	τεύξομαι, ἔτυχον, τετύχηκα, –, –
τύπτω	πατάξω/τυπτήσω, ἐπάταξα/ἔπαισα, πέπληγα, πέπληγμαι, ἐπλήγην
ὑγιαίνω	ὑγιανῶ, ὑγίανα, –, –, –
ὑπισχνέομαι	ὑποσχήσομαι, ὑπεσχόμην, –, ὑπέσχημαι, –
φαίνω	φανῶ, ἔφηνα, πέφαγκα (transitive) and πέφηνα (intransitive), πέφασμαι, ἐφάνθην (transitive) and ἐφάνην (intransitive)
φάσκω	–, –, –, –, –
φείδομαι	φείσομαι, ἐφεισάμην, –, –, –
φέρω	οἴσω, ἤνεγκα/ἤνεγκον,[28] ἐνήνοχα, ἐνήνεγμαι, ἠνέχθην
φεύγω	φεύξομαι, ἔφυγον, πέφευγα, –, –
φημί	φήσω, ἔφησα, –, –, –
φθάνω	φθήσομαι, ἔφθασα/ἔφθην, –, –, –
φοβέομαι	φοβήσομαι, –, –, πεφόβημαι, ἐφοβήθην
φράζω	φράσω, ἔφρασα, πέφρακα, πέφρασμαι, ἐφράσθην (with middle meaning)
φυλάττω	φυλάξω, ἐφύλαξα, πεφύλαχα, πεφύλαγμαι, ἐφυλάχθην
φύω	φύσω, ἔφυσα (transitive) and ἔφυν "grew, was," πέφυκα, –, –
χαίρω	χαιρήσω, ἐχάρην, κεχάρηκα, –, –
χράομαι	χρήσομαι, ἐχρησάμην, –, κέχρημαι, ἐχρήσθην
χρή[29]	χρῆσται, ἐχρῆν/χρῆν[30], –, –, –
ψεύδω	ψεύσω, ἔψευσα, –, ἔψευσμαι, ἐψεύσθην
ὠνέομαι	ὠνήσομαι, ἐπριάμην, –, ἐώνημαι, ἐωνήθην

---

[28] Unaugmented form ἐνεγκ-.   [29] Subjunctive χρῇ, optative χρείη, infinitive χρῆναι, neuter participle χρεών.
[30] These forms are really imperfects rather than aorists.

Vocabulary

All the information given in the right-hand column is essential and should be memorized with the words. Verbs with irregular principal parts are marked with an asterisk, and their principal parts, as listed above, should be learned along with the verbs. Words marked with a double asterisk are compounds for which the principal parts will be found under the simplex form in the list; compound verbs given only a single asterisk have their own entries in the list. Words marked "postpositive" do not come at the beginning of a sentence or clause. Deponents are middles unless otherwise indicated, and verbs that can take objects take them in the accusative unless another case is given.

2) always   ἀεί
    well   εὖ
    not   οὐ;[1] μή
    now   νῦν
    never   οὐδέποτε; μηδέποτε
    long ago   πάλαι
    again   πάλιν; αὖθις
    often   πολλάκις
    and   καί
    both . . . and   καί . . . καί
    also   καί (placed before the word it emphasizes)
    too   καί (placed before the word it emphasizes)
    even   καί (placed before the word it emphasizes)
    the   ὁ, ἡ, τό
    O (vocative particle)   ὦ (with vocatives)
    this   οὖτος, αὕτη, τοῦτο
    that   οὖτος, αὕτη, τοῦτο
    from   ἀπό (+ gen.)
    away from   ἀπό (+ gen.)
    out of   ἐκ/ἐξ (+ gen.)
    into   εἰς (+ acc.)
    to   εἰς (+ acc.)
    in   ἐν (+ dat.)

---

[1] Written οὐ before words beginning with a consonant, οὐκ before words beginning with an unaspirated vowel, and οὐχ before words beginning with an aspirated vowel.

on	ἐν (+ dat.)
after	μετά (+ acc.)
with (accompaniment)	μετά (+ gen.)
god(dess)	θεός, θεοῦ, ὁ/ἡ
stone	λίθος, -ου, ὁ
book	βιβλίον, -ου, τό
road	ὁδός, ὁδοῦ, ἡ
marketplace	ἀγορά, -ᾶς, ἡ
temple	νεώς, νεώ, ὁ
house	οἰκία, -ας, ἡ; οἶκος, -ου, ὁ
horse	ἵππος, -ου, ὁ/ἡ
sea	θάλαττα, -ης, ἡ
slave	δοῦλος, -ου, ὁ
master	δεσπότης, -ου, ὁ
brother	ἀδελφός, -οῦ, ὁ
sister	ἀδελφή, -ῆς, ἡ
young man	νεανίας, -ου, ὁ
messenger	ἄγγελος, -ου, ὁ
poet	ποιητής, -οῦ, ὁ
citizen	πολίτης, -ου, ὁ
government	πολιτεία, -ας, ἡ
courage	ἀνδρεία, -ας, ἡ
excellence	ἀρετή, -ῆς, ἡ
peace	εἰρήνη, -ης, ἡ
freedom	ἐλευθερία, -ας, ἡ
voyage	πλοῦς, πλοῦ, ὁ
allotted portion	μοῖρα, -ας, ἡ
dawn	ἕως, ἕω, ἡ
land	γῆ, γῆς, ἡ
language	γλῶττα, -ης, ἡ
mind	νοῦς, νοῦ, ὁ
good	ἀγαθός, -ή, -όν; καλός, -ή, -όν
beautiful	καλός, -ή, -όν
bad	πονηρός, -ά, -όν; κακός, -ή, -όν
shameful	αἰσχρός, -ά, -όν
free	ἐλεύθερος, -α, -ον
young	νέος, νέα, νέον
new	νέος, νέα, νέον

old	παλαιός, -ά, -όν
dear (to)	φίλος, -η, -ον (+ dat.)
friend (as substantive)	φίλος, -η, -ον
alone	μόνος, -η, -ον (alone or in predicate position)
only (after *the* or a possessive)	μόνος, -η, -ον (in attributive position)
only (not after *the* or a possessive)	μόνος, -η, -ον (alone or in predicate position)
middle (i.e. central)	μέσος, -η, -ον (in attributive position)
the middle of	μέσος, -η, -ον (in predicate position)
high	ἄκρος, -α, -ον (in attributive position)
outermost	ἄκρος, -α, -ον (in attributive position)
the top of	ἄκρος, -α, -ον (in predicate position)
the edge of	ἄκρος, -α, -ον (in predicate position)
(to) educate	παιδεύω
(to) have educated (i.e. cause to be educated)	παιδεύομαι
(to) eat	ἐσθίω*
(to) flee	φεύγω*
(to) learn	μανθάνω*
(to) find (out)	εὑρίσκω*
(to) have	ἔχω*
(to) carry	φέρω*
(to) have come	ἥκω*
(to) wish (to)	ἐθέλω* (+ inf.); βούλομαι* (+ inf.)
(to) deliberate	βουλεύομαι
(to) throw	βάλλω*
(to) hit	βάλλω*
(to) sacrifice	θύω*
(to) delay (*x* -ing)	μέλλω* (+ inf.)
(to) be about to	μέλλω* (+ fut. inf.)

3)	perhaps	ἴσως
	in vain	μάτην
	already	ἤδη
	immediately	εὐθύς; αὐτίκα
	almost	σχεδόν
	not yet	οὔπω; μήπω

still	ἔτι
no longer	οὐκέτι; μηκέτι
by (personal agent)	ὑπό (+ gen.)
prize	ἆθλον, -ου, τό
animal	ζῷον, ζῴου, τό
wild animal	θηρίον, -ου, τό
fruit	καρπός, -οῦ, ὁ
gift	δῶρον, -ου, τό
gold	χρυσός, -οῦ, ὁ
word	λόγος, -ου, ὁ
speech	λόγος, -ου, ὁ
work	ἔργον, -ου, τό
deed	ἔργον, -ου, τό
island	νῆσος, -ου, ἡ
disease	νόσος, -ου, ἡ
river	ποταμός, -οῦ, ὁ
war	πόλεμος, -ου, ὁ
battle	μάχη, -ης, ἡ
victory	νίκη, -ης, ἡ
judgement	γνώμη, -ης, ἡ
lawsuit	δίκη, -ης, ἡ
juror	δικαστής, -οῦ, ὁ
son	υἱός, υἱοῦ, ὁ
house-slave	οἰκέτης, -ου, ὁ
inhabitant	οἰκητής, -οῦ, ὁ
hoplite	ὁπλίτης, -ου, ὁ
guest-friend	ξένος, -ου, ὁ
stranger	ξένος, -ου, ὁ
sailor	ναύτης, -ου, ὁ
human (being)	ἄνθρωπος, -ου, ὁ (occasionally ἡ)
wise	σοφός, -ή, -όν
worthy (of)	ἄξιος, -α, -ον (+ gen.)
unworthy (of)	ἀνάξιος, -ον (+ gen.)
just	δίκαιος, -α, -ον
unjust	ἄδικος, -ον
able (to)	δυνατός, -ή, -όν (+ inf.)
impossible	ἀδύνατος, -ον
courageous	ἀνδρεῖος, -α, -ον

noble	γενναῖος, -α, -ον
lazy	ῥᾴθυμος, -ον
having authority (over)	κύριος, -α, -ον (+ gen.)
(personal) enemy (as substantive)	ἐχθρός, -ά, -όν
(military) enemy (as substantive)	πολέμιος, -α, -ον (usually in masculine plural)
prudent	φρόνιμος, -ον
(to) take	λαμβάνω*
(to) seize	ἁρπάζω*
(to) pursue	διώκω*
(to) judge (*x*, or between *y*)	δικάζω (+ acc. *x* or dat. *y*)
(to) suffer	πάσχω*
(to) drive	ἐλαύνω*
(to) lead	ἄγω*
(to) drag	ἕλκω*
(to) release	λύω
(to) dissolve	λύω
(to) ransom	λύομαι
(to) wash	λούω[2]
(to) wash oneself, take a bath	λούομαι[3]
(to) fall	πίπτω*
(to) teach (*x* to *y*)	διδάσκω* (+ acc. *x*, acc. *y*)
(to) have taught (i.e. cause to be taught)	διδάσκομαι*
(to) guard	φυλάττω*
(to) be on guard against	φυλάττομαι*
(to) die	ἀποθνήσκω*
(to) kill	ἀποκτείνω* (no passive)
(to) be killed	ἀποθνήσκω*
(to) arrive (at)	ἀφικνέομαι* (+ εἰς & acc.)

4)	here (no motion)	ἐνθάδε
	there (no motion)	ἐκεῖ
	elsewhere (no motion)	ἄλλοθι
	nowhere	οὐδαμοῦ; μηδαμοῦ
	(at) home (no motion)	οἴκοι
	from here	ἐνθένδε

[2] Often a contract verb λόω in Attic.   [3] Often a contract verb λοῦμαι in Attic.

from there	ἐκεῖθεν
from another place	ἄλλοθεν
from home	οἴκοθεν
here (of motion toward)	δεῦρο
there (of motion toward)	ἐκεῖσε
elsewhere (of motion toward)	ἄλλοσε
home (of motion toward)	οἴκαδε
at Marathon	Μαραθῶνι
Athens	Ἀθῆναι, -ῶν, αἱ
at Athens, in Athens	Ἀθήνησι
to Athens (of motion)	Ἀθήναζε
from Athens (of motion)	Ἀθήνηθεν
once	ἅπαξ
twice	δίς
sometimes	ἐνίοτε
suddenly	ἐξαίφνης
just now	ἄρτι
then (at that point in time)	τότε
then (next)	ἔπειτα
today	τήμερον
yesterday	χθές
late	ὀψέ
early	πρῴ
on	ἐπί (+ gen., dat.)
over	ὑπέρ (+ gen.)
through	διά (+ gen.)
under (of motion toward)	ὑπό (+ acc.)
near	ἐγγύς (+ gen.); πρός (+ dat.)
from (with people)	παρά (+ gen.)
onto	ἐπί (+ acc.)
to (with people)	παρά (+ acc.); ὡς (+ acc.)
toward, to (but not = into)	πρός (+ acc.)
beside (with people)	παρά (+ dat., acc.)
with	σύν (+ dat.)
together with (i.e. at the same time as)	ἅμα (+ dat.)
around	περί (+ dat., acc.)
before (in time or space)	πρό (+ gen.)
under (no motion)	ὑπό (+ gen., dat.)
beyond, exceeding	ὑπέρ (+ acc.)

because of	διά (+ acc.); ἕνεκα (postpositive, + gen.)
on behalf of	ὑπέρ (+ gen.)
about	περί (+ gen.)
instead of	ἀντί (+ gen.)
against (of attacks, etc.)	ἐπί (+ acc.)
against (of speeches, etc.)	κατά (+ gen.)
without	ἄνευ (+ gen.)
according to	κατά (+ acc.)
contrary to	παρά (+ acc.)
at the house of	παρά (+ dat.)
day	ἡμέρα, -ας, ἡ
drachma	δραχμή, -ῆς, ἡ
talent (6,000 drachmae)	τάλαντον, -ου, τό
foot	πούς, ποδός, ὁ[4]
stade (600 feet)	στάδιον, -ου, τό (plural οἱ or τά)
width	εὖρος, -ους, τό[5]
length	μῆκος, -ους, τό
height	ὕψος, ὕψους, τό
one	εἷς, μία, ἕν
none	οὐδείς, οὐδεμία, οὐδέν; μηδείς, μηδεμία, μηδέν
no one	οὐδείς, οὐδεμία; μηδείς, μηδεμία
nothing	οὐδέν; μηδέν
two	δύο
three	τρεῖς, τρία
four	τέτταρες, τέτταρα
five	πέντε
six	ἕξ
seven	ἑπτά
eight	ὀκτώ
nine	ἐννέα
ten	δέκα
twenty	εἴκοσι
fifty	πεντήκοντα
hundred	ἑκατόν

[4] Declined like θήρ (Smyth §259); for the purposes of this chapter it is only necessary to know the genitive plural ποδῶν.

[5] Εὖρος, μῆκος, and ὕψος are all declined like γένος (Smyth §263); for the purposes of this chapter it is only necessary to know the accusative singular, which is the same as the nominative singular.

five hundred	πεντακόσιοι, -αι, -α
thousand	χίλιοι, -αι, -α
ten thousand	μύριοι, -αι, -α
countless	μυρίος, -α, ον
first	πρῶτος, -η, -ον
second, next	δεύτερος, -α, -ον
third	τρίτος, -η, -ον
fourth	τέταρτος, -η, -ον
(to) be distant (*x* measurement, from *y*)	ἀπέχω** (+ acc. *x*, ἀπό + gen. *y*)

5)	because (+ clause)	ἅτε (+ participle); οἷα (+ participle)
	although	καίπερ (+ participle)
	nevertheless	ὅμως
	in the middle of (*x*-ing)	μεταξύ (+ participle)
	as if (+ clause)	ὥσπερ (+ participle)

shame	αἰσχύνη, -ης, ἡ
beginning	ἀρχή, -ῆς, ἡ
rule	ἀρχή, -ῆς, ἡ
weapon	ὅπλον, -ου, τό
comrade	ἑταῖρος, -ου, ὁ
prostitute	ἑταίρα, -ας, ἡ
lover	ἐραστής, -οῦ, ὁ
mainland	ἤπειρος, -ου, ἡ
tree	δένδρον, -ου, τό
forest	ὕλη, ὕλης, ἡ
wood (i.e. timber)	ξύλον, -ου, τό; ὕλη, -ης, ἡ
silver	ἄργυρος, -ου, ὁ
money	ἀργύριον, -ου, τό
shrine	ἱερόν, -οῦ, τό
offerings (to gods)	ἱερά, -ῶν, τά
crown	στέφανος, -ου, ὁ
advice	βουλή, -ῆς, ἡ
council	βουλή, -ῆς, ἡ
assembly	ἐκκλησία, -ας, ἡ
spectator	θεατής, -οῦ, ὁ
bandit	λῃστής, -οῦ, ὁ
thief	κλέπτης, -ου, ὁ

theft	κλοπή, -ῆς, ἡ
wisdom	σοφία, -ας, ἡ
sophist	σοφιστής, -οῦ, ὁ
philosopher	φιλόσοφος, -ου, ὁ
white	λευκός, -ή, -όν
mortal	θνητός, -ή, -όν
immortal	ἀθάνατος, -ον
capable (of *x*-ing)	ἱκανός, -ή, -όν (+ inf.)
cowardly	δειλός, -ή, -όν
terrible	δεινός, -ή, -όν
clever (at *x*-ing)	δεινός, -ή, -όν (+ inf.)
equal (to)	ἴσος, -η, -ον (+ dat.)
sacred (to)	ἱερός, -ά, -όν (+ gen.)
ready (to)	ἑτοῖμος, -ον (+ inf.)[6]
strong	ἰσχυρός, -ά, -όν
little	μικρός, -ά, -όν; ὀλίγος, -η, -ον
(too) few (to)	ὀλίγοι, -αι, -α (+ inf.)
(to) take pleasure (in)	ἥδομαι* (+ dat.)
(to) rejoice	χαίρω*
(to) enjoy (*x*-ing)	ἥδομαι* (+ participle); χαίρω* (+ participle)
(to) rule	ἄρχω* (+ gen.)
(to) begin (*x*, to *y*, *z*-ing)	ἄρχομαι (+ gen. *x*, inf. *y*, participle or inf. *z*)
(to) escape the notice of *x*, do without *x* seeing	λανθάνω* (+ acc. *x* & participle)
(to) stop (transitive)	παύω (+ acc. & participle in acc.)
(to) stop (intransitive)	λήγω (+ gen. or participle); παύομαι (+ participle)
(to) show	φαίνω*
(to) be obviously	φαίνομαι* (+ participle)
(to) seem to be	φαίνομαι* (+ inf.)
(to) beat to, do before *x* does	φθάνω* (+ acc. *x* & participle)
(to) obtain	τυγχάνω* (+ gen.)
(to) happen to	τυγχάνω* (+ participle)
(to) continue to	διατελέω** (+ participle)

[6] Later Attic accentuation ἕτοιμος.

(to) be ashamed (to have *x*-ed, of having *x*-ed)	αἰσχύνομαι* (+ aorist participle)
(to) be (too) ashamed to	αἰσχύνομαι* (+ inf.)
(to) become	γίγνομαι* (predicate adjective in same case as subject)
(to) send	πέμπω*
(to) receive	δέχομαι*
(to) accept	δέχομαι*
(to) increase	αὐξάνω*7
(to) burn (transitive)	καίω*8
(to) burn (intransitive)	καίομαι*9
(to) beat	τύπτω*; -πλήττω* (only in compounds)
(to) save	σῴζω*
(to) escape to	σῴζομαι* (passive) εἰς (+ acc.)
(to) harm	βλάπτω*
(to) write	γράφω*
(to) indict (*x* for *y*)	γράφομαι* (+ acc. *x*, gen. *y*)
(to) throw	ῥίπτω*
(to) leave	λείπω*
(to) turn (transitive)	στρέφω*; τρέπω*
(to) turn (intransitive)	στρέφομαι*; τρέπομαι*
(to) nourish	τρέφω*
(to) pray	εὔχομαι*

6)	but	δέ (postpositive); ἀλλά
	for (+ clause)	γάρ (postpositive)
	at least	γε (postpositive, enclitic)
	however	μέντοι (postpositive)
	and yet	καίτοι
	moreover	τοίνυν (postpositive)
	indeed	δή (postpositive)
	and	τε (postpositive, enclitic) . . . καί
	and (connecting large units)	δέ (postpositive)
	on the other hand	δέ (postpositive)
	on the one hand	μέν (postpositive)
	therefore	οὖν (postpositive); οὐκοῦν
	not therefore	οὔκουν

---

7 Sometimes αὔξω.   8 Sometimes κάω.   9 Sometimes κάομαι.

and not, but not	οὐδέ; μηδέ
or	ἤ
either . . . or	ἤ . . . ἤ
neither . . . nor	οὐδέ . . . οὐδέ; μηδέ . . . μηδέ
harbor	λιμήν, -ένος, ὁ
famine	λιμός, -οῦ, ὁ
plague	λοιμός, -οῦ, ὁ
(military) expedition	στρατεία, -ας, ἡ
army	στρατός, -οῦ, ὁ; στρατιά, -ᾶς, ἡ;[10] στράτευμα, -ατος, τό
soldier	στρατιώτης, -ου, ὁ
general	στρατηγός, -οῦ, ὁ
ally	σύμμαχος, -ου, ὁ
(army) camp	στρατόπεδον, -ου, τό
traitor	προδότης, -ου, ὁ
prisoner (of war)	αἰχμάλωτος, -ου, ὁ
hostage	ὅμηρος, -ου, ὁ
bird	ὄρνις, -ιθος, ὁ/ἡ
spring (season)	ἔαρ, ἤρος, τό
night	νύξ, νυκτός, ἡ
herald	κῆρυξ, κήρυκος, ὁ
guard	φύλαξ, -ακος, ὁ
shepherd	ποιμήν, -ένος, ὁ
woman	γυνή, γυναικός, ἡ[11]
wife	γυνή, γυναικός, ἡ
old man	γέρων, -οντος, ὁ
orator	ῥήτωρ, -ορος, ὁ
child	παῖς, παιδός, ὁ/ἡ[12]
Greek (person)	Ἕλλην, -ηνος, ὁ
Greece	Ἑλλάς, -άδος, ἡ
hope	ἐλπίς, -ίδος, ἡ
gratitude	χάρις, -ιτος, ἡ
body	σῶμα, -ατος, τό
corpse	νεκρός, -οῦ, ὁ

---

[10] Beware of the misprint στρατία in the middle-sized version of LSJ.

[11] Declined (in the American order of the cases) γυνή, γυναικός, γυναικί, γυναῖκα, γύναι; γυναῖκες, γυναικῶν, γυναιξί, γυναῖκας.

[12] Declined παῖς, παιδός, παιδί, παῖδα, παῖ; παῖδες, παίδων, παισί, παῖδας.

wild animal	θήρ, θηρός, ὁ
boundary	ὅρος, ὅρου, ὁ
mountain	ὄρος, ὄρους, τό
savage	ἄγριος, -α, -ον
big	μέγας, μεγάλη, μέγα
miserable	ἄθλιος, -α, -ον
hollow	κοῖλος, -η, -ον
empty	κενός, -ή, -όν
new	καινός, -ή, -όν
common	κοινός, -ή, -όν
ancient	ἀρχαῖος, -α, -ον
much	πολύς, πολλή, πολύ
many	πολύς, πολλή, πολύ in plural
funny	γελοῖος, -α, -ον
(to) gather	ἀγείρω*
(to) rouse	ἐγείρω*
(to) produce	φύω*
(to) arise	φύομαι*
(to) grow (intransitive)	φύομαι*
(to) lie	ψεύδομαι*
(to) go, march	πορεύομαι (passive)
(to) catch	καταλαμβάνω**
(to) have gone, be gone	οἴχομαι*
(to) wound	τιτρώσκω*
(to) exist	ὑπάρχω**
(to) vote (for *x*, to *y*)	ψηφίζομαι (+ acc. *x*, inf. *y*)
(to) weep	κλάω*[13]
(to) obtain by lot	λαγχάνω*
(to) sing	ᾄδω*
(to) make camp	αὐλίζομαι*
(to) treat with violence	βιάζομαι

7)	if (+ subjunctive)	ἐάν[14]
	if (+ indic. or opt.)	εἰ
	in no way	οὐδαμῶς; μηδαμῶς
	privately	ἰδίᾳ

---

[13] The endings never contract.   [14] Frequently written ἤν or ἄν.

treaty	σπονδαί, -ῶν, αἱ
danger	κίνδυνος, -ου, ὁ
name	ὄνομα, -ατος, τό
storm	χειμών, -ῶνος, ὁ
winter	χειμών, -ῶνος, ὁ
poem	ποίημα, -ατος, τό
necessity	ἀνάγκη, -ης, ἡ
truth	ἀλήθεια, -ας, ἡ
fortune	τύχη, -ης, ἡ
art	τέχνη, -ης, ἡ
honor	τιμή, -ῆς, ἡ
letter (of alphabet)	γράμμα, -ατος, τό
writings	γράμματα, -άτων, τά
reputation	δόξα, -ης, ἡ
affair	πρᾶγμα, -ατος, τό
thing (object)	χρῆμα, -ατος, τό
money	χρήματα, -άτων, τά
possession	κτῆμα, -ατος, τό
water	ὕδωρ, ὕδατος, τό
fire	πῦρ, πυρός, τό
spear	δόρυ, -ατος, τό
violence	βία, βίας, ἡ
life	βίος, βίου, ὁ
shout	βοή, βοῆς, ἡ
hand	χείρ, χειρός, ἡ
wealth	πλοῦτος, -ου, ὁ
guilty (of)	αἴτιος, -α, -ον (+ gen.)
responsible (for)	αἴτιος, -α, -ον (+ gen.)
not responsible (for)	ἀναίτιος, -ον (+ gen.)
difficult	χαλεπός, -ή, -όν
amazing	θαυμάσιος, -α, -ον
rich	πλούσιος, -α, -ον
on the left	ἀριστερός, -ά, -όν
on the right	δεξιός, -ά, -όν
(to) follow	ἕπομαι* (+ dat.)
(to) bring	κομίζω*
(to) hear	ἀκούω* (+ gen. of person, acc. of thing)

(to) be (well, badly) spoken of	ἀκούω* (+ εὖ/καλῶς, κακῶς)
(to) judge	κρίνω*
(to) persuade	πείθω*
(to) obey	πείθομαι* (+ dat.)
(to) run	τρέχω*
(to) fight (with)	μάχομαι* (+ dat.)
(to) hide	κρύπτω*
(to) remind (*x* of *y*)	ἀναμιμνήσκω** (+ acc. *x*, gen. *y*)
(to) remember	μέμνημαι* (perfect) (+ gen.)
(to) forget	ἐπιλανθάνομαι* (+ gen.)
(to) station	τάττω*
(to) steal	κλέπτω*
(to) perceive	αἰσθάνομαι* (+ gen. or acc.)
(to) kindle	ἅπτω*
(to) touch	ἅπτομαι* (+ gen.)
(to) strike	κόπτω*
(to) miss	ἁμαρτάνω* (+ gen.)
(to) err	ἁμαρτάνω*
(to) drink	πίνω*
(to) be a slave (to)	δουλεύω (+ dat.)
(to) bury	θάπτω*
(to) leave behind, abandon	καταλείπω**
(to) summon	μεταπέμπω**; μεταπέμπομαι**
(to) scatter	σκεδάννυμι*
(to) sow	σπείρω*
(to) be hated (by)	ἀπεχθάνομαι* (+ dat.)
(to) reproach	ὀνειδίζω (+ dat.)

8)	who, which (not interrogative)	ὅς, ἥ, ὅ
	where (no motion, not interrogative)	ὅπου; οὗ
	where (of motion toward, not interrogative)	ὅποι; οἷ
	from where (not interrogative)	ὁπόθεν; ὅθεν
	how, in what way, as (not interrogative)[15]	ὅπως; ὡς; ὅπῃ; ᾗ
	of what sort (not interrogative)	ὁποῖος, -α, -ον; οἷος, -α, -ον

---

[15] The English definitions for this and other words used in relative-correlative constructions are very inadequate; a wide range of different English terms not given in the vocabulary should also be translated with these Greek words under certain circumstances. For this reason it is better to think about a word's position in the chart at the end of this vocabulary unit than about its definition.

however much, as much	ὁπόσος, -η, -ον; ὅσος, -η, -ον
however big, as big	ὁπόσος, -η, -ον; ὅσος, -η, -ον
however many, as many	ὁπόσοι, -αι, -α; ὅσοι, -αι, -α
so, in this way, thus (adverbial)	οὕτω(ς);[16] ὧδε; τῇδε; ταύτῃ
such, of this sort (adjectival)	τοιοῦτος, τοιαύτη, τοιοῦτο(ν)
so much	τοσοῦτος, τοσαύτη, τοσοῦτο(ν)
so big	τοσοῦτος, τοσαύτη, τοσοῦτο(ν)
so many	τοσοῦτοι, τοσαῦται, τοσαῦτα
doctor	ἰατρός, -οῦ, ὁ
(non-Greek) foreigner	βάρβαρος, -ου, ὁ
crowd	ὅμιλος, -ου, ὁ; ὄχλος, -ου, ὁ
contest	ἀγών, ἀγῶνος, ὁ
fearful	φοβερός, -ά, -όν
bitter	πικρός, -ά, -όν
wretched	ταλαίπωρος, -ον
(to) live	ζάω*
(to) use	χράομαι* (+ dat.)
(to) ask (x for y)	αἰτέω (+ acc. x, acc. y)
(to) be general (of)	στρατηγέω (+ gen.)
(to) make clear	δηλόω
(to) disobey	ἀπειθέω (+ dat.)
(to) trust (in x or that y)	πιστεύω (+ dat. x, acc. & inf. y)
(to) distrust	ἀπιστέω (+ dat.)
(to) consider x worthy (of y)	ἀξιόω (+ acc. x, gen. y)
(to) inquire (about x from y)	πυνθάνομαι* (+ acc. x, gen. y)
(to) like	φιλέω
(to) love	ἐράω (+ gen.)[17]
(to) make	ποιέω
(to) fare (well, badly)	πράττω* (+ εὖ, κακῶς)
(to) do	πράττω*; δράω; ποιέω
(to) treat x well (i.e. do good to x)	εὖ δράω; εὖ/ἀγαθὰ ποιέω (+ acc. x)
(to) treat x badly (i.e. do bad things to x)	κακῶς δράω; κακῶς/κακὰ ποιέω (+ acc. x)
(to) charge, accuse (x of/with y)	αἰτιάομαι (+ acc. x, gen. y); κατηγορέω (+ gen. x, acc. y)

[16] Written οὕτω before words beginning with consonants and οὕτως before words beginning with vowels.
[17] The active is usable only in the present and imperfect.

(to) condemn (*x* for *y*, *x* to *z*)	καταγιγνώσκω** (+ gen. *x*, acc. *y*, inf. *z*)
(to) blame (*x* for *y*)	μέμφομαι* (+ dat. *x*, acc. *y*)
(to) conquer	νικάω
(to) win	νικάω
(to) sail	πλέω*
(to) help (esp. in military sense)	βοηθέω (+ dat.); ἐπαμύνω** (+ dat.)
(to) attack	προσβάλλω** (+ dat.)

CORRELATIVE WORDS[18]

Interrogative	Indefinite	Indefinite relative/ indirect interrogative	Specific relative	Demonstrative
τίς	τις	ὅστις	ὅς	οὗτος; ὅδε; ἐκεῖνος
πόσος		ὁπόσος	ὅσος	τοσοῦτος
ποῖος		ὁποῖος	οἷος	τοιοῦτος
πότερος		ὁπότερος		ἕτερος
ποῦ	που	ὅπου	οὗ	ἐνθάδε; ἐκεῖ; etc.
πόθεν	ποθέν	ὁπόθεν	ὅθεν	ἐνθένδε; ἐκεῖθεν; etc.
ποῖ	ποι	ὅποι	οἷ	δεῦρο; ἐκεῖσε; etc.
πότε	ποτέ	ὁπότε	ὅτε	τότε
πῶς	πως	ὅπως	ὡς	οὕτω(ς); ὧδε
πῇ	πη	ὅπῃ	ᾗ	τῇδε; ταύτῃ

9)	(an)other	ἄλλος, -η, -ο
	both	ἀμφότεροι, -αι, -α (takes predicate position)
	I	ἐγώ
	you	σύ
	who?, which?	τίς, τί
	why?	τί (neuter of τίς)
	him, her, it, them	αὐτός, -ή, -ό (alone in oblique cases)
	that (one)	ἐκεῖνος, -η, -ο
	this (one)	ὅδε, ἥδε, τόδε
	each	ἕκαστος, -η, -ον
	each other	ἀλλήλους, -ας, -α

[18] The point of this chart, which is an integral part of the chapter VIII vocabulary, is to show the relationship these words have to one another for the purposes of certain constructions. Some words given here will not be needed in this chapter, and therefore their definitions are reserved until the next chapter; in any case, for many of the words in this chart the definition is much less useful than the position in the chart as a guide to usage. It is recommended that this chart be learned so that one can reproduce it with each word in the correct row and column, as such knowledge will facilitate the understanding of a number of different kinds of sentences.

-self, -selves (intensifying)	αὐτός, -ή, -ό (in predicate position, or alone in nominative)
myself (reflexive)	ἐμαυτόν, -ήν
yourself (reflexive)	σεαυτόν, -ήν; σαυτόν, -ήν
himself, herself, themselves (reflexive)	ἑαυτόν, -ήν, -ό; αὑτόν, -ήν, -ό
him(self) etc. (indirect reflexive)	ἕ
themselves (indirect reflexive)	σφᾶς
each (of two)	ἑκάτερος, -α, -ον (takes predicate position)
which (of two)	ὁπότερος, -α, -ον
the other (of two)	ἕτερος, -α, -ον
neither (of two)	οὐδέτερος, -α, -ον; μηδέτερος, -α, -ον
which? (of two)	πότερος, -α, -ον
where? (no motion)	ποῦ
where? (of motion toward)	ποῖ
from where?	πόθεν
somewhere, anywhere (no motion)	που (postpositive, enclitic)
somewhere, anywhere (of motion toward)	ποι (postpositive, enclitic)
from somewhere, from anywhere	ποθέν (postpositive, enclitic)
how?	πῶς; πῇ
somehow	πως (postpositive, enclitic)
in some/any way	πη (postpositive, enclitic)
same	αὐτός, -ή, -ό (in attributive position)
who(ever), what(ever)	ὅστις, ἥτις, ὅ τι
some, someone (not followed by "other")	τις, τι (postpositive, enclitic)
any, anyone (not after a negative)	τις, τι (postpositive, enclitic)
what sort of?	ποῖος, -α, -ον
how much?	πόσος, -η, -ον
how big?	πόσος, -η, -ον
how many?	πόσοι, -αι, -α
when?	πότε
ever	ποτέ (postpositive, enclitic)
my	ὁ ἐμός, ἐμή, ἐμόν
our	ὁ ἡμέτερος, -α, -ον
your (you sing.)	ὁ σός, σή, σόν
your (you pl.)	ὁ ὑμέτερος, -α, -ον

(to) listen (to)	ὑπακούω** (+ gen.)
(to) marry (male subject)	γαμέω*
(to) marry (female subject)	γαμέομαι* (+ dat.)
(to) advise	συμβουλεύω (+ dat.)
(to) consult	συμβουλεύομαι (+ dat.)
(to) envy (*x* for *y*)	ζηλόω (+ acc. *x*, gen. *y*)
(to) spare	φείδομαι* (+ gen.)
(to) desire (*x*, to *y*)	ἐπιθυμέω (+ gen. *x*, inf. *y*)
(to) forgive	συγγιγνώσκω** (+ dat.)
(to) avenge (*x*, on *y*, for *z*)	τιμωρέω (+ dat. *x*, acc. *y*, gen. *z*)
(to) take vengeance (on *x* for *y*)	τιμωρέομαι (+ acc. *x*, gen. *y*)
(to) honor	τιμάω
(to) value (*x* at price *y*)	τιμάω (+ acc. *x*, gen. *y*)
(to) sell (*x* for *y*)	πωλέω* (+ acc. *x*, gen. *y*)
(to) buy (*x* for *y*, at price *y*)	ὠνέομαι* (+ acc. *x*, gen. *y*)

10)

archon	ἄρχων, -οντος, ὁ
dog	κύων, κυνός, ὁ/ἡ[19]
democracy	δημοκρατία, -ας, ἡ
leader	ἡγεμών, -όνος, ὁ
savior	σωτήρ, -ῆρος, ὁ
tent, stage	σκηνή, -ῆς, ἡ
lawcourt	δικαστήριον, -ου, τό
prison	δεσμωτήριον, -ου, τό

(to) say (that)	φημί* (+ inf.); λέγω* (1) (+ ὅτι)
(to) speak	λέγω* (1)
(to) assert (that)	φάσκω* (+ inf.)
(to) deny (that)	οὐ φημί* (+ inf.); οὐ φάσκω* (+ inf.)
(to) explain (that)	φράζω* (+ ὅτι)
(to) answer (that)	ἀποκρίνομαι* (+ ὅτι)
(to) report (that)	ἀγγέλλω* (+ ὅτι or participle)
(to) promise (to, that)	ὑπισχνέομαι* (+ fut. inf.)
(to) agree (with *x*, to *y*)	ὁμολογέω; ὁμολογέομαι (+ dat. *x*, fut. inf. *y*)[20]
(to) admit (that)	ὁμολογέω; ὁμολογέομαι (+ inf.)
(to) spend	ἀναλίσκω*

---

[19] Declined κύων, κυνός, κυνί, κύνα, κύον; κύνες, κυνῶν, κυσί, κύνας.
[20] Augments at the start: ὠμολόγησα.

(to) threaten (*x*, to *y*, that *y*)	ἀπειλέω (+ dat. *x*, fut. inf. *y*)²¹
(to) swear (by *x*, to *y*)	ὄμνυμι* (+ acc. *x*, fut. inf. *y*)
(to) go down	καταβαίνω**
(to) lead	ἡγέομαι (+ dat.)
(to) believe (that)	νομίζω* (+ inf.); ἡγέομαι (+ inf.)
(to) think (that)	νομίζω* (+ inf.); οἴομαι* (+ inf.)
(to) suppose (that)	ὑπολαμβάνω** (+ inf.)
(to) suspect (that)	ὑποπτεύω (+ inf.)²²
(to) be caught	ἁλίσκομαι*
(to) get to know (that)	γιγνώσκω* (+ participle)
(to) know (that)	οἶδα* (+ participle)
(to) be conscious (of, that)	σύνοιδα** (+ dat. & participle);
	συγγιγνώσκω (+ dat. & participle)
(to) hope (to, that)	ἐλπίζω (+ fut. inf.)
(to) expect (to, that)	ἐλπίζω (+ fut. inf.); προσδέχομαι**
	(+ fut. inf.)
(to) be ashamed (that, of)	αἰσχύνομαι* (+ εἰ)
(to) be surprised (that)	θαυμάζω* (+ εἰ)
(to) be surprised (at *x* because of *y*)	θαυμάζω* (+ acc. *x*, + gen. *x*, or + acc.
	x & gen. *y*)
(to) hear (that)	ἀκούω* (+ participle)
(to) see (that)	ὁράω* (+ participle)
(to) be silent	σιγάω*; σιωπάω*
(to) swim	νέω*
(to) give birth (to)	τίκτω* (no passive)
(to) be born	γίγνομαι*
(to) start	ὁρμάομαι*
(to) stay	μένω*
(to) wait (for)	μένω*
(to) cut	τέμνω*
(to) toil	κάμνω*

11)	interrogative particle	ἆρα
	then (i.e. therefore)	ἄρα
	perplexity	ἀπορία, -ας, ἡ
	strife	ἔρις, ἔριδος, ἡ
	love (sexual)	ἔρως, ἔρωτος, ὁ

---

²¹ Augments at the start: ἠπείλησα.   ²² Augments after the prefix: ὑπώπτευσα.

lack (of)	ἔνδεια, -ας, ἡ (+ gen.); ἀπορία, -ας, ἡ (+ gen.)
need	ἔνδεια, -ας, ἡ
desire (for)	ἐπιθυμία, -ας, ἡ (+ gen.)
fugitive	φυγάς, -άδος, ὁ
teacher	διδάσκαλος, -ου, ὁ
witness	μάρτυς, -υρος, ὁ
story	μῦθος, -ου, ὁ
law	νόμος, -ου, ὁ
letter	ἐπιστολή, -ῆς, ἡ
dream	ὄνειρος, -ου, ὁ
slavery	δουλεία, -ας, ἡ
tower	πύργος, -ου, ὁ
ramparts	πύργοι, -ων, οἱ
festival	ἑορτή, -ῆς, ἡ
bread	σῖτος, -ου, ὁ
belonging to someone else	ἀλλότριος, -α, ον
bare	ψιλός, -ή, -όν
useful	χρήσιμος, -η, -ον
beneficial	ὠφέλιμος, -ον
on foot	πεζός, -ή, -όν
eager	πρόθυμος, -ον
(to) ask	ἐρωτάω* (+ acc.)
(to) be	εἰμί*
(to) go, come	ἔρχομαι*/εἶμι* (see principal parts for distinction)
(to) destroy	διαφθείρω*
(to) corrupt	διαφθείρω*
(to) banish	ἐκβάλλω** (no passive)
(to) be banished	ἐκπίπτω**
(to) arrest	συλλαμβάνω**
(to) raise	αἴρω*
(to) take	αἱρέω* (no passive)
(to) choose	αἱρέομαι*
(to) acquire	κτάομαι*
(to) possess	κέκτημαι (perfect)
(to) be accustomed (to)	εἴωθα (perfect) (+ inf.)

(to) retreat	ἀναχωρέω²³
(to) speak in defense	ἀπολογέομαι
(to) call	καλέω*
(to) invite	καλέω*
(to) annoy	λυπέω
(to) be despondent	ἀθυμέω
(to) flow	ῥέω*

12) in order that   ἵνα; ὅπως; ὡς

priest	ἱερεύς, -έως, ὁ
seer	μάντις, -εως, ὁ
horseman	ἱππεύς, -έως, ὁ
man	ἀνήρ, ἀνδρός, ὁ
husband	ἀνήρ, ἀνδρός, ὁ
hero	ἥρως, ἥρωος, ὁ
king	βασιλεύς, -έως, ὁ
tyrant	τύραννος, -ου, ὁ
legislator	νομοθέτης, -ου, ὁ
Zeus	Ζεύς, Διός, ὁ²⁴
father	πατήρ, πατρός, ὁ
mother	μήτηρ, μητρός, ἡ
daughter	θυγάτηρ, θυγατρός, ἡ
old woman	γραῦς, γραός, ἡ
suppliant	ἱκέτης, -ου, ὁ
individual	ἰδιώτης, -ου, ὁ
ox, cow	βοῦς, βοός, ὁ/ἡ
flower	ἄνθος, -ους, τό
agreement	ὁμολογία, -ας, ἡ
wall	τεῖχος, -ους, τό
grave	τάφος, -ου, ὁ
ship	ναῦς, νεώς, ἡ
trireme	τριήρης, -ους, ἡ
sword	ξίφος, -ους, τό
missile	βέλος, -ους, τό
wine	οἶνος, -ου, ὁ
place	τόπος, -ου, ὁ
character	τρόποι, -ων, οἱ

²³ Augments to ἀνεχώρησα.   ²⁴ Declined (in Attic) Ζεύς, Διός, Διί, Δία, Ζεῦ.

state	πόλις, -εως, ἡ
city	πόλις, -εως, ἡ; ἄστυ, -εως, τό
town	ἄστυ, -εως, τό
acropolis	ἀκρόπολις, -εως, ἡ
head	κεφαλή, -ῆς, ἡ
factional strife	στάσις, -εως, ἡ
year	ἔτος, ἔτους, τό
memory	μνήμη, -ης, ἡ
family	γένος, -ους, τό
form	εἶδος, -ους, τό

(to) fear, be afraid	φοβέομαι*; δέδια/δέδοικα (perfect)
(to) take care	εὐλαβέομαι* (passive)
(to) contrive	μηχανάομαι
(to) bring it about that	πράττω*
(to) depart	ἀπέρχομαι**
(to) be absent	ἄπειμι**
(to) slander	διαβάλλω**
(to) breathe	πνέω*
(to) consider	σκοπέω*
(to) amuse	τέρπω*
(to) stretch	-τείνω* (only in compounds)

13)	so (with adjectives)	οὕτω(ς)
	so as, with the result that	ὥστε
	since	ἐπεί; ἐπειδή
	because	ὅτι; διότι
	on condition that	ἐφ' ᾧ; ἐφ' ᾧτε
	answer	ἀπόκρισις, -εως, ἡ
	nation	ἔθνος, -ους, τό
	custom	ἔθος, ἔθους, τό; ἦθος, ἤθους, τό
	character	ἦθος, ἤθους, τό

	bold	θρασύς, -εῖα, -ύ
	willing(ly)	ἑκών, ἑκοῦσα, ἑκόν (gen. ἑκόντος)
	unwilling(ly)	ἄκων, ἄκουσα, ἄκον (gen. ἄκοντος)
	true	ἀληθής, -ές
	like	ὅμοιος, -α, -ον (+ dat.)
	sensible	σώφρων, -ον (gen. -ονος)
	foolish	ἄφρων, -ον (gen. -ονος)

ignorant	ἀμαθής, -ές
impious	ἀσεβής, -ές
in need (of)	ἐνδεής, -ές (+ gen.)
swift	ταχύς, -εῖα, -ύ
healthy	ὑγιής, -ές
fortunate	εὐτυχής, -ές
happy (i.e. prosperous)	εὐδαίμων, -ον (gen. -ονος)
friendly	εὐμενής, -ές
unfortunate	δυστυχής, -ές
safe	ἀσφαλής, -ές
correct	ὀρθός, -ή, -όν
sweet	ἡδύς, ἡδεῖα, ἡδύ
whole	πᾶς, πᾶσα, πᾶν (in attributive position)
all	πᾶς, πᾶσα, πᾶν (with no article or in predicate position)
everyone, everything	πάντες, πᾶσαι, πάντα
deep	βαθύς, -εῖα, -ύ
heavy	βαρύς, -εῖα, -ύ
long	μακρός, -ά, -όν
short	βραχύς, -εῖα, -ύ
wide	εὐρύς, -εῖα, -ύ
black	μέλας, -αινα, -αν
trustworthy	πιστός, -ή, -όν
(to) resist	ὑπομένω**
(to) repent (of)	μεταγιγνώσκω** (+ acc.)
(to) go out (of)	ἐκβαίνω** (+ ἐκ & gen.)
(to) be in	ἔνειμι** (+ ἐν & dat.)
(to) accomplish	τελέω*
(to) enter	εἰσέρχομαι** (+ εἰς & acc.)
(to) rub	τρίβω*
(to) invade	εἰσβάλλω** (+ εἰς & acc.)
(to) fly	πέτομαι*

14)	anger	ὀργή, -ῆς, ἡ
	populace	δῆμος, -ου, ὁ
	device	μηχανή, -ῆς, ἡ
	strength	ἰσχύς, -ύος, ἡ; κράτος, -ους, τό
	ability	δύναμις, -εως, ἡ

wretched (i.e. good for nothing)	μοχθηρός, -ά, -όν
legitimate	νόμιμος, -η, -ον
precise	ἀκριβής, -ές
experienced (in)	ἔμπειρος, -ον (+ gen.)
skilled (in)	ἐπιστήμων, -ον (gen. -ονος) (+ gen.)
trivial	φαῦλος, -η, -ον
wicked	πανοῦργος, -ον
sharp	ὀξύς, ὀξεῖα, ὀξύ
easy	ῥᾴδιος, -α, -ον
clear	σαφής, -ές
conspicuous	φανερός, -ά, -όν
good	χρηστός, -ή, -όν
later, too late	ὕστερος, -α, -ον
(to) be present	πάρειμι**
(to) try (*x*, to *y*)	πειράομαι (+ gen. *x*, inf. *y*)
(to) neglect	ἀμελέω (+ gen.)
(to) disturb	κινέω
(to) deceive	σφάλλω*
(to) be disappointed (in)	σφάλλομαι* (+ gen.)
(to) befall	προσπίπτω** (+ dat.)
(to) go out, come out	ἐξέρχομαι**
(to) be in want (of)	ἀπορέω (+ gen.)
(to) stand by	ἐμμένω** (+ dat.)
(to) come next, come after	ἐπιγίγνομαι** (+ dat.)
(to) read	ἀναγιγνώσκω**
(to) get a share of (by lot)	μεταλαγχάνω** (+ gen.)
(to) have a share in	μετέχω** (+ gen.)
(to) oppose	ἐναντιόομαι* (+ dat.)
(to) plot against	ἐπιβουλεύω (+ dat.)

15)	outrageous behavior	ὕβρις, -εως, ἡ
	prayer	εὐχή, -ῆς, ἡ
	altar	βωμός, -οῦ, ὁ
	gain, profit	κέρδος, -ους, τό
	part	μέρος, -ους, τό
	end	τέλος, -ους, τό
	field	ἀγρός, -οῦ, ὁ
	trophy	τροπαῖον, -ου, τό

poison	φάρμακον, -ου, τό
bronze	χαλκός, -οῦ, ὁ
table, bank	τράπεζα, -ης, ἡ
position	τάξις, -εως, ἡ
archer	τοξότης, -ου, ὁ
country	χώρα, -ας, ἡ
(to) forbid (*x* to *y*, *x* from *y*-ing)	ἀπαγορεύω* (+ dat. *x*, μή & inf. *y*); οὐκ ἐάω (+ acc. *x*, inf. *y*)
(to) deny (that)	ἀπαρνέομαι (passive) (+ μή & inf.)
(to) allow (*x* to *y*)	ἐάω* (+ acc. *x*, inf. *y*)
(to) order (*x* to *y*)	κελεύω* (+ acc. *x*, inf. *y*)
(to) prevent (*x* from *y*-ing)	κωλύω (+ acc. *x*, inf. *y*); εἴργω* (+ acc. *x*, μή & inf. *y*)
(to) shut in or out	εἴργω*
(to) encourage (*x* to *y*)	παρακελεύομαι** (+ dat. *x*, inf. *y*)
(to) owe	ὀφείλω*; ὀφλισκάνω*
(to) help (in the sense of being useful to)	ὠφελέω
(to) put	τίθημι*
(to) open	ἀνοίγνυμι*
(to) show	δείκνυμι*
(to) give	δίδωμι*
(to) return	ἐπανέρχομαι**
(to) destroy	ἀπόλλυμι*
(to) perish	ἀπόλλυμαι*
(to) set up	ἵστημι* (see principal parts for meanings of tenses/voices)
(to) benefit	ὀνίνημι*25
(to) derive benefit (from *x*-ing)	ὀνίναμαι* (+ participle)
(to) be able (to)	δύναμαι* (+ inf.)
(to) know how (to)	ἐπίσταμαι* (+ inf.)
16) when(ever)	ὁπότε; ὅτε; ἐπεί; ἐπειδή
after	ἐπεί; ἐπειδή
before (+ clause)	πρίν (+ inf.)
until	ἕως; μέχρι; πρίν
while	ἕως
as long as	ἕως
ever since	ἐξ οὗ; ἀφ᾽ οὗ

---

25 Conjugated like ἵστημι.

gate	πύλη, -ης, ἡ
lie	ψεῦδος, -ους, τό
plain	πεδίον, -ου, τό
beauty	κάλλος, -ους, τό
benefit, use	ὄφελος, -ους, τό
(to) display	ἀποδείκνυμι**
(to) shout (to)	βοάω (+ acc.)
(to) laugh	γελάω*
(to) be with	σύνειμι** (+ dat.)
(to) give back	ἀποδίδωμι**
(to) sell	ἀποδίδομαι**
(to) sleep	καθεύδω*²⁶
(to) indicate	σημαίνω*
(to) collect	συλλέγω** (λέγω 2)
(to) cause *x* to revolt (from *y*)	ἀφίστημι** (+ acc. *x*, gen. *y*)
(to) revolt (from)	ἀφίσταμαι** (+ gen.)
(to) equip	στέλλω*
(to) embark	ἀναβαίνω**
(to) manage	διατίθημι**
(to) wrong	ἀδικέω
(to) distribute	νέμω*
(to) suffice	ἀρκέω*
(to) hand over	παραδίδωμι**
(to) (at)tend	θεραπεύω
(to) flatter	θεραπεύω
(to) destroy	καθαιρέω**
(to) cleanse	καθαίρω*
(to) fill (*x* with *y*)	πίμπλημι*²⁷ (+ acc. *x*, gen. *y*)
(to) enslave	δουλόω
(to) break	ῥήγνυμι*
17) tribe	φυλή, -ῆς, ἡ
soul	ψυχή, -ῆς, ἡ
(to) lie	κεῖμαι*
(to) have been put	κεῖμαι*
(to) send	ἵημι*
(to) enrage	ὀργίζω*

---

²⁶ Augments either at start (impf. ἐκάθευδον) or after the prefix (impf. καθεῦδον).
²⁷ Conjugated like ἵστημι.

(to) be angry (with)	ὀργίζομαι* (+ dat.)
(to) sit	κάθημαι*
(to) seat	καθίζω
(to) despise	καταφρονέω (+ gen.)
(to) laugh at	καταγελάω** (+ gen.)
(to) work	ἐργάζομαι*
(to) set x over y	ἐφίστημι** (+ acc. x, dat. y)
(to) prevail (over)	περιγίγνομαι** (+ gen.)
(to) surpass	διαφέρω** (+ gen.)
(to) betray	προδίδωμι**
(to) defend (x against y)	ἀμύνω* (+ dat. x, acc. y)
(to) resist	ἀμύνομαι* (+ acc.)
(to) punish (x for y)	ἀμύνομαι* (+ acc. x, gen. y)
(to) put on, inflict (x on y)	ἐπιτίθημι** (+ acc. x, dat. y)
(to) attack	ἐπιτίθεμαι** (+ dat.)
(to) make an attempt (on x, to y)	ἐπιχειρέω (+ dat. x, inf. y)
(to) let go	ἀφίημι**
(to) beg (x for y, to z)	δέομαι* (+ gen. x, gen. or acc. y, inf. z)
(to) imprison	δέω*
it is necessary (for x to y), x must y	δεῖ* (+ acc. x, inf. y); χρή* (+ acc. x, inf. y); ἀνάγκη ἐστί (+ dat. x, inf. y)
x ought to y, x should y	χρή* (+ acc. x, inf. y)
x needs y	δεῖ* (+ dat. x, gen. y)
x lacks y	δεῖ* (+ dat. x, gen. y)
it is possible (for x to y)	ἔξεστι** (+ dat. x, inf. y)
it seems best (to x to y), x decides (to y)	δοκεῖ (+ dat. x, inf. y)
x is a concern (to y)	μέλει* (+ gen. x, dat. y)
it is proper (for x to y)	πρέπει (+ dat. x, inf. y)
x is better off (y-ing)	λυσιτελεῖ (+ dat. x, inf. y)
it is advantageous (for x to y)	συμφέρει** (+ dat. x, inf. y)
x repents (of y)	μεταμέλει** (+ dat. x, gen. y)
x has a share (of y)	μέτεστι** (+ dat. x, gen. y)

18)	(to) establish	καθίστημι**
	(to) dwell	οἰκέω
	(to) throw into confusion	ταράττω*
	(to) dedicate	ἀνατίθημι**

(to) build	οἰκοδομέω
(to) spend time	διατρίβω**
(to) terrify	ἐκπλήττω*
(to) refute	ἐλέγχω*
(to) punish	ζημιόω (use δίκην δίδωμι as passive)
(to) have courage (in the face of *x*)	θαρρέω/θαρσέω (+ acc. *x*)
(to) approach	προσέρχομαι** (+ dat.)
(to) meet	ἀπαντάω* (+ dat.)
(to) dare	τολμάω
(to) be healthy	ὑγιαίνω*
(to) seek	ζητέω
(to) converse (with)	διαλέγομαι* (+ dat.)
(to) be at rest	ἡσυχάζω
(to) supplicate	ἱκετεύω
(to) please	ἀρέσκω* (+ dat.)
(to) love knowledge, study philosophy	φιλοσοφέω
(to) strive	σπεύδω
(to) strive, be serious (about)	σπουδάζω* (+ acc.)
(to) assign, command	προστάττω** (+ dat. of person & acc. of thing, or + dat. of person & infinitive)
(to) set free	ἐλευθερόω
(to) deceive	ἐξαπατάω
(to) prepare	παρασκευάζω
(to) make a treaty (with)	σπένδομαι* (+ dat.)
(to) transgress	παραβαίνω**
(to) go back and forth, go repeatedly to	φοιτάω (+ prepositions & acc.)
(to) outrage, treat arrogantly	ὑβρίζω
(to) associate with	συγγίγνομαι** (+ dat.)
(to) hate	μισέω
(to) praise	ἐπαινέω*
(to) bite	δάκνω*
(to) pity (*x* for *y*)	οἰκτίρω* (+ acc. *x*, gen. *y*)
(to) begrudge, be jealous of (*x* for *y*)	φθονέω (+ dat. *x*, gen. *y*)

Index to vocabulary

Under no circumstances should you need this section; all vocabulary should be memorized at the proper time and not thereafter forgotten. But just in case, here are the chapters in which each word appears.